European Security: Prospects for the 1980s

European Security: Prospects for the 1980s

Edited by
Derek Leebaert
Harvard University and
Massachusetts Institute of
Technology

Lexington Books
D.C. Heath and Company
Lexington, Massachusetts
Toronto

Library of Congress Cataloging in Publication Data

Main entry under title:

European security: prospects for the 1980s

    1. Europe—Defenses. 2. World politics—1955-   I. Leebaert, Derek.
UA646.E93   355.03'304   78-19539
ISBN 0-669-02518-6

Published simultaneously in Canada

Printed in the United States of America

International Standard Book Number: 0-669-02518-6

Library of Congress Catalog Card Number: 78-19539

For Diana Renee Dourif, without whom this book would not have been possible

Contents

Preface

For over thirty years, since the expediency of great-power wartime collaboration yielded to the tensions of the cold war, the military forces of the superpowers and their allies have faced the prospect of renewed fighting in Europe. This prospect has sometimes seemed remote. At other times immediate. Today it is tempting to regard warfare in Europe as an anarchronism, gone the way of clan feuds and social duels. But statements that "the final European war" has already been endured have unfortunately been among the most elaborately disproven assertions of this century.

Two years ago a group of faculty and fellows at Harvard's Center for Science and International Affairs convened to examine the contradictions of complacency and unease that have characterized European security. The subject lent itself well to the center's purpose, which is to bring together scholars and professionals whose major interests are the study of international security problems and related policy implications.

The group's working assumption was that shifting domestic priorities and political forces, both in Europe and in the United States, have combined with an array of newly emphasized issues to change the European defense calculus. Questions of energy supply, technological sharing, and ideological drift now intrude on the definition of security, which for thirty years largely involved such things as military strength, economic vigor, and national stability. These new defense considerations also exist side by side with long-standing military concerns such as the character of the Soviet threat, the cohesiveness of the two great defense organizations, and those areas of greatest military vulnerability. It is not simply a collection of new security problems that faces Europe in the next decade, but rather a mixture of old fears and new challenges.

There are many issues that this book does not address, despite the breadth of its title. China's professed association with NATO military objectives, the effect of what some see as the superpower naval disequilibrium, and the changes that may be brought by a new, post-World War II generation of European leaders without personal memories of the early years of the cold war are all subjects that might have been included. And the list could go on. We decided, however, to present a discussion that would be forward-looking as well as analytical, yet free from the conjecture that too often characterizes security studies. China's rhetoric has far surpassed its own defense preparations, naval and other hardware inventories lend themselves to a variety of contradictory measures, and shifts in leadership (as with Chancellor Schmidt's separation from Brandt's politics of contrition) are just beginning. Issues such as these will have to be dealt with elsewhere, when either more evidence has been accumulated or when far more detailed presentations can be accommodated.

While few believe that World War III is imminent, Soviet goals and intentions are the subjects of increasing debate within West European government and military councils. The ideological stridency that may have been appropriate in cold war confrontations is nearly universally regarded as anomalous in a time of what many see as enhanced international cooperation. Naturally, the Soviet Union continues to strive for an international environment compatible with its security and beliefs. Yet Soviet policymakers face the dilemma of continuing to desire an immoderate goal—the extension of the Soviet system—while having to rely primarily on the modest means of currently acceptable political activity. Since traditionally the Russians have looked to Europe for real and imagined military threats, it is there that this dilemma is most acute. The possibility of the Soviet Union's achieving a "consonant international environment" in Europe must be considered in light of the problems evidenced by NATO at the thirty-year mark.

The Soviet Union is not the only superpower that sees its first line of defense in Western Europe. American attitudes and the perceptions of American policymakers toward European security have been influenced consistently by intra-alliance disagreements, European efforts at unity, and three decades of alliance dominance.

Relations among Warsaw Pact members, as among those of NATO, are in a state of flux. There are differences of priorities within the Pact, tensions because of economic strain, and varying dictates of regime stability. Insofar as East European dislocation transcends the Pact, it can be regarded as a source of unrest for the continent as a whole and therefore merits thoughtful attention. The possible effects of the Conference on Security and Cooperation in Europe add a provocative twist to East-West relations.

Many of the political and military problems besetting Europe in the 1980s have existed since the North Atlantic Treaty's April 1949 pledge "to unite . . . efforts for collective defense and for the preservation of peace and security." But these problems are being addressed in a new, and perhaps post-cold war, context. More international negotiations involving European security have been pursued in the last decade than at any time since World War II (for example, the Strategic Arms Limitation Talks, the Mutual Balanced Force Reduction negotiations, and the Conference on Security and Cooperation in Europe). Yet détente has become elusive amid the charges that the Soviets are achieving the capacity for implementing their familiar blitzkrieg doctrine. The negotiations themselves have displayed an overcompartmentalization that avoids confronting the causes of fundamental tensions while dealing only with the effects.

It is against this background that *European Security: Prospects for the 1980s* examines the many facets of continental defense. These include the strength of the transatlantic commitment, the dynamics of the European military balance, the West's energy policy dilemmas, the impact of Soviet and East European affairs, and consideration of new influences on old political-military problems.

I would personally like to emphasize the seminal role played by the directors of the center in facilitating the group's research. This study has been sustained by their advocacy of collaborative analysis as well as by their generosity in providing a base for those of us who have worked for the last two years on the problems that follow.

Cambridge, Massachusetts, 1979   *Derek Leebaert*

Acknowledgments

A book such as *European Security: Prospects for the 1980s* contains by nature of its format and focus the contributions of a number of participants other than the authors. The mechanics of pursuing such a joint enterprise have required a rather extended effort: chapter drafts were circulated and assessed; the critiques of never-reticent colleagues were answered or incorporated; and the ministrations of the patient CSIA support staff were increasingly important as the months went by.

It is nearly invidious to attempt to cite individually those others involved with this study. But the advice and encouragement of several people have been significant. It would be unfortunate not to attempt to convey the extent of our obligation. In Europe, John Browne, Pierre Gallois, Waring C. Hopkins, and E. Gitz provided the benefits of unique perspectives and provocative debate at crucial times during the past two years. Meanwhile, in Cambridge and New York, professional direction and insights were given generously by William Kaufmann, Onno Leebaert, Robert Legvold, Michael Mandelbaum, John Palfrey, and Daniel Yergin. Valuable editorial assistance was provided by Melinda Nichols.

Precisely because this book is a collective effort by its authors, we believe it essential to emphasize that we alone are responsible for the analyses and opinions that follow. Indeed, there are several instances in which the authors' respective conclusions are less than complementary. The diverse views that are expressed may be the best illustration of the ambiguities and uncertainties that will continue to characterize questions of European security.

Part I
Reexamining Old
Assumptions

1 On Reaching Thirty

Derek Leebaert

Analyses of disharmony in the Atlantic Alliance risk being dismissed as either redundant or gratuitous. NATO's three decades have consistently shown European concern over the direction of U.S. defense policies, as well as Washington's despair when confronted by seemingly contradictory European signals. There has been no shortage of academic, military, or governmental prescriptions for remedying the alliance's variety of perennial shortcomings. But the second half of the 1970s has been a time of considerable ferment, even by NATO's standards. Changes of administration in the United States, a revivified debate over Soviet intentions, and continuing political uncertainties on the Continent have combined once again to bring the problems of European security to the forefront of international discussion. As NATO turns thirty, it reflects the shaken illusions, the reassessment of commitments, the preoccupation with self-examination, and, perhaps, the prospect of a new vitality that characterizes the passing of a generational span.

For thirty years NATO has served the functionally and geographically constrained mission of ensuring European security. It was established precisely along lines opposite those that had been required of collective defense during the interwar decades: in 1949 the threat impinged on all the members, and the allied military commitment was intended to be clear in advance of armed attack. Moreover, NATO would be part of a comprehensive alliance of which traditional regional security concerns would be only a part. It would be the backdrop for economic partnership. When the United States first offered a political and then military commitment, few worried at the time (at least out loud) of too much American participation or that U.S. domination would stifle fledgling European integration. Indeed, it was a European, not an American, preoccupation that stressed military rather than political mobilization. The extent and propriety of the U.S. role have been contentious ever since. With the definition of security now embracing nearly all of those factors which have a direct bearing on the structure of the nation-state system, the points of disagreement vis-a-vis the United States have increased exponentially. Yet the concepts of unity and collectivity have been advertised so frequently and so authoritatively that the casual observer can easily forget that so much of it is ethereal.

NATO members have all along had the extraordinary ability of proclaiming one thing at the highest governmental level while practicing the exact opposite in daily transactions. Although the United States has been accused of being the current villain of unilateralism as evidenced through SALT, energy, and monetary policies, NATO as a whole has been characterized by failure to concert political policies. Even at the end of its first decade, NATO members could look back upon a variety of instances in which anything but mutuality had been standard operating procedure: U.S. abandonment of its "united action" policy in Vietnam, the Suez adventure, the Jordan and Lebanon landings, the Quemoy crisis, and war in Algeria. The mischief was twofold: not only did all this determine that there would be no coherent Western policy in the extratreaty area as originally envisioned, but it meant that even political unity within the NATO region could not be guaranteed. As the purpose of a regional Western defense partnership is reassessed in the context of détente in Europe, there is pervasive unease about how to face the future.

The alliance must determine whether the problems that it now confronts are perpetual or merely transitory. After all, so much of the doom-saying of the early 1970s has been disproven. Toward the end of the decade Europe evidenced a renewal of confidence: Italy has not collapsed and has instead demonstrated a capacity for making the provisional work; the 1978 French elections have renewed the mandate of the Center; Germany seems cured of its near-nervous breakdown over the Baader-Meinhoff spree; and the British electorate is foregoing the temptations of fragmentary third-party politics. And out of all this has emerged, even if incompletely, a European monetary union. Will talk of NATO's obsolescence be shown to be nothing more than another example of poor forecasting? One thing is clear. With its regained confidence Europe is naturally enough less reticent in its criticism of the United States.

A host of new political, military, and economic concerns surround the familiar intra-alliance controversies of the past. Together they demand further examinations of NATO's effectiveness and solidity. Specific occurrences such as the 1971 U.S. break with gold, as well as the general tumultuous environment of the post-Keynesian world, all assure that the precarious U.S./European consensus on security is being further challenged. And complacency over NATO's success—at least in achieving its purpose of assuring deterrence—risks reviving those conditions that brought the alliance about in the first place. The alliance must contend not only with its own dynamics but with global political drift: increasing empathy with the Chinese perspective of the Soviet Union and the need for secure Middle Eastern oil supplies are among the influences that draw NATO concerns beyond Europe. Increased European weapon sales in the wake of U.S.-PRC normalization, as well as the uncertainties generated by the Iranian social crisis, have made the need for a shared global outlook imperative.

The crises surrounding the passing of a generation, according to the theorists of adult developmental stages, are characterized in the case of a partnership by a joint review of each party's aspirations. Each often perceives a lack of accord. But, renewed enthusiasm is an additional characteristic of this stage, as the aspirations of earlier years are given concrete goals or are reassessed altogether. For reasons more complicated than chronological coincidence—among them this paradox that the falsification of NATO predictions of the Soviet threat is an apparent confirmation of alliance success—the members have good reason to ask whether their continued relationship is now anything more than just a traffic in collective illusions.

The United States and the Illusion of Leadership

Washington retains its accustomed role of senior partner. After years of congressional squabbling, the United States now regards its more than five division equivalents in Europe (including guards of the theater nuclear weapons) as an established fixture of Atlantic defense. The products of the 1970s as an oft-proclaimed era of negotiations—the CSCE Final Act and the Berlin Agreement—help in pointing to the permanency of these troop placements. Unpleasantness results, however, when Europeans forget that despite this commitment NATO is only one instrument of global U.S. politics. This is especially true for the Carter administration, which prides itself in building political coalitions issue by issue. With such an approach, there is currently no area—including Europe—in which the United States is trying to achieve its objectives in isolation from other U.S. concerns elsewhere in the world.

Initiatives involving nuclear proliferation, arms sales, and human rights are among those issues that create notable contradictions. The alliance has been sustained for thirty years by the Europeans' assumption that the United States knows what it is doing—and by their resignation to the corollary that if the United States does not know what it is doing, it will do so anyway. Central to today's antagonisms is a conviction among the European allies—shared by sympathetic Amrican critics—that Washington has little idea where it is going vis-à-vis the alliance, and that its decision-making processes are so diffuse that it could not pursue a specific policy even if it is a misguided one.

The anxieties with which Europeans observe changes of administration in the United States are a constant in alliance politics. The evangelical image of the Carter presidency, however, has combined with a rhetorical tone reminiscent of Wilson and Dulles to cause special consternation. Doubts over presidential substance have become commonplace. Although by mid-1978 no president since Harry Truman had enjoyed less confidence among his countrymen in the handling of foreign affairs than did Carter, developments involving the Middle East, China, and Iran have complicated this image. In Europe, frustrations from dealing with an unusually distracted U.S. President are paralleled by larger and more disquieting questions related to American seriousness of purpose.

American dominance of the Atlantic Alliance is assured, for better or worse, by the superpower role. Even France's withdrawal from NATO left the country prudently under the nuclear aegis of the Atlantic Alliance, which, after all, spawned the original treaty organization. An estimated $40 to $60 billion are appropriated annually for what are described in Washington as NATO purposes. And, in addition to its other unprecedented prerequisites and obligations, the United States is ultimately responsible for nuclear conflagration in the West. In dealing with the Soviet Union—a country that keeps even its annual carrot production a secret—it is inevitable that American foreign policies will suffer some ambiguities. Yet despite customary European expressions of alternating euphoria and despair over the U.S. role in NATO, rarely has allied impatience with American contradictions been more justified than at the thirty-year mark.

The U.S. President is subject to repeated European demands (with the obvious exception of 50 million Frenchmen) for assertion of American leadership. State Department briefing papers, in turn, tend to support these exhortations enthusiastically. The Carter administration entered office with the intentions of overcoming the belief of its immediate predecessors that political/economic matters in Europe were in gross disarray. Whereas Kissinger's "Year of Europe" had withered from simple inattention, Carter's early focus on Europe—built upon the foundation laid by General Haig—indicated an initial effort (if only a psychological one) to put new momentum into NATO. The London pronouncements of May 10/11, 1977, which call for 3 percent annual defense budget supplements, were a generally pleasing result.

Despite early enthusiasm, problems of structure and personnel have led to disappointment in this administration's ability to adhere to the governing principles of the alliance—to consult together, to organize together, and to act together. The allies are even uncertain of how policies are actually being determined in Washington. The bureaucratic decentralization that involves a host of new governmental participants in defense affairs is perceived as a blurring of responsibilities. Allies now have to look to approximately a dozen different senior officials in the Defense and State departments, as well as in the Arms Control and Disarmament Agency, for explanations of U.S. policy (where it exists). Confused Europeans continue to ask, "Who is in charge here?"—especially after years of the Kissinger imprimatur. This disaggregation of responsibility now mirrors the difficulties that Americans have long had in listening to a cacophony of European voices.

The lack of clarity in U.S. decision-making is perhaps most apparent in the economic realm. And the greatest organizational deficiency is the president's inability to get his hands on any mechanism that can assist him in coherently pursuing his foreign policy objectives. Ambitious global issues have proven difficult to link with specific countries. Some policies, such as those concerning arms exports, have had to be reconsidered; others, such as weapon standardization, continue to stumble along while exacerbating interalliance relations.

Senator Arthur Vandenberg, Chairman of the Foreign Relations Committee, foresaw alliance weaknesses when he warned during ratifications of the NATO treaty in 1949 that "unless this treaty becomes far more than a military alliance, it will be at the mercy of the first plausible Soviet peace offensive."[1] Because of the necessary totality of the relations that evolved—political, economic, social, and cultural—NATO members have ironically permitted their respective sovereignties to be jeopardized by new and non-Warsaw Pact sources. Indeed, the following chapters best illustrate the U.S./European interrelation of factors such as energy policy, technology, and diplomacy. The allies have made themselves all the more susceptible to the transnational pathologies that are the dark side of an interdependent world.

American deficiencies have an especially pronounced effect upon the European partners. There is a fear that for the first time the United States has lost mastery over itself: inflation and the permanency of balance of payments deficits signify to some that the U.S. economy may be basically unsound; energy policy through European eyes can only be seen as perverse; the American refusal objectively to contemplate international monetary reform appears petulant; and fears generated by Watergate and the possibility of post-Vietnam isolationism are by now clichés.

Whether this all adds up to an abrogation of leadership is dubious. But Europe's leaders are hardly reticent as they observe such confusion, as well as endure its consequences. Bonn's criticism of U.S. monetary, trade, arms, energy, and East/West policies has been acerbic; France was so surprised by the American 1978 Non-Proliferation Act's requirement to renegotiate longstanding Euratom agreements that it simply ignored the pronouncement; and as an example of similar exasperation over U.S. insensitivity, Belgium's foreign minister has characterized the United States as "the spoiled child of the West."[2] Although U.S. officials find themselves comforted by Chancellor Schmidt's practice of being more circumspect in official circles, his personal observations that European nations may have to go it alone articulate allied fears. Despite three decades of—with one exception—rhetorical overkill, the reasons for allies now to broadcast the benefits of such devolution are hardly unpersuasive.

Economic and bureaucratic mistakes can be corrected. What might not be rectifiable are precedents set by unaccustomed U.S. acquiescence, first to the German-Brazilian understanding of suitable nuclear futures and second to the concept of permitting an allied veto for the first time over the development of an American weapon, that is, the neutron bomb. Regardless of the virtues of U.S. flexibility in these cases, this shedding of responsibility suggests a decrease in the concentration of alliance decision-making that has for more than thirty years been placed in Washington. Furthermore, Europeans are observing curious American concessions in SALT concerning continental military vulnerabilities. Defense Secretary Harold Brown, for example, has promised the NATO Planning Group on two occasions that the United States would not bargain away European access to the cruise missile—not even in a three-year protocol whose strictures, Europeans understandably suspect, would remain immutable. Once a pledge like this is compromised in superpower negotiations, there is little need to maintain the pretense of consulting allies.

The cohesion of the alliance is, as always, being scrutinized by the members. Although its viability may not be synonymous with U.S. leadership, a suspected absence of superpower backing detracts from the comprehensive advantages that Vandenberg and others envisioned. A variety of domestic constraints among the European members, in turn, also impedes a constructive intellectual exchange. Contentious matters such as Eurocommunism, comparative assessments of intelligence, and a proper position to take toward Africa cannot be discussed at the ministerial level within a NATO format, despite a shared ideological foundation among those concerned. It is clear that attempting to do so would imperil fragile parliamentary coalitions at home. The effort to sustain complementary alliance priorities and purposes is therefore further weakened.

Suggestions for stemming these centrifugal pulls come from all quarters: private study groups, academic conferences, government agencies, and military caucuses. Pleas for clear-cut U.S. leadership, for taking counsel before policies crystallize, and for using NATO as a building block for American purposes have all become proverbs. Official U.S. leanings on ill-defined military problems that are nevertheless central to the alliance—chemical warfare, civil defense, theater nuclear weapons, and so on—are generally only made available to allies through carefully structured briefings. Indications of U.S. views concerning the wider security issues of Soviet relations, international economics, and the pursuit of self-styled global issues largely go unshared—if only because Washington itself is too confused to realize or to remedy the impacts in Western Europe.

Assessing the Military Commitment

Issues that have been disruptive in the past are now appearing in new guises; the unfinished military debates of twenty years ago have been reopened.

European fears about the extent of the U.S. defense commitment, the hope that new military technologies will solve intractable political dilemmas, and the ambiguous role of nuclear weapons in Western Europe are all adding a sense of *déjà vu* to alliance politics. There is an apocryphal archaeological theory that could be applied to security studies, one named after General Curtis LeMay, the Air Force Chief of Staff who popularized the exhortation of bombing recalcitrant populations back to the Stone Age. The theory states that if today's analyst digs deep enough under the rubble of contemporary defense planning, he eventually comes across the Curtis LeMay civilization—a land dominated by the strategies and concepts of the late 1950s/early 1960s that are at the bottom of currently fashionable security problems and proposals. A generation of resurfacing alarms and responses within the alliance stands as the theory's proof.

Military woes are certainly nothing new. The so-called German neurosis of whether NATO would stick together if confronted by Soviet aggression makes for familiar reading. And the tongue-in-cheek Western strategy of "preemptive surrender" can always be depended upon to elicit nervous laughter. Ironically, the defense concerns of the European members are seen as reflecting apprehension about alliance military capabilities, even though continental political stability remains generally undisturbed. There is a heightened skepticism among the allies about both the strategic balance and Soviet military planning. These worries are strengthened by a steady flow of alarming Defense Department briefings and reconnaissance photos showing what, in more uncertain times, could be interpreted as a Warsaw Pact preattack preparation. Also, what to some Europeans were the comforting plans of limited nuclear options (in which U.S. strategic forces could in theory truncate an attack on NATO by striking selected Soviet military targets) are now highly ambiguous. But the fact remains that the Soviet threat is less compelling than it was. Unlike 1948, 1958, and 1968, Soviet tanks are at least not dramatizing actively a penchant for domination.

Why is alliance skepticism of its military defense once again coming into prominence? Two reasons for current European unease stand out. Paramount is the Soviet build-up and the way in which it is exercised. The Soviets have had their much-publicized blitzkrieg doctrine for years, but until recently neither the mobility nor the logistical support to execute it. This has changed profoundly, and with it have arisen renewed Western fears over Soviet intentions. There is a challenge implicit in the developing asymmetry of military strength; Soviet involvement in Africa—little understood as it may be—has added an immediacy to such concerns. In retrospect, reasons for international aggression often look bizarre. But Soviet criteria for assuming a risky international course may change; the possibility of a third installment in Europe's twentieth-century civil war cannot be ignored. The second reason for skepticism is a suspicion that the United States may be seeking strategic gains at the price of theater vulnerabilities. Although the popular stigma of dealing with the United States on defense matters has disappeared after Vietnam, the common cynicism involving the U.S. commitment to Europe remains. A dichotomy of interest is perceived. As the superpowers acknowledge strategic parity, there is a need to define the continuum between conventional and nuclear weapons in an environment of rapid technological change.

Considering TNW, Again

Thirty years ago, General of the Army Omar Bradley introduced one of the alliance's most provocative issues when he is said to have remarked of the Soviets, "When they get a bomb to neutralize ours, we better have an army to neutralize their army." We never did. European members of NATO originally drew solace from the belief that the conventional military imbalance was redressed in part by a near U.S. nuclear monopoly. But by the late 1950s, it was widely assumed that the Soviets' swift gains in strategic weaponry—including a lead in the development of ballistic missiles—had punctured the umbrella of SAC's previously superior thermonuclear power. Indeed, the American nuclear force was regarded by some as vulnerable to a Soviet surprise attack. Now formal assurances of parity have dredged up these old arguments of strategic decoupling and U.S. nuclear perfidy. The spats surrounding enhanced radiation warheads have, specifically, revived the hoary debate over theater or what used to be called "battlefield" weapons. Gaullist views concerning the primacy of national options in European defense—as well as the prolific writings of retired French Air Force General Pierre Gallois—are receiving renewed attention. Chancellor Schmidt's highly personal observation that Europeans may have to fend for themselves (insofar as SALT allegedly neutralizes U.S. strategic backing) updates Bradley's fears of military inadequacies.

The genesis of NATO's involvement with nuclear weapons may be the only part of the TNW relationship that all discussants agree upon. The United States deployed so-called tactical nuclear weapons in Europe during the 1950s and early 1960s on the basis of an exceedingly weak professional literature, one that nevertheless was sufficient to convince the respective administrations. Little consideration was given in Washington as to how these weapons would actually be used. Original impressions that they were an extension of field artillery to be linked with strategic weapons quickly proved unacceptable. The Europeans—especially the West Germans—have always seen nuclear weapons as preventing war, not just preventing an opponent's use of nuclear weapons. (Obviously both Americans and Europeans prefer deterrence with a minimal role given to the geographically limiting purpose of TNWs. The United States, on the contrary, could intend to postpone the moment of strategic escalation as long as possible.) It is probable that the only thing that these weapons would deter would be themselves, this being in harmony with the sally that all a big deterrent will deter is a big deterrent.

Herein lies the contradiction between European pressures to retain most of the Continent's 7,000 U.S. theater nuclear weapons (even more being afloat), yet not to contemplate their possible use or refinement. And what has been most apparent in current U.S. considerations of these weapons in Europe has been the emphasis placed on the credibility of use rather than on the stability of deterrence. There are few subjects which suffer more in discussion from abstraction than that of deterrence. Recriminations abound of inviting the use of nuclear weapons by considering to employ those versions that are claimed to calibrate the ensuring holocaust. But as in all treatments of the presumed political/military continuum between lower and higher kilotonnage, contrasting arguments can hardly be supported by fact, and one opinion is about as good as another.

SALT

As usual, Europe is hearing different things from different people in Washington. The sentiment behind Senator Sam Nunn's comment that "nuclear deterrence of major conventional attacks has been weakened by strategic parity" has been made all the more poignant by the way in which the United States has pursued its SALT negotiations.[3] Arms control is intended by the Carter administration to be an avenue to strategic stability. Unfortunately the semantic imprecisions that surround these talks are especially pernicious when they involve the alliance. What may be theater concerns for the senior partner are certainly nothing less than strategic imperatives for the associates. There is suspicion—not without cause—that the United States is pursuing a subterranean route to achieve its own objectives.

The secrecy and insensitivity of the U.S. SALT negotiations have given credence to those longtime critics who argue that the European and American defense loci are not inseparable. Those more sympathetic to the inextricability of the U.S. role in Europe (involving five Poseidon submarines at the disposal of SACEUR—the Supreme Allied Commander, Europe) have been undercut. The classic case of what passes as U.S. duplicity is the June 1977 visit of the Gelb delegation to Germany. As director of the State Department's Bureau of Political/Military Affairs, Leslie Gelb capably disparaged the cruise missile as a mainstay of national (that is, German) defense. Its penetrability was questioned, its cost-effectiveness doubted, and the overall impression was one of U.S. disappointment. Three weeks later, the president decided to scrap the B-1 and substitute the cruise missile, declaring that a major factor in his decision was "the recent evolution of the cruise missile as an effective weapon itself.''[4] Back went another delegation as conflicting U.S. opinion on the significance of the cruise missile continued to be articulated.

Contradictions multiplied further once the United States attached cruise missiles to ICBMs in SALT, rather than to unconstrained long-range Soviet theater systems such as the SS-20 IRBM. The fact that President Carter discussed—inconclusively—the SS-20 during his 1978 visit to Warsaw is uninspiring. European exasperation over this weapon epitomizes the differences with the United States. The American intention to place all weapons with a theater influence in the context of a distant SALT III is ironic insofar as a major accomplishment of SALT I is considered to be the segregation of the so-called gray areas. The leap of trust required of the Europeans is profound; they play no part in the negotiations, and they alone in the West are threatened by these weapons. For those so inclined, this is further evidence of nearly exclusive U.S. concern with its own defense priorities. Washington, for its part, has come to see such criticism as proof that the European allies are masters of the fancied slight.

There are many illustrations that can be cited as indicators of alliance dichotomization. The interminable Mutual Force Reduction talks in Vienna, for example, provide a less than central U.S. policy forum. But they have had the major benefit of getting all of the allies to consult with each other. SALT—the centerpiece of three administrations' vigorous arms control efforts—has had the opposite effect. Unsurprisingly, the dominant European perception is that the United States will listen on secondary issues but not on primary ones.

Military Disarray

How NATO would respond in a significant military crisis is anyone's guess. Its responses so far have been disturbingly unfocused both in theory and in practice. The rigid and insufficiently graduated structure has never endured an alert. The Berlin crisis of 1961 was the first occasion in which the alliance was forced to face the possibility of escalation in a realistic situation. The lessons derived are hardly reassuring. Although it was at that time that SACEUR (always an American) was given exclusive command responsibility for Europe under the peculiar *nom de guerre* Live Oak, it was months later, in fall 1962, that Professor Thomas Schelling ran tests among decision-makers concerning potential military responses involving the defense of Berlin. Try as he might to be provocative in the war-gaming, Schelling could not precipitate a Western commitment to fight. The fear of nuclear war was pervasive. To be fair, the theoretical alternative was bleak. In an early exercise that had a seminal effect on European popular opinion, the 1954 NATO exercise *Carte Blanche* simulated 335 atomic bomb drops in forty-eight hours to stem a Soviet attack—thereby discovering that over 1.5 million Germans would have been killed and 3.5 million wounded.

Schelling's practical demonstration of severe alliance reluctance to use force was both vivid and disturbing at the time. But it would be far more difficult today to offer even the pretense of a NATO military countermove. The United States cannot conceive of sending 40,000 combat troops toward the borders of Eastern Europe with neither NATO approval nor with agreement from Bonn as it did in 1961. Whether NATO could act expediently and in concert during similar circumstances today is problematic. It is also worth noting in a time of reassessment that a credible forward defense was the original quid pro quo for West Germany's entry into the alliance, a deployment that would give a purpose to German rearmament. It is the certainty of this defense that has been jeopardized by cavalier American discussions of retrenchments and territorial sacrifice.

Assurances of NATO resolve and cohesion have also been less than forthcoming during military challenges of the past decade. During the Czech invasion of 1968, attempts by individual unit commanders to reposition their forces were thwarted by their principals: U.S. General James Polk was prohibited from doubling the helicopter border patrols, and the RAF was ordered to quit disbursing its aircraft. These restraints may have been imposed prudently against the possibility of a catalytic war. But should conflict for some reason have spilled over into Western Europe, NATO would have found itself in less than desirable circumstances. And five years later when the Untied States was on a Defcon 3 nuclear alert during the October War, the Europeans were blissfully unaware and had gone home for the weekend.

If it had been found necessary for NATO to act with deliberation in any one of these three instances, its ability for effective action would have been found wanting. There is inadequate agreement over military concepts, doctrine, and command/control/communications mechanisms. Few trained personnel exist to oversee coordination of these elements. And at the most fundamental level, questions of weapon standardization are still believed to directly compromise the most sacrosanct of national ambitions.

The West Europeans must not pretend that they alone face a milieu of political contradictions and cross-purposes. Successive U.S. administrations have felt bedeviled by both transatlantic lethargy and criticism. Current sensitivity to the recrudescence of Gaullist/Gallois arguments is especially apparent. Why should U.S. strategic nuclear underwriting of Europe be questioned further because of declarations of parity? This condition has existed, it is answered, for nearly twenty years, since the consequences of a Soviet nuclear strike against North America would have been unacceptable all along to the United States. Moreover, the up to 800 Soviet

MRBMs that were targeted on Europe during the late 1950s were a convincing force in their own right. Unimpaired nuclear deterrence will continue to affect continental stability. And on the conventional level, past incidents of indiscipline and poor morale within the U.S. Seventh Army should not be interpreted simplistically as foreshadowing lackadaisical resolve in the face of Warsaw Pact armor. Deprecations of NATO's conventional abilities are too often simplistic. A paradox exists, however, in that the political aim of deterrence has been maintained without ever reaching the conventional force levels that the alliance continues to solicit.

Washington, for its part, is annoyed that not a single West European government is willing to come forward with its own proposals concerning the superpower nuclear balance and Europe. The Germans have come closest to stating a position on SALT and related nuclear matters (although little has been noted publicly on the cruise missile) but so far their internal debate continues unchecked. For example, there has been little commentary on details of enhanced radiation warheads other than the way in which the eventual U.S. nondecision was handled. Such reticence highlights the allies' ambivalence while vindicating Washington's long-standing position that it is unable by itself to construct appropriate dialogues.

All this reinforces the rather spurious argument that Europeans have few ideas to contribute to the arcane discipline of strategic studies. The ideas that are presented formally tend to be burdened by inhibitions; those that are presented informally are more often than not swallowed up in the U.S. bureaucracy. The Europeans believe, with justification, that the introduction of extraneous proposals into the superpower debate is less than welcome. The British and the Germans show great deference to the United States on these issues. There is no desire to initiate a demarche over alliance disagreements; it is felt alternatively that to resolve a specific problem satisfactorily is not worth jeopardizing the overall relationship, and that the day may come when it is more suitable to rock the boat. In the meanwhile, an ally can adjust to the U.S. directives in the accommodating manner of Britain which, during the first eighteen months of the Carter administration, began buying as many cruise missile parts and technologies as possible in anticipation of the U.S.-negotiated three-year restrictive protocol in SALT.

Toward the end of NATO's first decade, Field-Marshal Slim could instruct his countrymen that "when tempted to criticize an ally always remember that you are an ally yourself."[5] But such counsel can be endured only until it begins to discredit the concept of partnership. The disproportion between the influences of the United States and that of its alliance partners can make such dispassionate advice even more grating.

New Attractions

Two topics of special uncertainty are prominent in assessments of NATO military vulnerability. The first example involves the constant effort to exploit Western technological leads in weaponry; the second includes the apprehension arising from those political questions that have become emblematic of intra-alliance disarray.

  1. The new technical and political issues, such as the cruise missile controversy, that have emerged in the past five years add to the incredulity surrounding the NATO ideal of collegiality. While Kissinger's détente calendar complicated U.S. reexamination of European defense problems, a host of new weapons was added to the agenda. In the case of the air-breathing cruise, the sense of *déjà vu* is acute; some of the most virulent intra-alliance debates are spurred by an essentially World War II technology. What will be the role of this and the other newly introduced weapons in NATO, such as scatter mines, improved antitank weapons, and fuel-air explosives, during the coming decade? Will they revolutionize warfare and painlessly restructure the European balance, as some observers have hoped? Probably not. In fact, this weaponry may be only marginally helpful to the West and can best be characterized as an incremental benefit. Many of them give further advantages to the NATO defense and would presumably enhance the proverbial three to one advantage claimed already to be in favor of the defender. But as modern wars of mobility and political erraticism have shown, today's offense can be tomorrow's defense. Despite the fact that new weapons are exacerbating the effort at arms control, they do have advantages in that they complicate Soviet military decision-making, improve escalation control, and may be psychologically valuable to the Europeans—particularly the West Germans. But NATO has so many doctrinal as well as political problems that it will take more than enthusiasm over weapon refinements to remedy existing weaknesses. There has been no quick fix. Instead, old ideas resurface, such as the 1950's Von Bonin Plan of fixed German defenses based on anti-tank weapons.

  2. The best contemporary illustrations of political contradictions within the alliance focus on the uncertainties surrounding the NATO flanks, that is, those states to the north and southeast that are contiguous to the Soviet Union. Norwegians, for example, have been courting the French maxim that during a military crisis (especially one predominantly involving the interests of a single state, as in border incursions) they may be left to their own devices. Added to this is anticipation of the consequences that war in the West would entail—demonstrated in the case of Norway by the so-called social debate over the proper extent of allied force basings. But, ironically, there are simultaneous requests to SACEUR for prepositioned

NATO equipment. In the South, the Turkish refusal to permit the refueling of the Mogadisho-bound German commandos in 1978 is just one more instance of decay in the proverbial weak underbelly. The key to the endurance of a military alliance or compact is the conviction among its members that their security can be better protected by being inside the organization than by being out of it. This is clearly a matter of debate in several NATO foreign ministries.

Although Norway and Turkey have little more in common than an appreciation for hazelnuts, both have always warranted special consideration by their alliance associates: the former was pressured from the outset by the Soviet Union not to join NATO, and assurances that no foreign bases (or nuclear weapons) would be permitted during peacetime have done little to dispel Soviet apprehension. (Although Norway still adheres to the assurances made in 1949, it is also the only NATO country to reject a Soviet nonaggression pact.) Turkey similarly embodies unique concerns—notably the inability of both it and Greece to subordinate traditional hostilities to alliance needs. Indeed, during the late 1950s, when U.S. academic advocacy of independent nuclear forces was at its peak, a two-fold exception for Turkey was commonly made—that nuclear weapons might be used against Greece, or that Turkey might rashly use them against the Soviet Union. During the heyday of the Multi-Lateral Force, it was Turkey and Greece that had to drop out, for reasons not difficult to determine. This rivalry is discussed in detail in chapter 6, "Instability and Change on NATO's Southern Flank."

The undermining of NATO from within is reflected in the perennial and apparently insoluble problems that are currently most apparent in either or both of these states on the flanks: uncertainty about or unwillingness to accept support from other members, traditional antagonisms transcending NATO, ambiguity over the importance of the Soviet threat, opposition to foreign bases, fear of being used as a battlefield, and a prevailing demand to exercise national prerogatives. The flanks have long been featured in nearly all discussions of alliance vulnerabilities. Today's preoccupation with these peripheral defenses may even have its psychological roots in the classic encirclement strategies formulated in Europe by Clausewitz, established by Moltke, and refined by Schlieffen. As alliance commitments are weighed and its cohesion is reassessed, it is not surprising that West Europeans are conscious of more subtle forms of aggression than a frontal Warsaw Pact attack. And Russia's historical preference for not confronting its main enemy but instead concentrating on weaker areas adds to this concern. Herein lies the dilemma of three decades of successful allied military deterrence being flanked literally by the political dislocation that is more pernicious during a time of sustained peace.

The search for Western military security carries the warning that real or presumed overall Soviet superiority would have devastating political as well as morale consequences on both sides of the Atlantic. This is uncertain. But what is clear is that Europeans—whether on the flanks or in the North German plains—are increasingly weary of having the United States serve as fiduciary for their national destinies.

A variety of indigenous nuclear defense possibilities has therefore been entertained, at least since the American strategic vulnerability issue was raised in 1957. Development of a joint European medium-range ballistic missile to complement similar Soviet investment has been among the most disquieting—to both superpowers. Talk of such weaponry is nothing new. When the ill-fated nuclear capable Multi-Lateral Force was forsaken in 1964, its critics prophesied its revival. Interest in an independent and credible nuclear retaliatory capacity has not faded entirely in Europe. In a reincarnation of the MLF, there would be no guarantee that what was once hinted at as an ultimate relaxation of the American nuclear veto would not be dispersed with altogether. Increasing East/West force imbalances, the continually enticing prospect of augmenting continental defenses once and for all through nuclear weaponry, and the hope of repatriating strategic policymaking to Europe all assure that the attraction of such forces will continue to frame assessments of U.S. reliability.

A more fruitful venture for improving NATO security through mutual planning and reassessment as part of the Long Term Defense Program (LTDP) has been through the ten task forces established in 1977. These task forces, or workgroups, address such matters as in-place readiness, mobilization and reinforcement capabilities, force rationalization, and nuclear planning. But the LTDP is essentially an extention of earlier initiatives such as the U.S.-sponsored Alliance Defense 70 (AD-70) and the European Defense Improvement Program (EDIP).

This latest effort at collective planning is not immune to the familiar ailments of alliance introspection: the senior partner is reticent when discussing all nuclear weapons, and sudden overly enthusiastic U.S. initiatives are accused of injuring those specific national planning procedures that annually move apace. Despite these difficulties, the hope remains that the discussions within these disparate workgroups institutionalized the role that other than military influences have in the alliance's defense calculus. The German chancellor, among others, has already declared that European stability is wedded to U.S. economic and monetary policies. So, besides assuring that this conviction is understood in the United States, NATO as a whole must be flexible in defining its security while confronting those economic issues (inseparable from political and military priorities) that have become arbiters of the alliance's future.

Economic Self-Examination

As a structure that serves political ends by military means, the alliance is also in need of redefining its goals. The social and economic dimensions of security have been insufficiently treated at a time when defense of freedom is increasingly interpreted as meaning more than deterrence of external attack. American observers, especially, too often disregard the seriousness of European anxieties over economic security and internal stability. As the West enters an era of reduced industrial growth, strains in transatlantic relations have the potential for developing further as the United States continues to consume the largest share of world-wide marketable resources and products. Heightened sensitivity to the perils of economic—as well as political—interdependence has become painfully apparent.

Expositions on the quantum jump in economic interdependence are, by now, common. These linkages even appeared desirable until 1973, when what Herman Kahn has called "the beautiful era" suddenly ended. Now reliance on states not sharing Western goals and perceptions is a threat insofar as the resulting economic parameters affect the established order. But NATO does not have to look exclusively to outsiders as fomenters of commercial distress. Disputes over activities of multinationals, the 1973 devaluation of the dollar, foreign trade, fisheries, and access to technology have all ensured substantial intra-alliance contention. And as a negative example of NATO's quest for continuity, the last two problems have been festering practically since its inception.

Europeans are now worrying primarily about economic rather than military security, concern over the latter often being submerged beneath the sense of day-to-day complacency. Given this sense of priority everyone should have enough to worry about—at least through the early 1980s—until the ratio between jobs and workers changes dramatically. Calvin Coolidge's less than helpful observation that a loss of jobs causes unemployment has an unfortunate timeliness for much of the alliance. The postwar cooption of Europe's surplus agricultural population is over, and with it the extent to which urbanization itself brought unprecedented growth.

There is a collapse among all involved—especially economists and parliamentarians—about how to treat the pandemic of national and international economic and monetary ills. Insofar as the alliance's health is maintained at least as much by economic and social nutrients as by military capacities, loss of these nutrients would diminish NATO's defensive abilities just as surely as would depleted defense budgets. The political consequences of Europe's highly unfavorable demographic pattern are unknown. But the short-term pacifiers of artificial full employment and generous welfare cannot be maintained. Regardless of the effects of what has been called the emerging "politics of less," the point that remains indisputable is that these effects are inseparable from NATO futures.

The prescriptive literature for preserving European economic and social security is burgeoning; the problems remain unsolved. Two topics stand out as examples of intersecting economic, political, and military priorities. They each contain the possibility of as yet unchanneled benefits. But a constant danger of both is the temptation to regard exclusively one institution or proposal—as with the concept of independent European deterrent forces—as a remedy for an expanse of NATO failings.

1. The European Community has the potential to serve as a prime instrument for several pressing alliance purposes. Its potential is an extension of the original American ideology—urged first in the Atlantic Pact and subsequently in NATO—that a united Europe must be the prerequiscte for Atlantic cooperation and equal partnership. The EC provides links of solidarity that could be of political as well as economic utility. Rather than talking of the Community superseding NATO, as was done in the late 1950s, a more practical view is that a major function of the EC during the alliance's fourth decade can be that of tying troubled members to ideals of liberal European democracy.

The last expansion of the EC, bringing in Britain, Denmark, and Ireland, was complicated enough. The inclusion of Greece, Portugal, and Spain will be all the more difficult. Sacrificial as this expansion may be for the economies and budgets of the northern states, Britain and Germany believe that expansion is justified by the political imperative of democratic unity. An expanded Community could find itself more salable to the large electorates of the left than have been continued efforts at bilateral security ties and cooperation along traditional NATO lines. Moreover, the EC has additional potential to stimulate economic development through further integration. This, in turn, could give the voluble leftist parties a stake in any ensuing economic benefits, thereby buttressing their positions against their even more radical critics. Moreover, Europe's democracies might find it easier to have difficult economic decisions imposed by external (that is, EC) discipline than to be forced to make unpopular internal choices. One can argue that the franc has been linked to the mark precisely for this reason.

A final security-related virtue of the EC is that it could act as a forum for European views outside of a U.S.-dominated NATO. A unified Europe acting as a distinct counterpart to the United States is probably more welcome by the Carter administration than it would have been by previous administrations. The amalgam of people and parties descending on the May 1979 parliamentary elections may not be the appropriate harbinger of such a new power. Rather, a successful European monetary union will probably be the best catalyst for the long-envisioned emergence of Europe as an autonomous power. In these and a variety of other ways, the EC could be used more as a vehicle for improving the durability of what is fundamentally a defense compact among sovereign states. But the history of the EC has been no less tumultuous than that of NATO. In the desire for mutualism it must be noted that securing subscribers to expansive EC ambitions can be just as formidable as rallying allies to the increasingly nonmilitary needs of the alliance.

2. Weapon standardization is another, and more focused, topic that embraces an array of political/military concerns while being based on economic priorities. Moreover, it is the classic example of the single solution that is expected to repair alliance deficiencies through what—like European economic convergence—would appear to be common sense. The reasons why the fifteen states within the alliance have been unable to apply standardization criteria to a variety of weapons are implied in nearly all the difficulties that have impeded cohesion since the start.

Because it is a compact rather than a community such as the EC, NATO members are certainly not bound by the rules of central institutions. Fears of curtailed national defense options and of U.S. technological colonialism are therefore given free rein. Even though an agency for standardization and simple interoperability has existed for over a decade within NATO's organizational structure, it has been unable to overcome the governmental prejudices created by such fears. On a solely national level, the case of the British Steel Corporation is an instructive parallel. It now runs at only two-thirds capacity (break-even is 90 percent) and is heavily overmanned. But the national perpetuation of such an exceedingly redundant industry is considered imperative, if only to avoid the monopolistic leverage that Britain fears other states would exert if it did not make steel. The corporation's former chairman warned about foreign suppliers, "They'd put prices up as soon as we'd lost it. They'd ruin our engineering industry. They'd hold us for ransom."[6]

Similarly, NATO defense priorities often are second to traditional national assumptions that the fundamental requirements of sovereignty—such as economic independence—are assumed best through self-sufficiency. If nation X did not produce weapon Y, such atavism goes, precepts of sovereignty (that is, military freedom of action) could be too easily compromised. This is explained in detail by Robert Dean in chapter 5. The ensuing deficiencies in weapon standardization can be readily cited as a contributing factor in an alliance in which increased aggregate defense outlays do not ensure military superiority. Matters are further complicated by the fact that preferential treatment to EC members for development and production in militarily useful industries (that is, aerospace, electronics, and computers) conflicts with efficient use of resources among NATO members as a whole. Weapon standardization through trade liberalization in the civil sector, as well as a competitive approach to weapon development and procurement in the military sector, are needed in the larger NATO community, rather than the smaller European community. Efforts to bring about the larger integration as a matter of U.S. policy would complicate matters by requiring some sacrifice in European integration in order to further integration in the larger NATO framework.[7]

The reconsideration of standardization that followed President Carter's

London pronouncements has—like so many other NATO initiatives—been unable to disentangle the mesh of arms sales and national weapons production. The countries of Western Europe may be quite close to U.S. levels of productivity, and some may well pass the leader during the 1980s. But certainly in the case of France, and even in the case of Germany, with its labor unions having favored arms sales, reluctance to standardize goes beyond paeans of nationalism to include clear-cut economic reward. Arms exports have helped to recycle oil expenditures. Moreover, the U.S. emphasis on standardization, as well as its increased push for sales within NATO, is believed to really mean weapon standardization around U.S. designs. The result for Europe would be loss of civilian spin-offs, greater unit costs from shorter national production runs, and unemployment for European engineers and design teams. In addition, critics fear, the United States would increase its commercial advantage over its allies in this field, as in others. U.S. military exports already contribute more revenues to total exports, as well as to total GNP, than do those of Britain, France, and West Germany. For all of these reasons (and others as far back as postwar anticolonialism), the sentiment is often apparent that U.S. ethical stances on such matters as arms sales and standardization efficiencies are unlikely to inconvenience U.S. commercial interests. The example of U.S. nonproliferation policy can be used to quickly reinforce a mischievous if nevertheless persuasive European refrain: that given a confluence of economic, military, and strategic-political matters, the Americans are disturbingly close to a variation on Secretary of Defense Charles Wilson's dictum—that is, what is good for the United States is good for the alliance.

In a final review of the adequacy of the European economies to help underwrite Western defense, there is cause for optimism; this is reasonable despite the delayed recovery from the recession of 1974-75. The GNP of the EC is five-sixths that of the United States and is growing rapidly. All European NATO economies are currently running below capacity; the burden of defense in the West has become lighter (as a percentage of GNP) during the past decade while that of the Soviet Union has increased; and as NATO turns thirty it is clear that with its still unfulfilled defense capacities Western Europe can afford both guns and butter. Moreover, countries like West Germany, which spend a larger fraction of their product on civilian research and development than does the United States, could be in the forefront of many military technologies during the 1980s and beyond. This, two decades later, may finally satisfy the hope generated by *Sputnik* that the allies would lighten the American burden of weapons research and development. Britain's leadership on the frontiers of antisubmarine warfare is a case in point. In the conceptual clarifications that the future will require for the meaning of Western security, it is certain that West European economic vigor must be credited with a central role.

Paired with national economics in any alliance inventory is the social well-being of those populations to be defended. Youthful malaise and urban terrorism have both given rise to pundits' odd Nietzschean mutterings of antiseptic, technological modernism forcing young warriors to make war upon themselves. Unsurprisingly, nothing that is concrete and little that is profound stem from these discussions, except the satisfaction that Eastern Europe does not appear immune to at least the less dramatic indications of such unrest. Similar socio-psychological abstractions surround examinations of so-called Eurocommunism, a trend whose direction is only slightly better understood. Until recently, U.S. interest in this topic had been obsessive. Eurocommunism, however, can no longer be regarded as the extreme left, but rather as the extreme reasonable left. Kevin Devlin pursues this in chapter 10. From the perspective of alliance solidity, the ironies that arise are several. Rather than encouraging reaction within Germany and Italy, terrorism has, if anything, attracted popular attention to the plight of Europe's beleaguered entrepreneurial classes. One suspects that the reason Germany was so exercised over Baader-Meinhoff has far more to do with the country's own insecurity about political reaction than it does with fear of any systemic threat. Terrorism has also demonstrated the generic political and intellectual elasticity of modern European democracy. The phenomenon of powerful leftist socialist parties, for its part, has stressed the mingling of ideological and national affinities. In France, nearly all factions understand that national defense policy is independent only so long as it has NATO to be independent from—a wry observation being the leftist preference for the Gaullist policy of *tous azimuths*. With a different electoral arithmetic and political situation, the organized Italian left appears equally adaptable to the alliance status quo. The immutability of the outlooks of both France and Italy may be one of the most revealing of recent NATO developments.

Reports that NATO's contradictions foreshadow collapse have been commonplace for nearly a generation; cynicism has centered more on the members' ability to sustain political and economic vitality than on the prospect of the alliance's crumbling before Warsaw Pact threat or attack. So far, it is the national anxieties themselves that have proven the most damaging. But the predictions of NATO's demise that so frequently gain currency and then abate are always premature. Rather, there are indicators of calm in the midst of controversy. For example, the heavy European investment in the United States during the late 1970s certainly would have been seen as a classic flight of capital in less confident times. But it is instead viewed constructively on both sides of the Atlantic. William Butler Yeats's lament that "things always fall apart; the center never holds" has for thirty years been inapplicable as the alliance's economic foundation remains resilient.

Conclusion: Prospect of a New Vitality

There are continuities as well as differences between the traditional politics of military security and today's popularization of political and economic interdependence. An unambiguous European conviction is apparent (articulated forcibly even by the Dutch) as to the unacceptability of political benefits stemming from Soviet military potential. European recognition of the Gulag, the dissidents, and the profoundly conservative cast of the Soviet Union have all ensured that Moscow is far less of a model—certainly to radical youth—than it was in the past. The word "consensus" has become tedious after serving as a yardstick for NATO performance throughout the past generation. But in an alliance that has never been short on causes for internal discord, consensus of a sort emerges when the original NATO mandate of military defense is weighed against today's Warsaw Pact offensive capacity.

During NATO's first decade the slogan of interdependence arose nearly exclusively in a thermonuclear connotation; it was part of the phraseology used by civilian strategists during the debates over deterrence. When applied to a variety of modern nonmilitary security issues—energy, technology, monetary reform, and even ideologies—the contemporary impact of this phenomenon can be readily understood. But the original implication of U.S.-European strategic linkage still provides the firmament for the allied partnership. For the moment, the new vitalities within NATO are directed toward collectivity rather than dissolution: indicators include a reversed Canadian decision, and the subsequent purchase of Leopard tanks; an attempt at a 3 percent real term defense budget increase undertaken by all, albeit with ambiguities of accounting; a quiet rise in British defense spending that was virtually unquestioned by the left; and even a measured homogeneity with French military planning. Yet all this rests on a continuing assessment of U.S. political/military inextricability.

While U.S. and European critics speculate on the consequences of superpower parity, the fact remains that this is an old fear now surfacing from beneath the Curtis Le May civilization's rubble of strategic theorizing. As Alistair Buchan wrote in 1958, "The Soviet-American strategic deadlock is now fundamentally unbreakable."[8] But loose talk from rarified Washington sources, as well as a disturbing U.S. pliability in SALT, legitimizes those European critics who perceive a fundamental lack of military mutuality. America's portfolio of strategic weaponry, however, assures the superpower status quo. The much-vaunted dangers of optical parity are moot—insofar as rough equivalence has been a prime characteristic of the balance, from the European perspective at least, since Buchan's declaration.

Within the current West European context, the Soviets probably cannot use military force for political purposes, and the myth of Finlandization has generally been dispelled. But the problem returns to the members' original concerns of unity in extra-NATO military contingencies, most immediately the gray area of Yugoslavia. Despite the day-to-day complacency, the prospect of sudden high-risk Soviet policy has not been dismissed. This is especially true in the absence of effective confidence-building measures or those arms control agreements that might better try to limit Soviet options rather than numbers. As was the case in the alliance's beginning, Europe's two great powers are militarily committed elsewhere: Britain greets NATO's second generation with its troops in Ireland and with the possibility of involving them in Rhodesia; France, for its part, is distracted by its obligations in Africa. The alliance's attenuation is yet another one of those continuities that would be better abandoned. And new twists such as official German displeasure over the size of NATO's Reforger wargames keep alive doubts about overall coordination.

The Soviets, in sum, probably can be depended upon to cement the partnership, although their diminished stridency can also encourage complacency. The peace offensive that Vandenberg dreaded thirty years ago was, for better or for worse, never launched. Unless there is unforeseen and sweeping change in European governments, the Soviet Union will continue its roles as both opponent and unifier of the West. Therefore the alliance can continue to pursue (even in a stumbling fashion) its principle of collective defense, while having the durability of cultural, economic, and political interconnectedness go unchallenged.

If the allies had to agree unanimously on every act they took, NATO clearly would not and could not function. But for the United States, current policies of wishfulness (besides those de facto policies on matters where no policy exists) are as inappropriate in contending with international economic and monetary priorities as they would be if applied to U.S. military concerns. With the integration of all three, a need for overall political coherence is inseparable from any dedication to realizing the thirty-year-old goal of proximate Atlantic unity as a necessary supplement to European defense.

The question to be asked of NATO at the crossing of this generation span is the one that Marshall Foch posed in considering any prospective war or other military action: "De quoi s'agit il?" What specific policy objectives and national interests are to be served? How great is the value attached to them, and what is their fair price? And, in the long term, how might intellectual and cultural divergence between the United States and Europe affect common security interests a decade or two from now?

The requirements of deterrence are still being met, and at the same time the military framework has come to underpin Europe's economic development. The price incurred is the perpetual problem of alliance diplomacy, replete with the suspicions and contradictions that characterize such relations. But all these problems are manageable, and thirty years of the alliance indicate that the members at least believe that the price is worth paying. Like the predictions of Italian collapse, German paralysis, and British devolution, reports of NATO's demise are decidedly premature.

But current U.S. proclivities help to inhibit a common reply to Foch's question. And the ever-increasing number of security concerns in the 1980s could deemphasize further the traditional military indices of collective purpose. The objective of a supranational Western defense—based on politically equal and economically sound national constituencies—nevertheless remains paramount. Its value is inestimable if only because the alternatives imply far more unpleasant West European dislocations than have been caused by a generation of intra-alliance confrontations.

Notes

1. As quoted in Thomas K. Finletter, *Interim Report* (New York: Norton, 1968), p. 73.

2. *New York Times*, 3 May 1978.

3. Senator S. Nunn, *Policy, Troops, and the NATO Alliance*, 2 April 1974, p. 4.

4. *Washington Post*, 13 July 1977.

5. Sir William Slim, *Courage and Other Broadcasts* (London: Cassell, 1957).

6. *New York Times*, 28 May 1978.

7. "Trade Liberalization as a Path to Weapons Standardization in NATO," Charles Wolf and Derek Leebaert, *International Security* II (Winter 1978).

8. Alistair Buchan, "Their Bomb and Ours," *Encounter* XII (January 1959), p. 12.

2 Retreat from a Shared Vision

Stephen J. Barrett

Relations between the United States and Western Europe have gone through a number of redefinitions in response to changing circumstances that altered perceptions and possibilities. This chapter sets out to examine some features of past, present, and future transatlantic relations in an attempt to see how far, in the case of regional security, there can be said to be a sound basis for the links between the United States and Western Europe; how far the assumption of shared objectives is tenable, and whether the process of determining objectives across the Atlantic has more attributes of consultation and cooperation than of unilateral action.

Since the end of World War II there has been no marked shortage of concepts or models of transatlantic relations. The vocabulary has included the ideas of partnership, of Community and Grand Design, and, most recently of interdependence. Over the same period, the plane of analysis has shifted from the two-dimensional world of containment of Communist power to the three-dimensional world of architecture and engineering, with its own images of pillars and structures. To a great extent the changes in vocabulary have corresponded to shifts in relative power and to changes in the key problems of the day.

Difficulties in finding an enduring model have been reflected in much of the writing on transatlantic relations. The literature is strongly marked by diagnosis and prescription. It is no accident that a sense of malaise and dysfunction can be found in a row of titles that run from Henry Kissinger's *The Troubled Partnership* through Stanley Hoffmann's *Gulliver's Troubles* to the series of studies edited by David Landes under the title of *Western Europe: The Trials of Partnership*. Taken as contributions to an understanding of the problems of transatlantic relations, these and similar works are striking testimony to the difficulty of getting the relationship right, both analytically and operationally. However, they are also persuasive evidence for the view that relations between the United States and Western Europe are important in several unique respects. It is true that if relations between the Soviet Union and the United States go catastrophically wrong, the consequences may extinguish most of humanity. At another level, good relations between the United States and some of the principal oil-producing countries help guarantee that oil supplies to the Western world at large will not be disrupted. Nevertheless, there remains a *special* sense in which relations between the United States and Western Europe are critical to the survival of both continents, affect the influence each can wield elsewhere, and therefore can and should be better than they are.

The immediate postwar summit of transatlantic cooperation was based on a restored and revived Western Europe enjoying the protection of a military alliance with the United States, facing a Communist world that still appeared menacing in Western eyes. In outline, this was the general perception shared by Western Europeans and Americans alike. As a picture of the state of affairs at the time, it was not inaccurate. It might therefore have continued to serve as a valid principle of action if it had not been for developments which called into question the focus of the picture and began to break up the detail into more fragmented patterns and shapes.

From the mid-1950s onwards the latent assumptions began to be questioned or subjected to modification. At the global level, the changes had to do with the nature of the threat to the West and the sources from which it emanated. In two distinct ways the implications for the United States differed from those for Europe. First, the Soviet Union, which had exploded its first atomic device in August 1949, acquired over this period enough of a capability for attacking the United States to make it apparent that the American commitment to Western Europe had for the first time ceased to be virtually cost-free in terms of danger to the American homeland. Second, decolonization and the progressive loss of projectable European power outside Europe accelerated the process by which American interests were becoming increasingly global in character, with the consequence that Western Europe could no longer be entirely confident that its own interests would more or less automatically seem identical with those of the United States.

The shape of these new developments emerged slowly. Furthermore, American support for the progress of integration in Europe helped to brake an early tendency for one side of the Atlantic to fall out with the other. To some extent it can also be argued that the concentration of Western Europe on its own affairs made it less conscious of the potential for its interests and those of the United States to drift apart.

The familiar postwar image of a West digging in against a Soviet military threat and rebuilding the fabric of its society in the interests of preserving Western values did duty as a unifying principle of action for the first postwar decade. However, as new pressures and interests introduced a revised global agenda of issues in which there were also opportunities for different perceptions of the Soviet threat the image began to deteriorate. In purely transatlantic terms, the new factors can be grouped into several distinct categories and their impact charted accordingly.

Superpower Duopoly

The ending of the era of American nuclear monopoly ushered in a period during which the United States acquired an increasing strategic vulnerability to Soviet nuclear attack. It removed the near-certainty that the West possessed an effective deterrent, and substituted a calculus in which many could equate flexibility with doubt and faltering commitment. It raised the question of how the Europeans should respond to the changed military threat. And it required the alliance countries to evolve a new strategic doctrine to meet the new circumstances. These various forces set up some divisive cross-currents. The Europeans were clearly unhappy with the early formulations of the doctrine of flexible response, since it faced them, in effect, with a choice between the expense of increased outlay on conventional weapons—with the implication that they would be the foot soldiers in any European conflict—and accepting the early use of the tactical nuclear weapons, with devastating effects on the population and fabric of Western Europe. And there was also a third possibility that could not be ignored: that at the end of the day Western Europe might find that it had bought expensive but insufficient conventional strength and would have to be defended by the use of tactical nuclear weapons on Western European territory.

It is something of a paradox that as Soviet military power grew in the 1960s, so the Western view of the Soviet threat diminished. The political reasons for this include, on the European side, the desire to deal with the Soviet Union on the basis of European and national interests; the emergence of *Ostpolitik* in the Federal Republic; the hope among the Western European countries that exports to the Soviet Union and Eastern Europe could be increased, and a wish after the death of Stalin to explore the prospects for peaceful change in the Soviet Union and Eastern Europe. Then too there were stirrings of resentment against American predominance. In addition, the American side was involved in the early stages of the attempt to devise some way of managing relations with the Soviet Union with a view to minimizing the risk of war in Europe, and of the effort to work toward some measure of understanding and mutual restraint in other areas of the world where the superpowers had interests and there was potential for conflict. The combined effect was that the reality of the Soviet threat to Western Europe was called into question, while the United States began to downgrade NATO as the primary means of organizing its relations with the Soviet Union.

Economic Challenges

The postwar economic verities were bound to alter as the European economies revived and the European Economic Community gradually took on the character of a major economic grouping. Signs of strain came from various directions. In the early 1960s the U.S. administration could note that "when one partner possesses over 50 percent of the resources of an enterprise and the balance is distributed among sixteen or seventeen others, the relationship is unlikely to work very well" (Undersecretary of State George Ball in Philadelphia on 16 February 1962), and could use this thesis to gain support for the expanding Community and for President Kennedy's proposals for a Trade Expansion Act. Yet the economic consequences of U.S. involvement in Southeast Asia were to make the American support for a strong European economy as a counterpart to that of the United States wobble perceptibly in many instances. In 1966 Robert McNamara's attempts to persuade the Federal Republic of Germany to help the American balance of payments problem by purchasing arms from the United States helped to unsettle the government of Chancellor Erhard. And the intermittent rumbles over offset arrangements have been an indirect assertion that the strength of the West German economy requires a greater German contribution to the smooth running of the Western economic system.

At the regional level, the increased concentration of economic and commercial power in the enlarged EEC has made it easier for both sides to question the notion that what benefits Western Europe will automatically benefit the United States as well. Trade negotiations between Europeans and Americans over the last decade or so have reflected the new relationship. But the economies of the United States and Western Europe are likely to remain closely linked, despite the considerably lesser degree of American dependence on foreign trade. In terms of global power, the United States cannot easily ignore an area where the gross national product, steel production, and foreign trade all exceed that of the Soviet Union.

Some illuminating indicators of the nature of the economic nexus linking the United States and Western Europe can be formed from United States trade and investment statistics. Between 1974 and 1976 U.S. exports of goods and services to Western Europe did not fall below 27 percent of total U.S. exports of goods and services (the figures for exports of goods and services to the EEC was in the 20-21 percent region during the period). Over the same period, American imports of goods and services from Western Europe accounted for between 25 and 29 percent (EEC: 18-22 percent) of total United States imports. In 1975 over 50 percent of foreign investment in the United States was Western European in origin, while American investment in Western Europe represented about 22 percent of American investment abroad and provided nearly 60 percent of the contribution from overseas investment to the U.S. balance of payments.

However much economic and commercial links of this sort support the proposition that in some general sense there is a close and mutually beneficial relationship between the United States and Western Europe, they cannot disguise the existence of fundamental disequilibria. The inequalities stem from key asymmetries between the two regions. Although the gross domestic products of the United States and of the European members of the EEC are roughly equal in value, the in-built tendency of the United States economy to operate at a level of dependence on foreign trade only about a third as great as that of the major European EEC countries allows the United States a degree of insulation from the world economy. That insulation needs to be offset by a conscious effort by Washington to exercise a degree of responsibility for the world economy. In other words, while these may be cogent political and moral reasons for U.S. interest in the well-being of other democratic societies, there is probably no overwhelming economic reason for a continuing U.S. interest in the health of the economy of the rest of the Western world. To the extent that this is true, any particular set of measures taken in relation to the international arena may have to face the opposition of powerful interests in the United States. This is of course especially pertinent where imports into the United States are sensitive domestically and lead to demands for protection. It is not easy to play the role of the major actor on the international stage when the audience is prone to doubt the necessity for the drama in the first place.

A second and potentially more disturbing source of disequilibrium arises out of the double asymmetry in respect to the oil-producing countries. According to estimates prepared by the OECD (International Energy Agency), in 1980 the United States will be importing less oil than the European members of OECD and will be less dependent than the latter on imported oil both in proportion to total oil requirements and in proportion to total energy requirements. For Europeans there will remain the disturbing probability that if an energy shortage develops in the mid-1980s, the United States will be able to ensure that it continues to receive the lion's share. In any competition for a scarce resource the Europeans as a whole are likely to do less well than the United States, although one or two individual West European countries may be able to hold their own. There seems no reason to deny this central trend as long as greater factor mobility permits the American economy to remain generally more adaptable than the economies of Europe. For the Europeans there is thus a disturbing prospect that just as in conditions of no restraint on supply the American economy can obtain the oil required, so in more stringent times it will be European industries and workers rather than American ones that have to adapt to the shortages that may develop. In short, the European concern is that Western Europe lacks the projectable strength to ensure security of supply and that in time its community of interests with the United States will be enough to make it an attractive target for those seeking to put pressure on the United States, but insufficient to guarantee it American protection against disruption.

Based on this scenario, the 1980s could see increasing economic divisions among the OECD countries. The GNP of one set of countries may increase while there is near stagnation in others; conditions of recession and large-scale underemployment of capital and human resources may call into question the identity of political and social interests that has underpinned the transatlantic world since 1945; worst of all, a combination of rampant protectionism and an oil shortage could undermine not only the economic but also the political achievements of the Atlantic countries.

An Increasing Distance

There are already some signs of a separation of views between the United States and Western Europe over a range of societal issues. It is too early to say whether this represents a process that will continue, or whether it can be likened to an undocking of two space vehicles which thereafter continue to travel in a reasonably close relationship one to the other. The movement apart is on more than one plane. Along the philosophical axis, Europeans as a whole probably attach more importance than do Americans to equality of result—as opposed to equality of opportunity—within their society. On the practical plane, there appears to be a European preference for employment over growth and for stability of employment over readjustments to structural and innovation-caused changes in the work force. There preferences are not absolute (nor of course are they universally accepted within the respective societies). But for whatever reason and despite significant differences in detail, different approaches to the organization of society have emerged. The United States tends to see governmental and institutional intervention in society as desirable only when major changes of course are required or when equable relations between or among major social or economic groups have broken down. Europeans, on the other hand, expect their governments to order matters in such a way that stability of employment and income is achieved.

Thus the question arises whether these broad differences are likely to have any impact on the relations between the United States and Europe. Barring the total breakdown of Western cooperation, it seems intrinsically probable that the Western democratic tradition can assimilate without strain differences of this sort in political and economic objectives. This does not imply, however, that there will be a common view on the extent to which Western countries can accept an injection of Communist influence into the decision-making organs of the West without suffering a significant weakening of Western cohesiveness.

The problem is familiar—with one important difference. There is a past history of differences, at times forcefully expressed, about how to respond to communism. The process by which détente was added to the NATO objectives of defense and deterrence and the difficulties over *Ostpolitik* and trade with Eastern Europe are part of transatlantic history. But in these cases the problem concerned primarily contacts with external forces and did not entail any major alteration in the nature of Western society itself. However, the admission of a Communist party into a West European government will raise questions about the long-term direction of European society, just as it will introduce defense and security complications in proportion to the role of the country in the NATO alliance. The point is not whether or not Eurocommunism exists, or whether it or its national disaggregations will increase in influence, but whether the shared value-system of the Western countries can confidently and securely survive the implantation into Western society at the decision-making level of what is bound to be perceived as a significantly unreliable and alien set of influences.

Thus there is a broad canvas of issues where the assumption of an operationally significant identity of attitudes between the United States and Western Europe may be subjected to challenge and erosion over the next few years. The strategic identities have been wobbly; the economic cointerests remain powerful but conceal much potential for trouble; and on the ideological front there is some doubt about the impact of any close association of Communist parties with the governmental process in Western Europe.

A Problem in the Context of World Management

In addition to developments mainly within the Western alliance, there has been a major change in the way in which the United States regards Europe. What was once the major critical point of confrontation with the Soviet Union in the simplified power struggle during the postwar years has become at the most *primus inter pares* of American global interest areas. Europe remains a key component in the global scheme—its resources and commercial importance are likely to guarantee this status. But this status is one that the Europeans must share with other areas. The fact that the United States no longer construes the state of the global system primarily or exclusively in terms of the situation in Europe reflects two separate but mutually reinforcing developments. The first has to do with the rise in the relative importance attached to other parts of the world; China and the Far East have always had a particular place in American perceptions, but the Middle East and Africa are only the latest additions to a list of regions for which the United States must frame a policy. The second development has been the emergence of the United States and the Soviet Union as superpowers in the true sense, that is, as countries with the ability to project political, economic, and military force throughout the world.

Against this background, the primacy of Europe and its concerns was certain to be diminished. It is not without its ironic aspects that the dangers of a military confrontation in Europe and the risks of major political upheavals there have lessened at least in part because of the way in which the two superpowers, out-distancing all rivals, have encouraged or at least tolerated developments in the European context that make European conflict less likely. The move toward détente, *Ostpolitik*, the 1971 Berlin Agreements, and the Conference on Security and Cooperation in Europe represent some of the aspects of the attempt to set ground rules for East/West rivalry in Europe and to govern the rate and direction of change in both parts of Europe.

This trend has not been unwelcome in Europe. As has already been argued, the disappearance of the cold war has coincided with a wish to explore the prospects for a peaceful evolution of conditions in Eastern Europe and the Soviet Union, as well as the possibilities of trade with the communist countries. At the same time, there has been a price that West Europeans have had to pay for what some discern as peaceful coexistence and others as détente. This price is expressed in a threat of loss of strategic control over their destiny. With NATO ceasing to be the primary means by which the United States manages its relations with the Soviet Union, Western Europe is faced with a different and troublesome set of problems:

1. How to influence the growing superpower dialogue.
2. How to ensure that the strategic posture and doctrine of the United States satisfy European requirements and concerns.
3. How to ensure that what may be agreed between the United States and the Soviet Union under (1) or what is decided by the United States under (2) strengthens rather than weakens Western European power and, in a different area, assists rather than detracts from the prospects for a closer and more coherent Western European identity and influence.

From the American standpoint the superpower dialogue is a necessary feature of global management. To the extent that the crisis potential of Europe has been diminished, so purely European concerns tend to recede into the wider background where what really matters is not so much events within Europe as their effect on the world scene. At the same time, there is an evident connection between a regional military balance in Europe and the impact of the European situation on the world scene. This in turn means that if the balance of forces within Europe is perceived by either side to be politically destabilizing or military dangerous, there will be an enhanced risk that events in Europe will get out of hand.

Western Coordination

Within the Western alliance there will be a continuing desire to follow closely, and to influence where necessary, discussions between the Soviet Union and the United States—especially where these concern the present and future regional balance in Europe. American steps to keep NATO informed about SALT can be expected to continue. The MBFR negotiations also provide what is in principle an adequate means of ensuring intra-NATO consultation and participation where issues affecting the European balance are concerned, though the harmonization of American and Western European interests could be adversely affected if "gray area" questions are introduced into bilateral superpower discussions elsewhere. There have been suggestions that the interaction between the superpower discussions and those among the MBFR participants warrants the creation of more comprehensive European arms control negotiating machinery, so that the interconnection at the European level between strategic and tactical and between nuclear and conventional weaponry can be handled more efficiently. Setting aside the point that in the real world the establishment of new machinery nearly always involves significant bureaucratic and organizational discontinuities and loss of momentum, it may be doubted whether the situation is really one which would be improved by the devising of a new negotiation forum, at any rate for the present. The significance of weapons development in the 1980s has not gone unnoticed, and until there is an agreed Western position, a move to a fresh scene would in all probability lead to more frustration, mistrust, and disunity than to substantive progress. This is, however, an issue that should be kept under review since there may come a time when it will be advantageous to set up a new negotiating body charged with a wider range of European security issues. The entire question of the appropriate role of negotiations in ensuring European security is addressed in chapter 11.

Interdependence in Fact and Fiction

Regional security in Western Europe began by being focused primarily on the threat of Soviet aggression and on the dangers that prolonged economic disturbances would create for Western democracy. Since then it has had to justify itself in circumstances of detente and strategic parity and to accommodate itself to changing power relations within Western Europe. It has also had to guard against dangers of a routinization that called in question the case for a coordinated Western defense as generations changed in both East and West. Most recently it has had to prove a continuing relevance at a time when attention is directed more often to questions such as oil, the Middle East, and the problems of the third and fourth worlds than to the firepower disparities and geographical asymmetries along the East/West border. It is not surprising that the purely European aspects of regional security in Europe can appear as irritating factors in any American grand strategy, nor is it a cause for wonder that Europeans are concerned lest American preoccupation with global issues should blind the U.S. administration and congressional and public opinion to the possibility of a growing divergence between the political and economic objectives of the United States and those of its European allies. An anxiety of a different sort is felt by those in Western Europe who are confident that their structures and values are perceived as vital to American interests but who remain concerned that the span of attention of the United States will prove too short at some critical moment.

There have also been significant changes in the connotation of the term "interdependence." As was noted in the last chapter, interdependence was regarded in a positive light up to the 1970s. It offered a model of mutual support where both the powerful and the less powerful could feel they had a part to play. But by the late 1970s interdependence had acquired a strong element of dependence on outside powers. What was an attractive notion when the set of interdependent countries was defined as those in OECD and NATO lost some of its charm with the realization that the Western countries were linked with countries that might have different political and social goals. To adapt a phrase of James Thurber, dependence turned out to be two-thirds of interdependence as the Western countries began to face the implications of OPEC and the demands of the developing countries for a fairer share of the world's resources, markets, and wealth.

Part of the European adaptation to the new circumstances has taken the form of a deeper recognition that attention to the external responsibilities of the EEC is the best insurance against disruption of supply. At the same time Western Europe has had to relearn the old paradox that strength does not always convey invulnerability. In European eyes the issues of security of supply of oil and other raw materials loom larger than questions of the global strategic balance. In both these respects European interests have taken on a hue somewhat different from that of American concerns.

In analytical terms, what has happened in transatlantic relations over the last ten years or so can be considered as the consequences of subjecting established control and guidance mechanisms to new and unexpected inputs. The Western economies, based on a sound dollar, cheap raw materials, and adequate markets abroad, have experienced currency instabilities, raw material price increases, and domestic economic disturbances that have caused an undercurrent of protectionism. The North Atlantic Alliance has had to try to maintain its legitimacy in conditions of détente and at a time of change and uncertainty in military doctrine and weapons. Concurrently, questions arise about the long-term orientation of these West European countries where a Communist party is within striking distance of acquiring seats in the government. These new developments have put pressure on older institutions and the broad transatlantic consensus that had grown up since the 1950s. The Western response has been uncertain and halting—indeed, it is possible to construe the useful series of summit-type meetings of Western heads of government both as recognition of the existence of serious problems and as evidence that existing institutions and approaches are not able to deal with them properly. However, a measure of skepticism about arguments for another phase of institution-building seems warranted. Without a coherent group of new problems that can be divorced from other continuing issues, the case for a further international forum is not convincing and it seems better to use the familiar method of injecting high-level political pressure into existing bodies when circumstances so demand. What can be asserted with some confidence is that there are no signs of the sort of will to set up new machinery comparable to the drives and pressures that led to NATO, OECD, or the EEC.

Some Prospects for the Future

What continues to distinguish Western Europe from the other areas in which the United States is involved in regional security is that only in Europe are the forces of the two superpowers so positioned that they could directly and immediately become involved in a war. For their part, the West Europeans will see the maintenance of American forces in Europe as a guarantee of American protection, while the Final Act of the Conference on Security and Cooperation in Europe amounts to Soviet recognition of American participation in the management of European security. It is likely to continue to suit the Soviets to have to deal with the United States over the military aspects of European security. They will see the American presence as a safeguard against a German nuclear capability, and they may reckon that the degree of political stability provided by the American guarantee creates a more advantageous climate for their long-term political purposes than would the uncertain and potentially volatile situation that would follow withdrawal of the American commitment to Western Europe.

From the American standpoint, the case for maintaining the defense commitment to Europe may be expected to continue to prevail. The impact of the neo-isolationist wave that followed the collapse in Vietnam has largely been absorbed. In fact, the strong sense of underlying common interests between the United States and Western Europe has probably benefited from a contraction of American military involvement outside Europe. Pressures, mainly on economic grounds, to repatriate American forces from Europe will make themselves felt, but as long as the United States continues to sense its global responsibilities, it is unlikely unilaterally to destabilize the regional situation in Western Europe by major unrequited withdrawals of troops or weapons from the area. In short, it is probable that there will continue to be a good deal more than the necessary minimum of agreement between the United States and Western Europe on the importance of the defense of the region.

There may, however, be strains between the United States and Western Europe over broad economic and social questions as differences in economic vulnerability and social priorities manifest themselves. Although changes in power relationships cannot long be checked if the underlying realities provide the driving force, it will be desirable for the United States to demonstrate understanding and to work on the assumption that gradual changes over time may be acceptable, whereas abrupt and sharp discontinuities can disrupt societies and alliances. There will be a need for solidarity, even some short-term sacrifice of advantage, on the part of the United States in the interest of a constructive and satisfactory working relationship with a Western Europe which will be getting used to the idea that, like a latter-day Venice, its wealth and influence may be based on insecure foundations. This will require highly sophisticated leadership from the United States, where continuing domestic pressures for greater freedom of action may loom quite as large as recognition of the need to manage global matters in the interests of Western values.

From the vantage point of Western Europe the perspective will be different. Strategically, it will be necessary to acknowledge the global responsibilities of the United States and to see European concerns against this background. The countries of Western Europe must also live with the fact that their economic vulnerability causes them to be highly sensitive to global economic issues while they lack the American capacity to choose between influence and aloofness. The combination of economic interdependence with high societal expectations is likely to ensure that the issues will be politically charged when they are debated domestically in Europe. From this it follows that high-level brokering of issues across the board will be necessary and can be expected to characterize dealings between the United States and Western Europe for the foreseeable future.

For Western Europe, regional security is therefore never likely to be realized in the form of military or economic independence. The effective choice thus lies between various structures of interdependence, each offering a different role for Western Europe. The immediate external threat to Western Europe may have lessened; the risks of global war may have diminished; but in an interdependent age, where the chief dangers are internal uncertainty and the challenges of the changing world, the stability and security of Western Europe will probably remain closely bound to the United States. In terms of a different image, American and Western European societies appear to be traveling in the same direction, despite differences in construction and efficiency, lapses in convoy discipline, and a continuing requirement for better map-reading.

3 New Threat—or Old Fears?

Henry Stanhope

The Nunn-Bartlett report of January 1977 described a "new threat" to the North Atlantic Alliance. Against a background of strategic nuclear parity with the United States and advances in their tactical nuclear capability, the Soviets had endowed their forces opposite West Germany with the ability to initiate a potentially devastating invasion of Western Europe with as little as a few days warning.[1] It was not simply an enlarged threat, but one whose character had been deliberately retailored to exploit the very weaknesses in NATO's conventional posture which had always plagued the alliance.[2] This has provoked an ongoing controversy over the warning time that the allies might expect.

This chapter examines the military balance in the light of these perceptions, and offers conclusions on the significance of recent developments. It is concerned only with the Central Region of Europe, partly because this is the region upon which Senators Nunn and Bartlett, and others like Lieutenant General James F. Hollingsworth, have focused their attention, and partly because it does after all represent the NATO heartland. If the Central Region collapsed before an armed invasion, then NATO would assuredly expire with it.

This chapter makes only passing reference to the tactical use of nuclear weapons. While they have a place in the mechanism of flexible response, NATO's capacity to defend itself must be measured in conventional terms. Accordingly, this chapter foregoes discussion of the military implications of the so-called neutron bomb; the topic itself is addressed in chapter 11. It seems unlikely that NATO would make first use of nuclear weapons unless it has lost this capacity, and its forces have been reduced to those extreme circumstances which they are anxious to avoid. It remains quite possible that the Soviet Union would make first use of nuclear firepower, and some might consider it unrealistic to postulate any Central European conflict without taking this into account. But the likelihood of this happening, at least during the initial phase of any campaign, has receded in recent years.

Changing Perceptions

Perceptions of the conventional balance in Central Europe have changed continually and sometimes dramatically during the last fifteen years. Alain

Enthoven and Wayne Smith have demonstrated that NATO was born with a psychological complex about conventional weapons,[3] a complex which it has never fully outgrown. Through the 1950s and early 1960s military commanders at SHAPE commonly contrasted a total of 175 well-equipped, highly trained Soviet divisions with twenty-five or so ill-equipped, badly trained NATO divisions and drew the glum conclusion that the alliance could hold out for only a few days against a conventional assault before being forced to resort to nuclear weapons.[4]

It was only after the Systems Analysis Office in Washington had closely examined these long-held assumptions that a completely fresh assessment was made—though not universally accepted at first. In terms of overall manpower and materiel the two power blocs could be considered more or less equal.[5] A similar exercise indicated rough equivalence, if not NATO superiority, in tactical airpower—as against the previous contention that NATO was outnumbered three-to-one.[6] By 1967 Secretary McNamara felt able to declare with reasonable confidence that "even without the French forces NATO at present outnumbers the Warsaw Pact in terms of men on the Central Front."[7]

Thus the new assessments of the military balance helped to provide the rationale for NATO's eventual switch in strategy from one of massive retaliation to flexible response in 1967. It can be contended that the Systems Analysis Office merely proved what the U.S. administration had wanted it to prove, which was that allied reliance on American nuclear weapons could be reduced without detriment to European security, and indeed with considerable gain in credibility. But this is not to argue the rights and wrongs of the case.

Nor is it an attempt to apply the same findings to the current debate. The more conspicuous force improvements to which Nunn and Bartlett refer have been introduced by the Soviet Union since then. Moreover, Enthoven and Smith demonstrated only how conventional defense was made to appear "feasible" and went on to list a number of areas, such as troop deployment, manning and training levels, mobilization schedules and ammunition stocks, where there was room for considerable improvement in NATO's posture. It was not so much a prescription for complacency as a counseling against despair.

The point is that perceptions of the balance can change more swiftly and dramatically than the balance itself, and with results which are potentially as significant. It has been argued that the Soviet Union has won more than psychological satisfaction from the general assumption by Western nations that its forces are hugely superior to their own. "By translating what was at most a small measure of actual tactical advantage into the appearance of decisive strength, the Soviet Union has made tangible gains in the arena of East-West relations, and continues to do so."[8]

The start of the Vienna MBFR talks in 1973 stimulated a new wave of reassessments of the balance.[9] Criticism of NATO has since been directed from a narrower perspective. This post-Enthoven school of analysts, while largely conceding that NATO's input is adequate, has concentrated its attention on the output. NATO has enough resources, but does not use them to the best advantage. "Though the NATO aggregate strength is impressive, its defense posture as a whole is less than the sum of its parts. . . . Militarily NATO's crying need is not so much for more as for better."[10] Germane, if controversial, is the contention (discussed later by Robert Dean) that the alliance wastes at least $11 billion annually by not exploiting the advantages of common research and development, joint procurement and support functions.[11]

One specific criticism has been that NATO forces are configured to fight a protracted war, while the Warsaw Pact is prepared to wage a short one. The difference is not surprising, but it is not very sensible either. Forces designed to fight a short, violent engagement at least keep open the options of continuing to defend themselves in a longer engagement. Those which are structured for a long drawn out affair may simply not survive that long.[12]

Still more recently and rather more stridently, attention has been drawn to the danger of not only a short war but a sudden one. The assumption has been that it would start so swiftly and with so little warning that NATO would be unable to prolong it even if it wanted to. General Robert Close of the Belgian Army estimated in 1976, amid widespread publicity, that the Soviet Union could put thirty-nine divisions into the front line within forty-eight hours of mobilization, followed by sixty more within six days, while NATO could muster only twenty-two admittedly larger divisions, and would then have to rely upon British and North American reinforcements to make what could well be a hazardous journey to the European land-mass.[13] General Hollingsworth in his classified report in 1976 postulated an attack on fifty-four Pact divisions, twenty-seven of them Russian, in forty-eight hours.[14]

This then is the "new threat," also perceived by Senators Nunn and Bartlett. It does not rest upon an assumption that the Soviet Union would seriously contemplate a premeditated attack upon the West in Central Europe. The point has been made that during the last decade the Russians have scrupulously avoided celebrating their new superpower status by the expansionist policies and risk-taking adventures that some Western observers had predicted.[15] Even Senators Nunn and Bartlett dismissed any suggestion that a Soviet invasion of Western Europe was likely.[16] More credible is the "conflict arising from miscalculation during a period of tension," described by McNamara.[17] It is this kind of scenario to which overwhelming Soviet military power could be relevant.

Soviet Force Improvements

There is general agreement that the Soviet Union has improved its forces in Eastern Europe during recent years. There is less agreement over the scale of these improvements and still less over their significance. According to official British estimates, the number of tanks in the Central Region has increased by 31 percent, artillery pieces by 25 percent, armored personnel carriers (APCS) by 78 percent, and tactical aircraft by 20 percent.[18] However, SACEUR Alexander Haig has described the tanks increment at 40 percent and the artillery tubes at between 50 and 100 percent.[19] The Nunn-Bartlett report referred to a 200 percent increase in the number of Soviet fighter-bomber aircraft, which is a narrower definition than "tactical aircraft,"[20] and other estimates have included a 15 percent increase in tube artillery and a 25 percent expansion in battlefield missiles.[21] Such discrepancies may be the result of differences in timescale. Thus the British figures apply to the period 1968-76, while General Haig referred to "a persistent, long-term effort dating back to 1962 and perhaps earlier."

Manpower increases have also been variously assessed. Senators Nunn and Bartlett referred to "approximately 100,000" more Russian troops in Eastern Europe since 1968, and "thousands" more which were added after the start of the MBFR talks.[22] General Haig put the increase at 130,000.[23] The actual figure is probably nearer to 140,000, half of whom were left behind in Czechoslovakia after the 1968 invasion. The others may be accredited to the twenty Russian divisions in East Germany.

However, it is the qualitative rather than the quantitative improvements which have made the deepest impression. This is perhaps partly because NATO has become accustomed to enjoying a substantial lead in technology if nothing else. Now even this has seemed in danger of slipping away.

Thus the 2,000 more Russian tanks which are thought to have been added to Soviet forces in Eastern Europe have included the T-72, with its 122mm gun, automatic loader, laser range-finder, and superior track life to that of the existing T-62. (The T-62 can move on average only between 100 and 125 miles before needing extensive repairs, compared with the 150-200 miles expected of most Western tanks.[24])

The BMP-76 is possibly the most efficient APC in the world with a crew of three, eight infantrymen in the back, a 73mm gun, a 7.62mm machine gun, and a facility for launching Sagger antitank guided weapons (ATGW). More interesting than the numerical increase in artillery has been the switch in emphasis from towed to self-propelled guns—partly to afford more protection to the crews, but primarily to enable the batteries to keep pace with fast-moving armored columns. Ironically, the United States is now contemplating a switch back to towed pieces because they are cheaper.

Guns like the SP 122mm and 152mm howitzers were first identified in

Soviet forces in Eastern Europe in 1974. According to official U.S. estimates, the Soviet Army in Europe now has more than twice as many guns and heavy mortars as the United States.[25] Antiaircraft defenses have continued to improve, with the introduction of the Sam-8 and Sam-9, both of them effective against low-level aircraft, and of course the radar-directed, multi-barreled ZSU-23 gun. Minesweeping and minelaying equipment has been upgraded, and so have logistic systems—long considered a weak point in the Soviet inventory. The new Soviet seven-ton truck has been an important addition, along with a range of supply vehicles. Substantial stocks of petrol, oil and lubricants (POL) have been prepositioned, and so has more than one month's supply of ammunition for all combat units.[26] Then in 1975 the Russians surprised everyone by carrying out their six-monthly rotation of troops in Eastern Europe almost entirely by air, moving about 100,000 with combined fleets of military transports and Aeroflot civil aircraft. As a result the rotation was completed in two weeks, about a third of the time it used to take.[27]

Since 1973 the Soviet air force has been upgrading its aircraft in Eastern Europe, phasing in third-generation multi-role machines like the Mig-23 Flogger B and C, the Mig-21 Fishbed J, K, and L, the SU-17 Fitter C, the SU-19, and the Mig-25 Foxbat. Together with the Backfire bomber they represent a quantum jump in range and payload. The mix of aircraft also seems to reflect a fresh interest in ground attack/interdiction. The balance of the Soviet air force has until recently shown a heavy bias toward air defense. Recently there has been a growing interest in offensive use of air-power.[28] The number of ground-attack aircraft in the Soviet air force as a whole has risen from 600 in 1965 to over 1,700 today—in addition to several hundred Hind attack helicopters.[29] The average payload of these new aircraft, whose introduction into Eastern Europe is now nearly complete, has been assessed at six times that of the old Mig-17 in the 1950s.[30] NATO, it should be added, also improved its air forces during that time and it would be astonishing if the Soviet Union had not done so in its turn. But again NATO's alarm may be traced not so much to the improvements per se, but to the erosion of its technological advantage.[31]

Explanations for this Soviet improvement program are many and varied. One is that the Russians are concerned about internal security within Eastern Europe. There is certainly an element of this, as evidenced by the 70,000 troops which have remained in Czechoslovakia since 1968. In calculating its troop levels as a whole in Eastern Europe, the Soviet Union must consider the relative loyalty and camaraderie of its satellite states. It is relevant that the East European forces, while they theoretically comprise one-third of the Warsaw Pact's fighting capability, are much less well equipped and are kept at a lower state of readiness than the Soviet forces stationed alongside.[32]

Another contributory factor must be the MBFR talks—as is implied in the Nunn-Bartlett report. As Jane Sharp argues, arms-control negotiations can have the distressing effect of persuading either side to enlarge rather than diminish its forces, in the initial phase, anyway, while each stacks up bargaining chips. The practice has become an accepted accompaniment to the SALT dialogue, and it is possible that the 1,000 T-62 tanks moved into East Germany in 1973 were designated for this ignominious role.[33] (Actually, in any reduction of tank numbers, it would not be the T-62s themselves which would be withdrawn, but the T-54/55 which they would replace.) Such a practice could only have marginal effect if the Vienna talks ever resulted in the asymmetrical reductions and common ceilings, which have formed the basis of the NATO position. But it would be relevant to the symmetrical percentage reductions proposed by the Soviet bloc.

A third factor might be continuing Russian paranoia over Western intentions, or more realistically a simple action-reaction response to NATO force improvements. It is hard to believe that the Soviet Union still thinks it possible that NATO might carry out an unprovoked attack upon Eastern Europe. Soviet writings anyway have indicated a growing confidence in their own capabilities. But the Russians are equally aware of the danger of some accidental spillage from a political crisis in Europe—in which case they might well regard preemptive attack as the best means of defense.[34] Warsaw Pact exercises have looked like mirror images of those held by NATO, except that the roles of the wolf and Little Red Riding Hood are reversed, and that Little Red Riding Hood in the Pact's interpretation goes straight for a preemptive strike.

Weapons procurement has a momentum of its own in the Soviet Union, as it does elsewhere. Moreover the Soviet Union is influenced by two other inbred characteristics. One is an admiration for size and strength, which is reflected also in the strategic arms program. The other is a puritanical, miserly tendency to hoard. A weapon which is replaced is rarely thrown away. It tends to be driven into a warehouse and kept there—a comforting thought for a rainy day. Between 1968 and 1974 Soviet munitions factories produced no fewer than 24,300 T-55 tanks and 30,400 T-64s—with the T-72 still to come.[35] Given the momentum of a large production line, a fascination with mass, and a reluctance to throw anything away, the accumulation of arms in Eastern Europe may be seen more as a kind of disease than the product of controlled policy decisions.

The most common construction put upon Soviet force improvements, however, is that they are related to the blitzkrieg doctrine which the Russians seem determined to pursue. Purists may argue over the use of the term blitzkrieg to describe the Russian doctrine but it is a useful form of shorthand.

Renewed Soviet interest in conventional arms can be traced back to the late 1960s—as indeed might NATO's. It has even been dated with some precision as starting in 1967 (the year of NATO's official conversion to the flexible response strategy) when the Soviets held their first major exercise in which nonnuclear rather than nuclear weapons were starred.[36] Russian strategy is now thought to allow for a "relatively prolonged" period of conventional warfare in the opening phase of any general European conflict.[37] Nuclear forces would be held in readiness should the conventional option fail, or should the other side make first use of them. But the initial Soviet thrust would be made with fast-moving armor, mechanized infantry, conventional artillery, and tactical airpower. The Soviet forces would rely on surprise and mobility to strike before the enemy has had time to marshal his antitank defenses.[38] Presumably the plan would also include preemptive strike at the enemy's own nuclear weapons which, in NATO's case, tend to be concentrated for administrative and security reasons—in peacetime, anyway. By the time NATO had had time to reach a decision on whether or not to "go nuclear," it would be too late.

The quintessential concept would not be classical blitzkrieg in which speed and mobility are the primary factors, but rather what has been called "neutralization" of the battlefield. Mobility would be secondary to firepower.[39]

Important structural changes in the Soviet army have been inspired by this doctrine. Both the tank and motor rifle divisions have been increased in size by about 2,000 in either case. This has brought the tank division to about 11,000 and the motor rifle (MR) division to 12,000-13,500. The MR unit's tank strength has risen from 188 to 266, and both have acquired more artillery, the MR division's guns increasing from 105 to 165 and the tank division's from 36 to 72.[40]

The increased emphasis on conventional warfare had undoubtedly inspired this Soviet desire for greater concentration of firepower. But the changes can also be explained by a perceived need to repair a number of shortcomings in the balance of conventional arms.[41] The decision to introduce a more credible mix of armor, infantry, artillery, and air cover is silhouetted by the stress on the MR divisions, whose combination of arms would be a necessary function of warfare in the crowded urban environment of Western Europe. Of twenty new divisions most recently added to the Soviet Army, eighteen were MR units, embracing this combination of arms and heavy concentration on firepower. As a result, the ratio of MR to tank units has risen from 1.8 to one in the early 1960s to 2.2 to one today.[42]

There is also some evidence that the Soviet forces noted the lessons of the October War with as much interest as NATO. The tank/antitank debate seems to have been fiercer there than it was in the West—perhaps because of the place occupied by the tank in Soviet offensive doctrine.[43] After all, they were watching their own antitank guided weapons in action.

It also seems likely that they noted the vulnerability of armor when in-
adequately supported by infantry and artillery. The series of force improvements can therefore be regarded not as part of routine modernization
and upgrading, but as a specific program. Its aim has been to ensure that
Russian military capabilities live up to the blitzkrieg/neutralization doctrine
which is fundamental to the structure of the Soviet Army.

The Military Balance

The military balance as a statistical concept can be pushed and pummeled
like soft clay until one achieves the results that one wants. There are,
however, limits to its elasticity. It is difficult, for instance, to make it look
very favorable to NATO. How unfavorable one makes it depends to some
extent on how much realism one tries to inject. As a gross generalization it
might be said that the more realistic one tries to be, the less unfavorable to
NATO it becomes.

The following tables have been compiled from U.S. Defense Department figures by Professor William Kaufmann of the Massachusetts Institute of Technology.

The following points should be made. The four French divisions include
not only two which are stationed in Germany, but two more in Alsace-
Lorraine. The argument in favor of this is that France has declared its intention of lining up with the alliance on M-Day despite its resolve to remain
outside the military organization in peacetime. It is calculated that there is
as much probability of this happening as there is of, say, Czechoslovakia's

Table 3-1
Warsaw Pact M-Day Forces (Central Region)

| | Divisions | | | | | | | |
	Tanks	MR	Total	Other	Total	Men	Tanks	Aircraft
East Germany	2	4	6	–	6	70,000	1,400	300
Czechoslovakia	5	2	7	3	10	100,000	2,800	400
Poland	5	5	10	5	15	150,000	2,600	800
Total	12	11	23	8	31	320,000	6,800	1,500
Soviet Union	14	13	27	–	27	460,000	8,000	1,300
Total	26	24	50	8		780,000	14,800	2,800

Table 3-2
NATO M-Day Forces (Central Region)

	Divisions	Men	Tanks	Aircraft
Belgium	2	40,000	220	180
Britain	3	50,000	580	400
Canada	—	4,000	40	60
Denmark	2/3	20,000	90	130
West Germany	12	235,000	2,800	750
France	4	147,000	640	485
Netherlands	3	45,000	470	230
United States	5	185,000	1,250	550
Total	29 2/3	725,000	6,090	2,785

lining up with the Warsaw Pact. In fact there is a great deal more. Some Danish forces are included, which is not very unusual. But the Berlin brigades of Britain, France, and the United States are excluded, although it could be contended that despite their unique vulnerability in wartime, they would effectively tie down some Warsaw Pact forces, certainly in the initial phase. No account is taken of the French and British restructuring programs. In the case of Britain an additional division should be added to table 3-2—although the overall manpower will remain about the same.

On the Warsaw Pact side, table 3-1 accepts the common assumption that forces in Hungary would be deployed to the South and would take no part on the Central European front. The total manpower figure of 780,000 is substantially smaller than the 955,000 which is used by the Western powers at the MBFR talks. The 780,000 specifically excludes administrative noncombatant staffs, and is thus a more realistic total of the troops who might actually be deployed.

The only significant disparities on this assessment are in the number of divisions and of tanks. One reason for the discrepancy between the relative strengths of divisions and manpower is that Pact divisions are smaller than those in NATO. (Though the restructuring of the French and British armies will result in divisions being rather smaller than those of the Soviet Union.) NATO members on the other hand have more corps troops and independent brigades. An American division force equivalent including the division's initial support increment averages as many as 40,000 in peacetime and 48,000 in wartime, compared to a Soviet figure of about 21,000.[44] Moreover the Pact divisions include four—two in Poland and two in Czechoslovakia—which are Eastern European category-2 units. In peacetime these are kept at no more than quarter strength,[45] and should be regarded as no more than reserve units with active cadres. A still more

realistic profile would thus credit the Pact with only fifty-four divisions in
Eastern Europe, and Kaufmann believes that fifty would be still more accurate, since four more divisions are kept at a low state of readiness in
peacetime.

The tank figures, too, conceal the fact that NATO has 5,000 more in
West Germany, comprising war reserve and U.S. prepositioned equipment.
American stocks were badly depleted as a result of equipment being
diverted to Israel during the October War. At one time there was a shortfall
of almost 70 percent in tanks, 60 percent in APCS, and 50 percent in artillery.[46] And they did not reach their pre-1973 levels until December 1977.
There have been suggestions that the Soviet Union follows a similar reserve
practice, but there is no hard evidence to support this. The Soviet Army
keeps most of its tanks in storage for much of the time, retaining relatively
few for training purposes and rotating these round the squadrons. This
saves on maintenance and replacement costs but detracts from combat
readiness. On the other hand one should not count the NATO stocks in the
working total. They are, after all, only reserve stores, and are not much use
until there are crews to man them.

The military balance remains a one-dimensional concept when reduced
to tabular form. It takes no account of less quantifiable factors like the
quality of men and materiel, the interoperability of equipment—and hence
flexibility of forces in the field—the geographical distribution of manpower, and, most elusive of all, morale. But the numbers game has had a
mesmeric effect on the military and the media so that capabilities have often
been reduced to an arithmetical statement unrelated to any specific scenario
which could develop in Central Europe.

The "New Threat"

It is not that NATO has been unaware of Soviet military doctrine, or of the
way in which doctrine could be put into practice. It is rather that until
recently it was generally assumed that the Soviets did not have the
capabilities to sustain that kind of operation. McNamara declared:

> A surprise attack in the Central Region without a buildup might achieve
> some initial territorial gains, but it would sacrifice the potential advantage
> of a faster mobilisation capability and the simultaneous use of East Euro-
> pean forces. Unless reinforced with troops from the Soviet Union and with
> East European forces, the Soviet forces alone would be inadequate to sus-
> tain this kind of attack.[47]

But six years later Dr. Schlesinger used the "surprise attack" threat as his most powerful argument in resisting congressional pressure for U.S. troop reductions in Europe.[48] And in 1977 General Haig estimated NATO's warning time to be between eight and fifteen days—at least.

NATO's dilemma does not stem from an inadequate resource base. On the contrary, its forces in 1976, including the French, totaled 4,864,000 compared with the Pact's 4,772,000—including the forces of Hungary, Bulgaria, and Romania. Aggregate defense spending in the West amounted to $149.4 billion against the Pact's estimated $132.1 billion.[49] The Nunn-Bartlett report made the point that NATO's European member countries alone have a combined population greater than that of either superpower and a gross national product higher than that of the United States and more than double that of the Soviet Union. They also have the largest industrial plant in the world.[50]

Neither a fiscal sum nor a body count can provide a very accurate guide to military capabilities, as Israel has dramatically proved. But they indicate that NATO has the resources to defend itself, and moreover contributes a reasonable overall sum toward this purpose. What NATO needs above everything else is time. But will it be given that time?

The Soviet Army now comprises 168 divisions, whose distribution is summarized in table 3-3.[51]

Those divisions in the northern MDs would probably move against NATO's northern flank in wartime. Those in Hungary would turn south, while those in the Caucasian MDs normally face Turkey and Iran. Troops

Table 3-3
Soviet Divisions

| | Categories | | | |
	1	2	3	Total
East Germany/Poland/Czech.	27	—	—	27
Hungary	4	—	—	4
Western military districts	3	17	8	28
Northern military districts	—	7	2	9
Caucasian military districts	—	2	14	16
Moscow	2	—	—	2
	36	26	24	86
Central USSR	—	—	10	10
Southern USSR	—	4	17	21
Far East	20	21	10	51
Total	56	51	61	168

in the Moscow area would comprise a central reserve and those in the central USSR would also form a general reserve. It is sometimes suggested that the divisions in the Far East could be moved west in an emergency, which indeed they could. But even assuming that the state of Sino-Soviet relations allowed this, they would arrive too late to have a decisive impact on the short warning attack. If they were moved in advance the transfer would provide NATO with a useful indicator of Russian intentions. The usual assumption therefore is that the Soviet Union would deploy against Western Europe the twenty-seven divisions in Poland, East Germany, and Czechoslovakia together with the twenty-eight divisions in the western MDs. With the thirty-one East European divisions this would make up an invading force of eighty-six divisions. How quickly could such a force be put on line?

One estimate is that the twenty-eight divisions would move West at the rate of two divisions a day. Add two days, which the army would need to prepare the transfer, and one arrives at a possible D-Day sixteen days after the start of mobilization, or M16. A more realistic assessment is that the divisions would move at the rate of four every three days, and that the army would then need another week in which to get the reinforcements on line. On this reckoning the earliest possible D-Day timing becomes M30.

Assuming that NATO needs a week in which to satisfy itself that the Soviet intentions are not entirely honorable, and in which to decide what to do, M30 for NATO becomes M23, or, as it is more often expressed, M23/30. Even this timescale may be too generous to the Soviet Union. Only three of the twenty-eight divisions are Category-1 divisions, that is, between three-quarters and full strength. The seventeen Category-2 units are between half and three-quarters strength while the remaining eight Category-3 divisions have only about a third of their full establishment and may also have only obsolescent equipment. Taking these factors into account an M45 scenario might be still more realistic. But M23/30 is a useful discipline for Western planning purposes if only because it requires NATO to think in terms of rapid reinforcement by air. After that date one can start to think in terms of using sealift, too, and the problems become less difficult.

But would it be in the interests of the Soviet Union to wait that long? Table 3-4, again based on Professor Kaufmann's statistics, compares current NATO reinforcement rates with those estimated for the Warsaw Pact. The underlying assumptions are that only 50 Pact divisions would be ready to move on M-Day, but that the Soviet Union could then build up a capacity to transport two divisions a day.

The table assumes that by M2 the Soviet Union would have added one of the divisions from the western MDs and that the others would start to ar-

Table 3-4
NATO Reinforcement Rates Compared with Warsaw Pact Estimated Rates

	Pact			NATO		
	non-USSR	USSR	Total	U.S.	non-U.S.	Total
M-Day	23	27	50	5	25	30
M2	23	28	51	5	25	30
M3-6	31	28	59	5	25	30
M7	31	28	59	5	25	30
M8	31	32	63	5	25	30
M10	31	34	65	5	27	32
M11	31	36	67	5	27	32
M12	31	38	69	5	27	32
M13-16	31	45	76	5	27	32
M20	31	45	76	7	27	34
M23-25	31	51	82	8	27	35
M26-27	31	55	86	8	27	35
M35-37	31	55	86	9	27	36

rive at the rate of two a day, although the Category-3 divisions would not start to come on line until later. Soviet tactical air reinforcements might be expected to arrive by about M7, while a great deal of American aircraft might have been flown in by M12. (This would depend to some extent upon the availability of the Strategic Air Command's KC-135 tanker fleet.)

The peak periods at which it would be most advantageous for the Warsaw Pact to attack—in terms of firepower ratios, anyway—would seem to be M8-9, M15-16, and M26-29 (which is when all eighty-six divisions are on line). Robert Lucas Fischer, using different data and calculating in terms of divisional manpower, has put the current ratio in favor of the Pact at 1.36:1.[52] This climbs to 1.50:1 by M7 (or M-Day for NATO forces, given the seven-day decision-making pause), reaches a peak of 1.95:1 by M14, and falls back again to 1.50:1 by M28.

The convention that an attacking force needs a 3:1 advantage to be confident of breaking through the defense has little relevance to the Central European theater today. For one thing it presupposes that the defense is in a strongly fortified position, which is hardly the case. For another, it has been overtaken by advances in firepower and mobility. It is more likely that the attack could concentrate firepower quickly and forcefully enough to break through with a superiority of only 1.5:1.[53] In this case the Soviet Union might favor an attack on M6/7 when the ratio of advantage would not only be sufficient at 1.5:1, but would continue on a rising curve until peaking at 1.95:1 on M13/14.

Fischer calculates that the Pact could afford to put an overwhelming force of 235,000 into battle against one of NATO's eight corps by using only those immediately available forces.[54] Given the "garrison mentality" of NATO land forces[55] the prospects for a local breakthrough would seem to be extremely high. But it is unlikely that the Pact would seriously contemplate such a narrow axis of attack.

It is highly questionable how far the Soviet Union would accept the 1.5:1 breakthrough theory. Historically, they have been impressed by size and weight. Anyway, it is one thing for the defense to fear such odds, and quite another for the attack to risk them. Before the invasion of Czechoslovakia in 1968 they built up a 3:1 advantage against an enemy whose powers of resistance could hardly be compared with those of the Western alliance.

The rate of advance through Western Europe is also debatable. So much depends upon the ability of NATO forces to retreat in good order after an initial breakthrough, and then regroup. The Russian army has been credited with the ambition of moving at 112 kilometers a day. This would bring them to the Rhine in about forty-eight hours and to the Channel ports in less than a week. But it would be an incredible feat of military planning and logistics. Neither Guderian nor Patton managed to approach that rate of advance during the Second World War.[56] The effect of urban sprawl in Western Europe is an additional factor which must affect Soviet calculations as much as those of NATO.[57]

Kaufmann has estimated that a Pact force of eighty-six divisions could reach the Rhine in about nineteen days, if faced by only NATO's in-place units without reinforcements. They would start at a rate of 5.2 kilometers a day when their firepower superiority was 1.67:1. Nine days after D-Day, with a ratio of 5.56:1 after mutual attrition, they would be touching 92.3 kilometers a day. But this does not take airpower into account and is highly theoretical.

NATO Options

A rare selection of options have been proposed with the objective of correcting allied deficiencies in a sudden-attack scenario. A certain amount has already been done, or is programed, at least. General Haig has referred to a three-pronged force improvement plan designed to (a) increase the readiness of in-place forces, (b) rationalize forward defense measures, and (c) improve reinforcement capabilities.[58] Ammunition stocks are being moved forward (where in fact they become more vulnerable), alert procedures have been tightened, a better integrated command and control system with new communications network is being developed, and the interoperability of allied equipment is being pursued, if belatedly, as a more realistic alternative to standardization. More NATO airfields can now cross-service allied aircraft, even to the extent of rearming them.

The United States has made strenuous efforts to improve its teeth/tail ratio, with two additional brigades being stationed in West Germany to make up a total of five divisions—in exchange for 18,000 support troops. The number of divisions in the U.S. Army as a whole has been raised from thirteen to sixteen, and the size of divisions themselves is now being increased. A mechanized infantry division, for instance, will see its manpower rise from 16,500 to 17,800, with fifteen instead of eleven battalions, fifty-six more heavy guns, and fifty-four more tanks. As a result the combat/support ratio has moved from 50:50 to 70:30, and a number of commanders are now concerned because the fashion may have gone a little too far.

The list of other options which the alliance could take is almost infinite. The principal limit is how much the allies can afford or, more accurately, how much they are willing to spend. The United States, West Germany, Denmark, Norway, Belgium, and the Netherlands have recently increased their defense budgets in real terms,[59] and Britain has now followed their example. But to expect a "quantum jump" in firepower or manpower—if it were available—or a large-scale redeployment of forces in West Germany, might be unrealistic. There are certainly arguments for putting more artillery into the NATO package and for adding to the number of ATGW. But these might be considered adjustments rather than quantum jumps. It is also a regrettable historical accident that the U.S. Seventh Army, with its superior firepower, is stationed in the south rather than the north of West Germany. But the cost of moving it now, with all its supporting institutions, would be prohibitive. So it looks like an accident with which NATO has to continue to live.

There are two kinds of solutions to the questions which arise from a short-warning threat. One is to buy more time, and the other is to make more efficient use of the time that one already has. NATO could buy more time by delaying the enemy at the border. Ideally, one would meet him at the border, or as near to it as possible, and push him back over it. Senators Nunn and Bartlett have insisted that forces now stationed along the Rhine, or even West of it, should be moved toward the inter-German frontier, so that NATO would present a full frontal defense.[60]

But it is doubtful that the allies could flex enough muscle up front, particularly if the Soviets did, as was earlier suggested, concentrating over-whelming power on one small section of the border. An alternative, or perhaps an addition, would be to build a line of static fortifications along the frontier. This has been an unfashionable concept since the Maginot Line, and West German distaste for anything which might symbolize the division of the German people has made it still more unpalatable to Western armies. But the issue of the two Germanies has faded, and fashions do change. As a result, the idea still floats to the surface from time to time. On the other hand, it would not only be costly and unpopular, but it also might encourage one or two of the armies stationed behind it to pack up and go home.

At present, NATO buys time by trading space. Defense is not linear (as symbolized by a Maginot Line), but mobile. In effect, the allies would ride the enemy's punch, rocking back on their heels and allowing him to stretch forward until he is, hopefully, slightly off balance, then pushing him back again. This sounds easier than it is, and the task of regaining lost space from an enemy as powerful as the Soviet Union, with reinforcements to draw upon and a supply line overland to Russia, can be made to sound daunting. As an alternative to building up one's forward defense line, it might be bet-ter to concentrate on one's rear. If SACEUR had a strong mobile theater reserve to work with (in addition to the French and Canadians) he could switch it to that area of the battlefield where the punch had struck. One method might be to form the reserve from corps troops now in forward positions—who would be replaced in due course by American rein-forcements when they arrived.[61] It would, in theory, mean trading more space for time, which is not the way many feel NATO should go. But it would also improve chances of stopping the breakthrough, provided that the attack could be identified in time.

NATO would probably need to rely heavily on its airpower, anyway, if only because the disparity between the airforces is not very large—not if one takes account of NATO's superior technology and pilot training. Whether or not the West has the right mix of aircraft is another matter. Procurement policies have led to a preponderance of expensive, multi-role aircraft designed primarily for air superiority or deep interdiction. These are not, however, what NATO really wants. To bolster relatively weak land forces, the allies need plenty of cheap, fast, close-support aircraft which could attack enemy concentrations on D-Day and break up an armored of-fensive.[62] As it is, less than 20 percent of allied machines fall into this category.[63]

A strategy which would have bought more time for less money was outlined to President Carter by his national security advisers in 1977. Presidential Review Memorandum No. 10, whose initials PRM-10 still send a shiver of apprehension around Bonn, envisaged the loss of one-third of

West German territory in the event of a Soviet attack, as an alternative to spending more money on improved Western defense. But this appears to have been rejected for obvious political reasons.

The administration decided instead on the other option of making better use of the time that it has—with the help of a 3 percent real increase in defense spending for FY 79. More specifically, Defense Secretary Harold Brown in his Posture Statement in early February 1978 outlined proposals to increase the reinforcement rate for American troops in Europe.

At present only four more American divisions could reach Germany by M35, with six still to embark. And of the four, two would be those with equipment already prepositioned in Germany. The total capacity of the seventy C-5s and 234 C-141s which make up the American strategic airlift is 180,000 tons. But this includes only 70,000 tons of outsize cargo such as tanks and SP guns, which can fit only into the C-5s at a loading rate of 1,000 tons per aircraft. This is the most serious constraint.

One solution is to preposition more equipment in Europe, and there are plans to place two more division sets there in the early 1980s.[64] This does not help much on time because the Pentagon has found that it takes as long to move a continental U.S.-based division with prepositioned equipment into the line of battle as it does to move one together with all its kit across the Atlantic. However, prepositioning does alleviate the difficulty over outsize cargo. A division of men weighs about 3,000 tons and can be moved by wide-bodied jets without much trouble. So when this further prepositioning has been completed (at $500 million per division at plus $45 million annually for maintenance) the United States should be able to move six of its ten reinforcement divisions, leaving four more with all their equipment waiting for transport. Harold Brown announced proposals which would enable the Pentagon by 1982 to move five of these divisions and sixty extra squadrons of aircraft to West Germany within ten days of mobilization.

What the Defense Department would like to do is to complete its modification plans for the wide-bodied jets in the Civil Reserve Air Fleet. By strengthening the floors and fitting wide doors into the hulls, these jets can be made to accommodate outsize cargo. The total effect would be to add a further 91,000 tons to the outsize cargo capacity. When the other modification programs have been finished for the C-5s and C-141s, the CRAF plan should enable the Seventh Army to get close to its wartime establishment by a realistic date.

This might still leave the Warsaw Pact with one or two peak periods when its ratio of superiority would be disturbing. One solution to this might be to start thinking in terms of a quicker reaction time. If alert procedures could be tightened enough, American troops could be made ready for airlift that much earlier. Defense analysts have complained for some time that the seven-day pause which has so far been allowed as "reaction time" is unnecessarily long.

Conclusion

The Soviet Union has improved its forces in Eastern Europe. Firepower has been increased by an estimated 10 to 15 percent, and there have been significant additions to divisional logistics. The quality of equipment has been refined, and aircraft particularly are not only better, with improved range and payload, but have been given a more aggressive profile. The force improvements are in line with Soviet doctrine and seem to have been stimulated by (a) a switch in emphasis from nuclear to nonnuclear weapons in the opening phase of the battle, and (b) the lessons of the October War, which indicated the need for a better combination of arms.

Conclusions have been drawn from these force improvements to the effect that the Warsaw Pact is now capable of attacking Western Europe with little or no warning. Advances in Soviet firepower and mobility have made this possible, and the result is a "new threat" to NATO.

Before passing judgment on this perception, there are several points that should be made:

1. Of the fifty-eight in-place Pact divisions which would have to form such a force in the early stage of battle, thirty-one would come from East European powers. One could first reduce this to fifty-four on the grounds that four are little better than reserve units, and then one could cut it to fifty because four more are believed to be in a low state of readiness. But the other non-Soviet divisions, too, are less equipped, less well trained, and less well motivated than the Soviet troops. Not only might they not stir from their national boundaries, but the Soviet forces alongside might—for internal security reasons—need to stay with them.

2. Although NATO commanders fret, with some justice, over the maldeployment of some of their forces, their opposite numbers on the other side of the inter-German border might well do so too. Those in Czechoslovakia and Poland are some distance away, and two out of every three Russian divisions in East Germany are 100 kilometers back. On average they are further from the border than are the American troops in the West. The point is that it would take time and trouble to get them to the front. They would probably need to use cover and deception tactics, cloaking their movements beneath some gigantic military exercise. But an exercise involving all or most of the troops in Eastern Europe would hardly be ignored, even by NATO—especially if it coincided with a similar *Okean*-type exercise at sea. (Soviet ships would also need to escape beyond their historic chokepoints if the Russians were really contemplating global war.)

3. Although the Russians have built up their strategic airlift capacity, they would have to rely upon road and rail to carry divisions from the Soviet Union at the rate that has been predicted. But the road network through Poland is less than impressive, and the railway lines have a nar-

rower gauge than those in the Soviet Union. This implies more time and trouble—although it has been reported that two lines in Northern Poland are now being converted to the Russian gauge.[65]

4. Not only did the Russians wait to build up a 3:1 superiority on their Czech invasion, but their subsequent operation was not conspicuously efficient. Soldiers got lost, their vehicles broke down, their supplies ran out—much the same difficulties that any army encounters when it moves with 200,000 men or so and their equipment over roads they do not know and which were not built to receive them. It would be dangerous to base today's perceptions on yesterday's events, but the operation suggested at least that the Soviets are not supermen. Russian soldiers in general have similar limitations to those in other armies.[66] (Moreover, there are likely to be fewer of them in the future. Manpower of military age is declining at such a rate in the Soviet Union that to maintain forces at the present size on a basis of two years' conscription they would have to recruit 85 percent of all eighteen-year-olds by 1987.[67] This has no direct bearing on the present issue, but it is further indication that the Soviet Union has its problems. It is also arguable that the size of the Soviet army is not excessive, given the size and weight of its potential adversaries.[68])

One is led to the conclusion that there is, from a Western perspective, a worst-case contingency, in which the Soviet Union could mount an attack against the West with little warning. That this would take the form of an unprovoked attack, aimed perhaps at annexing part of West Germany or conducting some Communist crusade, seems so unlikely that it does not merit serious consideration.

It is conceivable that as a result of some political crisis in Europe, perhaps in Berlin or perhaps on the NATO flanks, the Soviet Union might consider that war was inevitable and that, given its military doctrine, a preemptive strike should be launched against the West. How much warning NATO would have received from this political crisis and how well the alliance may have heeded that warning is one of many imponderables. A worst-case analysis would assume that NATO had not reacted at all.

It is only right that military planners should draw attention to possible scenarios and should make plans for them. There are certainly several ways in which NATO could remove its deficiencies, as outlined above, without incurring crippling costs either in money or manpower.

But there are also limits in how far one should go in planning for a worst-case contingency. It seems unlikely that the Soviet Union would perceive itself capable of launching a sudden attack on the West with the forces now stationed in East Europe, even if it wanted to. A worst-case analysis on one side does not automatically look like a best case on the other. There is no evidence to suggest that the Soviet Union would view such an adventure with confidence. Nor is there evidence to suggest that forces in East Europe are better prepared than those belonging to NATO. If for some incredible reason NATO suddenly attacked the Warsaw Pact, the initial impact would probably be worse, since the attack would be even more of a surprise.

The military balance is not exactly a source of comfort to NATO. But it is not as bad as it is sometimes made out to be, and is open to a number of interpretations. There is also a tendency in the West to ignore force improvements among allied forces.

An alternative to "more forward defense" and "quantum jumps in firepower" is for NATO to meet the "new threat" by seeking an improved package of confidence-building measures. The forum could be the MBFR talks, which seem unlikely to achieve much if allowed to continue on their present course, although it is true that recent progress has encouraged a little more optimism. By switching their targets, they could be used to build upon the foundations laid in "Basket 1" of the CSCE agreement. Among the measures that could be sought are a limit on the size of exercises in Central Europe, a ceiling on the number of troops that could be moved into the region at any one time and the appointment of international inspectors to visit military installations on both sides.[69]

None of these would be easily achieved. But the results in terms of détente would be worth the effort. They might not only diminish the "new threat" but displace some of the old fears as well.

Notes

1. "NATO and the New Soviet Threat," presented by Senators Sam Nunn and Dewey Bartlett to the Senate Committee on Armed Services, January 24, 1977, p. 4.
2. Ibid., p. 2.
3. Alain Enthoven and K. Wayne Smith, *How Much Is Enough?* (New York: Harper and Row, 1971), p. 119.
4. Ibid., p. 133.
5. Ibid., p. 142.
6. Ibid., p. 146.
7. Statement before a Joint Session of the Senate Armed Services Committee and the Senate Subcommittee on Department of Defense Appropriations, on Fiscal Years 1968-72 Defense Programs, January 1967, p. 72.
8. Edward Luttwak, "Perceptions of Force and U.S. Defense Policy," *IISS Survival*, January-February 1977, p. 3.
9. Jane Sharp, "MBFR as Arms Control," in *Arms Control Today*, Vol. 6, No. 4, p. 1.

10. Robert Komer, "Ten Suggestions for Rationalizing NATO," *IISS Survival*, March-April 1977, p. 68.

11. T. Callaghan, *U.S./European Economic Cooperation in Military and Civil Technology* (Arlington, Va.: Im Tech, Inc., August 1974), pp. 22-36.

12. Steven Canby, "The Alliance and Europe Part IV: Military Doctrine and Technology" (IISS Adelphi Paper 109), p. 9.

13. Rowland Evans and Robert Novak, "NATO Fears of Soviet Supremacy," *Washington Post*, December 31, 1976.

14. Les Aspin, *Congressional Record*, House of Representatives, February 7, 1977, H911.

15. Hannes Adomeit, "Soviet Risk-Taking and Crisis Behavior from Confrontation to Coexistence" (IISS Adelphi Paper 101).

16. Nunn-Bartlett report, p. 7.

17. Robert McNamara, "Statement on FY 1969-73 and the 1969 Defense Budget," p. 81.

18. Statement on the Defense Estimates 1977, HMSO.

19. General Alexander Haig, speaking to the annual AUSA meeting, Washington, D.C., October 13, 1976.

20. Nunn-Bartlett report, p. 5.

21. *Aviation Week and Space Technology*, March 11, 1974, p. 43.

22. Nunn-Bartlett report, p. 4.

23. General Haig, AUSA meeting.

24. Richard Lawrence and Jeffrey Record, "U.S. Force Structure in NATO: An Alternative" (The Brookings Institution, 1974), p. 12.

25. General George Brown, "United States Military Posture Statement, FY 1978," p. 66.

26. John Erickson, "Soviet Ground Forces and the Conventional Mode of Operations," *RUSI Journal*, July 1976, p. 46.

27. General Richard Ellis, USAF, "Allied Air Forces Central Europe," *RUSI Journal*, July 1976, p. 6.

28. General Haig, AUSA meeting.

29. General Brown, "U.S. Military Posture," p. 79.

30. General Ellis, "Allied Air Forces," p. 6.

31. The Military Balance 1976-77 (IISS), p. 102.

32. Lawrence and Record, "U.S. Force Structure," p. 23.

33. Jane Sharp, "MBFR," p. 1.

34. Thomas Wolfe, "Soviet Military Capabilities and Intentions in Europe," in *Soviet Strategy in Europe*, ed. Richard Pipes (New York: Crane, Russak and Co., Inc., 1976), p. 158.

35. John Erickson, "Soviet Military Posture and Policy in Europe," in *Soviet Strategy in Europe*, pp. 171, 181.

36. Philip Karber, "The Soviet Anti-Tank Debate," *IISS Survival*, May-June 1976, p. 108.

37. Donald Rumsfeld, "Defense Department Report FY 1977," p. 188.

38. Karber, "Soviet Anti-Tank," p. 109.

39. Erickson, "Soviet Ground Forces," p. 46.

40. Ibid.

41. Ibid., p. 47.

42. Karber, "Soviet Anti-Tank," p. 107.

43. Ibid., p. 105.

44. Canby, "Alliance with Europe," p. 3n.

45. The Military Balance, p. 12n.

46. Erickson, "Soviet Ground Forces," p. 47.

47. Statement on FY 1969-73 and the 1969 Defense Budget, p. 82.

48. James Schlesinger Statement on FY 1975, p. 88.

49. The Military Balance, pp. 78-81.

50. Nunn-Bartlett report, p. 1.

51. Based on Professor Kaufmann's figures.

52. Robert Lucas Fischer, "Defending the Central Front: The Balance of Forces" (IISS Adelphi Paper 127), p. 25.

53. James Schlesinger Statement on U.S. Defense Policy FY 1976, pp. 111-115.

54. Fischer, "Defending the Central Front," p. 26.

55. General Haig, AUSA meeting.

56. Lawrence and Record, "U.S. Force Structure," p. 12.

57. Paul Bracken, *IISS Survival*, November-December 1976.

58. General Haig, AUSA meeting.

59. Drew Middleton, "NATO Military Aide Urges Allies to Raise Their Arms Budgets," *New York Times*, March 23, 1977.

60. Nunn-Bartlett report, p. 19.

61. Fischer, "Defending the Central Front," p. 38.

62. Canby, "Alliance with Europe," p. 38.

63. Lawrence and Record, "U.S. Force Structure," p. 36.

64. Donald Rumsfeld, Annual Defense Department Report, FY 1978, p. 234.

65. Erickson, "Soviet Ground Forces," p. 49, n9.

66. Herbert Goldhamer, *The Soviet Soldier* (New York: Crane, Russak and Co., Inc., 1975), p. 323.

67. Bernard Weinraub, "Soviet Union Facing Manpower Decline," *New York Times*, April 7, 1977, p. 8.

68. Jeffrey Record, "Sizing Up the Soviet Army" (Brookings Institution, 1975), p. 9.

69. Les Aspin, *Congressional Record*, H914.

**Part II
Dilemmas for the West**

4

America, Europe, and the Energy-Security Dilemma

Linda B. Miller

Six years after the Yom Kippur War and the oil embargo, certain truths about energy and security in the Western alliance context have emerged. It is well to state these at the outset, for political rhetoric obscures the actual state of affairs the alliance confronts. First, energy and security are linked for both America and Western Europe. No government defines its security exclusively on the basis of military forces-in-being or projected. For all industrial countries, access to fossil fuels is part of their security equation. "Security" implies a continuation of a standard of living dependent on imported resources, as well as a deterrent posture or defense capabilities. Second, no Western government has or is likely to have a comprehensive energy policy free from the constraints of domestic or global pressures. Put simply,

> it is . . . the political process operating within and among nations that will largely determine the extent to which economic efficiency and technological possibilities will control the future evolution of the world energy situation, and the extent to which other factors such as national security and prestige will come into play. Moreover, politics are the means for making key tradeoffs, nationally and internationally, between, for instance, cheap energy and secure supplies or between self-sufficiency and environmental quality.[1]

A third truth follows. "Key tradeoffs" take time to develop, hence the normal pulling and hauling of domestic political processes in the industrial democracies, together with the usual slow pace of intra-alliance bargaining, bear as much watching as the price-setting activities of OPEC. Fourth, superpower competition has not accelerated the rise of resource questions to the top of Western foreign policy agendas, nor will any conceivable Soviet-American accords yield solutions. Finally, energy politics highlight basic asymmetries between the United States and Western Europe, although both will be net importers in the 1980s. America's energy consumption is higher than Western Europe's, but so is its energy production and potential. In addition, a temporary (and dubious) advantage lies with the United States so long as it can trade advanced weapons for Arab oil.

If these "truths" tell us anything about the outlook for energy and security in the 1980s, it is that we must begin by looking at the setting in which American and European perceptions develop and then consider the hazards of dependence, independence, and interdependence. Too often energy is viewed as something apart, to be assessed as a "crisis" in which Western governments do not have choices—only imperatives. The contention here is that this perspective is distorted: the energy dilemma is now embedded in the domestic and foreign politics of the Western alliance and will remain so. The problem is long-term but may be susceptible to some manipulation if its fundamental characteristics are understood. Energy politics therefore illustrate splendidly the inherent features of international relations, "the science of uncertainty . . . the limits of action . . . the ways in which states try to manage but never quite succeed in eliminating their own insecurity."[2]

The Setting

Energy became a Western security issue when the questions of supply and price became threatening in 1973. Although access to Middle East oil had been a continuing preoccupation of the Western governments and Japan, the October War and the subsequent embargo revealed how complex the connections between energy and security had grown. It did not take observers or policymakers long to realize some of the implications of a new and frightening situation. Perhaps "only severe, sudden and *long-lasting* reductions in oil supplies can be considered *immediate* threats to national security" (emphasis added),[3] nevertheless "significant losses in employment and production"[4] could occur even with stockpiling or sharing schemes, if OPEC and the Arab states decided to play off Europe and Japan against the United States for political purposes. Consumer unity would seem to be critically important in denying producers' political demands. Why did such unity fail to develop in 1973?

The standard explanation for consumer disunity, stressing Europe's role as a "regional" power with limited responsibilities and America's as a "superpower" with global burdens, is incomplete. It emphasizes conflicting interests but glosses over divergent perceptions; it ignores the atmosphere within the alliance prior to October 1973, an atmosphere that shaped definitions of subsequent events.

American perceptions of Western Europe since the end of World War II have been remarkably tenacious and contradictory. On the one hand, American leaders have regarded Europe as an area of compatible values and institutions, the home of ancient cultures, languages, and traditions with unbreakable ties to the New World. Wilsonian scorn for Europe's power politics faded after 1945 as the former political center of the world sought its way in a changed environment. On the other hand, Europe has been viewed as "the prize" in the continuing Soviet-American contest, a region whose industrial base must remain firmly committed to the United States, even at the cost of restricting the European governments' internal political composition. U.S. warnings about Eurocommunism are thus consistent, if clumsy. At the same time, Europe has been feared as a "competitive sub-system," forming its own policies toward the Soviet Union, Africa, Latin America, Asia, and the Middle East, using its economic recovery to thwart varying American conceptions of European unity—"a partnership of equals," "twin pillars," or other Washington designs better left unremembered.

European perceptions of America have proved to be equally persistent and illusory. With the United States as their "defender," the Europeans could concentrate resources more heavily on wealth and welfare in circumstances of blurred distinctions between foreign and domestic policy. Yet America as the condominium partner of the Soviet Union has aroused Europe's suspicions. Seen from Washington, there was, in the 1960s at least,

> a certain irony in the way many Europeans imply that Soviet power is so great that they must repeatedly question the credibility of the American guarantee and at the same time assert that the Soviet threat has so declined that it is safe to reduce their own country's level of sacrifice for national and NATO security.[5]

These perceptions, revealing anxieties as well as rational calculation, are interesting precisely because they affected the behavior of governments in the months before and during the 1973 "crisis."

In April 1973, Henry Kissinger attempted to launch the "Year of Europe" before a generally unreceptive alliance audience. This elaborate and ultimately frustrated effort expressed U.S. concerns about Europe's lack of commitment to American policy preferences. The negative European reaction indicated visceral worries about American "hegemony." Neither the Americans nor the Europeans could deny that the military-economic bargain at the heart of Atlantic relations was in trouble, but they drew different conclusions about cause and effect, about illness and remedy. American officials argued that it was time for the Europeans to accept "linkage," to acknowledge the price of American security protection by granting better treatment to American goods in European markets and by increasing their defense outlays vis-à-vis Washington's. For the Europeans, the American Year of Europe looked like a public-relations gimmick that would legitimate American "linkage" with the Soviet Union in arms, trade, and possibly human rights, while relegating Europe's interests to the sidelines. Moreover, from a European vantage point, the implicit military-economic bargain struck with the United States in 1949 and again in 1958 was creaking but still acceptable, indeed more acceptable given the Community's economic strength than it had been in NATO's halcyon days.

Behind the U.S. proposals and Europe's lackluster response lay conflicting interpretations of security questions as the American and West European governments sought a competitive edge in their complicated relations. The United States, wanting both a special relationship with the Soviet Union and primacy in NATO, favored bilateral relations, while the Europeans, seeking leverage in Eastern Europe and the Mediterranean, insisted on separate declarations of principle on relations with the United States in the NATO and Community contexts. Unfortunately, this focus on maximizing marginal advantages, finally abandoned by the United States, tended to beg the question of whether the entire exercise of defining the nuances of Atlantic relations would have a political or other value for any of the participants. The time and energy devoted to tactical maneuvering over the form and content of the two declarations diverted attention from the need to adopt substantive Western positions on CSCE and MBFR, not to mention dealing with the looming energy dilemma.

It is hardly surprising then that the oil crisis should have caught the Western governments unprepared. Of course, the embargo brought to a climax forces set in motion decades earlier: the gradual shift from European coal and American domestic oil to Western reliance on Middle East oil, the rise of the independent oil companies, the relative decline of the "majors," plus the general loosening of structures in the international system. But the initial success of the oil weapon derived from the difficulties of finding petroleum substitutes quickly, together with unprecedented Arab unity against Israel and the absence of Western contingency plans. Governments reacted hastily, pragmatically and often incoherently, but, some would insist, "normally," for "governments have tended to deal with dislocations through adhoc daily decisionmaking, which reinforces attachment to the status quo and prevents governments from thinking about the effects of current policy on future options."[6]

While American officials disdained the frantic scrambling for bilateral European-Arab deals, without public appreciation of Europe's serious needs, most European countries had made a mockery of "impartial" stances as the Arab-Israeli fighting intensified and they contributed little to the climate of postwar negotiations. Both American and European leaders found it hard to accept their relative impotence vis-à-vis the oil companies as the multinationals distributed petroleum among importers according to *their* ideas of "equal suffering."

The crisis showed that Europe's "middle-rank" status was more limited than many political figures had appreciated: its economic power was vulnerable to external disruptions and its military weakness was self-evident.

Perhaps the biggest losers were the American and European theorists who had preached the virtues of interdependence and transnationalism. Interdependence among Western governments, far from diminishing conflict, exacerbated it in 1973-74. Moreover, national governments showed themselves to be most reluctant to yield control to nonstate actors. By reasserting themselves as states within the Community and by reviving the Atlantic connection, the European governments did demonstrate a chastened reality, especially an awareness of the differing national strengths and weaknesses found in the Nine. Yet, in the tension that gripped the Western governments, who could say whether they would "learn to live with a decline in their perceived economic power" or "imperiled by a sense of ebbing control and declining identity . . . strike out blindly against the others?"[7] Clearly, the traumatic events of 1973-74 were more than just an episodic crisis of confidence between the United States and Western Europe, more than an aspect of "global pluralism" or the "crisis of legitimacy"[8] in the industrialized world.

Avoiding a repetition of panicky consumer reactions was uppermost in the minds of American policymakers who urged the Europeans to join the new International Energy Agency in 1974. Despite French objections, the agency initially appealed to the other Europeans for whom tolerating American domination of the proceedings seemed less risky than being at the mercy of either the OPEC countries or the oil companies in the next crisis. The obvious U.S. reluctance to deal with the Community as a negotiating partner in the energy field left the Europeans with few choices, wary as they were of bilateral bargaining with Washington. Interestingly, whether consumer unity should be a desiderata for the alliance was not explored seriously in 1974 and in general has received less attention than it deserves, whereas the reassertion of American predominance has been widely debated.

Both what has and has not happened since 1973 form an important part of the setting. Western governments have continued to struggle with inflation, recession, unemployment, and balance of payments deficits. The international monetary system has not collapsed, but it is severely strained. Neither the European Community nor the United States has developed a coherent energy policy. While the Europeans have reduced their oil imports, the United States has increased its dependence on OPEC. World politics have become more complex, with few clearcut bilateral or multilateral relationships. "Linkage," judged to be costly, lacks a convincing regional or global rationale in the absence of American domestic support. Tradeoffs involving food, fuel, and arms are uncoordinated, but cartelization of additional commodities is a more remote prospect than it appeared to be in 1973. The Greek-Turkish dispute over Aegean oil and the cod war may be harbingers of future resource conflicts, but they have not become alliance-wide crises.

Increasingly, the Community appears to be a modified intergovernmental institution, a conclusion that will displease those who believe that the oil crisis has given the Europeans a new lease on a political and economic confederacy, who believe that the European states have found a new purpose or outlet as they look toward Mediterranean expansion. Whatever its virtues, enlargement of the existing Community to include such countries as Greece, Turkey, Spain, and Portugal will raise new problems in the energy field. The Community's resources will be stretched over a vast geographical area with uncertain benefits. North Sea oil is a palliative, and only for the British, at this stage.[9]

Within and beyond the Community's borders, there is more concern about the Soviet military build-up and less worry about the American guarantee. There is considerable bickering about war-fighting strategies versus more familiar deterrent stances. Détente has hardly changed habit in NATO; thus

> the West Europeans (still) criticize American rashness while questioning American cautiousness, . . . encourage East-West debate while fearing Soviet-American condominium, and . . . earnestly debate American political and strategic decisions after they have been made and are irreversible.[10]

Trends point in several directions as the United States and Europe ponder the West's energy-security dilemma. As oil consumers, arms suppliers, and food producers, alliance members are rivals as well as partners. Past history, hopes, biases, and cultural norms affect the state of mutual dependence as much as quantitative measures. Energy matters compete for attention with weapons standardization, the weakness of the dollar, the agenda for détente and North-South disputes. No structural solution provides a framework for the varied strands of Atlantic relations. As always, existing institutions like NATO, the EC, and the IEA, run the risk of becoming ends in themselves, rather than means to an end. The setting thus contains elements of both change and continuity that the catch phrases "American hegemony" and "European dependence" fail to clarify.

The Hazards of Energy Dependence, Independence, and Interdependence

Obviously, the choices for coping with the Western energy-security dilemma are neither one-dimensional nor cost-free. What should a national or regional energy policy offer? For some, an energy policy is simply a "device for allowing the most economic balance between different fuels to be found."[11] If the issue were really that simple, the U.S. Senate might well have passed President Carter's original energy bill in 1977 and German preferences for close ties with America would not have served as one of a number of constraints on the formulation of a Community energy policy. The profound domestic and global implications dictate a broader definition: "the assurance of sufficient energy supplies to permit the national or regional economy to function in a politically acceptable manner."[12] This approach acknowledges that even rich countries, if they are energy-importing, will have to be skillful in combining independent and interdependent moves. Domestic criticism of measures like rationing is almost inevitable and the international ramifications of diversification and stockpiling are unpredictable.

The record of adjustment to these new realities is understandably mixed. For instance, while the energy bill languished in conference, U.S. oil imports actually dropped. In a period of an oil glut, forecasters revised predictions of daily U.S. import requirements in 1985 downward from 12 million barrels to 7 million barrels a day, or about 50 percent of American petroleum needs.[13] Although the West is said to be ready for another disruption of supply with the IEA's emergency sharing plan, which calls for strategic stockpiles of seventy to ninety days of imports and emergency rationing to cut consumption 7 to 10 percent, fierce competition marks the activity of Europe's IEA members. They are using their national oil companies to try to increase control over supplies. One casualty of the "new oil nationalism" is the European Community's proposal to cut refining capacity in member countries, a plan pitting France, Belgium, Germany, and Italy against Britain, Iceland, and Denmark. A future victim could be the IEA's sharing plan, if national companies do gain additional control over oil supplies, and if environmental objections to fuller use of coal and nuclear power gain adherents in Europe.

The picture is still more complicated because governments must plan on the basis of widely divergent petroleum projections, coupled with domestic constraints on natural gas prices, off-shore oil leases, and nuclear power. Glaring inconsistencies abound, especially in U.S. policy. Washington has preached nuclear nonproliferation abroad while at the same time endorsing a more vital domestic nuclear industry. The Carter administration, reversing previous American policy, pressured both France and Germany to cancel sales of the complete nuclear fuel cycle to Pakistan, South Korea, and Brazil, citing the dangers of reprocessing. The United States also urged Japan and others to hold back on developing commercial versions of the fast breeder, despite the energy problems of these oil- and coal-poor countries. The compromise, a two-year international evaluation of the nuclear fuel cycle, is not likely to resolve the disputes between the United States and its allies on the controversial question of technology transfers. Japan has already announced its intention to proceed with reprocessing at Britain's Windscale.

More distressing is the continued failure of many governments to face some disturbing facts about the limits of consumer unity and energy "independence." As Robert Engler argues,

> A thoroughgoing reappraisal of the present energy system . . . demands a careful examination of its relations to the ongoing objectives of American foreign policy. If imports of oil and gas are to be accepted, their rate and prices must be attuned to public needs rather than corporate profitability. Banding together with other consumer nations, however understandable a defense against producer cartel attempts at what may be seen as economic blackmail or political reprisals, is a short-sighted strategy. It invites self-defeating military and diplomatic intrigue to widen fissures among the producer nations. This paradigm of economic sufficiency and security fuels the presumably abandoned cold war positions abroad. The United States still arms and finances racketeering ruling cliques who promise to deliver energy, markets, anticommunism, and populaces which ask few questions.[14]

As a result of a disinclination to reexamine the dangers of past policies, it is easier for Western governments to prepare for the last war, that is, a second oil embargo, rather than to probe more deeply into the tangled relationship of the oil companies and OPEC. While there is now much discussion of the need to limit oil imports, lest additional competition among advanced industrial countries result in an intra-European "North-South" split or a U.S.-German-Japanese preemption of available supplies,[15] there needs to be a deeper understanding of the "bilateral symbiotic oligopoly"[16] of the companies and the producer-governments, a factor that means Western governments cannot rely on the operation of price in the free market to correct shortages. As John Blair insists, "Quite apart from the fact that the oil industry bears only a passing resemblance to a free market, this approach to the energy crisis suffers from a fatal deficiency: both supply and demand are comparatively unresponsive to changes in price."[17] This insight has not been sufficiently appreciated by the major industrial powers, who called for a rise in U.S. domestic oil prices to the world level by 1980 at the July 1978 Bonn summit meeting.

Along with the failure to present to the public the pertinent information about supply and demand and the convoluted connections of the oil companies and OPEC, successive U.S. administrations have neglected to explain the inhibitions on American leverage. Again, Blair urges a more subtle appreciation of the behavior of the cartel and the companies:

> In predicting the imminent collapse of OPEC, the learned authorities and high policymakers had failed to recognize that, partly for the same and partly for different reasons, the countries and the companies had the same interests. Insofar as the countries are concerned, an ironic paradox is presented: those OPEC countries with the largest oil reserves have the least

need for additional funds to carry out ambitious industrialization programs, while those with the greatest need to industrialize have only limited
oil reserves. The former are unlikely to seek greater revenues by price sharing because they are already hard put to find uses for their existing
revenues; the latter are unlikely to cut prices because a greater volume of
sales would only accelerate the depletion of their limited reserves.[18]

While both the companies and the countries may put ceilings on production, the companies alone may set effective floors. Thus the United States
and other Western governments must have at least a two-pronged strategy
aimed at both key actors in the oil drama. Indeed, a three-pronged strategy
including the *individual* oil-producing countries would be a more appropriate objective because OPEC doesn't yet have the production control
program envisaged by some of its founders. It is not a classic cartel because
it does not have authority to set production controls, market shares,
penalties for violators, or mandatory export prices. Nor do members
delegate decision-making power to a central body. Nor are they likely to do
so as long as there are cleavages between "spender" versus "saver" OPEC
countries.[19]

This arrangement permits long-term deals between individual OPEC
members and Western governments, but does not provide any solution to
the Western alliance's problems of energy and security. It is against this
background that criticism of America's failure to develop and sustain an
energy policy should be placed. Is malfeasance or misperception at fault?
Believers in malfeasance blame the government, consumers, environmen-
talists, or the oil companies acting alone or in combination. Advocates of
misperception stress the lack of political will in America's acceptance of recent oil price increases. To be fair, dealing with OPEC is difficult. Even if
the cartel's internal political conflicts become intractable, its economic
strength grows with increasing demand, even in a time of comparative glut.

Of course, there is no dearth of suggestions for dealing with OPEC's
challenge, although most of them have serious drawbacks. The General Accounting Office asserts that the U.S. government should take an activist
role vis-à-vis the oil multinationals and OPEC, using trade terms and
technology or service exports as levers on OPEC,[20] but it does not specify
whether these efforts should be unilateral or collaborative. Others, believing that all confrontational tactics are discredited, urge an American
withdrawal from the world oil market but are unsure how to implement it.
M.A. Adelman has urged the use of sealed bids for U.S. imports as a way of
encouraging dissension in OPEC. Will this scheme work? What will prevent
seller collusion in this process? Another proposal, a three-class system of
tariffs for United States oil imports, would benefit non-OPEC countries in
the American market. Yet there are mechanisms open to the cartel to resist
such barriers, and the impact on Europe and Japan could be deleterious.

If there are no easy answers, there are at least lessons to be applied in the near future. It is evident that industrial countries will find it more difficult to increase the security of a constant oil supply than to promote conservation or the establishment of alternative sources. In addition, more elaborate multilateral relations between oil producers and consumers, transcending petroleum and embracing other commodity issues, will be required. Obviously, the idea of American "self-sufficiency" is misleading, if it is assumed that European and Japanese oil supplies will be assured by lowering American dependence on foreign imports, or that energy independence can be accomplished without additional inflation, recession, unemployment, and environmental damage. Finally, it must be admitted that oil is a wasting, exhaustible asset. Thus, conservation and price stability should be America's principal objectives.[21]

Gradually, the idea that conservation is critical to the future of Western societies is gaining strength. The Europeans are substantially ahead of the United States in conservation efforts, according to studies of the International Energy Agency.[22] Failure to conserve or change consumption patterns will become more serious if Saudi Arabia is unwilling or unable to increase its production in the 1980s, and if alternate sources are slow to develop. Conservation is at the heart of proposals for "soft-energy" choices versus "hard" choices, especially nuclear power. These ideas, associated with Amory Lovins, emphasize improving energy efficiency by technical fixes and matching tasks with appropriate energy sources. While coal could be accommodated within the soft-energy path, nuclear power could not. Although some of these ideas have already found official acceptance, others are likely to remain speculative. They have appeared at a time when it has become evident that the pursuit of energy "independence" would require huge capital investment in nuclear power, a choice that may endanger international security if it hastens the plutonium economy and present intolerable safety risks to local communities.

Similarly, strip-mining, additional pollution, inflation, recession, unemployment, or other ills may be unacceptable domestically. To be sure, "the domestic costs of energy self-sufficiency are only beginning to emerge. On the one hand, a concerted drive for energy development could produce jobs. On the other, a highly-funded U.S. federal energy program could drive up taxes. Tensions between energy conservation and development are likely" if conservation is relegated to a less prestigious environmental protection agency.[23]

President Carter's hastily drawn energy proposals stressed conservation, conversion from scarce oil to plentiful coal, and a different tax base. The plans proved confusing. The administration could not manage to arrange the key tradeoffs that would make a national energy policy realistic. There are still doubts that oil and gas can be "conserved" without stunting economic growth, doubts that the successful balancing acts of Sweden, Germany, and Japan could be repeated in the United States. The oil and gas lobbies attacked, as did consumer groups who feared that the well-head tax would simply drive up the price of domestic oil to world levels, with no break for the nonindustrial consumer.

The chief drawbacks to the Carter plans were procedural as well as substantive. After the president set an unrealistic deadline for submission to Congress, he failed to consult key party leaders. Later he retreated from the stance that the United States had to declare the "moral equivalent of war" on energy. As in other areas of domestic and foreign policy, the president appeared to retreat ineptly under pressure. The Carter proposals did serve a useful purpose in the domestic and alliance debate insofar as they abandoned the slogan of energy independence and tried to promote smaller, gas-efficient automobiles. Nevertheless, they do not add up to a coherent two- or three-pronged strategy directed at the oil companies, individual OPEC members, the cartel, or U.S. domestic interests.

Implementing the Carter proposals is posing problems. In the field that touches on alliance politics most directly, nuclear power, energy officials have developed legislation designed to speed the licensing process, but the bill has been the subject of an intense battle within the administration. In that battle, the Department of Energy and the Nuclear Regulatory Commission have been opposed by a vast array of other agencies, not just the Council on Environmental Quality but also the Office of Management and Budget and others. Officials in those departments are firmly opposed to the further use of nuclear power.

Apart from these U.S. bureaucratic squabbles, another row threatened to break out between the United States and the Community over the tightened regulations on exports of U.S. nuclear fuel, calling for prior American approval of reprocessing. A deal whereby renegotiation of the 1960 treaty could proceed by excluding all subjects being discussed in the international fuel cycle evaluation has eased the situation, and U.S. exports of enriched uranium to the Community will resume. The Community is also diversifying its purchases of enriched uranium to ensure supplies from the Soviet Union, and it is building its own enrichment facilities in Holland, Britain, and France. Obtaining Canadian and Australian supplies of raw uranium will be contingent on improved EC safeguards. Given the security implications, it is clearly in the interest of the Community to avoid depending on the Soviet Union for more than 10 to 20 percent of Europe's enriched uranium supply. According to the Community's Commission, the projected generating capacity of Europe's nuclear reactors through 1990 will not have to be scrapped for lack of fuel. The lead time for building enrichment plants is regarded as sufficient to prevent shortages.[24]

The years since the oil embargo have demonstrated that for Western governments energy dependence is uncomfortable, energy independence is chimerical, and energy interdependence is uncertain. A number of constraints are apparent. If Europe were less dependent on Arab oil and U.S. uranium, the problem of developing alliance responses to the twin challenges of OPEC and nuclear energy would be easier. If the United States had no interests in the Middle East other than access to oil at an acceptable price, the domestic consequences of a failed confrontation stance against OPEC might be contained. If nuclear proliferation were a less obsessive American concern or if massive U.S. conventional arms sales to the Persian Gulf[25] were not a source of alliance tension, a collective and comprehensive Western energy policy might be conceivable. For the next decade, at least, such an objective seems too ambitious. Instead, a complex assortment of risks centering on energy will affect Western security in the 1980s.

The Outlook for Energy and Security in the 1980s

The United States and its European allies will prepare for these risks on the basis of some shared perceptions and many unresolved questions. As a result, conclusions or prognostications seem especially speculative. Yet it is useful to consider the content of these perceptions and questions, for they suggest that skillful diplomacy will be needed to avoid being caught between allies and interests.

The 1970s have not been totally barren of specific achievements in allied energy planning, despite false starts. The IEA is at least a Western "energy conscience."[26] The need for the United States to do more with existing domestic resources like oil shale and to conduct research on solar, geothermal, biomass, and other "exotic" alternatives is acknowledged. The dangers of nuclear power, particularly the waste disposal problem, have attracted attention. The agreement on a safeguards code to prevent nuclear exports from being used for military purposes is a useful beginning. But it is not clear whether the American legislation to cut off supplies of nuclear fuels and technology in the absence of full-scope safeguards after eighteen months will prove effective.

At a more general level, it is widely known that the United States and its allies have different resource vulnerabilities and that the political consequences for security involve domestic constraints as well as international considerations. Governmental choice in energy affairs on both sides of the Atlantic is restricted by Europe's lagging political and economic unification and by the asymmetrical nature of interdependence. Pragmatic adjustments rather than joint decision-making are the rule, and the area of foreign economic policy is particularly contentious.[27] Resource-rich countries like the United States have discovered that domestic reactions to petroleum shortfalls and gluts or nuclear power hazards constrain bureaucracies. Yet it is not obvious that threats from at home are perceived as more "real" than threats from abroad in energy affairs. The management of interdependence may have to begin at home, but it cannot stop there. Nevertheless, the differing domestic costs and benefits of choices facing Europe and America cannot be ignored, especially when these choices will be made by a generation of political and business leaders accustomed to affluence and the rhetoric of détente as well as to the limits of European economic and defense capabilities.

In the 1980s, Europe will not be an independent, integrated subsystem fully responsible for its own defense or its own industrial growth. If actual fighting on the Continent were expected, the situation would appear more worrisome. To be sure, popular concern over the Soviet military build-up and the fate of the neutron bomb and cruise missile indicate that traditional concepts of defense and deterrence are still high on foreign policy agendas. Yet the rapid depletion of scarce resources and the intensifying competition to protect access to supplies has produced new approaches to security guarantees. The Western economies are highly dependent on obtaining energy resources at a socially bearable cost. Policymakers must give serious thought to the ways in which conflicts over energy resources may be anticipated or resolved via bilateral or multilateral means, just as they earlier worried about a Soviet surprise attack. With respect to energy and security, then, the major accomplishments thus far lie in the realm of perception rather than policy.

There are other shifts in understanding that may prove equally important in the years ahead. For example, few Western policymakers appear to believe that the increasing volume of transactions and common tasks in world politics will erode hostilities or that problems of interdependence are psychological rather than structural.

While the United States and OPEC have ways of creating stresses for each other, oil politics have had the most deleterious effects on the older European middle-rank states whose lack of certain high technologies accentuates alliance tensions. Western unity will be rendered more elusive in the 1980s by separate interests and by probable failures of political leadership or administrative skills. Consumers may be able to affect the operation of OPEC by supporting internal coalitions that favor controlled prices, although some sacrifices may be entailed.

Despite these widely accepted ideas, there are numerous problems that could impede the formation of Western strategies. There are no definitive methods for ascertaining whether energy scarcities are real or contrived. There are no simple combinations of national, regional, or multinational arrangements for continued access to energy supplies that are compatible with both the minimum requirements of a world order and the foreign policy objectives and instruments of the United States, Western Europe, and Japan. While some observers argue that earlier crises in Atlantic or OECD relations could be instructive in dealing with possible oil and uranium supply interruptions, many critics insist that Western energy problems are *sue generis*. There is less disagreement on the fact that the behavior of nonstate actors—for example, the European Community, OPEC, the oil companies, and the IEA—does complicate, as well as facilitate, national decision-making. Not only are these actors qualitatively different, they also do not command domestic allegiances that are the precondition of energy tradeoffs.

Clearly, the outlook for energy and security in the 1980s involves both technical and political aspects that current theories of interdependence or bureaucratic politics explain partially, at best.

Notes

1. Mason Willrich, *Energy and World Politics* (New York: The Free Press, 1975), p. xii.

2. Stanley Hoffmann, "An American Social Science: International Relations," in *Discoveries and Interpretations: Studies in Contemporary Scholarship, Deadalus*, Summer 1977, p. 57.

3. Edward Krapels, *Oil and Security: Problems and Prospects of Importing Countries, Adelphi Paper* No. 136 (London: International Institute for Strategic Studies, Summer 1977), p. 29.

4. Ibid.

5. Warner R. Schilling, William T.R. Fox, Catherine M. Kelleher, and Donald J. Puchala, *American Arms and a Changing Europe* (New York: Columbia University Press, 1973), p. 192.

6. Edward L. Morse, "The New Europe: A Unified Bloc or Blocked Unity?" in Robert A. Bauer, *The Interaction of Economics and Foreign Policy* (Charlottesville: University of Virginia Press, 1975), p. 126.

7. Raymond Vernon, "Economic Sovereignty at Bay," *Foreign Affairs*, October 1968, p. 122.

8. For additional discussion of these points, see Edward L. Morse, "The Atlantic Economy in Crisis," in *Atlantis Lost*, James Chace and Earl Ravenal, eds. (New York: New York University Press, 1976), chapter 7.

9. N.J.D. Lucas, *Energy and the European Communities* (London: Europa Publications, 1977).

10. Schilling, *American Arms*, p. 149.

11. John Maddox, *Beyond the Energy Crisis* (New York: McGraw-Hill, 1975), p. 208.

12. Willrich, *Energy and World Politics*, p. 67.

13. *International Herald Tribune*, May 29, 1978.

14. Robert Engler, *The Brotherhood of Oil* (Chicago: University of Chicago Press, 1977), p. 241.

15. See, for example, "International Energy Supply: A Perspective from the Industrial World," Rockefeller Foundation Working Paper, May 1978.

16. John Blair, *The Control of Oil* (New York: Pantheon Books, 1976), p. 293.

17. Ibid., p. 323.

18. Ibid., p. 280.

19. For additional details on this distinction, see Robert S. Pindyck, "OPEC's Threat to the West," and S. Fred Singer, "Limits to Arab Oil Power," *Foreign Policy*, Spring 1978, pp. 36-67.

20. *New York Times*, January 4, 1978.

21. Linda B. Miller, "Energy, Security and Foreign Policy," *International Security*, Spring 1977, p. 120.

22. See, for instance, *World Energy Outlook*, OECD, Paris, 1977.

23. See Amory Lovins, *Soft-Energy Paths: Toward a Durable Peace* (Cambridge: Ballinger Publishing, 1977). He credits his ideas with the capacity to offer "jobs for the unemployed, capital for business people, environmental protection for conservationists, enhanced national security for the military, opportunities for small business to innovate and for big business to recycle itself, exciting technologies for the secular, rebirth of spiritual values for the religious, traditional virtues for the old, radical reforms for the young, world order and equity for globalists, energy independence for isolationists, civil rights for liberals, states' rights for conservatives."

24. For additional discussion, see Lucas, *Energy and the European Communities*, pp. 108-110.

25. U.S. sales to Saudi Arabia alone total $12 billion in the years 1973-1977. The Saudi arsenal includes: 110 F5E fighters, 250 M-60 battle tanks, 400 Maverick air-to-surface missiles, 6 batteries of Hawk surface-to-air missiles and 2,000 Sidewinder air-to-air missiles. The Carter administration will sell 60 F15 bombers to Saudi Arabia as part of a package deal involving the sale of 50 F5 fighters to Egypt, and 15 F15s and 75 F16s to Israel. U.S. spokesmen have consistently tried to downplay Saudi Arabia's emergence as a confrontation state in the Arab-Israeli conflict as a consequence of these acquisitions. Since 1976, the United States has sold to Iran 350 Sidewinders, 350 Sparrow air-to-air missiles, 424 Phoenix air-to-air missiles. The fate of the 160 F16s promised for delivery in 1979-1983 is problematic. For additional details, see *The Military Balance, 1977-1978*, International Institute for Strategic Studies, London, p. 97.

26. Daniel Yergin, "Killjoy of the Western World," *The New Republic,*
February 25, 1978, p. 20.

27. For an analysis of this problem, see essays in *Between Power and
Plenty: Foreign Economic Policies of Advanced Industrial States, International Organization,* Autumn 1977.

5 The Future of Collaborative Weapons Acquisition

Robert W. Dean

Over the last half decade the obvious diseconomies in European defense planning and production have commanded new attention because of pressures to reduce defense budgets and the build-up of Warsaw Pact conventional forces. Widely acknowledged deficiencies in NATO's conventional force posture and the strain on national resources have led to a declaratory consensus that increased defense cooperation—specifically, the pursuit of standardization, interoperability, collaborative acquisition and general rationalization—can significantly redress the East-West military imbalance without placing major new demands on national defense budgets. This impulse is reinforced by the postulate that advances in conventional arms technology—notably in antitank and antiaircraft guided weapons—have altered the tactical environment, shifting the balance of military advantage, to an even greater degree, to the defense. Outfitting European forces with the most advanced weapon systems is seen as a means of compensating for the Warsaw Pact's quantitative advantage. The military logic is debatable. What is not subject to question is the perceived need of the larger NATO European states to maintain the capability to develop and produce high-technology weapon systems.

But highly sophisticated technology has also changed the economics of defense, placing the national development and production of many weapon systems beyond the reach of individual countries. Insufficiently large national markets for costly advanced systems logically dictate that their development and production be undertaken cooperatively. As a result of these factors, collaborative acquisition has captured the attention of officials and defense planners on both sides of the Atlantic.

The weapons acquisition process in the NATO countries is carried out domestically, and defined by national military and industrial objectives. Acquisition decisions remain the prerogative of individual governments. In comparison to the resources devoted to developing and procuring weapons nationally, the extent of past international collaboration has been small. NATO organizations have worked to encourage a variety of forms of collaboration. And yet progress toward a more systematic, internationalized acquisition process has been meager.

This chapter seeks to generalize on the basis of nearly two decades of

European experience in collaborative acquisitions, primarily that of Britain, France, and Germany, since in the aggregate the three acount for approximately 75 percent of non-U.S. NATO defense expenditures. The determining motive has been to preserve and extend an independent defense industrial base for national political and economic reasons, recognizing at the same time that maintaining technical progress and industrial capacity depends in important part upon the success of international industrial consortia producing for markets larger than national needs. Each country has been guided by the urge to protect future weapons and technology sources, as well as domestic employment and weapons export markets.

The obstacles to collaborative acquisition in Europe are considerable. Each country's options and interests are governed by the industrial bases from which existing weapons inventories have come, by current and future resources, and by the military requirements and replacement schedules which determine national acquisitions decisions. Collaborative programs oblige agreement between prospective partners on costs, and on development and production schedules. They also oblige firm commitments on long-term major expenditures, with each participant having only limited power to vary that expenditure unilaterally. National military requirements and technical specifications, themselves the product of national staff planning procedures and service interests, must be made to conform where technological risk and uncertainty are often high. It is these incentives and constraints, the politics of the *national* defense acquisitions process, which have influenced the extent and shape of collaboration efforts in Europe. And it is only an appreciation of the national process which permits a realistic estimate of the future of the international collaborative process.

**The National Motives and Pressures behind
European Collaboration**

Utilization and Preservation of Existing Capacity

The impulse to utilize and to preserve existing capacity is a strong determinant in national weapons acquisition, and is no less important in collaborative acquisition. Those countries which have significant research, development, and production capabilities often feel compelled to choose a national product if feasible, or to ensure that national industries are utilized to the maximum extent in collaborative projects.[1] Since the overriding factor governing the prospects for joint acquisitions is the interest of the major European countries in the health and competitiveness of domestic defense industries, collaboration could be defined as the pursuit of national ends through international means. Thus collaboration has involved integration of specific equipment markets, but not the long-term integration of research and development (R and D) or production capabilities based on national specialization.

Specific national motives for collaboration have varied from project to project. In all cases, however, they appear to have been as much the product of economic and industrial considerations as of strategic and military objectives. Furthermore, *production* costs and *production* efficiency have been important, but secondary, concerns. For Britain and France, collaboration has proved to be the means to maintain existing capacity which might otherwise have succumbed to rising resource restraints. For the FRG, collaboration was and is a way of establishing new defense industrial capacity, and developing technology and design capabilities. The MRCA project is representative of these objectives.[2]

Since the mid-1960s the European defense industry as a whole has adapted to intense American competition, as well as to higher R and D costs, through increased concentration. This trend has seen the disappearance of smaller firms through a process of amalgamation. The most important mergers have included Dassault and Breguet (1971) in France, and BAC and Hawker-Siddely (1974) in Britain; in Germany all indications are that VFW-Fokker and Messerschmitt-Boelkow-Blohm will be merged in the near future. The relatively smaller national demand for military aircraft and other advanced weapon systems in Europe as compared with the United States is another pressure which has argued for the amalgamation of aerospace and other high technology defense *markets*.[3]

Distribution of High R and D Costs through
Expanded Exports

The central problem for Britain, France, and Germany is that of rising unit costs due in large part to the higher development costs of advanced technology. One way to hold down unit costs of new systems is to amortize the costs of R and D and tooling over longer production runs. Further industrial contraction and production stretch-outs are not attractive options. Decreasing production does not decrease R and D costs which remain constant or grow, but are more difficult to support at existing levels because of decreased production. Indeed, "to survive at all," in the words of a French official, "[the European armaments industry] must keep up its present level of output."[4] A steady, uninterrupted effort to continue technological progress is regarded as possible only if current capacity is preserved. That capacity, in the view of policy level officials, can only be maintained on the basis of exports.[5] The attraction of collaboration as a means of distributing R and D costs and of ensuring the expansion of exports is obvious.

International collaboration does derive from the desire to economize. But rationalization across national boundaries is supported only to the extent that it does not compromise preservation of extant defense-industrial facilities and related national objectives associated with maintaining an advanced, comprehensive defense-industrial base. There is advocacy of greater commonality of weapons produced, as well as larger production runs of individual series, but scant support for further rationalization which might involve long-term national specialization or the relinquishing of national capacity. It appears to be established practice that considerations of cost effectiveness and industrial efficiency must avoid creating disequilibria in the socio-economic environment, which is one effect that sectoral optimization in defense industries would have.[6]

Maintenance of a Diverse National Technology Base

One reason for the absence of a more integrated, specialized, and comprehensive approach to defense R and D is the strong national reluctance to become technologically dependent upon allies by relinquishing national capabilities. High R and D costs and insufficient national markets constrain European governments to collaborate. (Indeed, in the case of some high-cost, complex systems it may be a question of collaborating or doing without.) Obviously, some form of dependence ensues. The process of collaboration, however, has been governed by the desire to limit dependence as much as possible, to ensure that technological progress deriving from collaborative efforts results in the maintenance of national technological diversity, not in rationalization and specialization. Each of the three major European powers wants at the least to maintain *its own* aerospace, electronics, and communications industries, and, what is directly related, an advanced defense industrial base. These objectives militate against technological integration.

Specialization in R and D has also been difficult to achieve for political reasons. The national technology policies of Britain, France, and Germany in the defense sector transcend economic motives of national profit and employment, and of ensuring a proportionate "just return" from collaborative efforts. Their competition for power and influence within Europe, as well as national political and economic ambitions which extend beyond Europe, are also important determinants. Genuine interdependence (that is, specialization) has its political preconditions, which do not necessarily involve the surrender of national sovereignty, but which would oblige a level of political trust and certainty with respect to future patterns of cooperation in Europe which does not now exist and which is unlikely to be achieved in the foreseeable future. It is a reflection of such basic attitudes that until now national governments have shown a willingness to pay a premium in order to avoid dependence of a permanent sort within the framework of collaborative European defense projects.

The effort to limit dependence is evident in the insistence by each participant that it retain access to all technologies, and in the case of the three major countries, national production capability for the weapon systems as a whole. (French, British, and West German defense officials have claimed that each country retains the technology and production know-how derived from collaborative projects which would enable domestic production of all jointly developed weapon systems. This is something which could hardly be achieved, however, without incurring large penalties in both cost and time.) One visible result of the national objectives to avoid technological integration is that—at least until now—no international industrial mergers have resulted *from the collaborative process.* Another is the reluctance of European governments to assign exclusive prime contract responsibility of full design leadership for *total* system development to other European firms in important part because of the potential technological dependence which such division of labor implies. For example, five firms from three countries share responsibility for the MRCA airframe.[7] One possible result of this process is the international spread of R and D capabilities (each country benefiting from joint developments) accompanied by the greater national concentration of R and D resources into the larger and technologically strong firms which have collaborated in the projects.

Preservation of National Defense Capabilities

The practical possibilities of greater defense specialization, of limiting national military industrial capacities and relinquishing balanced national forces, are circumscribed by a host of considerations central to national sovereignty and economic well-being and by political uncertainties which could alter national defense needs in the future. Such specialization, even of a limited sort, presupposes political decisions which would embody a qualitatively enhanced political commitment to the alliance. Failing such a commitment, could a state which had relinquished its navy to depend upon that of a neighboring state rely on its ally in crises now unforeseen and unpredictable? Would that ally submit to prior pledges of military support which could involve it in crises in which it had less than a vital interest? Are not apprehensions justified that defense collaboration which breeds specialization would relegate a nation to second-class technological status in certain critical areas in comparison with its defense partners—with disadvantages for its advanced industries as a whole?

A certain amount of de facto specialization in force structures has taken place over the past two decades: few European armies have comprehensive military capabilities or are equipped or trained to fight anywhere but in their immediate national neighborhood.[8] If operational limitations have been imposed upon national forces, however, they have been the result of national decisions calculated on the basis of national strategy or resources, and the reduction of expenditures and the scaling down of national defense postures. Nowhere has the issue been addressed of relinquishing national capabilities in favor of surrendering them to allies. Few collective efficiencies, military or economic, have resulted.

Reservations about depending on weapons imports, and misgivings about the political dependence this may breed, have encouraged most European states to maintain and develop indigenous weapons industries, however limited. The procurement policies of Britain and France have been the most comprehensive. In the first two decades following World War II a broad defense base was considered necessary to support foreign policies which might have obliged military action far from Europe, and independent of allies. These ambitions have been less important during the last fifteen years. But both in size and capabilities their force structures and industries still reflect military strategies that dictated preparedness for a wide variety of conflicts, and a need for unhindered domestic weapons sources. Furthermore, the impulse is still strong to ensure unrestricted national access to and use of military hardware. Since the early 1960s, however, the pressures of rising defense costs and shrinking resources have forced both Britain and France to moderate a strong preference for unilateral weapons acquisition. But collaborative projects continue to be guided by the objective of minimizing encumbrances of any sort on the use or supply of jointly acquired hardware.

Since West Germany entered NATO, procurement policy has been politically determined in large part by its security dependence on the United States. Bonn's heavy dependence on American supplies, however, permitted the rapid outfitting of the Bundeswehr with a broad range of weapons, and reinforced Germany's political/security dependence. In the mid-1960s German purchases of U.S. defense equipment were used by agreement to offset U.S. troop costs. Military purchases from Britain served the same purpose. Germany's second-largest supplier has been France, a policy also politically motivated, at least in the 1960s, by Germany's view of weapons purchases as part of the general policy of Franco-German reconciliation.[9]

Budget Restraints and Savings through Collaboration

A prevailing political climate of détente, European expenditure commitments in the social sector, economic malaise, and inflationary crises have combined to make major increases in European defense budgets unlikely. Equally as significant as the prospect of limited growth in European defense budgets is the change in their structure. As a proportion of total defense expenditures, manpower and operating costs have risen over the past decade while allocations for equipment have generally fallen. The key question is the extent to which research, development, and procurement budgets in particular have fallen victim to reduced GNP growth rates and to increases in social costs. Specific and detailed analyses or comparisons are difficult to make. But one thing is clear: when cuts come in European defense budgets they tend to come in equipment expenditures. The trend is likely to continue. Moreover, the cost of replacement systems has been considerably greater than the cost of the systems they are designed to replace.[10] While it is subject to qualification, the choice, simply put, is to accept a qualitative decay of force structures or to modernize at the cost of a reduction of numbers.

This brings us to the issue of the presumed savings associated with collaboration. There seems to be a common assumption that collaborative procurement can produce considerable savings. But there is every reason to question *the extent* of possible savings. At a West European Union symposium held to address problems of armaments cooperation, officials and industrialists questioned whether collaborative programs and the way in which they have been organized thus far had proved to be more cost efficient than the proliferation of individual national programs.[11]

Many estimates of potential savings through collaboration are based on assumptions that alliance-wide specialization can be achieved and duplication eliminated, especially in R and D. Aggregate estimates of R and D duplication in Europe and within the alliance as a whole, and possible collective alliance efficiencies (such as appeared a few years ago in the so-called Callaghan Report), are macroeconomic appraisals which only make plain that egregious diseconomies exist. One of the weaknesses of such analyses is that they have done little to point the way toward practical means of savings. Estimates of possible savings have varied from $1 billion to in excess of $10 billion per year in comparison with existing aggregate expenditures. But such savings could be achieved only if NATO were a more, if not fully, integrated alliance and acquisition could be fully rationalized. This would call for each country's acceptance of the principle of international comparative advantage in regulating its defense acquisition, and probably its role in NATO strategy as well. In short, it would mean the acceptance of specialized and limited role, a politically unrealistic prospect.[12]

Despite the acknowledged diseconomies in weapons acquisition, much suggests that the difficulty of verifying economy of scale savings accruing from joint acquisition is itself an obstacle to achieving those savings. This is due in part to the fact that no precise analysis of the structure and capacities of European defense industries has been available. No broader, let alone comprehensive, view of rationalization has ever been realistically possible.[13] Furthermore, to the best of the writer's knowledge, no successful efforts have been made thus far to quantify specific losses of efficiency or potential savings in areas realistically amenable to collaborative policies or, for that matter, to specify actual savings derived from past or current European collaborative programs. The paucity of detailed comparative cost data means that it is difficult, if not impossible, to verify the economies which might result from greater collaboration.[14] More systematic, detailed, quantitative analyses could enable calculation of potentially high pay-off collaborative acquisition opportunities.[15] The shortage of data is to blame not only for the failure to initiate more collaborative projects, but probably also for the cancellation of a number of projects already under way in which rising costs, delays, and market shrinkage were more difficult to anticipate.

It is unlikely that a general rule can be established for savings or cost increase in collaborative weapon systems programs. Potential savings and cost increases will probably vary with each case. For one thing, it is difficult to verify the exact increase in the cost ratio because there is never an identical project to which the collaborative one can be compared. For another, because the typical weapon system involves procurement of at least a few hundred items, costs depend heavily on factors such as how development and production work is distributed among participants, their relative efficiencies, the availability of supplies, local labor supply, industrial capacity and backlog, and the extent to which national requirements can be harmonized in a single product, that is, how many versions of the same basic system must be produced to satisfy all the nations involved. In this connection it should be noted that there are more factors involved in cost reduction than simply producing a greater number of units. The relationship between cost reduction and units produced tends to be a direct one when those units are produced by a single production line and when they are identical. Multiple production lines and variations of a basic design tend to diminish the cost-reducing effects of larger production runs. All of this suggests that each weapon system which is a candidate for collaboration must be examined separately and in detail to determine the economic effect of an increased production rate.

Standardization

Another motive for collaboration is presumably the standardization of military equipment. But here motives differ on either side of the Atlantic. To oversimplify, we in the United States have endorsed collaborative procurement as a means of achieving standardization—compatibility in military equipment, as well as in logistics, doctrine, and procedures, which may extend from their complete identity to their simple "interoperability"—and we tend to emphasize the collective benefits in military efficiency which, it is assumed, will accrue. On the whole, the Europeans acknowledge the military benefits of at least a degree of standardization but, reflecting economic priorities, have endorsed it rather as a means for achieving collaborative acquisition. Thus, the priorities are reversed. It is less the pursuit of collective military efficiencies which motivates the Europeans than the perceived economic necessity of collaboration. One indication of the European attitude is that although the military benefits conferred by standardization through joint acquisition may be acknowledged, such approval has been insufficient to persuade European nations to collaborate where technological and financial pressures have not been overriding.[16] Thus far, joint acquisition projects like the British-German-Italian Multi-Role Combat Aircraft represent ad hoc responses to economic pressures, limited budgets, the spiraling costs of advanced technology, and the need for larger markets to offset costs and distribute the investment burden. Such problems are not unimportant or unfamiliar to American defense planners, but their magnitude and immediacy are considerably greater in Europe.

Standardization and collaborative acquisition, all too often regarded as one and the same, are in fact quite separate issues. Given the wide variety of existing weapons, even partial standardization (that is, different national forces deploying the same weapons) can only be an incremental process. Furthermore, in the past, collaborative acquisition has not necessarily resulted in wholly standardized equipment. Such weapons are intended for incorporation into national forces under national command; different national versions have been produced and—for example, in the case of the Jaguar and MRCA—they have been subject to national modification. Even where existing systems have been produced under license in Europe, the product has often differed significantly from the original design. Because there were no provisions for standardization and interoperability with U.S. aircraft, the F-104G produced in Germany, for example, was considerably different from its U.S. counterpart.

The postulate that standardization of equipment translates directly into greater military effectiveness is not universally accepted either among students of the problem or professional officers. Despite commonly held assumptions about the military value of standardization, putative gains in military effectiveness are often difficult to demonstrate. This may account for the dearth of quantitative, as opposed to qualitative, appraisals, even in the specialized literature. Pentagon officials responsible for standardization have acknowledged the difficulties thus far in devising convincing quantitative measures. Precisely because standardization questions have only been addressed hypothetically, questions remain. For example, should one nation forego a better weapon, or one which conforms precisely with its own military requirements, for the uncertain military benefits of standardization? If national commands retain the responsibility for providing logistics support, why would standardization of equipment necessarily confer significant military advantage, apart from emergency interoperability? Standardized equipment would enable the joint procurement of support items like spare parts. But if there were no central planning or administration of logistics, not only would life-cycle economies be limited, but military effectiveness could be curtailed, standardized equipment notwithstanding. National armies would still be restricted to their own defense sectors, to their own logistic "tails." In other words, standardization of equipment without more genuine military integration might contribute only marginally to military effectiveness.[17]

The Shape of Collaboration

Concentration in High Technology Areas

Those forces which both encourage and restrict collaboration also shape the collaborative effort. European projects have been concentrated in what national participants evidently see as seminal military technologies, above all in aerospace and electronics. This is probably because:

a. these technologies are regarded as strategic to maintaining advanced national defense industries and competitiveness positions in third markets, even if they are to be shared;
b. they would require unacceptably high R and D budgets to support strictly national programs;
c. they are perceived as having a high "spillover" value for related civilian industries.

As the relatively small number of major projects (some ten to twelve) thus far suggest, the United Kingdom, France, and the FRG have shown themselves willing to collaborate primarily when the national quantity required is too small to justify the development costs, or if a single nation does not have the technology or the development capabilities available. This also helps to explain the concentration on major weapon systems: if the weapon can be developed and produced within national means at acceptable cost and the national market is sufficient, the preference appears to be not to collaborate.

The relatively greater distribution of collaborative projects in the more advanced equipment—combat and other fixed-wing aircraft, helicopters, and guided weapons—reveals where the economic and technological incentives to collaborate are strongest. The more technologically advanced a weapons project is, the greater is the prospect of escalating costs, inadequate research and development capabilities, and ultimate failure, and the more compelling is the logic of risk-sharing and joint investment. More conventional systems and technologies such as armored vehicles either require proportionately less R and D expenditures, or the United Kingdom, France, and the FRG have sufficiently large national production runs to obviate the need for collaboration. There is little reason to expect that this pattern of selective European collaboration in aircraft and missiles will change in the future.

Lack of Longer-term Industrial Integration

Another characteristic of collaboration has been the lack of long-term industrial integration. Thus far, each codevelopment project has been ad hoc and self-contained: each has been negotiated on the basis of the principles that each participating country receive a share of the benefits proportional to its costs (or the number of units to be procured), and that this be achieved within the framework of that particular project. There has been little equalization of costs over several projects (although some interproject balancing has occurred.) There has been no overall planning which would permit the disproportionate allocation of tasks among different projects to exploit specific national advantages, and the determination of equity by systematically extending the costs and credits derived from one project to another, a process which could imply continuing industrial integration. Achieving equity has often involved constant renegotiation during the life of a project against a background of cost escalation and changing currency parities to insure the agreed distribution of benefits. Notwithstanding the separate character of each collaborative project, the cumulative effect of a number of them may adumbrate a form of industrial integration, a subject which will be addressed later.

Restricted Number of National Participants

The advantages of distributing high-risk development costs and creating larger markets to reduce unit costs argue for increasing the number of collaborative participants. But inherent in the collaborative pursuit of national defense industrial capabilities and commercial competitiveness are the apparent tendency and the incentive to restrict the number of countries in any one project. The complexities of managing a collaborative project increase with the number of participants, as, apparently, do the costs and schedule delays. This has made officials in all three countries apprehensive that collaboration will "deteriorate" as the number of nations involved in a particular project grows. While there are advantages to collaboration, there are also disadvantages and inefficiencies, and the latter tend to grow at a faster rate than the former in proportion to the number of participants. For these reasons, the main European collaborative development projects have consisted of two or three participants. Indeed, the MRCA project stands out as one of the new major development undertakings to integrate the work of three nations. Other major efforts have generally been Franco-British or Franco-German in composition.

Even where collaboration is longer term and successful, participant nations remain reticent about expanding industrial consortia. Euromissile, the Franco-German consortium that has successfully developed and produced three tactical missile systems since 1963, will presumably be expanded to include the British Aerospace Corporation for the joint development of an antiship missile (under the tentative rubric of Anti-Ship Euromissile—ASEM). The inclusion of Italy as a fourth participant, however, has evidently been resisted. The tendency to limit the number of national participants in individual projects suggests that it is unlikely that future collaboration in development of total systems, especially in the aircraft field, will come to include more than three participants, let alone grow into more inclusive European endeavors.

Collaboration as a Political Process

It should be apparent that by its very nature collaboration is bound to be intensely political. Participants in collaborative acquisition programs seek a common product, but they also seek a comprehensive return—in technology acquisition, employment benefits, allocation of production and sales, and other outputs—proportionate to their share of program inputs. This can be a very different thing from simply obtaining a fixed number of aircraft or missile systems which corresponds to a percentage of program equity. Those pressures and interests which influence national acquisition policies quite naturally seek to influence international programs to ensure optimal national or sectoral outcomes. Furthermore, in order to reach agreement on collaboration, efficiencies must often be traded off to assure equity.[18]

European experience in international industrial projects generally has shown that in negotiating agreements governments are prone to advocate the cause of national suppliers. Given the strong official interest in supporting the progress of national industries, the tendency is for government support to be shifted into international negotiations on collaboration. A national requirement, industrial capability, or design may be put forth as the model for international acceptance. Or compromises might be sought in the interest of compatibility and reaching agreement, but to the maximum degree possible they will accommodate all national objectives. The degree to which these objectives will influence individual collaborative efforts will vary. The point to be emphasized is that the dynamics of collaboration may subordinate objective consideration of performance standards or cost effectiveness considerations. In the language of one analysis, "the setting of a technical specification to fill [a] performance requirement may derive rather from the relative (bargaining) power of the participating [firms or governments] than from technical and cost considerations."[19]

Other outcomes are also possible. Rather than expressing genuine single or unitary requirements, the requirements of collaborative systems are liable to be an amalgamation of various national requirements, reflecting compromises made in the program formulation phase (compromises which may continue), and suggesting that the participants have not given absolute priority to overall program requirements over certain national demands such as the incorporation of certain specifications.[20] Furthermore, in order to reach agreement on a basic design, individual nations may be obliged to purchase capabilities they do not necessarily need. One view of collaboration as a highly politicized process is set forth by Mr. Allen Greenwood, chairman of the British Aerospace Corporation. The past few collaborative projects (the reference apparently includes the MRCA) have been governed more by political than strategic considerations, according to Greenwood. Companies have frequently been chosen for reasons "which are based on criteria neither of industrial efficiency nor technical quality. The management of these enterprises is often bedeviled by political pressures."[21]

Renegotiation appears to be a continuing process and problem. Changes in specifications or other project areas, depending on their magnitude, can often be negotiated within the international program management organization. But program changes (especially equipment specifications) often have to be ratified by authorities within the national defense establishments. Decision authority at the program level, in other words, has been typically diluted by the need to consult with and to coordinate the positions of authorities in two or more governments. Vital decisions may therefore be as much the product of political-social-industrial considerations in individual countries as those limited to the program itself.[22] Strictly national programs are not immune to such pressures. But the nature and number of pressures in international programs often differ. For example, maintaining originally agreed-upon national equities obligates the redistribution of work between nations once the project is underway in response, for instance, to changed currency parities. This introduces a dimension of complexity into the management of collaborative programs which does not obtain on a national basis. The need for continuing compromise over a collaborative program's life is obvious, although the extent of the penalties which a program might incur as a result (in delays, for example) is not clear.

It is probably a safe generalization that, the newer and more sophisticated the technology of a collaborative weapon system is, the more difficult program management problems are likely to be. The prediction of technological and cost risks is rendered more difficult. Establishing and maintaining a common international requirement naturally give rise to more debate within the national services. As a result, the number and complexity of program decision points increase.

Generating Common Military Requirements

The existence of similar, if not identical, operational concepts clearly facilitates collaboration in weapons acquisition. But within NATO operational concepts have been established, by and large, according to national rather than collective criteria, and by national defense ministries and services. The result is that national military concepts, and therefore operational requirements, differ markedly. The lengthy and ultimately unsuccessful efforts of Britain and Germany to reconcile contrary tactical concepts of tank mobility in order to collaborate on tank design and production provide an example of differing national concepts. The British emphasize the tank's role as the focus around which cluster ground combat units; the Germans stress high mobility, speed, and the tank's capacity as a basic fire unit. Technical problems encountered in the MRCA project, to cite another example, arose in large part from the fact that the aircraft's initial requirement fused the divergent operational needs of Britain, Germany, and Italy in a way that forced designers against technical boundaries. Such examples are numerous. The point is that in the absence of a common concept, achieving coherent, feasible military requirements is difficult. The most recent German White Paper singled out a "unanimously agreed analysis of the threat and a common (operational) concept [as a] prerequisite to harmonizing military requirements."[23]

Commonly agreed-upon operational concepts can facilitate actual collaboration in acquisition, but as NATO's history in this area shows, they do not assure it. If nations cannot agree on how a weapon will be used, that is if they cannot define common operational requirements, either they cannot build it cooperatively or must modify it once built. The failure of the joint German-American MBT-70 development was due, among other factors, to such typical differences over requirements as the U.S. Army's insistence that maximum engine horsepower be available at a temperature of 125 degrees Fahrenheit. That specification incorporated a need for potential worldwide deployment of the tank, and the army was willing to bear the additional expense in achieving such a performance level. The FRG, its threat environment limited to the European theater, had little interest in such a level of performance. Similarly, the United States withdrew from the four-party Field Howitzer-70 project to begin its own development program because the U.S. Army insisted that any major howitzer be air-transportable, a requirement which arose from the need in Vietnam for air-mobile artillery.

Even when similar operational concepts permit the launching of a collaborative project, participating nations may still disagree on technical problems of development, that is, on operational requirements. In adapting the Franco-German surface-to-air Roland missile system for use by the U.S. Army, one fundamental alteration was the adoption of a more powerful radar tracking unit, the result of differing estimates of operational needs. The U.S. estimate of the potential Soviet Electronic Counter Measure (ECM) threat was greater than that of France and Germany. Furthermore, the French and German versions were planned for integration into a dense radar network in Europe, whereas the U.S. version had to be capable of being deployed by itself.[24] The U.S. requirement was therefore for a more powerful unit. Such changes have lessened the compatibility of national systems and forced production costs higher.

Driven by economic imperatives toward greater collaboration, European nations have been willing to bend national military requirements in the interests of getting a project off the ground. A question remains, however, about the extent to which operational requirements can be genuinely harmonized at the outset and retained intact over the life of a project. To the maximum degree possible there should exist both a clear *national* and an international consensus on user requirements to minimize the necessity for renegotiation. Some renegotiation of the original requirement will be inevitable, because of the impossibility of anticipating the technical problems which normally attend the development of new and complex systems. Examples abound of projects interrupted or canceled because of diverging national needs. The Mallard program, a joint U.K.-Australian-Canadian-U.S. effort to develop a secure tactical communications system, foundered on the continuous need to negotiate common user requirements. This resulted in program delays, cost escalation, and the tendency of participants to reassess their commitment to the project.[25] In this case the United States dropped out. Both American and European experience points to the need for effective machinery for agreeing on common requirements between military service staffs at the senior level in the early concept phase of acquisitions planning. And throughout program life the need is to identify and to coordinate tactical concepts and staff requirements as early as possible, and to ensure that they continue to be monitored in a spirit of compromise at the same senior level.

Issues in U.S.-European Collaboration

Much has been written about the "technology gap" between the United States and Europe, the relatively greater rate of American technological advance. Though the phrase may have lost its currency, an American advantage in advanced weapons technology still exists, the product of larger annual R and D expenditures, a larger home market in which unit costs are usually lower, and normally shorter development times.[26] The United States produces more sophisticated weapons over a wider range than any European competitor. But the European capacity and potential are considerable and, on the whole, European industry's ability to satisfy European defense requirements has increased over the past two decades. This is due in part to the diffusion of technology which began with the licensed production of American weapon systems in the late 1950s and early 1960s and also to the independent advance of European industry itself.[27] Precisely where and by how much U.S. defense-related technological capabilities exceed Europe's—collectively or nationally—are questions which have not been answered satisfactorily. Accurate estimates are difficult, and often impossible. A recent Defense Department study cited as a fundamental problem the lack of information available on European systems development work, on production and engineering capabilities, and even on newer systems in production.

What the U.S. lead means in practice is that the possibilities for "Europeanizing" the acquisition of advanced weapons are limited. The level of dependence on U.S. technology is already high, and pressures for continued transatlantic cooperation are strong. For the Europeans this is in some areas a partnership born of necessity. The degree of specialization in electronics equipment, for example, is such that parts required for modern weapon systems may have only one or two sources, and these are often in the United States or controlled by U.S. patents. Furthermore, a large share of the European electronics industry is U.S. owned. One study estimated that "every advanced aircraft produced in Europe (civil as well as military) contains a number of components of American origin for which there is no European source."[28] The MRCA has an avionics package much of which is of American origin.[29] In sum, the growth of European defense technology industries, and their ability to develop and produce complete weapon systems, depend upon some form of cooperation with the United States. A strategy whereby European governments would seek to fashion their own unity in opposition to the United States, at least in the crucial field of advanced weapons technology, would be highly improvident, and is unlikely. In practice, there is every effort on the part of the Europeans to encourage collaboration with the United States but to channel it into high-technology areas where the U.S. lead is considerable and where the technological payoff to the Europeans is greatest.[30]

Earlier coproduction of U.S. systems in Europe under license—among the more important were the Hawk surface-to-air missile, the Sidewinder air-to-air missile, the Bullpup air-to-surface missile, and the F-104G combat aircraft—was accomplished by means of separate intergovernmental agreements involving the export of U.S. equipment and technology. In some cases, European nations lacked the technology to produce similar items. In other cases they did not: Britain and France were producing independently designed weapons with equivalent functions and therefore participated, respectively, only in the Bullpup and Hawk programs.[31] In each case the Europeans adopted an American model to satisfy a military requirement, and then produced it under license. Consortia were formed, each participant receiving contracts proportionate to its share of the collaborative program. A management organization was established for each project under a formal NATO umbrella but was staffed only by people from the participating countries. The advantages for the Europeans were that equipment could be rapidly incorporated into their forces; each country's expenditures remained mostly in its domestic economy; cost advantages were achieved as a result of large-scale production (albeit at greater cost than direct purchase); and new missile and aircraft technology, as well as American management techniques, was learned. Furthermore, new industrial capacities were created for each of the participants; for the Germans, the F-104 was the first production of a major advanced weapon system. The project was seminal in enabling the growth of an advanced domestic aircraft industry.[32]

There were considerable disadvantages as well for the Europeans in these four collaborative production projects. Above all, the United States reaped the commercial benefit and gained a sure place in the European market. One result was that in the decade of the 1960s the United States sold ten times as much military equipment to Europe as it imported from the Continent. These early collaborative efforts demonstrated to European governments the extent to which they could become the hostage of U.S. technology, but also—equally as important—the feasibility of carrying through such large-scale and complicated projects. The F-104G program was in fact the most ambitious collaborative program ever implemented within the alliance, and it served as an impetus for the Anglo-French Jaguar fighter aircraft project begun in 1965. This and the bilateral Martel air-to-surface missile involved the two European countries for the first time in a degree of complementary military industrial specialization. The Jaguar project was among the first in which decision-making in the development of a major advanced weapon system for national forces had to take into consideration the defense requirements of another country.[33] This was the first case, in other words, in which operational requirements were made to coincide. It was a political departure for the participants, necessitating a reciprocal scrutiny of tactical concepts, compromise on requirements, and reconciliation of vested service and defense industrial interests.

In sum, what the larger European states collectively fear is not cooperation with the United States, which all recognize as essential, but an overreliance on American weapons technology which might vitiate European R and D capacities and future commercial competitiveness. This extends to nonmilitary industries as well. Generally speaking, the perception seems to hold sway in Britain, France, and Germany that it is only the growth of indigenous capacity which can attenuate what is often regarded as American "technological colonialism." The desire to limit dependence creates a strong impulse, if not a preference, for collaborative acquisition projects on a European basis. The perception is that direct imports of finished American weapons will do little to maintain indigenous European R and D capacities, or to sustain a competitive European sales position in third markets. Coproduction under U.S. license, each country building a portion of a system for European assembly, is economically advantageous inasmuch as it preserves or creates jobs in Europe. But because such collaboration does not do enough to maintain or stimulate independent European R and D capacities, the apprehension is that in the longer run coproduction is a solution to the "two-way street" problem which would transform European advanced weapons industries into the step child of U.S. technology.

The Two-way Street

Between 1971 and 1976, NATO countries purchased military equipment from the United States in the amount of $4.5 billion; U.S. purchases of military equipment in Europe amounted to $846 million, a 5:1 ratio. While reciprocal purchases of defense equipment in the alliance have been skewed heavily in favor of the United States, total dollar expenditures by the United States in NATO countries during the same period were well in excess of $4.5 billion, almost three times as much, according to one Defense Department estimate. In addition, five U.S. division equivalents in Europe save the European states from additional large military expenditures. Yet another consideration is the U.S. deficit in the bilateral balance of payments with some European states, above all Germany. It is, in any case, difficult to establish a generally accepted definition of equity in the transatlantic defense account. But is it equitable to characterize the defense trade balance simply in terms of equipment purchases?

It appears that what some European governments desire is an equivalent of the bilateral U.S.-Canadian Defense Equalization Act, which provides Canadian manufacturers with nondiscriminatory access to the U.S. defense market, in competition with U.S. industry. Canadian firms which offer competitive price, delivery, and quality can obtain substantial U.S. contracts. Legislative provisions remain, however, which restrict the scope of Canadian participation in U.S. defense programs. Nevertheless, the result has been an approximate balance in dollars spent by each country in the other for defense equipment.[34] It was argued earlier, however, that Britain, France, Germany, and other European nations seek more than a simple financial balance in a two-way street. Through the expansion of markets they seek to maintain a high-technology defense base, and the vitality and competitiveness of their own defense industries. The extent to which the Defense Equalization Act helps Canada maintain such a defense base is doubtful, for, with some exceptions, Canada sells low-technology items to the United States. All the same, the IEPG is examining the U.S.-Canadian agreement to decide if it or a similar system of reciprocal purchases provides a model for similar European-American arrangements.[35]

One hypothetical arrangement that has been suggested would have Europe buy the F-15 and the F-16 off-the-shelf from the United States for the air superiority mission. The United States and other allies would in turn buy the MRCA and the Alpha Jet from Germany, Britain, Italy, and France for the interdiction and training missions. CNAD would maintain a system of "NATO purchase accounts," under which domestic and foreign purchases of defense equipment would be recorded, and a record of national credits and debits established. Parties to the agreement would oblige themselves to compensate one another and to redress an imbalance after a period of five years, perhaps through nonmilitary purchases.[36]

These particular systems aside, for an arrangement of this sort to be practicable a host of political and economic obstacles would have to be overcome in the United States. The suggestion, however, reflects the attitude of many officials in Britain, France, and Germany that a system of *large-scale reciprocal purchases of major finished systems* must be established if the transatlantic financial imbalance is to be offset. There is considerably less interest in a two-way street in licenses because the smaller financial return on license purchases is unlikely to affect the present imbalance substantially. American production under license of Roland is an example. According to some senior French Ministry of Defense officials, had the United States bought the Franco-German-produced Roland, the sale would have amounted to some 7.5 billion francs in export orders. As it is, the return to France from the sale of the license is only some 150 million francs.[37]

From the British, French, and German standpoints, collaboration is preferable from the outset, that is, from the development phase of acquisition. This is because codevelopment is seen as a means of fostering indigenous technological capabilities over the longer term. Coproduction does not exclude this, but it often involves unwelcome restrictions on the use of U.S. technology. Senior European government and industry officials have repeatedly stressed that proposals for improving the efficiency of acquisition in the alliance through collaboration will not succeed if that is to be done on the basis of U.S. equipment, either through off-the-shelf purchases or through coproduction.[38]

The preference for codevelopment of certain weapon systems has an even more fundamental reason. It is increasingly the case that precision guided munitions (PGM) weapons are organically integrated with their delivery platforms. This is becoming especially true for air-launched weapons, which are interwoven into spaces on the aircraft itself.[39] There is, therefore, some apprehension in Europe that in the future subcomponents of U.S. technology will be difficult to integrate into European designed and produced platforms, and as a consequence, Europe will be less able to buy selectively from the United States. The fear is that, at worst, a buy-all-or-nothing situation might develop. At the least, greater dependence upon U.S. air weapon systems means potential economic penalties for the European aircraft industry. Codevelopment—as interpreted in Europe—means that European firms will have an unencumbered share of the technological benefits of collaboration, and not just a more equitable financial balance achieved either through offsets or through production under license.

Yet another reason for the British, French, and German stress on codevelopment is the importance attached to beginning collaboration early in system development, before entrenched national and service interests become involved which can frustrate international programs. Transatlantic *ab initio* collaboration has not been the practice in the past. Once national requirements have been separatively generated (or development begun on two or more similar national projects), experience shows that coordinating them is more difficult.[40]

Central to any expansion of U.S.-European collaboration will be the policies which govern third-country sales of collaboratively produced weapons. The preemininent question is how greater collaboration with the United States will influence the European ability to export freely; the answer is to be found partly in the degree to which the attraction of incorporating advanced American technologies into European weapon systems or in developing technologies in collaboration with the United States will in the future be offset by U.S. restrictions which impede the export of that equipment.

Those restrictions will have two sources. The first derives from a natural

American predisposition to protect the competitive advantage of U.S. firms in third markets. The source of the second will be the Carter administration's enunciated policy of seeking to reduce arms exports. Although the transfer of weapons and related technologies to NATO has been declared exempt from such restrictions, the right of NATO nations to reexport such items has not.[41] We have noted the importance which Britain and France, in particular, attach to weapons exports as a means of sustaining advanced defense industries. There may be a contradiction, therefore, between a U.S. policy which seeks to foster greater collaboration with the Europeans on the one hand, and which seeks to restrict their third-country arms sales on the other. "Third country sales," according to one senior European defense industry executive, "are absolutely vital to any continuing arrangement in licensing and co-production between U.S. and European manufacturers. [They are] the 'swing factor' between a profitable and an unprofitable arrangement."[42] The view of this executive, widely held in Europe, is that implementation of the administration's arms sales policy will lead inevitably to a reduction of U.S.-European weapons collaboration. Furthermore, Machiavellian though it may seem, suspicions exist in Europe at the official level that through greater collaboration the United States seeks to encourage dependence in high-technology defense industries on American-controlled sources of supply as a means for influencing European export policies. The hypothesis that by expanding collaborative arms acquisition, thereby expanding markets for European weapons, the United States can reduce existing incentives to export to non-NATO states and reduce interallied arms competition is regarded with some skepticism in Europe. Generally speaking, one can postulate that to the extent the United States imposes third-country export restrictions, the effect may be to discourage the Europeans from collaboration. But obviously there are bound to be many exceptions where restrictions are accepted because of the decisive importance of a specific weapons technology.

Prospects

National acquisition policy can be said to have essentially four driving forces: the satisfaction of operational requirements; the desire to make technological progress; the maintenance of broad defense technological and industrial capabilities and skilled labor; and the satisfaction of national economic imperatives (for example, maintaining employment levels or a satisfactory trade balance). These last three mean that defense decisions on collaborative procurement are usually industrial policy decisions as well. A central factor determining the future of collaborative acquisitions is therefore the extent to which these desiderata are subject to international solutions in collaborative programs. The problem is one of reconciling national acquisition policy and processes and national defense policy with international collaboration.

This may be more probable now than in the past because the national acquisitions choices have been narrowed by resource constraints. Joint European undertakings over the last fifteen years must be viewed within the changing context of the economic and industrial situation. Against the background of presently strained economies and defense budgets, the interest in and the prospects for a more sustained effort at collaboration in Europe are encouraging. At the same time, while collaborative effort may be more necessary than ever, the following points deserve emphasis. *First*, the degree to which economies of scale can be achieved solely on the basis of the European market is probably limited. *Second*, even if the political will is present, the scope for the expansion of joint acquisition programs will be restricted by budget limitations. (The MRCA program, for example, has reportedly absorbed some 25 percent of the FRG's military R and D funds annually.) Collaboration is likely to expand selectively, future joint acquisition of major systems limited for the most part to a small number of high technology projects in the aerospace and electronics industries. These will conform essentially to national military requirements. Obviously, the possibilities for collaboration will be limited further by the number of types of systems to be built. *Third*, in addition to simple defense resource limitations, the proliferation of collaborative procurement projects is excluded by national politico-military objectives and economic considerations discussed earlier. *Fourth*, it is unlikely that future collaboration in development of total systems, especially in the aircraft field, will come to include more than three full participants, let alone grow into more inclusive European endeavors.[43] For the general pattern of collaborative acquisition in Europe to change considerably, more extensive dovetailing of national defense planning and budgetary processes—which now take place independently of one another—would have to be initiated.

Within these limitations, however, European collaboration may have a cumulative effect. The processes of choosing and managing collaborative projects may become more routine and the programs less easy to dissolve. Certain industrial, economic, and technological interests and objectives may begin to transcend the demands of individual projects and lead to de facto defense industrial integration, or at least to new degrees of mutual dependence. Some present programs may presage the development of quasi-permanent international industrial consortia which preserve the national integrity of participating firms, but in which a strong mutual interest and rationale prevail in continuing the arrangement. Euromissile, the German MBB and French Aerospatiale consortium, may be an example.[44] A similar tendency toward the continuation of collaboration may be evident in the

Airbus venture with possible follow-on development of new transport aircraft.[45] Such signs suggest that interdependence, regardless of how governments try to limit it, may impose itself as an increasingly necessary goal of national policy. A decisive factor is whether or not existing industries will continue to exist as nationally viable industries. This deserves a more thorough analysis than is possible here. In sum, however, it seems safe to suggest that collaboration has not progressed to the point where structural change or the division of development and production work in or among the British, French, or German aerospace or electronics industries is not irrevocable, albeit at considerable expense to the partners.

Finally, it should be clear from the discussion that "success" with respect to collaboration can only be defined in terms of a variety of national objectives. These may or may not encompass cost savings. (Here one would have to distinguish in each case between original motives and expectations, and actual program outcomes.) Collaborative programs have proved advantageous in some respects: they have provided the vehicle for the acquisition of a limited number of advanced systems and the meeting of national mission needs; on the face of it, certain programs have enabled savings to be achieved which would have been unlikely, if not impossible, in comparable national programs; they have permitted national technological capability and momentum to be maintained in some areas of advanced weapons development which might otherwise have been impossible because of insufficient national resources; except for tradeoffs in requirements, collaboration has not restricted the peacetime military choices of individual nations.

This said, however, collaboration is unlikely to offer the means for maintaining *comprehensive* national defense R and D and production capabilities or weapons inventories at lower cost. This is, first, because its scope will continue to be determined by available resources which will limit the number and types of projects which states can acquire concurrently, and second, because the overall savings to be achieved are problematic, calling into question any assumption that more systematic collaboration would permit savings sufficient to sustain both national defense-industrial and force structure capabilities otherwise impossible on a national basis. Finally, in itself collaboration does not promise to alleviate the need for fairly comprehensive national capabilities because it has not constituted (and it is improbable that it will come to constitute) military or broad defense-industrial integration.

Notes

1. Cf. United States Department of Defense, *Rationalization/Standardization with NATO*, (A report to the U.S. Congress by Donald Rumsfeld,

Secretary of Defense), Second Report, January 1976, p. 51. According to the most recent German Defense White Paper, "Equipment collaboration is a problematic issue above all for those allies whose defense industries are highly developed. For them these industries are an essential factor of their employment and export policies." *White Paper 1975/1976*, "The Security of the Federal Republic of Germany and the Development of the Federal Armed Forces," Press and Information Office of the Government of the FRG, 20 January 1976, p. 59.

2. See K. Pavitt, "Technology in Europe's Future," *Research Policy I (1971/1972)* p. 244.

3. Cf., the table in Roger Facer, *The Alliance and Europe: Part III, Weapons Procurement in Europe—Capabilities and Choices*, Adelphi Paper No. 108, International Institute for Strategic Studies, London, 1975, p. 19.

4. Address by General Marc Cauchie, *Assembly of Western European Union Committee on Defence Questions and Armaments,* A European Armaments Policy Symposium, March 1977, p. 23.

5. Ibid.

6. The attitude of one leading Italian industrialist is typical of those who advocate greater commonality of weapons produced, as well as larger production runs of individual series, but who shy from further rationalization. Greater commonality and larger production runs are viewed as, "the limit which should be imposed on cost reduction; to go beyond this, reducing the number of production lines and concentrating them in a few production areas, chosen on grounds of maximum economy of production and technical reliability, would lead to a disturbance of the European human environment similar to the ecological disturbance caused by the pollution of a sea. *Optimization must therefore observe the existence of present production lines . . .*" The views of Gustavo Stefanini, president of Oto Melara. *Assembly of WEU,* op cit., Emphasis Added. See also, North Atlantic Assembly, Military Committee, Report on the Activities of the Subcommittee on European Defence Cooperation, presented by Mr. Klaus G. DeVries (Netherlands), Rapporteur, *International Secretariat*, November 1976 (T 166, MC/EF [76]).

7. K. Pavitt, "Technology in Europe's Future," *Research Policy I (1971/1972)* p. 231; W.B. Walker, The Multi-role Combat Aircraft (MRCA): A Case Study in European Collaboration, *Research Policy II, (1974)* pp. 289-290.

8. Cf. Bernard Burrows and Christopher Irwin, *The Security of Western Europe: Towards A Common Defence Policy*, Chas. Knight and Co., Ltd., London, 1972, p. 92.

9. Cf. John Calmann, *Defense, Technology and the Western Alliance,* Number One, *European Cooperation in Defense Technology: The Political Aspect,* ISS, April 1967, London, p. 16.

10. Although these figures may not be representative, one estimate of the increase in unit cost between generations (based on an average of 13 U.S. systems) identified a general increase in R and D costs of 5.4:1, and in production costs of 4.2:1. Roger Facer, *The Alliance and Europe: Part III, Weapons Procurement in Europe—Capabilities and Choices*, Adelphi Paper No. 108, International Institute for Strategic Studies, London, 1975, p. 4.

11. *Assembly of WEU*, op. cit., p. 23.

12. Geoffrey Ashcroft in *Military Logistic Systems in NATO: The Goal of Integration, Part I: Economic Aspects*, Adelphi Paper No. 62, International Institute for Strategic Studies, London, Nov., 1969, pp. 4-7. For some comparative estimates of savings and duplication, see U.S., DoD, *Rationalization/Standardization* . . . (1976) op. cit., p. 51 and Callaghan, *US/European Collaboration* . . ., op. cit., pp. 17, 24-27, 37.

13. Johannes Steinhoff, "Der Zwang zur Verteidigungskooperation Westeuropas," *Europa Archiv*, Folge 14/1974.

14. A recent U.S. DoD report concluded that "no precise formula to determine savings has been found." A Rand Report cites the inadequacy of comparative cost data as a primary obstacle to joint acquisition planning, noting that only 60 percent of NATOs 600 five year force proposals for 1973 were able to be even crudely costed.

15. A suggestion made some years ago. Cf., Ashcroft, op. cit., *Military Logistic Systems in NATO:* . . . *Part II*, p. 12.

16. Ibid., pp. 5-6.

17. Ibid., pp. 5-6. For a critical appraisal of the scope and potential for NATO logistics standardization and resulting economies, see Ashcroft, *Military Logistic Systems in NATO: The Goal of Integration, Part I: Economic Aspects*, Adelphi Paper No. 62, International Institute for Strategic Studies, London, Nov. 1969. Also see Carstens and Mahnke, op. cit., pp. 194-210.

18. Cf. Jack N. Behrman, *Multinational Production Consortia: Lessons from the NATO Experience*, U.S. Dept. of State, Office of External Research, Bureau of Intelligence and Research, Aug. 1971, pp. 1, 8-9. Behrman provides a useful discussion of the politics of negotiating technical and financial issues.

19. Cf. Harlow, *Some Reflections on European Technological Cooperation*, OEDC Document, DAS/D/68. 3071, 19 March 1968, as cited in Pavitt, op. cit., p. 230.

20. *Assembly of WEU*, op. cit., p. 88.

21. Greenwood continues, ". . . the quality of the product is usually excellent but . . . the cost is often higher than had been forecast . . . when [a] particular program is completed the partnership ceases and the process starts all over again with a fresh piece of defense equipment, new partners,

new management and the educational sequences are repeated." *Assembly of WEU*, op. cit., pp. 24-27.

22. "The Quandary of Cooperative Weapons Development with European Allies," *Industrial College of the Armed Forces*, Washington, D.C., Eugene J. Vitetta, Class of 1972, p. 29.

23. White Paper 1975/1976, "The Security of the FRG and the Development of the Federal Armed Forces," Press and Information Office of the Government of the FRG, 20 January 1976, p. 58.

24. *North Atlantic Assembly, Military Committee*, op. cit.

25. Vitetta, op. cit.

26. See, for example, Alistair Buchan, *Defence, Technology and the Western Alliance*, No. 6, *The Implications of a European System for Defense Technology*, October 1967, Institute for Strategic Studies, London, p. 3; K. Pavitt, op. cit., pp. 216-219; John Calmann, *Defense, Technology . . .*, p. iii.

27. Trevor Cliffe, *Military Technology and the European Balance*, Adelphi Paper No. 89, International Institute for Strategic Studies, London, August 1972, pp. 27-28.

28. Facer, *The Alliance and Europe: Part III*, op. cit., p. 22.

29. Walker, op. cit.

30. Johannes Steinhoff, "Der Swang. . . . ." op. cit., *Europa Archiv*, Folge 4/1976, pp. D86-D109; and Folge 19/1976, pp. D526-D533; See also United States Senate, Subcommittee on Research and Development and the Subcommittee on Manpower and Personnel of the Committee on Armed Services, *Hearing on European Defense Cooperation*, 94th Congress, Second Session, March 31, 1976, U.S. Gov't. Printing Office, Washington, 1976., pp. 155-156.

31. Mary Kaldor, *European Defence Industries—National and International Implications*, ISIO Monographs, First Series, No. 8, Institute for the Study of International Organization, University of Sussex, England, 1972., p. 39.

32. Rhodes James, op. cit., pp. 11-19.

33. Martin Edmonds, "International Collaboration in Weapons Procurement," *International Affairs* (London), Vol. 43, No. 2, April 1967,. pp. 252-253; Ashcroft, *Military Logistic Systems*, Part I, op. cit., pp. 20-21.

34. North Atlantic Assembly, op. cit., p. 8. A similar Memorandum of Understanding was concluded between the U.S. and the U.K. in 1975.

35. North Atlantic Assembly, op. cit., Appendix 2.

36. The views of Carl Damm, Member of the German Bundestag, and of the Sub-committee of the North Atlantic Assembly on European Defense Cooperation. "Views from the North Atlantic Assembly," in Meeting Report, *International Symposium on NATO Standardization and Interoperability*, American Defense Preparedness Association, March 1978, pp. 25-32.

37. *Assembly of WEU*, op. cit., p. 21 and author's interview with General Marc Cauchie, November 1977.

38. See, for example, the address by George R. Jefferson, Chairman and Chief Executive, British Aerospace Dynamics Group, in Meeting Report, *International Symposium on NATO Standardization and Interoperability*, American Defense Preparedness Association, March 1978, pp. 39-42.

39. See James Digby, *The Technology of Precision Guidance—Changing Weapon Priorities, New Risks, New Opportunities*, P-5537, The Rand Corporation, Santa Monica, November 1975.

40. *Assembly of WEU*, op. cit., p. 23; North Atlantic Assembly, op. cit., p. 3.

41. According to recently articulated U.S. policy, if an American firm is not denied permission for a third country sale, the same treatment will be accorded to a European licensee. Speech by V. Garber in Meeting Report, *International Symposium on NATO Standardization and Interoperability*, American Defense Preparedness Association, March 1978, op. cit., pp. 127-133.

42. Count Corrado Augusta, in Meeting Report, *International Symposium on NATO Standardization and Interoperability*, American Defense Preparedness Association, March 1978, op. cit., pp. 77-83.

43. Cf. Ashcroft, *Military Logistic Systems, Part 1,* op. cit., p. 21. Limited national participation in the form of sub-contracting, however, may very well extend beyond three nations.

44. "The two firms concerned," according to Guenther Kuhlo, Head of the MBB Dynamics Division, "have gradually achieved a kind of integration and neither could envisage an end to cooperation which for both firms, as for their employees, would be disastrous." *Assembly of WEU*, op. cit., p. 87.

45. *Aviation Week and Space Technology*, Vol. 108, No. 10, March 6, 1978, p. 28.

6

Instability and Change on NATO's Southern Flank

A Work Group Analysis

Of all the challenges facing the United States today, one of the most crucial is the restoration of sense of direction and purpose to its policy on NATO's southern flank. For many years Greece and Turkey were among the staunchest members of the Atlantic Alliance, contributing together some 750,000 troops to NATO. Each maintained a special relationship with the United States dating back to the late 1940s. At that time the United States, under the Truman Doctrine, granted both countries large-scale economic and military assistance which allowed them to resist internal and external threats to their security. The military ties initiated under the Truman Doctrine were later expanded and buttressed by a variety of important political and economic ties which served to further cement the bonds between the United States and its two southern allies.

One need only take a cursory glance at the southern flank today to see how radically the situation has changed. On the bilateral level, U.S. relations with both Greece and Turkey have seriously deteriorated. On the alliance level, Greece has withdrawn from the military structure of NATO, while Turkey is threatening to reduce her commitment and could at some point even drop out entirely. Meanwhile, the Cyprus issue continues to fester, poisoning relations between Greece and Turkey and exacerbating tensions over other issues in the Aegean. Lastly, domestic trends in both countries raise troubling questions about the long-term viability of their democratic institutions.

The Military Dimension

These developments highlight the growing disarray on the southern flank in recent years. This disarray has been lent greater importance, moreover, by the changing military balance in the area, particularly the naval balance. The geographic differences between the Central Front (where there is a single line of contact with the Warsaw Pact stretching from the Alps to the Baltic) and the southern flank (where various theaters are separated by rugged terrain) make seapower critical for resupply and reinforcement of ground troops. Without effective sea control a coherent defense of the

107

region is impracticable. For many years this was not a problem because the Sixth Fleet could operate virtually unhindered in the Mediterranean. In the last fifteen years, however, the Soviet Union has greatly expanded its presence in the Mediterranean. In 1963, for instance, there were no Soviet ships in the Mediterranean. Today there are some forty-two—half of them combatants. While Soviet naval strength in the Mediterranean has declined somewhat in recent years, because of the loss of port facilities in Egypt, in less than a decade and a half, the Soviet Navy has changed from a coastal navy whose main function was to show the flag to one with significant sea-denial capabilities.[1] This directly affects the ability of the Sixth Fleet to support any land battle in Greece and particularly in Turkey.

In short, there is currently an uneasy balance in the Mediterranean as a result of the Soviet naval build-up. On the one hand, the United States can no longer exercise undisputed control of the sea. On the other hand, the Soviet Union cannot entirely deny its use to the United States. The determinant of whether the United States can control the sea or whether the Soviet Union can deny us its use (either for military purposes or to interdict strategic supplies such as oil) is likely to be land-based airpower. Here, too, the Soviet Union has made important gains. As a result of the introduction of the Backfire bomber, Soviet land-based aircraft can now reach out into the Mediterranean basin, making what was once a haven for the Sixth Fleet an area that will have to be fought for. From the American point of view, this underscores the vital importance of land-based aircraft in any Mediterranean conflict, particularly of tactical aircraft presently stationed in Greece and Turkey. Without the protection they would afford, the Sixth Fleet would become even more vulnerable.

Another important development has been the expansion and modernization of Soviet land and air forces. On the southern flank this has been neither as large nor as intense as on the Central Front, but it has still exceeded that of NATO and has served to give the Warsaw Pact both a numerical and technological advantage over the NATO forces.[2] In northern Greece and Turkish Thrace, for instance, twenty-three Greek and Turkish divisions face an estimated combined force of thirty-two Warsaw Pact divisions, most of which are mechanized and possess a favorable tank ratio of 3:1. Farther East, the Soviet Turkish-oriented forces stationed in the Caucasus have been modernized and now possess a significant air mobile threat. Combined with technological advances in night vision, hand-held air defense weapons, and communications this could change the character of the war in the area to NATO's disadvantage. Soviet air capability has also been enhanced by the deployment in the Ukraine of the Backfire with increased range and payload, which during conflict would probably be directed against the NATO maritime force in the Black, Aegean, and Mediterranean Seas, and quite possibly against Greece and Turkey as secondary targets. Last, there is the deployment of intermediate-range ballistic missiles (IRBMs), among them the SS-20, situated in the northwest Crimea and in the northern fringes of the Transcaucasus. Presumably some of these would be used against targets on the southern flank.

By contrast, much of the equipment used by the Greek and Turkish forces is rapidly approaching block obsolescence. While both countries have begun to undertake large-scale modernization programs, these have been handicapped by the dwindling support within Congress for FMS (Foreign Military Assistance) credits in favor of direct commercial sales. This imposes additional burdens on both countries, particularly Turkey, which has been faced with one of the severest economic crises in its postwar history. In the case of Turkey, moreover, the effect of these measures has been compounded by the impact of the arms embargo which, according to NATO estimates, reduced the military effectiveness of Turkey's armed forces in some areas by as much as 80 to 90 percent.[3] While the decision to lift the embargo should help to alleviate some of the most serious military problems facing Turkey, the need for modernization is so great that even with the resumption of full-scale U.S. military assistance significant military weaknesses are likely to exist for some time.[4]

The Political Dimension

The above discussion highlights the shifting military balance on the southern flank. However, it is not the Soviet build-up and the expansion of the Soviet military presence in the Mediterranean that is at the heart of resulting security dilemmas. For the most part Moscow has been a residual factor, responding to and benefiting from a disarray which it has neither created nor been able to harness. The problems faced by the United States on the southern flank are essentially *political* in nature and have been only tangentially related to the growth of Soviet power. They have their roots in social, economic, and political changes in Greece and Turkey over the past decade as well as in changes in the international system at large.

Among the most important of the factors contributing to the erosion of alliance harmony on the southern flank have been:

The Decline of the Perceived Immediacy of the Soviet Threat. The entry of Greece and Turkey into NATO (1952) was essentially a response to the fear of direct Soviet attack. As long as the threat was perceived as direct and immediate, Greece and Turkey were willing to subordinate themselves to the dictates of U.S. policy in return for U.S. protection. Once this threat no longer seemed immediate, both countries began to be less willing automatically to follow the U.S. lead on every issue and to put alliance interests—or in this case, U.S. interests—ahead of other national interests.

Détente. The process of East-West détente that began to emerge in the mid- and late 1960s eased the sense of external threat and deflected attention toward pressing domestic issues. As a result, an increasing number of people in both countries began to question the need to maintain a defense establishment oriented toward a threat which seemed less and less real. This led to a growing debate in each country as to the value of the alliance and at the same time a desire to expand relations with the Soviet bloc.

The New Importance Lent to Energy Questions Since the Oil Embargo. Both Greece and Turkey, particularly the latter, are heavily dependent on Middle Eastern oil,[5] and in the last few years both countries have sought to expand their relations with the oil-producing states in the Middle East. Consequently, today neither country can be counted on to support U.S. Middle East policy—a fact well illustrated by the refusal of both countries to allow U.S. overflights to supply Israel during the October War.

Domestic Changes in the United States, especially the more assertive role that Congress has begun to play in foreign policy lately. The president no longer has a pre-Vietnam/Watergate flexibility and latitude in foreign affairs. Traditional majorities within Congress have also begun to dissipate. The overall result of this process has been to make foreign policy a much more complex and unwieldy process and to allow for the greater intrusion of domestic political factors, particularly "ethnic politics," into the decision-making process. There have been a number of recent examples, the most relevant here being the ability of the "Greek lobby"[6] to maintain the arms embargo against Turkey for nearly four years.

Cyprus. This problem has perhaps been most responsible for today's troubled situation on the southern flank. The beginning of the erosion of alliance harmony can be traced back to the 1963-64 crisis. This revealed the frailty of apparent congruent interests, and it invoked the first major expressions of dissatisfaction with U.S. leadership. While U.S. intervention managed to prevent an outbreak of war, it did so at considerable cost to relations with both allies, each of which accused the United States of supporting the other.

For a while the issue remained quiescent, in part because the head of the Greek junta, George Papadopoulos, consciously sought to avoid becoming embroiled in a dispute which might lead to the collapse of his regime. His successor, Dimitri Ionnides, showed no such restraint. The Greek-inspired coup to overthrow Archbishop Makarios in July 1974 touched off an international crisis that led to the fall of the junta and the restoration of democracy in Greece, the invasion and occupation of 40 percent of Cyprus by the Turks, and the withdrawal of Greece from the military structure of NATO.[7] Moreover, it left a festering sore that has seriously eroded alliance solidarity and which remains a constant threat to regional stability. The U.S. arms embargo, rather than making the Turks more pliant, as was its intention, hardened their resolve not to yield to pressure. While Bulent Ecevit, the current Prime Minister, has shown more flexibility than his predecessors, for domestic reasons he has been afraid to make too many concessions. At the same time, the death of Archbishop Makarios in August 1977 removed from Cyprus the one man who had the prestige and stature to make the politically difficult decisions needed to help break the current stalemate. Thus, despite some occasional signs of progress, the Cypress problem continues to be a major source of tension on the southern flank.

The Aegean. The reeruption of the Cyprus dispute has exacerbated other issues between Greece and Turkey, notably those over national rights to the continental shelf and control of Aegean airspace. These issues are actually more serious and potentially more explosive than the Cyprus dispute because they directly affect the sovereignty and vital interests of both countries.[8] The Greeks regard the Turkish demands for a share of the continental shelf as little more than a pretext for the resurrection of Turkish claims to a number of the Aegean islands and as part of a more militant and expansionist Turkish policy since 1974. As a result, Athens has strengthened its defensive capabilities on a number of islands off the Turkish coast, despite the fact that such actions are prohibited by the treaties of Lausanne and Paris. While Ankara has been careful not to formally challenge Greek sovereignty over the Aegean islands, it has protested the violations and has sought to build up a special Aegean army.

The Greeks have insisted that the continental shelf issue must be resolved on the basis of part precedents of international law. The Turks, on the other hand, have argued that the case must be settled on the basis of equity and "special circumstances" existing in the Aegean. Talks between the two countries have gone on for several years without visible results—in large part because both Ecevit and Caramanlis fear the domestic political consequences of making concessions on important national issues. As long as the issues remain unresolved, there exists a danger of some minor incident escalating into a major clash—as almost happened in the summer of 1976 when Turkey sent an exploratory vessel into the disputed area of the Aegean.[9]

Taken together, these developments have led to a dangerous decline in security on the southern flank and a sharp deterioration of the U.S. position there. They underscore the need to give serious consideration to the region and to restore a sense of purpose and direction to U.S. policy in the Eastern Mediterranean. This is all the more important because internal developments within Greece and Turkey in the next few years could contribute to further regional instabilities.

To better understand the calculus it is useful to take a closer look at developments in both countries since the 1974 Cyprus crisis.

Greece

In the more than four years since the 1974 Cyprus crisis, Greece has made impressive strides toward the restoration of parliamentary democracy and the restructuring of its foreign policy. Much of the credit for the smooth restoration of stability belongs to Greece's Prime Minister Constantine Caramanlis. Despite the impressive achievements of the last four years, however, there remain a number of troubling uncertainties.

One of these is the present state of U.S.-Greek relations. These are at their lowest ebb since the end of World War II. A strong current of anti-Americanism exists which puts objective constraints on the room for maneuver of any Greek government, even one as favorably disposed toward the United States as the Caramanlis government generally is. While such sentiment is strongest on the Left and among the youth, it is by no means confined to these groups. It is shared in varying degrees by groups which a decade ago could have been counted among the strongest supporters of the United States.

The deterioration of U.S.-Greek relations and the rise of anti-Americanism have two particular causes. The first is U.S. policy toward Greece under the junta. While there is little evidence that the United States actually engineered the 1967 coup, failure to make more energetic efforts to ensure the restoration of democracy served to undermine support for the United States, as well as for NATO. The Johnson administration did suspend shipments of heavy arms to the colonels, but spare parts and other military equipment continued to flow. Under the Nixon administration, moreover, the United States resumed shipment of some heavy arms and even sought an expansion of the U.S. military presence by negotiating a "homeport" agreement providing for the stationing of a navy carrier force near Athens. At the same time a number of high-ranking officials—including Vice-President Agnew—visited Greece, and those visits were given great play in the controlled Greek press. All this contributed to the impression that the United States supported the junta—a view that is still widely entertained in Greece.

A second and perhaps even more direct cause of the deterioration in Greek-U.S. relations is U.S. policy during the 1974 Cyprus crisis—particularly what many Greeks regard as a U.S. "tilt" toward Turkey. The perception that the United States could and should have prevented the Turkish invasion of Cyprus led to the outbreak of virulent anti-Americanism, and made some sort of response by the newly installed Caramanlis government unavoidable. Under public pressure, Caramanlis was compelled to withdraw from the military structure of NATO and begin a reassessment of U.S. relations.

One of the consequences of reassessment was the termination of the home-porting agreement, which was widely regarded as an offensive symbol of U.S. support for the junta. Another outcome of the reassessment was the initiation of bilateral talks over the future of U.S. installations in Greece. These talks culminated in the initialing of a new Defense Cooperation Agreement (DCA) in July 1977.

The new DCA is intended to modernize and replace the 1953 U.S.-Greek Defense Agreement and other bilateral security agreements. Valid for a period of four years, the new agreement allows continued use of four military installations—the Hellenikon airbase in Athens, a communications station at New Makri near Marathon, a port and airfield at Souda Bay (Crete), and an electric listening post at Iraklion (Crete). In accordance with the new agreement, these facilities will be under Greek control. There are also provisions for the sharing of intelligence. Last, the United States agrees to provide Greece with $700 million in assistance, part of which will be in grant aid.[10]

The Greek government has yet to sign the agreement, however, and at present it is unclear whether it will do so. The decision to lift the arms embargo to Turkey—however justified in terms of U.S. national interest—has complicated relations with Athens and is likely to lead to a further cooling of U.S.-Greek relations, at least in the short term. Moreover, domestically, it has served to strengthen the hand of Andreas Papandreou, the leader of the Pan Hellenic Socialist Movement (PASOK) and Caramanlis's main political rival, who has touted the move as further proof of America's pro-Turkish bias and the general bankruptcy of Caramanlis's policy. How much political capital Papandreou will be able to reap from the repeal of the embargo remains to be seen, but if the Turkish Defense Cooperation Agreement (signed in March 1976) is renegotiated, as now seems likely, then Caramanlis could find himself under considerable pressure to demand the renegotiation of the Greek DCA, and to impose tougher terms than are contained in the present draft.

As far as NATO is concerned, here too Greece's relationship remains uncertain. Greek withdrawal was more a trial separation than a divorce. While it recalled its representatives from the NATO command at Izmir, Athens has continued to maintain military attachés at a number of embassies in Europe and at NATO headquarters outside of Brussels—an indication of its basic desire to remain in the alliance. Moreover, recently Greece has shown a willingness to undertake some limited cooperation with NATO. In September 1977, for instance, Greece participated in NATO maneuvers for the first time since it formally withdrew from the military structure of the alliance in 1974.[11]

Caramanlis has indicated that he would like to see Greece reintegrated into the military structure of the alliance and negotiations aimed at defining the terms of Greece's eventual reintegration are currently underway.[12] However, Greece's ultimate relationship to NATO depends upon a number of factors. The first is the approval of Turkey, which to date has been unwilling to agree to the proposed terms of reintegration—in large part in order to put pressure on Greece to be more forthcoming on other bilateral issues. The second factor is Greece's domestic political situation. Anti-NATO sentiment remains strong and has to some extent even been intensified by the lifting of the embargo. Moreover, since the November 1977 elections, the strength of the anti-NATO forces (principally PASOK) has increased, narrowing Caramanlis's room for maneuver.

Papandreou has sharply attacked Greece's ties to NATO on the grounds that they result in a "loss of national independence" and make Greece "subservient to an outside power center." As an alternative, he has advocated closer ties to the third world, the development of an indigenous arms industry along Yugoslav lines, and he has even suggested that Greece should consider acquiring nuclear weapons.[13] To some extent, this may be more rhetorical than realistic, but if Papandreou's strength continues to grow, Greece's reintegration into NATO could become more difficult. And should he come to power in the near future—a possibility that should not be excluded—Greece would probably withdraw from NATO entirely.

Western and Eastern Europe

The reassessment of U.S.-Greek relations has been paralleled by an effort to expand and deepen Greece's ties to Europe. The keystone of Caramanlis's European policy has been the decision to press for full membership in the European Economic Community. Greece's application to join the EEC represents an historic opportunity to weave the country more tightly into the economic and political fabric of Europe. It thus not only has important political and economic implications but significant security dimensions. These ties are likely to become even more important in the coming years, in view of the weakening of Greece's traditional ones to the United States.

Caramanlis would like to see Greece in the EEC by 1980. However, over the last two years, a number of developments have threatened to upset his timetable. First, there has been a growth of the anti-EEC forces, principally

PASOK. Second, the applications of Spain and Portugal have raised new doubts about the advisability of immediate expansion and have forced the Community to confront larger issues that it has so far avoided.

Many members doubt whether the Community is ready to absorb the poorer Mediterranean countries without undertaking a number of structural reforms, particularly concerning agriculture. Some also worry about the costs that any transfer of resources will entail.

These fears have led some leaders to advocate a "global" approach by which Greece, Spain, and Portugal would enter the EEC simultaneously.[14] Such an approach, in their view, would allow the EEC—and the countries themselves—to undertake those reforms that would facilitate a smooth transition and minimize the dislocations caused by their entry. For its part, Greece has viewed talk of a global approach with concern because this would tie its fate to that of Spain and Portugal and could delay its entry for an undetermined period. Instead, Athens has argued that it should be treated as a "special case" because of its long-standing links with the EEC, which predate the applications of Spain and Portugal by some fifteen years, and that any problems posed by its accession can be solved within the framework of existing institutions.[15]

Whatever the validity of the economic arguments for treating Greece, Spain, and Portugal as a package, these must be weighed against the potential political repercussions of such a policy. A prolonged delay on Greece's application could cause considerable disillusionment within Greece and spark a backlash that could ultimately strengthen the effect of the anti-EEC forces in the country. Moreover, if Greece's entry were to be delayed too long, it could possibly be nullified by political changes within Greece itself. Should Papandreou come to power before 1980—the earliest date when accession now seems possible—he might use the delay as a pretext to withdraw Greece's application altogether. Thus an historic opportunity to bind Greece politically and economically to Europe—and thereby strengthen the prospects for stability in southern Europe as a whole—would be lost.

Greece has also begun to expand relations with Eastern Europe, particularly its Balkan neighbors. Soon after coming to power, Caramanlis visited Yugoslavia, Romania, and Bulgaria, and in the last few years, cooperation with all the Balkan countries, particularly Yugoslavia, has intensified considerably. Greece was also the spearhead behind the convocation of the inter-Balkan conference held in Athens in January 1976 to discuss ways of increasing cooperation in the fields of energy, transport, and culture.[16]

To a large extent, Greece's more active policy in the Balkans has been aimed at gaining support for its position on Cyprus and outflanking Turkey. But it should also be seen as part of a general effort to diversify its foreign policy and reduce its dependence on the United States. Greece's intensified Balkan policy has given rise to speculation about a possible revival of the interwar Balkan entente. However, given the very different socioeconomic systems and political allegiances that exist today in the Balkans, there are objective limits to which the effort to forge closer ties can be pushed—a fact that has been underscored by Bulgaria's negative attitude toward a follow-up of the Athens Balkan conference. However, under Papandreou, the Balkan option might take on greater prominence. He has been favorably impressed by the manner in which both Tito and Ceausescu have managed to pursue a relatively independent policy, and he has consciously sought to develop contacts with both the Romanian and Yugoslav parties.[17] Closer Balkan cooperation—possibly even in the field of defense[18]—would be a logical extension of his general foreign policy orientation.

After a period of stagnation—in large part because of Greek suspicion of Soviet efforts to court Ankara—relations with Moscow have also begun to improve. In September 1978 Greek Foreign Minister George Rallis paid an official visit to Moscow—the first visit by a Greek foreign minister since the establishment of relations between the two countries in 1924. In addition to providing for the establishment of a Soviet consulate in Salonika and a Greek consulate at the Black Sea port of Odessa, it is expected to lead to the expansion of cooperation in a number of fields, including culture, trade, and merchant shipping. In fact, the visit has already had one important result: in September 1978 two Greek destroyers made an historic cruise through the Turkish straits to visit Odessa. This visit was reciprocated by a Soviet fleet visit to Piraeus, the traditional port-of-call in Athens for the U.S. Sixth Fleet in the Mediterranean, in late October 1978.[19]

The significance of the Rallis visit and other recent initiatives in Greek-Soviet relations should not be overdramatized, however. They simply represent a long-overdue attempt to normalize relations with Moscow, not to change Greece's basic foreign policy orientation.[20] Nonetheless, they underscore the degree to which Greece has begun to seek greater autonomy and scope for independent initiatives in its foreign relations in the last few years. Even more importantly, they bear witness to a more active interest in Greece by the Soviet Union. Encouraged by the strong showing of the Left in the last elections (November 1977) and aware of the pressure for change within Greece, Moscow seems to be looking ahead to the "post-Caramanlis era" and the changes that this may bring.

Domestic Politics: After Caramanlis, What?

This points to one of the key question marks surrounding Greece's evolution—the prospects for domestic instability and the effect this might have on both its internal development and foreign policy orientation. At first glance there would seem relatively little reason for concern. Since the dark days of the Cyprus crisis in the summer of 1974, Greece has achieved a degree of prosperity and political stability few would have thought possible several years ago. The army has returned to the barracks and been purged of the most recalcitrant supporters of the junta; inflation—which had been running at nearly 30 percent during the last years of military rule—has been drastically reduced; unemployment has been cut; the monarchy has been abolished, thus removing one of the most divisive issues in Greek politics; the foundations of parliamentary rule have been reestablished and freedom of speech has been restored; and the country's foreign policy has been reoriented along lines more in keeping with Greek national interests.

There are reasons for concern despite these many positive changes. Many of the basic problems that have hindered Greece's development in the past remain unresolved: the "parasitic" nature of the Greek economy, particularly the channeling of capital into nonproductive sectors such as tourism, luxury real estate, and shipping; the underdevelopment of agriculture; the gross inequities of income; the growing gap between city and country; the backwardness of the educational system, which forces many of the best students to study abroad and often not return; and the "personalistic" nature of Greek party politics. In short, while outwardly Greece has succeeded in reestablishing parliamentary rule, many of the ingredients needed for it to function successfully in the long run remain absent.

Moreover, there are indications that the political stability that has characterized Greek politics over the last four years may be more fragile than initially thought. After the collapse of the junta, Caramanlis was widely perceived even by many on the Left as the man most capable of resolving Greece's crisis and preventing a return of the tanks. As a result, his New Democracy party won an overwhelming majority in the November 1974 elections. This seemed to belie fears that the Greek electorate had been radicalized by seven years of military rule. As the memories of the dictatorship have started to fade, however, dissatisfaction and pressure for change have mounted and Greek politics are beginning to display signs of growing polarization.

This growing pressure for change was reflected in particular in the results of the elections, which showed a marked erosion of support for Caramanlis's party. While the New Democracy won 43 percent of the popular vote and 174 seats in Parliament, this was far short of the unprecedented 54.37 percent of the vote and 220 seats which it had won in 1974. For the first time in postwar history the Left broke the 30 percent barrier, gaining 37 percent of the popular vote and swamping the center. At the same time the far Right also made a surprisingly strong showing. The

National Rally, a party set up by former Prime Minister Stephanos Stephanopoulos only two months before the elections, won nearly 7 percent of the vote—a significant gain which suggests growing dissatisfaction on the Right from elements that have traditionally supported Caramanlis.[21]

On the Left, the pro-Moscow Communist party, KKE (Exterior), which was legalized soon after Caramanlis came to power, received 9.36 percent of the vote—a sizable increase over its showing in the 1974 election. The KKE has unabashedly hewed the Soviet line, opposing Greece's entry into the EEC, participation in NATO in any form, and any U.S. presence in Greece. Domestically it has called for an extensive program of nationalization. However, while the KKE has considerable support among Greek students, most of its adherents are old-line Stalinists, and unless it changes its orientation the KKE is not likely to increase its strength significantly.

Surprisingly, the Communist Party of the Interior, a ''Eurocommunist'' party with an orientation similar to that of the Italian Communist party, did rather poorly. The leftist alliance, of which the Interior was a part, managed to gain just under 3 percent of the vote. Programatically, the Interior has opposed Greece's membership in NATO and the retention of U.S. bases on Greek soil, but it has supported Greek accession to the EEC. While it has the support of a number of Greece's leading intellectuals, the party has been hindered by lack of money and poor organization, and its poor showing in the 1977 elections has diminished its chances of playing a major role in Greek politics in the near future.

By far the most significant result of the elections was the strong showing of Papandreou's Pan Hellenic Socialist Movement (PASOK). Papandreou's party captured 25 percent of the vote against only 13.5 percent in 1974 and increased its representation in Parliament from thirteen seats to ninety-three, displacing the Center Union (EDIK)—which received just under 12 percent of the vote (against slightly over 20 percent in 1974)—as the second-strongest party. Particularly noteworthy was the fact that PASOK did well in rural areas that have been traditionally conservative strongholds.

PASOK's success in the November 1977 elections established it as the most important opposition party in Greece today. An outgrowth of the resistance movement PAK (Pan Hellenic Liberation Movement), founded by Papandreou while in exile, PASOK embodies a variety of elements ranging from Swedish social democracy to the vague radicalism of third world national liberation movements. Although it calls itself Socialist and has sought ties with other Socialist parties, particularly the French, it actually has more in common with many of the radical populist parties of Latin America in the 1930s and 1940s. It draws its support primarily from the lower middle class—the small shopkeepers, peasants, and lower-echelon civil servants and white-collar workers. PASOK also has been able to attract a large number of young, well-educated technocrats, many of whom were radicalized by seven years of military dictatorship and favor fundamental structural change. While it is one of the few parties besides the KKE with a real grass-roots organization and structure, it remains essentially a "personalistic" party, and Papandreou has shown little tolerance for internal dissent or deviation.

On the domestic front, PASOK has advocated a program of broad social and economic change, including the "socialization" of basic areas of the economy such as energy, banks, and transport. In foreign policy it has called for a number of sweeping changes.[22] In particular Papandreou has opposed Greece's planned accession to the EEC, and advocated instead a loose association along the lines of the Norwegian model. On relations with Turkey he has taken an equally uncompromising stand. He denounced the meeting between Ecevit and Caramanlis in March 1978, claiming that it resulted in unilateral concessions on the Greek side, and he proposed the extension of the Greek territorial waters from six to twelve miles—a move which, while justified under international law, would be likely to exacerbate relations with Ankara and confirm Turkish suspicions that Greece was trying to turn the Aegean into a "Greek lake." Moreover, during the tension over the Turkish dispatch of an exploratory vessel, the *Sismik I*, into the disputed area of the Aegean in the summer of 1976, Papandreou suggested that the Greek government should respond by sinking the ship, which certainly would have led to war.

The degree to which Papandreou will be able to increase his support over the next several years is uncertain. However, the results of the 1977 elections have produced a more fluid political situation. Caramanlis's room for maneuver has been narrowed, and in the future he is likely to face increasing criticism both from the right and the left. The election results point to a trend that could have long-term implications for Greece's internal and external policy. They suggest that the consensus that has existed on a number of important domestic and foreign policy issues since the end of World War II is breaking down.[23]

This trend is all the more unsettling because of the uncertainties surrounding the future of the New Democracy. The problem is that the New Democracy is a typical "clientelistic" party, a coalition of notables held together more by the strength of Caramanlis's own personality than by any common ideology or political outlook. Caramanlis is seventy-two, however, and there are signs that after four trying years he is beginning to tire. He apparently would like to relinquish the post of prime minister once many of his major goals—accession to the EEC, reintegration of Greece into NATO, and normalization of relations with the United States—have been achieved. It is widely believed that when the current term of President Tsatsos runs out, Caramanlis will step up to that office.

The key question, therefore, is: After Caramanlis, what? While over the last year Caramanlis has moved to broaden the base of his party by bringing into the cabinet a number of prominent political figures associated with the Center, such as Constantine Mitsotakis, this has done little to solidify the party or prepare it for Caramanlis's eventual departure. At present there is no chosen successor—though two men, Evangelos Averoff, the current defense minister, and George Rallis, the foreign minister, seem the most likely contenders for Caramanlis's mantle. Of the two, Averoff has the best chance, particularly because he has the trust of the army. Yet neither Averoff nor Rallis has the prestige and authority enjoyed by Caramanlis; there is a strong possibility that the New Democracy could split into a number of warring factions after Caramanlis departs. Such a situation could lead to the type of political maneuvering and instability which precipitated the 1967 coup.

To be sure, much has changed in the last twelve years. The army's image has been tarnished by its mismanagement of affairs during the dictatorship. However, the norm of civilian supremacy is not as firmly rooted in the Greek officer corps as it is elsewhere in western Europe. The armed forces have intervened in Greek politics seven times in this century, and despite the junta experience they continue to regard themselves as the "custodian of the nation" and symbol of national unity. If there were a precipitous decline in internal security—especially if it coincided with a deterioration of relations with Turkey—the military could be provoked to intervene. Thus, while the situation in Greece now appears stable, developments in the coming years bear watching.

Turkey

Sitting astride the Dardanelles, Turkey occupies a key strategic position in the Mediterranean. Although a Moslem country with over 96 percent of its territory in Asia, Turkey has been engaged in a process of Westernization for almost one hundred years. The real turning point in this process, however, was the establishment of the Turkish Republic in 1923 by Kemal Ataturk, which marked the beginning of a systematic attempt to transform Turkey into a Western state. Since then, Turkey has evolved from a one-party authoritarian state into a parliamentarian democracy. At the same time, through its membership in NATO, its ties to the EEC, and its participation in the Council of Europe, Turkey has manifested a strong commitment to the West in its foreign relations. Today Turkey is passing through one of the most difficult periods in its postwar history. Internally, it has been wracked by a crisis which has severely tested its social order and democratic institutions. Externally, there has been growing Turkish disillusionment with its Western ties—especially the United States—and calls for a reorientation of the country's foreign policy.

These calls have their origin in a number of different developments. The first is the emergence of détente. The second is the renewal of tension with Greece, which has shifted the sense of imminent threat to the East and made some reallocation of Ankara's defense forces seem more compelling. A third factor has been the recent decline in the Turkish economy, which has made it increasingly difficult for Turkey to sustain a large defense structure—particularly one oriented against a Soviet threat that is regarded as increasingly unreal. A fourth factor has been Turkey's growing sense of isolation in its relations with the European Economic Community, which has been exacerbated by Greece's application to join the EEC.[24]

Last, and perhaps most important, has been the increasing strain in relations with the United States and a growing uncertainty about the reliability of the United States as a major ally. The origin of the deterioration of U.S.-Turkish relations can be traced back to the 1963-64 Cyprus crisis, in which U.S. intervention was highly resented. The sharp tone of President Johnson's famous letter to Turkish Prime Minister Inonu and particularly the suggestion that the United States might not come to the aid of Turkey in the event of a Soviet attack came as a profound shock.[25]

One of the most important consequences of the Turks' ensuing foreign policy reevaluation was a reexamination of bilateral defense arrangements. This resulted in the signing of a new Defense Cooperation Agreement in July 1969 giving the Turkish government more control over indigenous U.S. bases. Another consequence was the initiation of efforts to improve relations with the Soviet Union. A third was an attempt to expand relations with the Arab world.

During the late 1960s and early 1970s relations were further strained by a host of other issues: U.S. policy toward Vietnam; port visits of the Sixth Fleet; differences over the pace and methods of modernizing the Turkish armed forces; the gradual reduction of U.S. economic assistance; the progressive reluctance of the U.S. Congress to fund military aid; and U.S. efforts to curtail Turkish poppy cultivation in order to reduce the drug-abuse problem in the United States. To this must be added other more general factors such as the growth of extremism and the growing polarization of Turkish politics, which finally precipitated the intervention of the military in 1971.[26]

The most serious cause of friction has been the arms embargo imposed on Turkey by the U.S. Congress in the aftermath of the 1974 Cyprus crisis. The embargo was regarded by Turkey as an unjustified slap at a loyal ally which over the years had contributed heavily to collective defense. In particular, it raised further questions in the minds of many Turks about U.S. reliability. In essence, Turkish security was seen as being held hostage to the vagaries and peculiarities of U.S. domestic politics.

The overall impact of the embargo was a serious strain on Turkish-U.S. relations and the belief that Turkey had to reduce its dependency on the United States. Over the last few years there has been a growth in the sentiment that Turkey should pursue a more "multi-faceted" foreign policy, one which would take into greater consideration Turkey's unique geographic position and historic role as a bridge between East and West.[27] This attitude draws on traditions strongly rooted in Ataturk's foreign policy and is widely held within the Republican People's party (CRPP), the current governing party led by Bulent Ecevit, which came to power in January 1978. It has been made all the more compelling by these recent economic problems.

It is against this background that recent and future developments in Turkish foreign policy should be viewed. While the lifting of the embargo has removed the most important irritant in U.S.-Turkish relations, it nevertheless seems likely that some adjustments in Turkey's foreign and defense posture will occur. Since January 1978 Ecevit has stressed the need for a new "National Defense Concept," and representatives from the Defense and Foreign Ministries, the General Staff, and the economic planning organization are currently working on the outlines of such a scheme.

This is not to suggest that Turkey intends to withdraw from NATO. Ecevit has reiterated the importance he attaches to Turkey's membership. However, it does seem likely that Turkey will reduce its manpower commitment and shift some of its forces away from the Soviet-Turkish border to areas more contiguous to Greece. At the same time, it will probably intensify its efforts to develop an indigenous arms industry and diversify its source of military hardware.

Lastly, Ankara may also seek changes in its bilateral military relationship with the United States. Exactly what this will entail is difficult to predict. To date, Turkey has allowed four of the most important U.S. military installations, closed in July 1975, to be reopened.[28] However, these are on an interim status pending an overall review of U.S.-Turkish military ties, and it is likely that Ankara will insist on a renegotiation of the defense cooperation agreement (DCA) signed in March 1976 but never ratified by the U.S. Congress.[29] In fact, Ankara may seek to use the U.S. installations as a bargaining chip to induce the United States to increase its economic and military assistance. Given the current mood in Congress and its general antipathy toward bilateral aid, such pressure could provoke new tensions in U.S.-Turkish relations. Moreover, there remain differences of approach between military issues. For instance, in looking at Turkey's military needs, the United States is likely to emphasize the acquisition of defensive weapons that will enhance Turkey's ability to defend the 300-mile border with the Soviet Union rather than some of the more expensive and prestigious offensive weapons such as the F-5 fighter-bomber currently desired by the Turkish military. Turkey is also concerned about the U.S. approach to the

Multi-lateral Balanced Force Reductions (MBFR) negotiations in Vienna, where it is an observer, and would like to see the present negotiating area expanded to include all NATO countries. Thus, while the embargo has removed the most important obstacle to an improvement in U.S.-Turkish ties, relations in coming years are hardly likely to be problem-free.

Western Europe, NATO, and the EEC

These recent strains in U.S.-Turkish relations have lent greater importance to Turkey's ties to western Europe. Turkey has already signaled its interest in increased European cooperation regarding weapons manufacture, and it clearly hopes that some members of NATO will provide greater financial and military assistance. Indeed, the willingness of the West to be responsive to Turkey's economic plight could significantly influence its future relationship to NATO, as well as the West as a whole. The European response has been less than hoped for—a fact that has increased Ankara's sense of isolation and abandonment.

At the same time, Turkey's relations with the EEC have become more contentious. In part, the difficulties originated in Turkey's association with the EEC in the early 1960s and in the assumptions that surrounded Ankara's application. The application was motivated more by political considerations than economic realities (that is, Greece's decision to apply to the EEC). A related factor was Turkey's desire to draw closer to the West as the cold war persisted. Turkey's association with the EEC was regarded therefore as a supplement to Ankara's ties with NATO.[30] While the EEC had reservations about Turkey's ability to weather stiff economic competition, it felt a certain obligation to be evenhanded and develop relations in tandem with Greece.

The original terms of the 1963 association have not proven capable of preparing the Turkish economy for full integration.[31] In recent years difficulties have intensified between the EEC and Turkey to bitterness and misunderstandings. First, Turkey's growing balance of payments deficit with the EEC has risen from 86.1 million in 1970 to 1.7 billion U.S. dollars in 1975. Second, the implementation of the EEC's Mediterranean policy—particularly the negotiation of preferential trade agreements with virtually all Mediterranean countries—has reduced the value of agricultural concessions granted to Turkey. Third, the economic recession in Europe led to pressure on the part of some EEC members, especially West Germany, to halt the flow of emigrant workers. The result of this policy was an increase in unemployment in Turkey, which added to Turkey's already formidable economic problems. The drop in remittances from Turkish workers abroad threatened one of the main sources of revenue used by Ankara to offset its balance of payments deficit. The recession also made many EEC countries more reluctant regarding the amount of financial assistance they were willing to channel to Turkey. A fourth reason was Greece's application to join the EEC, which sparked new fears that Athens would use its membership to block Ankara's entry into the EEC and to generally thwart Turkey's interests. Such feelings were to some extent reinforced by the general lack of sympathy which the Community displayed for Turkey's position on Cyprus, despite its official position of impartiality and the skillful manner in which Caramanlis has sought to intensify Greece's ties to Europe since 1974.

All these reasons in one way or another have contributed to the deterioration of Turkey's relations with the EEC and have given rise to growing doubts in Turkey regarding the value of EEC ties. The growth of anti-EEC sentiment has manifested itself most clearly within the National Salvation party (NSP), which until the formation of the Ecevit government in January 1978 had been the linchpin of every governing coalition since 1973. Motivated by Islamic ideas and a desire to see Turkey return to its former greatness, the NSP advocates increasing ties with the Arab world and is opposed to entry in the EEC, arguing among other things that the Arab world provides a better market for Turkish industrial goods than does industrialized Europe. The two leading parties, the Justice party (JP) and the Republican People's party (RPP), have generally favored membership. However, the RPP has shown some reservations about the effect that a customs union might have on state planning, and some Turkish commentators have recently suggested that membership in the EEC is incompatible with the Turkish Constitution.[32] Even the Justice party, which is the most favorably disposed toward the EEC, has pressed for readjustments to the Association treaty in order to offset the impact of recent changes in EEC policy.

These questions are likely to be raised with increasing intensity in the coming years as Greece comes closer to full membership, and, unless some compromise is worked out, they could become a source of conflict with the EEC in the future. In Turkish eyes, the Community's willingness to accommodate its demands could well become the acid test of the Community's attitude toward Turkey generally. Thus the issue is an explosive one.

As Mehmet Ali Birand has recently noted: "If Turkey is not allowed some sort of presence in the context of the political mechanism of the Community, it will be assumed that Europe has made its choice and the repercussions could be incalculable."[33] Taken together with the difficult economic problems related to Turkey's integration into the Community, a failure to work out some *modus vivendi* could intensify doubts—already prevalent in some circles—about the value of Turkey's association with the Community and the West in general.

The Soviet Option

Turkey's recent troubles with the West have given rise to speculation about a possible "Soviet Option." Good Soviet relations were a cornerstone of Ataturk's foreign policy—a fact of which Moscow constantly reminds the Turks. Relations between the two countries deteriorated at the end of World War II as a result of Stalin's pressure for a revision of the 1930 Montreux Convention and his attempt to raise claims against the Turkish regions of Kars and Ardahan. In the wake of the 1963-64 Cyprus crisis, however, Ankara embarked upon a policy of rapprochement with Moscow. This culminated in a visit to Moscow by Turkish Prime Minister Suleyman Demirel in October 1967.

In the decade since Demirel's historic visit, relations have improved, particularly in the economic field. Under an economic agreement signed in March 1967, the Soviet Union agreed to aid Turkey in the construction of a number of major projects including an iron and steel mill at Iskenderun, a large oil refinery at Izmir, and a major aluminum plant at Seydisehir as well as a dam and glass factory. In recent years, Soviet economic assistance for these projects has been expanded through a series of additional agreements. For instance, in July 1975 a $700 million credit deal—the largest ever between the two countries—was signed. In it the Soviet Union agreed to supply parts and machinery for the expansion of the steel mill at Iskenderun and also for other projects.[34] During Foreign Minister Caglayangil's visit to Moscow in March 1977 Turkey signed an economic agreement in which Moscow pledged a $1.2 billion loan.[35]

Today, some eleven major projects have been or are being built with Soviet aid. Most are examples of "co-production" in which the Soviet economic assistance is repaid with finished projects from the plants themselves or with Turkish exports. The steel mill at Iskenderun is one of Moscow's largest aid projects in the third world. In fact, in 1975, Turkey received more than half of all Soviet aid given in that year[36]—a good indication of the importance which Moscow attaches to improving relations with Ankara.

Moreover, relations in the political/military sphere have also shown signs of improvement. In April 1978, for instance, Soviet Chief of Staff Nikolai Orgakov paid an official visit to Turkey—the first visit of a senior Soviet military official to Turkey since the visit of Marshall Kliment Voroshilov in 1933—and two months later Ecevit made a much-publicized trip to Moscow, where he signed a "document on friendly relations and cooperation" with Moscow. While the document essentially reiterated many of the basic principles of the Helsinki Agreement and fell considerably short of Moscow's main goal of a nonaggression pact, the fact that Turkey was willing to sign such a document underscores the changed climate of relations in recent years.

Moreover, even if Moscow has not succeeded in attaining its main objective—weaning Turkey away from NATO—its courtship of Ankara has met with some success. In July 1976, the Soviet aircraft carrier *Kiev* entered the Mediterranean, despite the fact that the passage of aircraft carriers is prohibited by the Montreux Convention, which both Turkey and the Soviet Union signed. The Turkish government accepted the Soviet description of the *Kiev* as an "antisubmarine cruiser," although the *Kiev* mounts a large-scale flight deck and carries helicopters and thirty YAK-36 vertical short takeoff and landing (V-STOL) jet aircraft. The Turkish willingness to accept the Soviet classification of the *Kiev* was generally considered to reflect a desire on Turkey's part to avoid any controversy with the Soviet Union, and it is an important example of the manner in which Moscow has been able to cash in on the improvement in relations.[37]

One should not, of course, exaggerate the degree of improvement in Soviet-Turkish relations or its implications. At present, Turkey is primarily interested in tapping Moscow's economic potential and it remains wary of Russia's long-term political intentions. Turkey has fought some thirteen wars with the Soviet Union, and for most Turks, especially those within the higher echelons of the military, Moscow is still regarded as the major threat to Turkish security. Turkey's policy options are narrowing. If it cannot obtain the weapons it needs to modernize its army to keep pace with the augmentation and modernization of Soviet forces stationed across the Turkish border in the Caucasus, then some accommodation with Moscow is almost certain to occur.

How far this process of rapprochement will proceed will depend upon the course of relations with the West, especially the United States. While no dramatic shift in Turkish policy is likely in the near future, the long-term prospects are less certain. There are elements within the RPP, not to mention the radical Left, which favor closer relations with Moscow and which no longer regard the Soviet Union as a particular threat. At present their influence is not great, but it could increase and find greater resonance if U.S. relations deteriorate further and if the present sense of bitterness and isolation continues to grow.

The Middle East and Third World Option

In the last few years Turkey has also undertaken a conscious effort to expand ties with the third world. Ankara applied for observer status at the Sixth Conference of the Nonaligned, held in Colombo (Sri Lanka) in August 1976 (its application was opposed by India, however), and plans to apply for guest status at the meeting of foreign ministers of the nonaligned countries next year. Turkey has also been courting the Group of 77, and in August 1978 played host to a conference on the New International Economic Order.

The area in which this trend has been most clearly manifested, however, is the Middle East. Historically and geographically, Turkey has had strong ties to the Middle East, and in recent years there has been a growing feeling that Turkey ought to play a greater role in the region.[38] This belief has been given greater impetus by the new status of the Middle Eastern countries since the energy crisis, and by Turkey's mounting economic difficulties. Turkey is heavily dependent on outside oil, and it was hard hit by the quadrupling 1973 prices.[39] As a consequence, Turkey has sought to strengthen its relations with Iran and Pakistan within the framework of the Regional Cooperation for Development (RCD), the economic-cultural arm of CENTO. These efforts have met with only moderate success.[40] Turkey has also sought to increase cooperation with Libya and Iraq, from whom it imports over 40 percent of its oil. Ankara's main interest has been in obtaining credits to finance its increasing oil imports.

Politically, Turkey's interest in improved relations in the Middle East has been prompted by a desire to obtain Arab backing for its position in regard to Cyprus, and since 1974 Ankara has increasingly voted with the Arab states against Israel. To some extent, Turkey's efforts to expand relations with the countries of the Middle East have also been influenced by religious and cultural ties. While constitutionally Turkey is a secular state, Islam still plays an important role in Turkish society, especially in the rural areas which were less directly affected by Ataturk's reforms.[41] During the period when the Muslim fundamentalist National Salvation party was a key member of the ruling coalition (1973-77), its leader Necmettin Erbakan used his influence to push for increased contacts with the Arab world. The convocation of the Seventh Conference of the Islamic Foreign Ministers in Istanbul in May 1976 was an important reflection of this policy.

Yet there are objective limits to how far this policy can be pushed. Turkey's Arab opening has failed to bring the hoped-for support for Ankara's position on Cyprus. Nor have any of the Middle Eastern countries (with the exception of Libya) shown a strong willingness to help bail Turkey out of its financial difficulties. Moreover, there are historical and psychological factors that inhibit a significant expansion of Turkish ties to the countries of the Middle East. As a non-Arabic state and a former colonial power, Turkey is still regarded with considerable suspicion—in some cases, antipathy—by many of the countries in the area. Thus, while Turkey is likely to continue to try to expand its relations with the Arab countries, these ties are hardly likely to develop to the point where they could offer a substitute for Turkey's ties to the West.

Turkey's Domestic Crisis

The deterioration of Turkey's relations with the West, particularly with the United States, is more unsettling because it has coincided with and to some extent has been given impetus by growing domestic tensions. Today, in fact, Turkey faces one of the most serious domestic crises in its modern history. Since the late 1960s there has been in increasing polarization of Turkish political life which has until recently hindered the formation of a stable and effective government, capable of resolving Turkey's mounting internal and external problems. This paralysis and polarization in national politics has been accompanied by an alarming rise in domestic violence, much of which has been precipitated by clashes between right-wing and left-wing students. In 1977, more than 250 persons were killed in acts of political violence, and by the end of 1978 the death toll had risen to 1000, provoking the introduction of martial law in thirteen provinces. The violence has important cultural as well as political roots, with various youth groups mobilized in defense of antagonistic traditions. Moreover, in some areas, such as Eastern Anatolia, which is heavily populated by Kurds, the violence has also reflected the emergence of traditional and ethnic conflicts.

The domestic violence and growth of extremism has been reinforced by a sharp deterioration in Turkey's economy. This economic crisis has its roots in a number of developments: the reduction in U.S. aid and the shift of U.S. policy away from bilateral to multilateral funding; the recession in Europe after 1973 which caused a decline in remittances from Turkish workers abroad; the Cyprus crisis,[42] which resulted in large defense outlays and the diversion of scarce resources to the military sector;[43] and most importantly, the quadrupling of oil prices since 1973 which led to a sharp rise in Turkey's trade deficit (about $3 billion in 1977). As a result of these dislocations, inflation has been running about 25 percent to 30 percent a year since 1974 and unemployment has reached 2 million out of a work force of 16 million. Since coming to power in January 1978, the new government, headed by Bulent Ecevit, has taken a number of measures designed to bolster the economy—including a devaluation of the Turkish lira of 30 percent against the dollar—and has actively sought financial assistance from organizations like the International Monetary Fund (IMF). However, despite these measures, the fundamental problems facing Turkey in recent times are likely to continue to pose major obstacles to economic growth in the future. The population (presently about 42 million) is increasing by almost 3 percent per year and is expected to double by the year 2000. Without a drastic reduction in the birth rate, it will be impossible for Turkey to achieve rapid economic development.

This is not to suggest that Turkey's problems are insoluble. But it does highlight the real difficulties the country is likely to face in the coming years and the dangers these pose for domestic stability. If these problems are not faced squarely, domestic violence is likely to continue to mount—and with it the political potency of extremist groups. Over the long run, this could erode support for Turkey's democratic institutions and undercut further the country's ties to the West.

Toward a New Policy for the Southern Flank

Five years after the eruption of the Cyprus dispute the southern flank remains in crisis. Without immediate action the situation is likely to worsen. Yet despite the great concern over the fissures on the southern flank, there is very little evidence that the problems are receiving the systematic attention and the creative thinking they deserve. Many of the concepts and axioms which lay at the heart of the U.S. approach to the region are carryovers from the late 1940s and 1950s. Today they are no longer an adequate basis for policy toward a region that is undergoing rapid economic and political change. In the complex and pluralistic milieu of the late 1970s and 1980s, alarmism about the growing Soviet threat is unlikely to be an effective source of policy. This is not to imply that the Soviet threat no longer exists. But today the threat is less immediate and less direct. Most importantly, it is no longer regarded by Greece and Turkey as the main source of their insecurity. An effective policy toward the region must address itself to the real sources of insecurity and at the same time attempt to reestablish a basis for genuine cooperation which will blunt any attempt by the Soviet Union to exploit the instabilities, both real and latent, on the southern flank. This is all the more important because of the potential for instability elsewhere in southern Europe—particularly in post-Tito Yugoslavia.[44]

The problem of containing Soviet power in the eastern Mediterranean must be seen in a broader context—a part of the larger problem of managing political change. In the coming years, both Greece and Turkey are likely to seek greater autonomy in their foreign relations, reducing to some extent their former dependence on the United States. The United States can hardly prevent this. Nor should it try to. The most likely result of such a policy would be to alienate further Greece and Turkey as well as weaken their ties to the West. The United States should adopt instead a flexible approach. It should recognize that such efforts are a part of a natural attempt (belatedly) to adapt themselves to a changing international environment, and it should seek to channel and guide these efforts in directions which enhance the security of both countries without undermining the foundations of the alliance as a whole.

The lifting of the embargo offers the chance to set U.S. relations with Greece and Turkey on a new footing and to reestablish a sense of purpose in our policy toward both countries, a sense which has been sadly lacking in recent years. What is needed is a new approach that balances the need for military cohesion with the impulse toward political change. Today more than ever, Greece and Turkey must feel that they are valued members of a wider community of shared goals and ideals which includes—but extends beyond—the narrow boundaries of common defense. Only under such circumstances will both be willing to contribute to the collective defense, and only under such conditions will the United States be in a position to begin to repair the fissures on the southern flank and reestablish genuinely cooperative and harmonious relations with both allies.

At the same time, the United States, in concert with its West European allies, should intensify its efforts to get Greece and Turkey to resolve their differences through negotiations. Given the complexity of the issues and the differing perceptions on each side, this will not be easy. However, recent experience has underscored the fact that progress toward resolution of such intractable disputes cannot be obtained through sporadic discussions, but requires a commitment to intensive and sustained negotiations. This is the lesson of Camp David.

The starting point of such efforts should be Cyprus. The Cyprus issue may prove more amenable to such a process than the Aegean because it involves both protagonists less directly. Progress toward a settlement on Cyprus would create a better psychological atmosphere for the resolution of other bilateral issues and could pave the way for a gradual improvement of political relations between both countries.

None of these measures in and of itself is likely to solve all the outstanding problems on the southern flank. However, taken together they would be indicative of a positive new direction in U.S. policy in the Eastern Mediterranean and could help to restore a greater degree of stability in an area which in the future could pose a growing threat to European security and alliance cohesion.

Notes

1. For a detailed discussion of the Soviet naval build-up in the Mediterranean, see Barry M. Blechman, *The Changing Soviet Navy* (Washington, D.C.: The Brookings Institution, 1973).

2. "Security in the Mediterranean—a NATO Perspective," Presentation by General William A. Knowlton, Commander LAND-SOUTHEAST (Izmir), May 20, 1977, p. 5, mimeographed.

3. *New York Times*, May 23, 1978.

4. The Turks have estimated, however, that it will take $600 million worth of spare parts alone to make up the losses caused by the embargo.

5. In 1975, for instance, Greece received 69.1 percent of its oil from OPEC countries while Turkey received 90.7 percent.

6. On the role and methods of the Greek lobby see Morton Kondracke, "The Greek Lobby," *New Republic*, April 29, 1978, pp. 14-16. Also Russell Warren Howe and Sarah Hays Trott, *The Power Peddlers* (New York: Doubleday and Co., 1977), pp. 406-468.

7. For a particularly good analysis of the crisis and the U.S. behind-the-scenes diplomacy, see Lawrence Stern, "Bitter Lessons: How We Failed in Cyprus," *Foreign Policy*, Summer 1975, pp. 34-37.

8. The Aegean issue is extremely complex and no attempt to analyze the issue in detail can be undertaken here. For a balanced treatment that addresses both the political and the legal aspects see Barry Buzan, "A Sea of Troubles? Sources of Dispute in the New Ocean Regime," *Adelphi Paper 143* (London: International Institute for Strategic Studies, 1978), pp. 28-30.

9. In fact, Andreas Papandreou, the leader of the Pan Hellenic Socialist Movement (PASOK), called upon the government to sink the *Sismik*, a move which would have almost certainly led to the outbreak of hostilities between the two countries.

10. See "Principles to Guide Future United States-Greek Defense Cooperation," *Department of State Press Release* No. 180, April 15, 1976.

11. Greek participation was limited to naval and air units and was made possible by the manipulation of the NATO command structure. Normally, exercises would have been directed out of NATO's regular headquarters in Izmir (Turkey). Instead, to assuage Greek sensitivity, they were directed from the regular headquarters in Naples; this put the exercises under the command of a British admiral rather than a Turkish one.

12. The actual terms of the negotiations have not been revealed. However, Greece is thought to be seeking a special status within the alliance in which its armed forces would come under NATO command only in case of major conflict. With this arrangement, a new allied headquarters under a Greek commander would be established in Larissa (central Greece) similar to the headquarters in Izmir. Each of the two headquarters would have a national commander and an American deputy commander. Structurally, they would be subordinate to NATO's headquarters in Naples (CINC-SOUTH). Part of this plan has already been implemented. At the end of June 1978 a Turkish general took over command of the allied headquarters at Izmir, which until then had been under the control of a U.S. General.

13. Nicholas Gage, "Opposition Leader in Athens of Two Minds about U.S.," *New York Times*, April 12, 1978.

14. See in particular Wilhelm Haferkamp, "Chancen und Risiken der Zweiten EG-Erweiterung," *Europa Archiv* 19/1977, pp. 617-626.

15. See John Pezmazoglou, "Greece: A 'Special Case' for EC Membership," *European Community*, September-October 1977, pp. 7-9.

16. For a good discussion of the Athens Conference and its implications see Richard Clogg, "Balkan Kaleidoscope," *World Today*, August 1976, pp. 301-307.

17. Papandreou met with Tito in Yogoslavia in February 1978, and in September a Yogoslav party delegation headed by Stane Dolanc, Secretary of the Yugoslav Central Committee Presidium and the prime candidate to replace Tito as head of the Yugoslav party, visited Greece for an exchange of views with PASOK. See Papandreou's remarks in *Politika* (Belgrade), September 10, 1978, noting the similarity of views between the two parties' approach to Balkan cooperation.

18. Contact between Yugoslav and Greek defense officials has increased considerably in recent years. In June 1978 Yugoslavia's defense minister, General Nikola Ljubicic, paid an official visit to Athens, while in October 1976 Greek defense minister Evangelos Averoff visited Belgrade. These visits have been supplemented by other exchanges at a lower level. While Greece and Belgrade have denied that they are considering concluding a defense agreement, Papandreou has claimed that Yugoslavia is prepared to go into joint arms production with Greece. See Nicholas Gage, "Opposition Leader of Two Minds about U.S.," *New York Times*, April 12, 1978.

19. *Christian Science Monitor*, September 14, 1978.

20. This was underscored by the visit to Athens of Chinese Foreign Minister Huang Hua in September 1978, only a few days after Rallis returned from Moscow.

21. A Rightist party that ran in 1974, The National Democratic Union, received only 1 percent of the votes and no seats in Parliament.

22. For a good synopsis of PASOK's platform and Papandreou's views see "Socialist Transformation," PASOK No. 2 (Athens, September 1977) and "Foreign Policy," PASOK No. 4 (Athens, September 1977), particularly Papandreou's position paper prepared for the Malta Conference of Socialist Parties of the Mediterranean, June 1977, "Toward a Liberated and Socialist Mediterranean," in ibid., pp. 13-24.

23. Richard Clogg, "Greece: The End of Consensus Politics," *World Today*, May 1978, pp. 184-191.

24. See Bulent Ecevit, "Turkey's Security Policies," *Survival,* September-October 1978, pp. 203-208.

25. For the text of the Johnson letter and Inonu's reply see *Middle Eastern Journal*, Summer 1966, pp. 386-393.

26. For a good discussion of these issues and their impact on U.S.-Turkish relations see George S. Harris, *Troubled Alliance* (Washington, D.C., and Stanford, California: American Enterprise Institute and Hoover Institute on War, Revolution, and Peace, 1972), pp. 125-147.

27. See in particular the article by Observer, "A Multi-faceted Foreign Policy as a New Approach," *Dis Politika* (Foreign Policy), Volume 6, Nos. 3-4, June, 1977, pp. 7-17. The author was reputed to be a high official in the Turkish Foreign Ministry.

28. These installations are intelligence-gathering bases at Sinop on the Black Sea Coast, Diyardakir in Eastern Turkey, Belbasi near Ankara, and a navigation station at Kargabrun, north of the Marmara Sea. For a discussion of the functions of these bases and their importance to the overall U.S. intelligence-gathering effort, see *United States Military Installations and Objectives in the Mediterranean*, House Committee on International Relations, 95th Congress, first session (Washington, D.C.: U.S. Government Printing Office, 1977) March 27, 1977, pp. 37-47.

29. The agreement provided for greater Turkish control over the installations and expressly prohibited their use for any purpose not authorized by the Turkish government. It also agreed to provide $1 billion in loans, grants, and credits over a four-year period.

30. See Mehmet Ali Birand, "Turkey and the European Community," *World Today*, February 1978, pp. 52-61.

31. The association agreement signed in Ankara on September 12, 1963, gave Turkey privileged access to the EEC markets and special financial assistance as well as promising special employment opportunities for Turkish workers within the EEC. The agreement also set out detailed schedules for the reduction of tariffs and the elimination of trade barriers, to a full customs union. The goal of these measures was explicitly stated as full membership within the EEC.

32. See Udo Steinbach, "Auf dem Wege nach Europa? Die Beziehungen zwischen der Turkei und der Europaeischen Gemeinschaft durchlaufen eine Kritische Phase," *Orient* 1/77, pp. 79-101; also Sefik Alp Bahadir, "Europa und die Turkei, Eine Oekonomische Studie," *Dritte Welt*, Sonderheft 1975, pp. 154-185.

33. Birand, "Turkey and the European Community," p. 60.

34. Reuters, July 9, 1975.

35. Tass, March 18, 1977.

36. Christopher Wren, *New York Times*, August 20, 1976.

37. For a good discussion of the *Kiev* incident and its strategic implications, see Barry Buzan, "The Status and Future of the Montreux Convention," *Survival*, November-December 1976, pp. 242-247.

38. As Prime Minister Ecevit recently noted: "Historically and geographically Turkey is primarily a Balkan, Middle Eastern and Eastern Mediterranean country. This certainly does not exclude the fact that Turkey is also a member of the community of Europe, but our starting point is the Balkan area, the Middle East and the Eastern Mediterranean. Therefore we should give greater emphasis to these historical and geographical realities." Bulent Ecevit, "Turkey's Security Policies," *Survival*, September-October 1978, p. 205.

39. In 1977, for instance, Turkey's expenditure for the import of oil was $1.5 billion—nearly equal to the total volume of its exports ($1.7 billion).

40. See Rolf-Roger Hoeppner, "The Future Course of the RCD—Iran, Turkey, Pakistan," *Aussenpolitik*, 2/77, pp. 227-236.

41. For an insightful discussion of the revitalization of Islam in Turkish life see Arnold Hottinger, "Kemal Ataturk's Heritage," *Encounter*, February 1977, pp. 75-81.

42. It has been estimated that the first year of Turkey's military presence in Cyprus entailed an expenditure of about TL 35 billion, or about $2.5 billion—the equivalent of 40 percent of the national budget for that year.

43. Turkish defense expenditures as a percentage of government spend-

ing have been 26.6 percent (1975), 29.4 percent (1976), and 21.1 percent (1977). All figures from *The Military Balance*, 1977-78 (London: International Institute of Strategic Studies, 1977), p. 83.

44. For a fuller discussion of this question and its implications for regional and international stability see F. Stephen Larrabee, "Balkan Security," *Adelphi Paper 135* (London: International Institute for Strategic Studies, Summer 1977).

Part III
The Pan-European
Dimension

7

The Soviet Perception of European Security

Coit Dennis Blacker

The Soviet Union is a superpower with global interests and policies. Its ability to influence events around the world and to realize its foreign political goals is equaled only by that of the United States. Yet in a very real sense the Soviet Union is preeminently a European power. It is the dominant country on the continent, possessing human, material, and military resources that no individiual state in the area can rival. Moscow's involvement in the politics of the region is both constant and inevitable. As a function of this geopolitical reality, the Soviet leadership devotes considerable attention and energy to its relations with the countries of Western Europe.

The purpose of this chapter is to analyze comprehensively Soviet perceptions of and attitudes toward the problem of security in Europe. The first two sections examine the military and political aspects of the problem as seen from Moscow. The third section concentrates on the Kremlin's apprehensions as it confronts a Western Europe caught in the midst of major social and systemic change. Each part also focuses on the spectrum of policies that the Soviets have pursued in their efforts to meet and overcome these challenges. Frequently, the factors which shape Soviet diplomacy, both internal and external, are discussed in a theoretical vein, as abstractions. The intention here is to explore how Kremlin leaders have sought to attain their foreign policy objectives in a specific region of the world.

Military Security

One of the most important aspects of the relationship between the Soviet Union and Western Europe is, of course, the military dimension. At first glance, it would seem that Moscow has little cause for concern. The Soviet Union has attained a degree of military power on the Continent, and, in fact, throughout Eurasia, that is without peer. The two principal contenders, Germany in Europe and China in Asia, are at a level qualitatively below that of the Soviet Union in existing capabilities. Yet the Kremlin argues that security in Europe remains tentative and unstable, largely, if not exclusively, as a result of the partnership between the United States and the major capitalist countries of Western Europe. It is "Atlanticism," in the Soviet view, that allows the United States and its allies to exercise considerable control over political and economic developments within Western Europe and

137

thoughout the non-Communist world. It is, moreover, the military apparatus of the alliance which comprises the core of the Atlantic connection and which poses a substantial and continuing threat to the security and well-being of the Soviet and Warsaw Pact states. When the partnership shows signs of stress or decay, as it did in 1973 after the October War, Soviet analysts carefully assess those strains in an attempt to decipher what they portend for the alliance. While the emergence of tension among the Western allies is held to be a reflection of deep and inevitable "intra-imperialist contradictions," the Kremlin has also noted the basic resilience, durability, and vitality of the Atlantic bond. For Moscow, NATO and its related institutions represent the most powerful of the imperialist collectives and the most developed mechanism through which the Western countries coordinate their foreign and domestic policies.

The American Presence in Europe

The Soviets contend that while most of the Western European governments actively support the policy, it is the Americans who are the principal architects of and the driving force behind the Atlantic connection. For Washington, the alliance is an invaluable vehicle with which to safeguard its extensive economic and political interests on the Continent. By conditioning its pledge to defend the member states of NATO on Europe's adherence to the principles of Atlanticism, primarily anti-Communist governments and pro-American trade and commercial policies, the United States has placed largely implicit limits on Soviet access to the material and human resources of the region. With Washington acting as a highly visible guardian in residence, the Kremlin's ability to influence and/or meddle in the affairs of Western Europe falls short of the optimal. Thus, in some ultimate sense, the disintegration of the Atlantic alliance and the withdrawal of American military power from the region are in the interest of the Soviet Union.

The Kremlin's hostility to the presence of large numbers of U.S. forces in and around Europe was an especially strong theme of Soviet diplomacy in the early to mid-1960s. The underlying contention was that the American "occupation" was one of the central causes of regional instability, a condition that would persist until such time as Washington was compelled to reduce or withdraw its military contingent. In July 1966, the Warsaw Pact states issued a declaration on European security that focused on the pernicious effects of American military policies. The declaration alleged that the United States and its NATO allies were attempting to perpetuate the division of Europe by promoting an arms race and by exacerbating international tensions; in pursuit of these ends, the Pact argued, troops of the United States are still kept in Europe, their military bases are located in Western European countries, stockpiles of nuclear weapons are being created, nuclear submarines are sent to the seas that wash Europe, the American Sixth Fleet sails in the Mediterranean and planes carrying nuclear bombs fly in the skies over European countries.[1]

To ameliorate the confrontation in Europe, the Pact states urged the "withdrawal of all foreign troops from other countries' territories to within their national frontiers," or as a first step, the liquidation of the military organizations of NATO and the WTO.[2]

With the advent of détente and the improvement in superpower relations, Moscow has continued to convey its opposition to American military power in Europe but with a much greater degree of subtlety than in the 1960s. Sharply worded condemnations have been replaced by the vocabulary of conciliation and reason. For example, the Soviet international affairs specialist, Dmitri Proektor, writing in the September 1973 issue of *Mirovaya ekonomika i mezhdunarodniye otnosheniya*, sketched a blueprint for European security that had as one of its cardinal features a gradual weakening of the two blocs' military functions and, as a final step, their complete "atrophy."[3] While the article did not explicitly call for the withdrawal of the 300,000 United States armed forces, the implication of Proektor's analysis was clear. The abolition of NATO could, from the Kremlin's perspective, permit the defense of Western Europe to be decoupled from American conventional and perhaps strategic power by severely undermining the rationale by which the United States maintained its military presence in the area thirty years after the Second World War.

That Moscow would look kindly on at least a partial redeployment of NATO-assigned American forces to bases within the continental United States seems evident. Yet Soviet leaders must develop their policies not from generalized and rather abstract conceptions but from realistic assessments of existing political realities. Surely the Kremlin does not regard an American departure from the Continent as imminent, but as a fairly distant prospect, coming, if at all, at the end of a long period of declining imperialist cohesion—at a time when the Europeans would grow less tolerant and more resentful of American political and economic hegemony. The Soviets seem to feel, however, that by steadily improving their relations with the capitalist states of Western Europe they can persuade the NATO allies that their dependence on the American security guarantee is not only expensive and inhibiting but superfluous as well. To draw these countries away from the United States gradually and without arousing latent suspicions about Soviet intentions has been one of the central objectives of the Kremlin's bilateral diplomacy in Europe.

What the Soviet political authorities clearly do not want are American withdrawals which unleash in their wake a wave of anti-Sovietism. A hasty pullout by the United States executed without careful consultations with the Western Europeans, while perhaps destabilizing in the short run, would not necessarily work to the advantage of the Soviet Union. Reawakened fears about Russian hegemonial aspirations could prompt NATO Europe to spend significantly more on defense, not less. In this instance, Moscow's objective is to ease the United States out of Europe in stages, while at the same time seeking to dissuade the NATO allies from rushing in to fill the vacuum. The Kremlin's participation in the Central European force reduction talks is based in part on the perception that the negotiations might result in a phased and orderly American withdrawal that the Western Europeans will accept as a natural and inevitable consequence of the relaxation of international tensions. Thus it is the goal of Soviet leaders to have a constant input into how, under what circumstances, and at what rate the United States recalls its forces from the region. For the Politburo, the timing of the withdrawals and the context in which they proceed are critical considerations, at least as important as the magnitude of the reductions themselves.

Short of a direct military engagement, the Soviet Union cannot compel the United States to remove its forces from Europe. At most, the Kremlin can help to shape an international political environment that is conducive to such a retrenchment. By simultaneously, but independently, cultivating better relations with the United States and the Western European countries, by quietly exploiting the latent and not so latent tensions that exist among the Atlantic states, and by pursuing a policy of moderation that encourages fragmentation rather than consolidation within the West, the Soviets can anticipate a gradual and uneven weakening of the bonds that link Washington to NATO Europe, a process which could lead over time to a smaller and less powerful American military presence on the Continent.

West German Military Power

After the United States, the Soviets regard the armed forces of the Federal Republic as the greatest potential threat to their security and to the security of Europe. It is the combination of West German and American military power which embodies for them the very essence of "Atlanticism." The *Bundeswehr*, with almost 400,000 men, comprises over 50 percent of NATO manpower along the central front; the airforce of the Federal Republic, the second largest in Western Europe, has the capability to deliver nuclear weapons to targets within Eastern Europe. Consequently, the Kremlin is extremely sensitive to any changes in those force levels. The Soviets also suspect that should the United States tire of its European responsibilities or surrender a portion of its obligations through formal diplomatic agreement, the Federal Republic would not hesitate to assume the preeminent role within NATO and upgrade its armed forces to coincide with the elevation in status. Moscow enjoys a robust economic relationship with Bonn and, since the advent of *Ostpolitik*, comparatively cordial political relations as well. Yet from the Soviet perspective, the primary obstacle to the development of a more permanent détente between the two countries is the maintenance by the Federal Republic of a sizeable and well-equipped military establishment.

As in the case of the American military presence in Europe, the Soviets have no formal or officially sanctioned way to control the size of the West German armed forces. They cannot instruct the Federal Republic to reduce the *Bundeswehr* by 25 percent; neither can they insist that the airforce be barred from carrying nuclear weapons. Yet they can influence the defense decision-making process in West Germany in several ways. They have, for instance, gone to great lengths over the past decade to reassure Bonn that their intentions are peaceful. Since 1970, the Soviets have emphasized that with the confirmation of the territorial status quo in Central Europe, relations between the two countries can develop in a normal fashion, based on the principles of peaceful coexistence and mutual advantage. The Kremlin doubtless hopes that a prolonged détente with the West Germans, buttressed by economic links and regular high-level political consultations, will induce Bonn to reduce or, at a minimum, not increase that portion of its gross national product devoted to military expenditures. Although the Federal Republic has, in fact, raised the level of defense spending in recent years, the Soviets may take solace from the fact that without the relaxation of tensions, the increase might have been much larger.

A second way in which the Soviets have attempted to check West German military capabilities has been through mutual force reductions. The Warsaw Pact countries have advanced several initiatives in the course of the negotiations which, if they were to become part of an agreement, would prevent the Federal Republic from adding to the numerical strength of its armed forces. Soviet sponsorship of national subceilings in Vienna has, for this reason, met with the resistance of the NATO states; the proposal has on several occasions been rejected by the Western negotiators.

Thus, even with the general improvement in Soviet-West German political relations, and in spite of the impressive build-up in Soviet military capabilities, the Kremlin leadership continues to view the largely potential power of the *Bundeswehr* with trepidation. Furthermore, the Soviets are likely to remain extremely vigilant and, to a degree, uneasy, until such time as either de facto or negotiated limits are placed on the armed forces of the Federal Republic.

Western European Military Integration

In addition to American and West German military power, the Soviets view the prospect of accelerated Western European defense cooperation as a potential threat to their security. The Soviets would prefer that NATO Europe forego the option of integration and remain largely as it is—a loose collection of independent states with minimal collaboration on defense-related issues. A constellation of small and medium-sized powers, confronting Moscow as individual national actors, poses a much less formidable challenge to Soviet interests than would a militarily (and perhaps politically) cohesive Western Europe.

Soviet analysts point to three vehicles by which the Western Europeans have sought to advance the cause of military integration. First, they have noted and criticized recent discussions in the West concerning the possible resurrection of the European Defense Community and the future role of the Western European Union.[4] The Soviet leadership is also concerned about the possible transformation of the European Economic Community into a political-military "bloc."[5] What the Soviets find especially disturbing is not the economic cooperation that currently exists within the EEC (which they have come to accept as an international fact of life and which they see as having potential benefits for the Socialist countries) but the possible "spillover" of integration into the areas of foreign and military policy.

Finally, Soviet policymakers are alarmed by the prospect of a Western European nuclear consortium. When the United Kingdom joined the Community in 1973, suddenly it appeared much more likely to the Kremlin that the British and the French might coordinate their research efforts and combine their nuclear arsenals to produce a deterrent force of considerable strength.

Soviet leaders can do very little in the way of direct action to halt the process of Western European military integration. Fortunately, from their perspective, the problem is not an especially acute one at the present time. Although NATO Europe has taken some tentative steps in that direction in recent years, defense policy continues to be, almost exclusively, a national rather than an international prerogative. What they can do and have done is to publicize their opposition to integration and to put their trust in what Robert Legvold has called "a gradual, random, unforeseen series of disruptions" within NATO to undercut the cooperative impulse.[6] Moscow recognizes no doubt that its ability to control developments in this area is severely limited and that the establishment of a European Defense Community is best deterred through the preservation of East-West détente. Military collaboration seems much less likely to make significant progress during a time of ostensible relaxation than in a period of heightened international tension.

This, in turn, helps to explain Soviet participation in the force reduction talks. Merely the process of negotiation can act as an impediment to further integration by altering threat perceptions. The Soviets also look to an MBFR agreement as a vehicle to freeze NATO Europe's defense efforts at some arbitrary level, either implicitly, by the creation of a psychological inhibition to augment military capabilities, or explicitly, by the imposition of national force ceilings. At a minimum, the Kremlin leadership seems to feel that the Vienna talks are a low-risk venture that can serve Soviet interests by producing a sense of complacency among the Western states on defense-related issues.

Soviet security interests in Europe are not gravely threatened either by the American presence or by West German armed forces; even less are they threatened by the prospect of a Western European military union. The primary danger, in Moscow's view, is that these three relatively distinct forms of Atlantic military power will in some fashion be cojoined; namely, that the Germans will assume a more central role in alliance defense, that the European NATO states will succeed, however imperfectly, in elaborating a common military policy, and that the United States will nurture both developments while at the same time maintaining a contingent of several hundred thousand troops in the region. Whether or not NATO evolves along these lines is a matter to be decided over a period of years by the members of the alliance; moreover, those decisions will turn largely on domestic rather than international political considerations. Lacking a formal input, the Soviets can only express their opinions and perhaps influence the general outcome of the debate by their diplomatic and military conduct. Thus it seems reasonable to assume that Soviet leaders will avoid abrupt shifts in both the tone and the content of their Western European diplomacy, shifts that the Atlantic countries might interpret as provocative or destabilizing. The cultivation of better bilateral relations, a grudging tolerance for the American presence on the Continent and a strong preference for negotiation instead of confrontation are currently and will probably remain the favored mechanisms by which the Kremlin seeks to arrest the futher aggrandizement of NATO Europe's military potential.

Political Security

Soviet authorities are concerned at least as much with the political aspects of security in Europe as they are with the military dimension. They have, after all, been able to guarantee the physical security of the Soviet state and the Warsaw Pact countries by the maintenance of large and modern armed forces, equipped with sophisticated conventional and nuclear weaponry. As the Kremlin must be aware, it is beyond the capability of the NATO allies to dislodge the Communist regimes by the application of military power. The Soviets have found, however, that the achievement of security in a political sense has been a somewhat more elusive goal.

For most of the last thirty years, Soviet diplomacy in Europe had a decidedly defensive orientation. Until the first part of this decade, the

Kremlin's primary objective was to consolidate the postwar "gains of socialism" by obtaining from the West formal recognition of the political order in Eastern Europe. With the arrival of détente and, in particular, with the normalization of relations between the Federal Republic and its Communist neighbors, that objective has been largely realized. Eastern Europe has become for Soviet leaders a problem of much more manageable proportions. As a consequence, the way in which Moscow defines its security interests in Europe has undergone a significant alteration. With greater confidence in their ability to control events in Eastern Europe, the Soviets have sought to involve themselves directly in the politics of Western Europe—in other words, to have a permanent input into the decision-making process of the Atlantic states. In short, the Kremlin's policies toward Western Europe have shed many of their reactive characteristics and have grown markedly more innovative. In a basic and profound sense, the Soviets have come to regard security in Europe from a truly continental perspective, as a problem not only of forestalling undesirable change within the Socialist community but also, and perhaps more importantly, of encouraging certain types of change within the capitalist countries.

Security in Eastern Europe

Before they could embark on this more ambitious policy, it was imperative for the Soviets to gain Western acceptance of the political and territorial status quo in Eastern Europe. In the absence of a general European peace treaty, the NATO countries, and most prominently the Federal Republic, were in a unique position to confirm the results of the Second World War. At the core of the problem was the refusal of the major Western states to recognize as legitimate the East German regime. As long as the Atlantic states withheld recognition, Bonn could continue to claim that the division of Germany was a temporary condition and that it had the right to speak for and represent Germans on both sides of the demarcation line. In addition, the Federal Republic had yet to acknowledge the legality of the transfer of German territories seized by the Poles in 1945, further complicating the West's relations with the Communist countries. Under these conditions, Eastern Europe remained a constant source of international tension; what stability did exist in the region was provided by the presence of Soviet armed forces rather than by any kind of shared political consensus.

When West German Chancellor Willy Brandt took the first tentative steps to normalize relations with the socialist countries of Europe in 1969, the initial Soviet reaction was one of suspicion. The Kremlin regarded the German initiative as insincere, as an attempt to meddle in the affairs of, and undermine Soviet hegemony in Eastern Europe. Brandt persisted nonetheless in his efforts to open a dialogue with Moscow and in late 1969 the two former adversaries began negotiations on a renunciation of force agreement. Eight months later, in August 1970, the Moscow Treaty was signed by representatives of the two countries. The Kremlin eventually abandoned its negative posture toward *Ostpolitik* and warmed to the policy as it became apparent that in exchange for a rapprochement the Federal Republic was prepared to accept as binding the de facto international frontiers in Central and Eastern Europe, thereby indirectly affirming the existence of a sovereign and independent East German state. The West Germans concluded similar accords with the Poles in 1970 and the Czechs in 1973, thus signaling Bonn's acceptance in a wider sense of the political situation in Eastern Europe. The relationship between the Federal Republic and the German Democratic Republic proved to be a somewhat more intractable problem; while the two German states did sign a treaty in 1972 elaborating various principles of relations, the agreement stopped short of requiring Bonn to extend full diplomatic recognition to the Communist regime.[7]

With the ratification of the treaties between West Germany on the one hand and the Soviet Union, Poland, and Czechoslovakia on the other, the Soviets made appreciable strides toward their goal of enhancing stability in Eastern Europe. As recently as 1974, the Kremlin was still emphasizing that it was the détente with the Federal Republic that had supplied the critical foundation for the reduction of tension in Europe.[8] From the Soviet perspective, the system of treaties spawned by *Ostpolitik* comprised an indispensable beginning. With Bonn's sanction of the Central and Eastern European status quo, Moscow's latent fears of German revanchism were measurably reduced. More importantly, the Soviets might have reasoned that the United States, Britain, and France would be much more inclined to accept "the inviolability of European borders" in light of the Moscow Treaty than had such an agreement failed to materialize. For Kremlin leaders, then, one of the most promising aspects of West Germany's new Eastern policy was that it could lead to a more general Western endorsement of the changes wrought by the events of 1945. For this to take place, it was essential that the exclusively bilateral nature of *Ostpolitik* be transformed into a multi-lateral process.

The vehicle which the Soviets selected to accomplish this goal was the Conference on Security and Cooperation in Europe. The overriding purpose of the CSCE, in Moscow's view, was to impart legitimacy to the German settlement.[9] To do so, the Soviet delegation sought Western support for a series of principles on which to base Europe's political relations. The most important of these principles was the inviolability (or what Moscow preferred to call the "the immutability") of the existing interstate borders. The Atlantic countries, in response to West German reservations on the issue, proposed that a provision be added to permit the nonviolent revision of frontiers. Although a similar clause had been included in the Soviet-West German treaty at Bonn's insistence, the Kremlin argued against such an amendment at the CSCE.

For almost two years the two sides were unable to devise a workable compromise because of their respective convictions that a matter of considerable importance was at stake. The issue was finally resolved by the incorporation of both provisions in the Final Act of the CSCE. Thus the "inviolability of frontiers" was enshrined as one of the cardinal principles of European security along with a clause allowing for the "peaceful revision" of international borders.

The confrontation over the question of frontiers was one of several serious disputes that arose between East and West at the all-European conference. The most disturbing development, from Moscow's vantage point, was the aggressive Western sponsorship of various human rights proposals. Yet in spite of these complications, the primary Soviet objective at the CSCE was realized. Thirty-five European countries, the United States, and Canada, in signing the Final Act, symbolically sanctioned the political and geographic consequences of World War II. No less significant, the Soviets now had sufficient confidence with regard to their position in Eastern Europe to undertake a larger and more sustained role in the affairs of Western Europe.

More recently, Soviet leaders have sought to bolster the Socialist regimes by promoting greater economic cooperation between the COMECON and Common Market countries on a bloc-to-bloc basis.[10] On one level, the Kremlin's interest in more extensive trade relations with the Western Europeans can be explained in national rather than international terms. Declining growth rates, difficulties in passing from "extensive" to "intensive" industrial development, and severe agricultural problems have plagued the planned economy of the Soviet Union in recent years; an influx of capital and technological expertise could help to alleviate these crises. Yet without diminishing the significance of this factor, Moscow also looks to the Common Market as a way to assist the troubled economies of Eastern Europe. By solving some of the region's most vexing problems, such as outdated production techniques, inefficient distribution systems, and the slow pace of modernization, the Communist governments would, presumably, improve their economic performance and, as a result, be in a better position to satisfy popular demands for a higher standard of living; this could, in turn, relieve domestic political pressures. As long as COMECON-EEC cooperation does not interfere with or unduly complicate the process of integration within the bloc, Moscow has reason to encourage the growth of closer commercial ties between the Socialist and capitalist countries of Europe.

The Soviets manifest their interest in greater cooperation both by promoting exploratory discussions between Common Market and COMECON officials (such meetings have, in fact, taken place regularly since 1975) and by asserting that the European Community, in and of itself, is a poor candidate for integration, lacking the requisite "socio-political homogeneity," "foreign-political solidarity" and "ideological compatability." They also contend that the increasing economic difficulties plaguing the EEC, especially acute in the wake of the 1973 Arab oil boycott, are a function of the "long cold war" which led to the unnatural division of Europe. As an alternative to this discriminatory arrangement, Soviet writers argue against self-imposed economic blocs and for the development of a more inclusive structure that would transcend ideological and political differences.[11]

The major drawback of stronger and more numerous East-West trade links, in the Soviet view, is that the Western countries might then be afforded a much better opportunity to "subvert" the Eastern European governments, both by exposing those societies to capitalist economic and political values and by revealing to them in a highly visible fashion their relative material deprivation. To guard against these twin dangers, Moscow is sure to seek maximum control over the pace, as well as the extent, of intersystemic cooperation.

Interestingly, the Soviets encountered a very similar problem at the CSCE. They were able to obtain Western endorsement of the European status quo only by pledging to support "the freer movement of peoples and ideas." It is as yet too early to judge which side paid the higher price. The critical question is whether Western confirmation of an existing political reality will turn out to have as great an impact on Europe's future as might a reduction in the Kremlin's ability to manage as effectively as in the past the rate and nature of change within the "Socialist commonwealth." It is hardly a coincidence that the most concerted Soviet drive for Warsaw Pact unity and solidarity in recent years occurred during the height of the debate over human rights at the European conference. Since the conclusion of the CSCE, the calls for vigilance have, if anything, become more frequent.[12]

Security in Western Europe

In a sense, détente has freed Soviet diplomacy in Europe from many of its traditional constraints. Standing guard over their empire in Eastern Europe, a task to which Kremlin leaders once assigned enormous political and military resources, no longer seems to require their undivided attention. With the ratification of the status quo in the East, the Soviets have begun in a pervasive and systematic way to make their presence known to the Western Europeans and to inject themselves into the politics of the region. Their policies toward the Atlantic countries retain many of their reactive characteristics but, in contrast to earlier periods, now display a strong element of activism. In particular, the leadership seems to have acquired in recent years a fairly clear conception of how it would like Western Europe to develop over the next decade; no less important, the Soviets have formulated and conducted policies in pursuit of these objectives that are creative, patient, and responsive to shifts in the international environment.

As an ideal, the Soviets would probably prefer a Western Europe detached from the American security guarantee and composed of politically independent and economically competitive states, governed by leftist parties sympathetic to Moscow. For the short term, however, they must base their policies on more modest and attainable goals. In this context, the most serious and enduring threat to Soviet interests in Europe is, once again, Atlanticism. Yet it is not simply the military component of the alliance that concerns Moscow, but the political and economic dimensions as well. Atlanticism, Kremlin spokesmen allege, provides the organizational and structural framework that enables the Western allies to orchestrate their foreign economic policies, that safeguards the extensive commercial and financial investments of the United States on the Continent, and that allows the governments in Washington, London, Paris, and Bonn to chart the course of non-Communist Europe's political development. Although it must inevitably decline in strength as the correlation of forces "shifts decisively in favor of socialism," the Atlantic partnership remains for Moscow the most potent expression of imperialism's determination to resist the expansion of Soviet power in the West.

Despite the numerous and obvious frictions that have emerged among the partners, the Kremlin seems reconciled to the continued existence of this capitalist community, at least for the foreseeable future. As such, the near-term Soviet objective is not to sever the Atlantic bonds, but to weaken them; not to dismantle the collective from without, but to encourage quietly and from afar disintegration from within. Soviet authorities might hope that, through such a process, Western Europe will suffer a kind of crisis of identity, a gradual erosion of self-confidence that will prompt the countries of the area to seek an "accommodation" with Moscow.

The Soviets are also disturbed by the tendency among the European capitalist states to move in the direction of greater integration. While their ultimate fear is of a British, French, and West German military consortium, they view with disfavor any action which might lead to the transformation of the region into an "intermediate power center." A Western European union, however limited or incomplete, would pose several dangers from Moscow's perspective. First, it could impart new vitality to the shaky structures of Atlanticism if the Europeans were to coordinate their efforts with the United States and if the Americans were to adjust their trade and economic policies to reward rather than penalize progress toward integration. Second, it would tend to accentuate the "closed" nature of the EEC and thus complicate Soviet plans to promote "all-European" cooperation. And third, it would enhance West German economic and therefore political weight within Western Europe which, in light of Bonn's intimate ties to Washington, the Kremlin could only regard with alarm. As Legvold has observed, the Soviet leadership wants "the Bonn-Paris-London triangle to be sufficiently strong to assert its independence from the United States, but sufficiently divided to prevent it from overcoming the 'contradictions' of integration. And they do not want a single power to dominate the Community, let alone bring it back to partnership with the United States.[13]

Moscow has pursued three distinct strategies in order to undercut Atlantic cohesion and to deflect the impulse toward integration. The first and perhaps most important has been the fostering of close bilateral relations with three of the largest countries in the area—France, the Federal Republic, and more recently, Italy. It has been the Kremlin's intention to turn bilateralism into a permanent feature of the European political landscape. The Soviets have concentrated, in particular, on cultivating long-term economic commitments (through trade agreements and joint commercial ventures such as the Fiat automobile plant in the Ukraine) and on making high-level consultations a regular and familiar practice (witness Brezhnev's meetings with Pompidou in January 1973 and Giscard d'Estaing in June 1977, and the general secretary's visit to the Federal Republic in May 1973). Clearly, they see this as a vehicle for keeping abreast of trends in Western Europe and for conveying their views to and influencing the policy decisions of the French, West German, and Italian governments. On balance, the Soviets seem satisfied with the accomplishments of the bilateral approach and they consistently emphasize its contribution to East-West détente. The notable exception has been the United Kingdom; Moscow's relations with London have been neither as cordial as those with Paris nor as commercially rewarding as those with Bonn.

The Kremlin has also revealed its opposition to Western European integration through its EEC policy. While they have come to accept the EEC as an unpleasant reality and have even sponsored preliminary contacts between the Nine and their East European counterparts, the Soviets would probably prefer that the developmental process within the Community be arrested or, if possible, reversed. Thus they continue to negotiate exclusively bilateral trade arrangements with the Western European countries, effectively ignoring the Common Market as an economic entity. They also remind the member states, in an uninterrupted flow of articles and analyses, that the institutions of the EEC cannot ensure the political stability and economic growth of the region. Finally, they are extremely sensitive to any enlargement of the Community; following the entry of the United Kingdom, Denmark, and Ireland in 1973, the Kremlin reacted negatively, claiming that the architects of the merger were attempting to unite the whole of capitalist Europe into a single imperialist federation. The difficulties that the Nine have encountered in devising a common agricultural policy and in achieving significant movement toward a monetary union would seem to indicate that Moscow's anxieties are largely unfounded. Nonetheless, the Soviet campaign against the Common Market remains an important part of their diplomacy.

A third way in which the Kremlin has sought to undermine the Atlantic connection and to hamper integration is by advocating the dissolution of NATO and the Warsaw Pact. As a substitute the Soviets urge the creation of a pan-European security system. While a Europe without blocs has been a recurring theme of Moscow's foreign policy since the 1950s, it was not until the advent of détente that the concept became something more than a rhetorical device by which the Socialist countries communicated their hostility to NATO and to Western "militarism." With the easing of cold war tensions and more specifically with the convocation of the CSCE, the Soviets seemed to detect for the first time a certain receptivity to the idea among "progressive circles" in the capitalist countries of the Continent.

In the absence of the two alliances, tranquility would be assured through collective security. At the outset, peace would be preserved by the "universal and compulsory implementation of definite principles of relations between states," such as those adoptèd in Helsinki, including the nonuse of force, respect for territorial integrity, and the inviolability of interstate borders.[14] In the second phase, the European countries would jointly issue "material guarantees" that would "rule out the very possibility of arms being used by an aggressor."[15] *Izvestiya* in July 1973 asserted that these guarantees would "protect" states from aggression though the article did not explain how, nor did it suggest what kinds of mechanisms might be required both to enforce the peace and, if necessary, to punish a transgressor.[16]

Just as the Soviets do not expect the EEC to collapse as a consequence of their opposition to the organization, they do not anticipate the break-up of NATO through their sponsorship of an "all-European" security system. Moscow's objectives in both cases are to advance alternatives to the existing relationships and to generate support within the West for their acceptance. In this regard, it is interesting to note that the Soviets explain their participation in the MFR negotiations not only in terms of reducing the probabilities of a violent conflict in Central Europe but also in terms of facilitating the transition from a security arrangement based on bipolarity to one founded on multilateral assurances. They see the Vienna talks, then, as having the potential to weaken NATO over a period of years by rallying popular sentiment against the notion of blocs. Western European electorates which do not sense an overarching military threat from the East are less likely to elect political representatives who describe the preservation of the Atlantic alliance as a central thrust of their foreign policy than they are those who focus on other issues.

What emerges from this survey of Soviet attitudes toward the political aspects of the security problem in Europe is that although Kremlin leaders have no great affection for the institutions of Atlanticism, including the Common Market, their aim is not so much to destroy those institutions by force of arms as it is to transform them beyond recognition, both by encouraging changes which they would define as advantageous and by the subtle application of pressure at vulnerable points and at opportune moments. At this level of abstraction, Soviet goals appear precise and fully coordinated; in practice, the leadership undoubtedly reacts to developments pragmatically, without reference to a "grand design" if, in truth, such a schematic exists at all. In any event, Moscow can only hope to influence political decision-making in Western Europe in a rather general way. Because of this, it seems prudent to argue that the degree to which the Soviets succeed in realizing their objectives will be less a function of what policies they adopt than of how the United States and its allies respond to a host of challenges currently confronting them—internal, as well as external.

A Changing Calculus

Beyond the more visible military and political dimensions, there is a third aspect to the problem of security in Europe that is of obvious and immediate concern to the Soviet leadership. As events from Portugal to Greece to Norway have demonstrated, the countries of Western Europe are in the midst of a process of fundamental political, economic, and social change. While the crises that have plagued the Atlantic and Mediterranean states over the last decade—the decline of confidence in existing governments, the twin phenomena of inflation and economic stagnation, the rise of racial, ethnic, and subnational tensions, and an increasingly polarized political environment—have been largely internal rather than external in origin, the Kremlin is keenly sensitive to the fact that domestic factors have a profound impact on the direction and content of a country's foreign policies. Consequently, Moscow recognizes that the changes which take place within Western European societies will necessarily and directly effect the interests of the Soviet Union and the Socialist community. For the Kremlin then, what transpires in France or Italy or Spain within the next several years is not merely an absorbing, if largely academic, question, but a matter of considerable practical significance as well.

Moscow and the Problem of Change in Europe

As the Soviets look toward Western Europe, they see four relatively distinct regions where change of some magnitude is either imminent or already underway. To the north, Moscow's relations with the Scandinavian countries have grown less peripheral and more complex than at any point in the recent past. Politically, the area seems to have undergone a moderate shift to the right, as evidenced by the election in Sweden of a "conservative" government in 1976, the first time the Left Social Democrats have been out of power in that country since before the Second World War. In Finland, the small but influential Communist party, while it retains several ministerial posts, finds itself increasingly at odds with the ruling Center-Left coalition of which it is a part. Economically, the seas contiguous to Northern Europe have become progressively more important to the Soviet Union over the last ten years. With the discovery of major oil reserves in the North Sea and with the possibility that other, equally rich petroleum and natural gas deposits might be found in the Barents Sea off the North Cape and the Kola peninsula, the Kremlin's relations with Norway, already complicated by the persistent problem of fishing rights, have entered a new and delicate phase.

Yet, more than other single factor, it is the military significance of Northern Europe that accounts for Moscow's deep and abiding interest in the area. The Northern Fleet of the Soviet Union, with 180 submarines (ninety of them nuclear powered), nine cruisers, fifty-five destroyers, and over 200 smaller vessels, is entirely dependent on the 400 mile gap between Spitzbergen and the Scandinavian mainland for egress into the Atlantic Ocean. The Soviets have watched with alarm as NATO, responding to a perceived threat, has stepped up the level and sophistication of its aerial and electronic surveillance of the region over the last several years. For Moscow, guaranteed passage out of Arctic waters is a critical issue, essential not only for defensive purposes (narrowly defined) but also for the effective projection of naval and air power far beyond the territorial boundaries of the Soviet state. Because of this, the Kremlin closely monitors, and is harshly critical of, any Western efforts to redress the military balance, or imbalance, along the northern flank.[17]

In Southeastern Europe, change along two fronts, in one case actual and in the other case probable, directly affects Soviet interests on the Continent. While the Soviets have not sought in an overt sense to exploit the virtual collapse of NATO's southern flank, they, rather than the antagonists, have been the principal victors in the intermittent conflict between the two ancient adversaries. As the Americans have become less popular, the Kremlin has attempted to increase its leverage in the region by improving relations both with the left-leaning regime in Greece and with the traditionally Russophobic Turks. To date, Moscow's diplomatic campaign has met with only limited success.

Although the Soviets are clearly concerned with developments in Greece and Turkey, it is Yugoslavia, and in particular Yugoslavia after Tito's exit, that preoccupies them as they survey conditions and trends in contemporary Southeastern Europe. Given a choice, Moscow would probably prefer a unified Yugoslav state, fully integrated into the Socialist community with membership in the Warsaw Pact and CMEA. Failing that, it is difficult to gauge with any degree of accuracy what the Soviets would regard as the most acceptable alternative. They might, for example, look favorably on the break-up of the south Slavic federation; they might, in fact, support such a dissolution by assisting the various movements for national autonomy. They could then seek to establish a client-patron relationship with one or more of the emerging republics on the assumption that the victory of a pro-Soviet faction in Serbia or Slovenia would better serve the cause of socialism than the preservation of the status quo. Were Tito's successors to jettison outright the policy of nonalignment and attempt to lead Yugoslavia into the Western camp, the Kremlin would no doubt seek by every means at its disposal, up to and perhaps including the use of force, to forestall such a shift. In such a situation, it seems likely that a major East-West confrontation would ensue.[18] To avert a Balkan crisis of significant proportions, it is in Moscow's interest to maintain the best of relations with Belgrade by promoting the extension of political and economic ties, by lobbying for the creation of new ones, and by avoiding any action, military or otherwise, that might prompt the Yugoslavs to turn to the Americans to safeguard their independence and national integrity. In short, as the Soviets reach out to embrace their renegrade Communist brothers, they must be careful not to crack any ribs in the process.

With regard to the Iberian peninsula, the central problem facing Soviet policymakers, as in the case of Yugoslavia, is how to influence political developments during a period of transition. The differences between the two situations are, however, more compelling than the similarities. As a measure of last resort, the Kremlin could convey to Belgrade its intention to intervene militarily. Moscow would then have the option of translating words into actions or of using the threat of invasion to extract concessions. Whatever the decision, the threat would be a credible one. Only under extraordinary conditions, similar to those which existed during the 1936-39 civil war, might the Soviets be seriously tempted to commit significant quantities of material aid, not to mention manpower, to assist "antifascist" forces in Spain. The same would apply for Portugal. In light of the security agreement between Washington and Madrid and Portugal's membership in NATO, a large-scale intervention in the region following a prolonged internal crisis would seem to be a less than viable option for Soviet decision-makers, assuming for the moment they possessed the will and had at their disposal the requisite capabilities.

In Italy and France, Soviet authorities have reason both to welcome and to fear the coming to power of the Communist parties. On the positive side, their election would signify a dramatic defeat for the forces of "Atlanticism." A Socialist Italy or France would, it seems safe to assume, pursue policies more comforting to Moscow than to Washington. Even if both countries were to retain their formal membership in NATO, the presence of Communists in sensitive governmental posts would inevitably undermine the political cohesion and thus the military effectiveness of the Western alliance. It is difficult to imagine how NATO could continue to function as a credible anti-Communist as well as an anti-Soviet alliance with the PCI in power, although it could, in all probability, survive the eventual election of a Socialist and Communist regime in France.

Yet the equation is hardly that simple. For the Kremlin, Italian and French Communists in positions of national leadership might prove more disturbing than reassuring. Because of their campaigns to chart a course independent of Moscow, an electoral success for the PCI or the PCF would be widely interpreted as a victory for "national" communism rather than a triumph for the Soviet Union, acting in its capacity as the self anointed leader of the world's revolutionary and progressive forces. Such a development would tend to accentuate existing polycentric tendencies and to reinforce the legitimacy of the concept of "different roads to socialism," a view first enunciated by the Yugoslavs. The effect would be to undercut further the CPSU's claim to exalted status within the international Communist movement. Even more troubling from the Kremlin's vantage point, Marxist-Leninists sharing power with bourgeois elements in the West would offer a stark contrast to the monopolist practices of the Workers' and Peasants' parties in Eastern Europe. Communism shorn of its repressive character, in other words "socialism with a human face," could exert a strong and, in the Soviet view, dangerous influence on political thought and behavior in the various Peoples' Republics.

What this survey suggests is that Soviet leaders are probably as concerned with the rise of the Left and what that portends as they are with any other single issue in contemporary Western Europe. How the Kremlin will respond to events in Northern Europe, in Yugoslavia, and on the Iberian peninsula will be determined in part by the political success or failure of the largest and most powerful of the region's Communist parties. For this reason, it is impossible to gain an accurate understanding of how the Soviets perceive the problem of security in Europe without a careful examination of their attitude toward phenomenon—later examined by Kevin Devlin—of Eurocommunism.

The recent debate over the utility of the concept *dictatorship of the proletariat* epitomizes in a sense the growing tension between Moscow and the Eurocommunists. The phrase was originally a Soviet one and refers to the retention of supreme political power by a Communist party even after the creation of a genuine "workers state." By the early 1960s, the PCI had quietly dropped the slogan from all party documents and speeches, on the apparent assumption that the work "dictatorship" had an excessively authoritarian ring that was likely to alienate more voters than it would attract. The formulation also seemed inappropriate in light of the fact that the Italian Communists had long argued for a sharing of political power *beyond* the bourgeois-democratic phase of the revolution. To resolve the dilemma and to enhance its "democratic" credentials, the *dictatorship of the proletariat* disappeared from the PCI's lexicon.

For similar reasons, the Central Committee of the French party voted to excise the term from its vocabulary in early February 1976, citing its lack of utility as an intellectual tool and its inapplicability to the class structure of the PCF. Coming from the party that had once been the most Stalinist in Western Europe, the decision seemed to stun Moscow momentarily. In response, the Soviet press released a spate of articles and speeches that defended the concept as a central tenet of Marxism-Leninism, with undiminished relevance for Communists everywhere.

The conflict between the Kremlin and the Eurocommunist parties moved into the open shortly after the French action during the twenty-fifth CPSU Congress in late February 1976. Several West European party leaders, including Marchais and Spain's Santiago Carrillo, chose not to attend the conference. The PCI's Berlinguer did journey to Moscow but, in a speech the Soviets sought without notable success to censor, strongly affirmed the right of all Communist states and parties to pursue "different paths to socialism," free from foreign interference. The Kremlin was quick to react. In his remarks to the Congress, Brezhnev subtly disavowed the rationale for "national" communism by underlining the universal nature of the ideology and by stressing the transcendent importance of *proletarian internationalism*. The CPSU general secretary said in part:

> From our viewpoint, the renunciation of proletarian internationalism would mean depriving the Communist Parties and workers' movements in general of a powerful and tested weapon. This would also do a good turn for the class enemy, which, by the way, is actively coordinating its anti-communist actions on an international scale. We Soviet Communists consider the defense of proletarian internationalism the sacred duty of every Marxist-Leninist.[19]

Brezhnev went on to state that compromises on matters of "principle" were inadmissible as "both right-wing and far left revisionism are by no means inactive and because the struggle for the Marxist-Leninist foundations of the Communist movement and against attempts to distort or undermine them remain the common task of everyone."[20] Unmistakably, Berlinguer had struck a sensitive chord in his address, the implications of which were not lost on his hosts and which they hastened to rebut.

The polite sparring between Berlinguer and Brezhnev at the CPSU Congress proved to be only a foretaste of things to come. The more dramatic, if still muted, confrontation between the "loyalists" and the "autonomists" occurred before and during the June 1976 conference of European Communist parties held in East Berlin. The meeting, first proposed in October 1974, was conceived by the Soviets as a vehicle to arrest the various heretical trends then in evidence and as a first step toward the convocation of a World Party Congress. By obtaining a general confirmation of their position as the first among equals, the Soviets expected the conference to strengthen their hand not only in terms of the European parties but also in dealings with the Chinese. The Eurocommunists, who at first resisted the call, agreed to the meeting on the condition that it take place on the basis of full equality; namely, that Moscow be accorded no special status. When the representatives of twenty-nine European Communist parties finally met in Berlin on June 29, Soviet leaders must have seriously questioned whether the benefits to be gained would be commensurate with the enormous effort involved in planning and executing the conference.

Their anxieties were well founded. The wording of the declaration was a significant victory for the Eurocommunists. As Devlin has noted elsewhere, "It was a lowest common denominator text based on the new principle of consensus, itself a formal recognition of the equality and autonomy of all Communist parties; it contained no criticism of the Chinese and no praise for the Soviets; it dealt with political action and not with ideology; and it was not binding upon the participants (in fact, it was not even signed by any of them)."[21]

One of the most striking features of the declaration was the absence of the phrase *proletarian internationalism*. Europe's Communists merely pledged themselves to "comradely and *voluntary* cooperation" while "strongly adhering to the principles of equality and the sovereign independence of each party, non-interference in internal affairs and respect for their free choice of different roads in the struggle for social change . . . and for socialism.[11]

As discomforting to Moscow as the declaration itself were the remarks made by several prominent West European Communists both during and immediately after the conference. From Madrid, the PCE rejected the contention that the CPSU enjoyed any extraordinary rights or privileges vis-à-vis fraternal parties in Spain, Italy, France, or elsewhere. Berlinguer reasserted the PCI's conviction that the construction of Socialist societies in the West must of necessity be founded on "the principles of the secular, non-ideological nature of the state and its democratic organization; the plurality of political parties and the possibility of the alteration of government majorities; the autonomy of trade unions; religious freedom; freedom of expression, of culture, and of the arts and sciences." Marchais declared, in a comment that was unlikely to have won him any additional friends in Moscow, that "conferences like this one do not appear to us [the PCF] to correspond any longer to the needs of our time." He also stated that henceforth any elaboration of a "common strategy" among Communist parties was "absolutely ruled out."[22]

For Communists in the West, the link to Moscow is a link to their own past. Their legitimacy as "revolutionaries," as *bone fide* Marxist-Leninists derives in part from their ties to the "Fatherland of Socialism." To break irrevocably with the Kremlin would deprive them of their uniqueness. While younger party members might welcome the decision, the "antifascist" veterans of the 1930s and 1940s might resist it as a betrayal of principle—the adoption of social reform as a goal, rather than social revolution. Were the Eurocommunists to reject Moscow and abandon their Marxist-Leninist philosophy, they would run the risk of becoming ideological eunuchs or, at a minimum, indistinguishable from their ancient rivals, the Social Democrats. Their popular appeal—as a viable alternative to the "reformism" and "trade-unionism" offered by the Socialists—would be seriously eroded.

On a more practical level, once the connection had been severed, the Eurocommunists could no longer look to the Soviet Union as a source of aid and comfort in the ongoing struggle against imperialist reaction. The financial assistance rendered the PCI and the PCF by the CPSU, through import-export operations, "joint" commercial ventures between capitalist entrepreneurs and Soviet agencies, and "laundered" campaign contributions (originating in Moscow but dispersed locally by Italian and French nationals) would almost certainly come to an end. Deprived of a major source of income, the West European Communist parties might find it much more difficult to compete with conservative and Rightist forces. Reduced funding might also mean reduced media access to the voting public and a less potent political organization; one consequence could be fewer electoral victories and thus a diminished power base from which to challenge the capitalist "ruling circles." While the Soviets may not be the most desirable of allies, the West European parties may well feel that Moscow's support is too valuable to sacrifice without a readily available substitute.

For the Kremlin, too, the advantages of preserving the bond currently outweigh the disadvantages. A public rupture with the PCI, the PCF, and the PCE, when added to the defection of the Chinese, the Yugoslavs, and the Albanians, would leave the Soviet leadership in a situation not unlike that which confronted the Vatican during the Reformation: that of an aging, cautious, and inflexible oligarchy attempting without notable success to reestablish ideological conformity in a world run rife with schismatics, heretics, and infidels. More concretely, the Eurocommunists represent for Moscow a vehicle to influence, though not determine, political developments in Western Europe. Whatever level of anti-American and anti-German sentiment presently exists on the Continent is in part a result of the enhanced visibility and respectability of the PCI and the PCF. In the last decade, Communists have enjoyed considerable success in mobilizing popular discontent in West Europe; they have provided an organizational and theoretical focus to the campaigns against "monopoly capital," "bourgeois oppression," and "American hegemony." Whatever the inspiration for these assaults, the Soviets, perhaps to an even greater extent than the Eurocommunists, have benefited from these tactics. Quite obviously, a Western Europe, rent by class antagonism and afflicted with serious psychological, sociological, political, and economics ills, poses a less formidable challenge to the Soviet Union than a more self-assured and vital community of states.

Finally in this context, what undoubtedly saves the Eurocommunists from more direct and pointed Soviet criticism is their enduring attachment to the concept of "democratic centralism" as the sole method of intraparty decision-making. Despite the "liberalization" of the PCI and the PCF, both parties remain faithful to the traditional Leninist notion of decision by consensus with no allowance for subsequent dissent. Although Berlinguer and Marchais constantly reaffirm their respect for pluralism and the mechanics of "bourgeois democracy," so far they have been unwilling to permit any significant democratization of their respective political organizations. When, for instance, the PCF voted to abandon the phrase "dictatorship of the proletariat" in 1976, the vote of the Central Committee was a disturbing 1,700 to 0.

The rigid discipline imposed on the members of the PCI and the PCF is precisely the characteristic of those parties which most pleases and reassures the CPSU; conversely, it is also the feature which most unnerves the democratic parties in the West. As long as the three most powerful European Communist parties evidence virtually no inclination to de-Stalinize from within, their capacity to act as guardians of both individual and institutional freedoms in Italy, France, and Spain must remain suspect. It is this intolerance for dissent which, more than any other factor, raises serious and alarming questions about the "transformation" of Western European communism.

Because both sides have more to gain than to lose by maintaining at least the facade of unity, it is improbable (which is not to say impossible) that the debate will erupt into an open confrontation. Moscow seems prepared for the time being to tolerate the numerous and frequent deviations of the Eurocommunists; the alternative is to force a showdown that could easily result in a complete breach of interparty relations. As long as the Eurocommunists do not adopt blatantly "anti-Soviet" positions and policies, and as long as the rise of the Left does not precipitate a violent Western reaction, Kremlin leaders have reason to encourage their unorthodox brethren in their pursuit of political power. How much assistance the Soviets may be willing to provide their fellow Marxist-Leninists as they carry on their struggle is a separate issue.

Prognosis

Clearly, the obstacles that confront Soviet decision-makers as they attempt to translate their conception of a "pacific" Europe from vision to reality are formidable. This suggests, in turn, that for the Kremlin the achievement of something approaching "absolute" security is an unreachable goal, as it is for virtually all countries that share frontiers with states whose national interests do not coincide with their own. Barring the sudden departure of the United States from Europe, the political and economic collapse of the NATO countries, and the triumph of orthodoxy over heresy within the Eurocommunist parties, the Soviets must coexist in an environment where their power is far from unlimited and where their ability to realize their objectives falls short of the optimal. Consequently, Moscow seeks relative advantages and imperfect solutions in its struggle against Atlanticism and the forces of reaction.

Soviet policies in Europe reflect these constraints. Policies have been carefully conceived and pursued, for the most part, with patience and flexibility. Moscow seems fully sensitive to the fact that more assertive behavior, while yielding perhaps a temporary advantage, could lead to a costly, if not cataclysmic, confrontation between the two world systems. Yet after a decade of détente and a tangible amelioration of tension on the Continent, Western Europe and the Soviet Union and will remain, in all probability, locked in a basically adversarial relationship. Thus mutual insecurities and a largely implicit form of instability seem destined to persist.

Notes

1. United States Arms Control and Disarmament Agency, *Selected Background Documents Relating to Mutual and Balanced Force Reductions,* Disarmament Document Series Reference No. 611, 1973, "Declaration on European Security by the Political Consultative Committee of the Warsaw Pact States, July 6, 1966," p. 4 (hereafter cited as *ACDA I*).

2. *ACDA I,* p. 11.

3. D. Proektor, "Evropeskaya Bezopastnost: Nekotoriye Problemi," *Mirovaya ekonomika i mezhdunarodniye otnosheniya,* Number 9, September 1973, pp. 87-98.

4. The EDC, a plan authored in Washington and Paris for the unification of the French, German, and Benelux armed forces, was ultimately

vetoed in 1954 by the French National Assembly after a tortured eighteen-month gestation period. The Soviets greeted its passing with relief.

5. Several of the Western European specialists in the Soviet Union have argued that the "Atlanticists" have as one of their paramount goals the acceleration of regional military integration, which might then provide the Community with a substantial defensive capability. See V. Cherkasov, " 'Six' and 'Four' Make 'Ten,' " *International Affairs,* Number 4, April 1972, p. 89-90; and M. Mikhaylov, "A Peace Code for Europe," *Izvestiya,* January 17, 1974, p. 5; see also Nikolai Kononov, commentary, "Intensify the Struggle against the Intrigues of the Opponents of Detente," February 10, 1974 (*FBIS,* "Soviet Union," February 11, 1974, p. A7).

6. Robert Levgold, "The Soviet Union and Western Europe," from *The Soviet Empire: Expansion and Detente,* Wm. E. Griffith, ed., Lexington, Mass.: Lexington Books, D.C. Heath, 1976, p. 238.

7. Press and Information Office of the [German] Federal Republic, *The Treaty Governing Principles of Relations between the Federal Republic of Germany and the German Democratic Republic,* Bonn, 1973.

8. See V. Rostovtsev, "USSR-FRG: Developing Relations," *International Affairs,* July 1974, p. 46.

9. Although the United States had extended formal diplomatic recognition to the German Democratic Republic in September 1974, as had the United Kingdom and France several months earlier, the Soviets were eager to confirm the existence of two German states, and the legitimacy of their respective frontiers, multilaterally, through the auspices of the all-European security conference.

10. The Soviet Union's strong preference for bloc-to-bloc negotiations between the EEC and COMECON is an obvious reflection of the Kremlin's fears concerning the ability of the Western countries to hamper the integrative process within Eastern Europe. If Poland, for example, were to develop close economic relations with the Common Market, Warsaw would be less inclined and perhaps less able to seek cooperative ventures with the other Socialist states, including the Soviet Union. As a consequence, the Soviets might lose a degree of leverage over the Poles, as Warsaw grew less dependent on Moscow for both short-term and longer-term economic assistance.

11. Cherkasov, " 'Six' and 'Four' Makes 'Ten,' " *International Affairs,* April 1972, p. 90.

12. See, for example, "Speech by Comrade L.I. Brezhnev at the Seventh Congress of the Polish United Workers' Party," *Pravda,* December 10, 1975, pp. 1-2.

13. Levgold, *The Soviet Empire: Expansion and Détente,* p. 238.

14. Fedorenko and Yermachenkov, "For Peace and Security in Europe," *Soviet Military Review,* January 1973, p. 61.

15. Ibid.

16. A. Grigoryants and M. Zubko, "A Forum for All Europe," *Izvestiya,* July 3, 1973, p. 1.

17. Soviet ground, air, and naval forces stationed in and around Murmansk have been described as the heaviest concentration of conventional military power anywhere in the world. By comparison, NATO's northern flank is lightly defended. See John Erickson, "The Northern Theater: Soviet Capabilities and Concepts," *Strategic Review* IV (September 1976):67-82.

18. See William Zimmerman, "The Tito Legacy and Yugoslavia's Future," *Problems of Communism* XXVI (May-June 1977):33-49, for an interesting analysis of what might take place in that Balkan country, both internally and externally, after Tito's death.

19. Speech by Leonid Brezhnev at the 25th CPSU Congress, "The Report to the CPSU Central Committee and the Party's Immediate Tasks in the Fields of Domestic and Foreign Policy," *Pravda,* February 25, 1976, pp. 2-9 (*Current Digest of the Soviet Press,* XXVIII [March 24, 1976]:1.

20. Ibid, p. 13.

21. Devlin, "The Challenge of Eurocommunism," *Problems of Communism* XXVI (January-February 1977):15.

22. Devlin, "The Challenge of Eurocommunism," p. 16.

8

Security, Change, and Instability in Eastern Europe

N. Edwina Moreton

Eastern Europe today, as in the past, presents a complex and at times contradictory picture to the outside world. Time and again events in the region have confounded attempts to predict its future evolution, so that the parameters of change within the Warsaw alliance could only be defined in retrospect and then only in the negative sense of what had ultimately gone beyond the bounds of Soviet toleration.

Over the past few years the contradictions which seem to characterize the political development of Eastern Europe have again come under scrutiny as the two halves of Europe, and in particular the two superpowers, the Soviet Union and the United States, have buried a sufficient number of their differences at least to review the possibilities for increased economic, political, cultural, and even military cooperation. Yet in many ways a degree of confusion and uncertainty extends even to this European security process itself. In the wake of the Helsinki conference of 1975 and the 1977 Belgrade follow-up conference, it is clear that the motives and expectations of several of the major participants have undergone radical change.

The impact of these negotiations on Eastern Europe has been contrary to that initially expected by both superpowers. Rather than promoting a degree of internal flexibility in the East, the wave of dissent throughout Eastern Europe over the past four years has had precisely the opposite effect. The ruling regimes have responded by reinforcing the trend toward ideological consolidation and integration. This response has been adopted even by those regimes, such as Romania, which in the past have shown signs of dissatisfaction with Soviet attempts to encourage or impose greater discipline and control.[1]

There are other issues which have likewise become prominent in recent years and which might be expected to have some impact on the pattern of relations within the East European alliance. Indeed, the present picture of the region is one of ferment. A combination of international developments suggests a pattern of change on a scale and at a pace perhaps not seen in the past. Among these developments are: an apparent transformation in the political climate in Western Europe; problems of domestic dissent; economic difficulties in the wake of recession in the West; the increasing scarcity and high price of raw materials, particularly energy supplies; and

163

the challenge to the Soviet model of economic, social, and political development posed by Eurocommunist heresies.

Yet, although CSCE focused public attention on these developments and to that made a contribution to the process itself, the Conference did not create any of these issues. The issues all have their roots in earlier history and are not hard to trace. The difficulty lies once again in trying to assess implications for future security, change, and stability in Eastern Europe. Thus, one of the central questions which must be addressed is this: Is the current process of European security irrelevant to the political future of Eastern Europe? The obverse question is also of direct concern: namely, What impact might the political development of the Warsaw alliance have on the future security of Europe?

Answers to both these questions must take into account not only the assumptions behind the evolving concepts of security in the region, but they must also take a critical look at previous assumptions concerning the nature of relations between the East European states and the Soviet Union, in terms of both formal and informal alliance mechanisms. The point to be made is that these constraints should be seen to operate at several different levels, with varying consequences at each.

Against this background some attempt can be made to assess the present implications and future consequences for Eastern Europe of current economic, military, and political developments in the region and hence understand the complex relationship between developments in the wider European context and the political development of the East European alliance.

The Concept of Security

It is generally recognized that a security problem exists in Europe—and has existed throughout the postwar period. However, outside the narrower definitions of the physical security of the two opposing military alliances, NATO and the Warsaw Pact, there is considerably less clarity concerning the broader concept of security and its relationship to the political future of Europe.

In fact, the absence of any clear concept of security, beyond the mere absence of war, is the essence of the current problem and derives from the inability of the four major wartime allies to come to a common understanding of what would constitute an acceptable state of security for the Continent in the period immediately following the Second World War. Inevitably, in the zero-sum power game that resulted, the interests of individual states were for many years so closely identified with and subordinated to those of their protective alliance leader as to be virtually indistinguishable.

In recent years, particularly in the wake of the more organized détente between East and West (the treaties between West Germany and the Soviet Union, Poland and East Germany the Four Power Berlin Agreement, SALT, CSCE, MBFR), the concept of security in Europe has taken on a far broader aspect than the term's accustomed usage of previous decades. As the sights of both sides have been raised from their previously exclusive focus on the continental as well as global military-strategic balance, it has become clear that the present and future security of Europe is inextricably bound up with such problems as trade, technology transfer, energy dependency, and inflation. Although it might be assumed that the more ties created between East and West in Europe the greater the stake of both in the political future of the process, paradoxically the long-term political implications of current policies are being deliberately side-stepped. The result is that Europe seems to be becoming an area of lesser, rather than greater concern to Western governments, the Carter administration's public posture on the issue of human rights notwithstanding.

There are several reasons why the East European component of the current process of European security and détente no longer seems as vital. To a considerable extent, the relocation of emphasis by the two superpowers, away from potential political conflict and toward more pragmatic problems of trade and economic cooperation reflects a declining interest in considering political alternatives to the present configuration of states in Europe.[2]

Secondly, despite the increased publicity given in the West to dissident movements in the Soviet Union and Eastern Europe, it is apparent that the current level of interchange—both economic and political—at the interstate level has been achieved on the basis of a recognition of and commitment to the status quo, as defined by the two superpowers. Currently, as in the past, Western policy toward the states of Eastern Europe is a function of this superpower relationship in Europe.

Thirdly, the very concept of an organized détente has at least deemphasized the traditional concerns of European security, namely the ambiguous future of Berlin and the so-called West German threat—whether political, psychological, physical, or mythical—to the status and security of East Germany and the postwar boundaries in Europe. These had all originally been considered agents of bloc cohesion in both alliance systems and, if nothing else, had maintained the focus clearly on what divided the two halves of Europe. The implicit assumption behind the Helsinki process that the political status quo will remain or can be forced to remain static imputes a degree of certainty to the future which would seem at least premature. Indeed, as the wave of dissent in Eastern Europe increased during 1976 and most of 1977, it became clear that, in the context of a divided Europe, even limited agreement on the status quo could unleash a potentially disruptive internal dynamic of its own.

The role of the Warsaw Pact in the affairs of Europe is changing in response to the changing relationship between the individual East European states and their Soviet sponsor. The more dramatic upheavals in Eastern Europe have always been followed closely by observers in the West but little credit has been given to the possibility of more subtle, but potentially equally momentous, changes at work within the Pact. In the complex of interdependencies being established in the bilateral and multilateral relationships which characterize present-day Europe, any changes taking place in Eastern Europe are likely to have more direct impact than in the past on the conduct of East-West relations. Furthermore, the doctrine of "peaceful coexistence" proclaimed by the Soviet Union and its Warsaw Pact allies implies the greater involvement of these latter in the political future of Western Europe.[3] These factors, combined with the growing phenomenon of Eurocommunism, would seem to argue against the maintenance of a static East-West balance. These uncertainties make the Warsaw alliance deserving of continued focus—and not simply as an adjunct to Soviet power in Europe.

Problems of Analysis

It is impossible to overlook two major parameters to change in Eastern Europe. First, Soviet military, economic, and political power of course far outweighs that of the rest of Eastern Europe. This asymmetry of power within the Eastern alliance is reflected in its persistent, though modified, hierarchical structure and the inequality which has characterized relations between the Soviet Union and its allies.[4] At various times this relationship has resulted in a threat to and transgression of the physical security of the respective East European states.

A second distinction must also be made—that between physical security, which may be threatened from either East or West, and regime security, which for present purposes may be summed up in the distinction between the common interests of ruling elites in the Warsaw Pact states and the various aspirations of the East European populations.

Security in the East European context has always been an ambigous concept. The failure or reluctance to differentiate between these various facets of security is reflected in the failure to appreciate the complexity of the triangular, and at times contradictory, relationship between the East European regimes, the Soviet Union, and the West. Hence the apparent difficulties experienced in the past by Western governments in formulating coherent policies toward the region.[5]

Perhaps inevitably, given the origins of the division of Europe, the anchor point of all assumptions about and policies toward Eastern Europe has been the role assigned to ideology. As the hostile confrontation of the 1950s gave way in the 1960s to a hesitant, if more pragmatic, pursuit of détente by the two superpowers, possibilities were seen for overcoming the political division of Europe:

> In Europe, politics and economics conspire against the communist ideology and portend the erosion of its universalistic perspectives. European politics reflect the renewed vitality of nation-states; European economics underline the ideological neutrality of the technological revolution. They present opportunities for the lifting of the social and cultural Iron Curtain by the use of enlightened trade policies. The gradual subordination of ideological to domestic considerations may still leave paramount the political and power factors that caused the partition of Europe. But the erosion may gradually open the way to dealing with these political factors on their own terms, unaffected by the emotional and absolutizing consequences of ideological dogmas.

The passage cited above, though written in the early 1960s, would hardly seem out of context fifteen years later.

It is never entirely clear what were the nature of the state interests that were to emerge as the wave of ideology ebbed. Implicit in the model, however, is the assumption that the term ''national'' in Eastern Europe is necessarily synonymous with ''anti-Soviet'' and therefore by definition more attuned to Western ''democratic'' traditions. Translated into practice, it seemed to be assumed that a threshold existed in East-West contacts in Europe, which, if triggered, could induce a particular regime to move away from the Soviet orbit and toward the West.

It now seems clear that the fundamental premise of the erosion of ideology and concomitant assertion of (more acceptable) state interests has proven false. Whether the ideological community of interest which can bind together such apparently diverse regimes as Romania, East Germany, Poland, Hungary, Bulgaria, and Czechoslovakia is thought to be based on a ''self-interest rooted in weakness''[7] or a more positive awareness of common ideological outlook and interests, the events of the last decade would seem to suggest that there is more to the cohesion of the Warsaw alliance than simply the ultimate reality of Soviet power.

The unclear relationship between nationalism and communism is partly attributable to the growth away from the overtly ''satellite'' status of the Stalin era and toward the political diversity and uncertainty which has characterized the past decade in East European—Soviet relations. The invasion of Czechoslovakia notwithstanding, since the mid-1960s there have been numerous signs of a growing interdependence between the Soviet Union and its allies, despite the obvious and continuing inequality of power within the alliance.[8]

There may be considerable uncertainty at times as to the extent to which the East European regimes enjoy the support of major segments of their population. But the interests of those regimes—and these may be defined differently and in different combinations on different issues—are a vital element in the pattern of relations in Europe and in the Warsaw alliance in particular.

This aspect is of direct relevance to the current debate in the West over the political leverage, if any, and therefore the political purpose, behind East-West trade and technology transfer—one of the key elements in the current process of European security. If the ideological component of the Warsaw alliance still operates at the level of the ruling regimes, then any Western attempt, conscious or unconscious, to use economic inducements as a substitute for confronting the political issues dividing Europe is doomed to founder on this ideological/political threshold.[9]

The Political Development of the Warsaw Alliance

Although the treaty setting up the Warsaw Pact was signed in 1955, for the first decade of its existence it lay dormant as a political mechanism. The upheavals of 1956 and after were dealt with unilaterally by the Soviet Union and not even discussed at the (infrequent) meetings of the Pact's Political Consultative Committee—allegedly the highest political organ of the alliance. When it did meet, the PCC concerned itself exclusively with such issues as the German problem, Berlin, disarmament, and a Peace Treaty for Europe. This preoccupation was hardly accidental, since one of the immediate motives for setting up the formal alliance structure in 1955 was to provide the Soviet Union with a symbolic counterposition to NATO at the Geneva conference of that year, in response to the inclusion of West Germany into the Western military alliance. Furthermore, its organizational structure followed closely that of NATO. Although there was evidently debate at the time over the future role of the Pact in Soviet foreign policy,[10] Khrushchev preferred to use other channels in dealing with his "junior allies," namely the attempted supranational integration of the East European economies within the framework of the Council for Mutual Economic Assistance (CMEA, also known as COMECON) and the international Communist gatherings of 1957 to 1961.

Krushchev's grand design for a "Socialist commonwealth" with Moscow as its natural center fell victim to the combined assault of the Sino-Soviet dispute, which destroyed the unity of the wider Communist movement, and opposition to his economic plans from several East European states—notably and most effectively from Romania. His replacement in 1964 saw an upgrading of the Warsaw Pact—both as a military and political alliance. However, just as Khrushchev used de-Stalinization as a weapon in his struggle for power in the 1950s and had to live with the increasing differentiation in Eastern Europe, so the decision to revitalize the Warsaw Pact has imposed its own constraints on the current Soviet leadership.

Brezhnev apparently hoped to use the Warsaw Pact to facilitate the cohesion and discipline of the Eastern alliance, both by military coordination and the coordination of foreign policy among the member states under Soviet leadership. But he was to be challenged consistently on both counts.

Joint military exercises involving the armed forces of the Warsaw Pact had begun in 1961. By 1965 the northern tier of Poland, East Germany, and Czechoslovakia—the states of greatest military-strategic importance in the East-West conflict—had emerged as the "first strategic echelon" in Soviet military strategy in Europe. This, together with Romania's refusal from 1964 onwards to commit troops to joint exercises (Romania did not even participate in staff exercises until the 1970s) reinforced a trend already discernible within the alliance in economic affairs, namely the differentiation between the more industrially advanced states of the north and the more agricultural south. Moreover, beginning in 1965, an appreciation on the part of all the East European states of the political implications behind Soviet attempts to reorganize and strengthen the Pact as a means of effecting greater cohesion provoked sharp divisions within the alliance, which themselves had an impact on its future development.

For example, Romania began calling for the abolition of military blocs and the withdrawal of foreign military bases from Europe and, according to Western press reports, in May 1966 circulated a document to its East European allies demanding that the post of supreme commander be rotated between the member countries and criticizing Soviet domination of the military structure, the absence of consultation procedures on the use of nuclear weapons, and the burden on member territories of financial contributions toward the upkeep of Soviet forces.[11] The Soviet Union was again evidently forced to make a tactical retreat, since the final declaration of the PCC meeting of July 1966 in Bucharest made no reference to closer integration. It emphasized instead the principles advocated by the Romanian party for the conduct of bloc affairs; that is, the observance of formal channels of consultation and discussion and the principles of party and national sovereignty.[12]

Romania was not alone in criticizing the structure of the alliance. Although both Poland and East Germany, by virtue of the unresolved nature of the German problem, evidently regarded close integration within the Warsaw alliance at that time as the ultimate and sole defense of their sovereignty and territorial integrity, the other member of the "Iron Triangle," Czechoslovakia, also criticized the exclusive appointment of Soviet officers to the Pact's high command and the inadequate use of the Pact's political machinery for effective consultation.[13]

Despite the demonstration of force in the invasion of Czechoslovakia, reactivation of the formal machinery of the alliance in the postinvasion period saw also a revival of the basic disagreements and pressures for reform which had been held in abeyance but in no way resolved or removed by the invasion. In March 1969 the PCC met briefly (the official session lasted only two hours) in Budapest to ratify a series of changes to the Pact's military structure: 1) a committee of defense ministers was established and declared the supreme military consultative organ of the alliance; 2) the joint command of the Warsaw Pact Joint Armed Forces was reconstituted, so that deputy ministers of national defense rather than the ministers themselves became deputy Warsaw Pact commanders under the Soviet commander-in-chief; 3) a military council was established; 4) a permanent joint staff was established, with East European deputy chiefs of staff at the major-general level; 5) a new organ was established to coordinate weapons development; 6) a new statute was established for the Joint Armed Forces.[14]

Although very little information has been supplied by East European or Soviet sources concerning the practical implications of these modifications, the available evidence would suggest that, far from facilitating the supranational integration of the Warsaw Pact armed forces under Moscow's control—as was speculated at the time in the West—the new system has very possibly reinforced the principle of *national* control and injected a permanent East European presence in institutional form into the consultation process in military affairs.[15]

There is little doubt that the Budapest PCC meeting was merely the formal conclusion to some lively debate on the future of the military alliance.[16] Yet despite the closer coordination in military affairs, proclaimed in the interests of military efficiency, the subsequent statements and actions by both the Soviet Union and the East European regimes testify to Moscow's continued inability to force through any reorganization which would deprive East European governments of national control over their armed forces in peacetime.[17] In effect, the 1969 reforms in practice appeared to take up the threads of the pre-1968 pressure on the part of several East European states for improved access to the channels of command and increased consultation in military affairs, although in each branch of the new structure overall command was to be retained by Soviet officers.[18]

More recently, the reorganization of the Pact's military infrastructure has been complemented by a readjustment of its political suprastructure. At a meeting of the PCC in Bucharest in November 1976 it was decided for "the further improvement of the mechanism of political cooperation within the framework of the treaty . . . to create the committee of foreign ministers and the united secretariat as organs of the Political Consultative Committee."[19]

Again it has not been made explicit or yet become apparent just how these changes will affect the practical political operations of the alliance. The communiqué spoke of cooperation, not integration, which would suggest that even if Brezhnev had been pressing his allies for a more "integrated" alliance structure, he failed to gain their collective approval for any such plans.[20] The analogy to the organizational changes endorsed in 1969 would seem strong. As with the Committee of Defense Ministers, the new Committee of Foreign Ministers merely gives institutional form to an existing political reality. The foreign ministers of the Warsaw Pact states had met on a number of occasions on an *ad hoc* basis, their meetings usually dealing with the less controversial (and often more propagandistic) issues, such as the preparations for a European Security Conference. However, over the longer term—and depending on future developments in Eastern Europe—it may be that these meetings of Pact foreign ministers will perform a regular consultative role, based on a recognition that the PCC—a meeting of top party leaders—is not always the most useful forum for discussion. Certainly, the increasing number of top-level bilateral summits and fairly regular multilateral gatherings (for example, party congresses, COMECON council sessions, the more informal Crimea "vacation" meetings) must inevitably reduce the need for formal PCC meetings. Unlike in the 1950s and early 1960s, the less than regular PCC meetings are by no means indicative of the absence of top-level consultation.

These modifications to the political structure of the alliance and the institutionalization of consultation at a number of different levels may also be a sign that the Warsaw Pact as an institution is becoming less ritualistic, both in the face of the self-assertion of individual East European member states and also in the wake of the settlement of some of the issues which have fed its previous symbolism and maintained the role of the PCC as a propagandistic forum in the East-West conflict in Europe.

Of the several major issues which in the last decade have provided the focus for Pact declarations—such as the West German threat, European security, the war in Vietnam, and the Middle East conflict—in almost every case the issue has either been eliminated (Vietnam), regulated (the German problem), or become the subject of joint crisis management between the superpowers (the Middle East). In contrast, the November 1976 PCC declaration concerned itself almost exclusively with the various aspects of the CSCE process, the issue of disarmament, and relations between socialist states.

It is again possible to speculate that in November 1976 Brezhnev was attempting to exert pressure through the issue of institutional reform to coordinate more effectively Pact positions prior to the second round of the CSCE, due to begin in Belgrade in June 1977. This is especially plausible since the Conference of European Communist Parties in the spring of 1976, far from demonstrating Soviet primacy, had very publicly endorsed the notion of "institutionalized diversity"—a price the Soviet Union had had to pay for Romanian and Yugoslav participation, among others. Both had boycotted the previous conference in Karlovy Vary in 1967.

In the past, one of the major obstacles to the PCC's ability to function as a genuine policymaking forum has been the Soviet Union's repeated attempts to use the Eastern alliance to coordinate the policies of its allies (ostensibly against the West) in a manner conducive to Soviet hegemony and control. Where the political channels have broken down the Soviet leaders have fallen back on the other—military—aspect of the alliance. Thus, the Pact's dual function in Soviet eyes of defending Soviet interests and promulgating Soviet policy has inevitably come into conflict with individual East European states' desires to preserve national autonomy, promote their own national aspirations, and establish *two*-way channels of communication.[21]

As a result, individual East European states have at times sought to restrict, rather than expand, the use of the Warsaw Pact as a foreign policy mechanism, even though it remains their only formal channel of foreign policy formulation and conflict regulation. The real political issues affecting the future of Eastern Europe (China, intra-alliance cooperation, and so on) have remained essentially "shadow" issues to be dealt with behind closed doors, often bilaterally. Yet, given the changes in the international environment in the present decade, it is these shadow issues which may well emerge in sharper relief, refocusing attention on the original parameters to political change: the predominant position of the Soviet Union and the relationship between the ruling Communist regimes and their populations. These are still the dominant factors around which all other issues cluster.

In sum, the modifications both to the military and political structures may well represent an attempt to reorganize the Pact on a more rational basis, fitting the requirements of the alliance itself rather than those of international diplomacy. Although the combined impact over the long term of recent changes, both in alliance structure and the international environment, must remain the subject of speculation, the current situation displays elements of continuity and change which may be significant pointers to the future.

**Dimensions of Security and Change:
The Current Situation**

In solely military terms very little has changed in the relationship between the East European states and the Soviet Union. If anything, on the surface the situation has deteriorated. There are now thirty-one Soviet divisions stationed in Eastern Europe. Before 1968 there were twenty-six—the five extra being those currently stationed in Czechoslovakia, which prior to the invasion had no Soviet troops stationed on its territory. On the basis of Western estimates, therefore, the East European states provide roughly 60 percent of all Warsaw Pact divisions in the European region outside the Soviet Union.[22]

Taking just the northern tier of strategically important states, Poland, East Germany, and Czechoslovakia, the East European proportion drops to roughly 50 percent.[23]

However, leaving aside any considerations of the political weight to be derived from this balance of forces, the picture is clouded by several other related factors. For example, the military balance becomes much less favorable to the East European states if included in the number of Soviet troops are those stationed in the western regions of the Soviet Union. Although Soviet preponderance is more evident in the northern and central regions than in Southeastern Europe, the overall imbalance is clearly in the Soviet Union's favor.[24]

The effectiveness of East European military capabilities is further reduced by the virtual monopoly enjoyed by the Soviet Union in production and supply of armaments.[25] Similarly with respect to strategic weapons, although the East European armed forces have been supplied with Soviet delivery vehicles, these are generally not the most modern. What is more, as far as is reliably known, the Soviet Union has not placed any of its nuclear warheads in Europe at the disposal of its East European allies.[26] Presumably to reassure its allies in view of their lack of strategic capabilities, Soviet sources lay heavy emphasis on the Soviet nuclear shield as being the reliable defense of all Warsaw Pact states.

Finally, although in numerical terms the East European contribution to Warsaw Pact troop strengths and defenses is important—at least in peacetime—there has always been doubt voiced in the West concerning the political reliability of these troops in wartime. If the invasion of Czechoslovakia can be taken as indicative of Soviet behavior in the event of war, it may be assumed that the Warsaw Pact "is not intended to be a wartime or operational command-and-control headquarters." Rather, judging from this experience, it is intended more as an "administrative, politico-military authority" designed to coordinate the East European armed forces "in the most rational way in the interests of Soviet defense policy and strategy" and under Soviet command.[27] Hence the Soviet Union's continued refusal to permit East European officers to occupy key posts in the military command of Pact forces.[28]

Yet, as seems evident from the 1969 and 1976 reforms, the Soviet Union has been unable to translate all its military advantage into political control. That is not to say that the East European regimes are not loyal members of the Warsaw Pact, interested also in improving the efficiency of the alliance. However, alongside the elements of continuity there are manifestations of change: Romania is no longer, if indeed it ever was, a lone critical voice in Warsaw Pact affairs. There are rumblings from several quarters concerning such issues as nuclear strategy, offset costs from Soviet troops stationed in Eastern Europe, the need for the development of national East European military doctrines, and the need to satisfy the aspirations of the various national officer corps.[29]

Even to the extent that the East European countries, including Romania, have cooperated in joint exercises aimed at increasing the strength and efficiency of the Joint Armed Forces, it has become clear that as long as individual states retain national control over their armed forces, efficiency is a two-edged sword, since it injects a degee of East European presence into the operation of the alliance which—in peacetime, at least—Moscow cannot readily ignore. A good example of this would be the East European states' rejection of Soviet attempts to expand their alliance commitments beyond Europe to Asia, and specifically to the Soviet border dispute with China.

In this respect it is worth noting too that in the post-*Ostpolitik* era in Europe the Soviet Union is not the only guarantor of Polish and East German borders. To the extent that these two states had previously been inhibited by such uncertainties, their role as traditional supporters of the Soviet Union within bloc councils could conceivably be modified in the future.[30]

Since Honecker's accession to power in East Germany in 1971, and particularly since the regulation of relations between the two German states and the acceptance of the GDR into the mainstream of international political life, relations between East Germany and the Soviet Union have displayed a far greater degree of stability than was the case certainly in the last few years of Ulbricht's leadership.[31] Both sides point to this new relationship as a model of Socialist fraternal relations, and clearly the interests of the two regimes do coincide on all fundamental issues. Yet this is only part of the picture. There are issues where East German and Soviet interests diverge.

One prominent example is the apparent collapse of a Soviet-West German energy deal in the face of East German opposition to plans for West Berlin to be connected to the West European power grid, across East German territory.[32] While this issue was of direct concern mainly to bilateral East German-Soviet relations, on a broader level it remains to be seen what the future implications will be insofar as both the Berlin agreement and the Basic Treaty came about only in the face of at times considerably East German opposition.

Certainly, whether by (East German) accident or (Soviet) design, East Germany seems to be assuming a more prominent and clearly defined role in bloc affairs.[33] In fact, several of the East European states have adopted a more accentuated profile in recent years: East Germany became Moscow's liaison channel with the West European Communist parties—with mixed success—in the preparations for the East Berlin conference in the spring of 1976; Romania has already established a reputation for itself in international affairs as a useful mediator in several parts of the globe; Hungary, too, in the pursuit of a quiet life, has often been suspected of playing a similar role within the Warsaw alliance.

Thus, the kind of relationship that might be expected to evolve between the Soviet Union and its allies in the future would presumably be based on a more differentiated concept of loyalty, less flattering to any particular Soviet regime and based on a more rational assessment of the common interests of the ruling elites. It was certainly by no means insignificant that the document which finally emerged from the East Berlin conference of European Communist parties in 1976 proclaimed "respect [for] free choice of different roads in the struggle for social change of a progressive nature and for socialism" and asserted that "the Communist Parties do not consider all those who are not in agreement with their policies or who hold a critical attitude toward their activity as being anti-communist."[34] By no means insignificant also was Brezhnev's speech to the conference in which he ignored the painful compromises achieved in the conference document and reemphasized the principle of proletarian internationalism. Clearly he intended his remarks to be a cautionary admonition to the East Europeans. But the fact that the Soviet Union felt obliged to restate its position so promptly and so pointedly indicates a degree of unease on the part of the leadership.

It is not surprising that similar elements of continuity and change are evident in the economic sphere also. Once again the Soviet Union is by far the dominant force in the COMECON,[35] in terms of energy, raw materials, industrial output, imports, and exports. Again, since the early 1960s successive Soviet leaderships have sought to bring about the supranational integration of the East European economies, presumably in the interests of both economic efficiency through specialization and alliance cohesion through economic interdependency. Yet, although the degree of cooperation and integration within the COMECON has increased markedly over the past decade, according to the "Comprehensive Program" adopted after the twenty-fifth Council session in Bucharest in July 1971, economic integration will take place

in accordance with the principles of socialist internationalism and on the basis of respect for national sovereignty, independence, and national interests, of non-intervention in the internal affairs of nations, and of total equality, mutual advantage, and comradely reciprocal aid.

Furthermore,

"socialist economic integration is carried out on an entirely voluntary basis and is not accompanied by the creation of supranational organs."[36]

The practical effect of this has been that as far as joint projects and the setting up of COMECON agencies are concerned, participation by all

Warsaw Pact states has been by no means automatic. Again Romania stands out as the most nonconformist ally, declining to participate in projects or agencies it feels do not further Romania's own aspirations for rapid industrialization, economic diversification, and national sovereignty.[37]

On the other hand, the last three years have seen signs of a growing rapprochement between Romania and the Soviet Union. There have been more frequent top-level political, economic, and even military contacts and a projected sharp increase in bilateral trade for the period up to 1980. These moves appear to have been conditioned by a number of factors, such as Romania's own economic difficulties, manifestations of internal dissent, and a changing international environment which perhaps inhibits somewhat Romania's ability to manipulate its ties with the West, China, and its Balkan neighbors to bolster the pursuit of relatively independent policies within the Warsaw alliance. Yet, at the same time, this improvement in bilateral relations has not been matched by any shift away from Romania's principled opposition to the supranational integration of the East European alliance or its traditional concerns of sovereignty and national independence.[38]

In addition, there are now a significant number of bilateral projects underway which do not involve the Soviet Union, ranging from joint industrial ventures to joint exploitation of natural resources, particularly among the three most industrially advanced states, Poland, East Germany, and Czechoslovakia. And although the Soviet Union still occupies a disproportionately large share in the foreign trade of these states, rather than one-sided dependency on the Soviet Union, the picture that emerges is one of interdependency. (The surprise decision of the Council session in June 1978 in Belgrade to admit Vietnam to full membership of the COMECON could well present further obstacles to any far-reaching plans for the integration of the economies of the member states.)

This increasingly complex relationship can be illustrated by the recent history of Eastern Europe's energy problem. With the exception of Romania, which maintains an independent petroleum industry, all the remaining East European economies have been heavily dependent on the Soviet Union for energy imports in the form of oil and natural gas. Before 1974, the Soviet Union supplied oil to the East Europeans at prices well below the world market price, in effect providing a substantial subsidy to the economies of its allies. In 1975, at Soviet instigation, revisions to the COMECON pricing system on a whole range of commodities had the particular effect of increasing significantly the price of Soviet oil. As was pointed out at the time, one side effect of this restructuring of the price system was to improve the Soviet Union's terms of trade with Eastern Europe, forcing these countries to increase their exports to the Soviet Union and correspondingly restrict the volume of goods available for domestic consumption and for export to the West. The net effect would be a disruption of the current economic plans and the closer integration of the economies of Eastern Europe with that of the Soviet Union.

The disruptive effect of such price changes is indisputable. However, the political implications behind the move are more complex. For example, as a result of the 1975 price adjustments the intra-CMEA terms of trade moved in favor of the Soviet Union by an estimated 10 percent. Yet it has been shown that had actual world market prices been applied, the improvement would have been considerably greater—roughly 30 percent.[39] Thus, although the East European situation has since been less favorable, in comparison to current world markets the Soviet Union is still indirectly subsidizing the economies of its allies.[40]

Presumably one of the reasons for the relatively moderate adjustments was an awareness of the possible repercussions of a more drastic action in economic, social, and political terms within Eastern Europe. (This awareness is evidenced also by the granting of large Soviet credits to Poland to help alleviate the economic situation following the price riots of 1976 and by the flexibility in applying the new pricing system in trade with individual East European states—for example, Hungary.) Yet, judging from the results of the thirtieth COMECON Council session in East Berlin in July 1976, no obvious alternative political price was exacted by the Soviet Union in return.

More recently, the notion that the energy dependency of the East European states must inevitably increase Soviet political influence on its allies has come in for even more fundamental reassessment.[41] In fact, since the late 1960s at least, the Soviet Union has been encouraging its East European allies to diversify their sources of energy imports and rely less on increased Soviet energy supplies—particularly oil—though with very limited success. However, at the thirty-first COMECON Council session in Warsaw in June 1977, the Soviet Union evidently made clear its own inability to meet the increasing energy demands of its allies and its domestic economy, while at the same time it sold oil abroad for much-needed hard currency. The result was a decision on the part of the Soviet Union to slow down drastically the rate of growth of oil supplies to Eastern Europe. This will undoubtedly effect trade patterns to some extent, as the East European countries are forced both to cut back domestic demand and look for additional supplies from the Middle East and the West. However, given the community of economic and political interests binding the Warsaw Pact states, predictions of far-reaching political consequences or reorientations in Soviet-East European relations resulting from this decision[42] are likely to be as wide of the mark as were the previous predictions that oil would constitute the ultimate Soviet weapon for reimposing monolithic conformity on the Warsaw Pact.

On the second—domestic—level of analysis, relations between the East

European regimes and their populations have been undergoing rapid change in response to increasing industrialization and accompanying social pressures. There are a number of identifiable sources of instability which have presented themselves as recurring themes from the early post-Stalin years: nationalism, the minorities question, the alienation of parts of the intelligentsia, and rising expectations resulting from relative economic and political stability leading to increasing demands on the leadership to be accountable to popular demands. The Polish riots of 1970 and then again of 1976 have been the most dramatic examples in recent years—and the most potent. (The Czechoslovak crisis of 1968 was qualitatively different, in that the initiative for reform came first from the party.) In 1970 the Polish riots resulted in Gomulka's fall from power and his replacement as party leader by Gierek. In 1976 the almost instantaneous decision to rescind the most important price increases in the face of worker hostility was further testimony to the leadership's sensitivity to popular unrest and the potential power of worker dissent.

In Hungary, too, there has been evidence of modification of economic policies in response to pressures from below. In this case a degree of worker opposition to the introduction of further economic reforms designed to expand a system of wage differentials and incentives bespeaks the potential conservatism of the working population.[43] In both cases, though more obviously in the case of Hungary than Poland, opposition to government policies was restricted to economic, and therefore more bargainable, issues. To some extent this may be seen as confirmation of a trend toward the depoliticization of the citizenry in Eastern Europe—partly in response to the defeat of the reform movement in Czechoslovakia and partly in response to an increasing standard of living.

None of the potential sources of instability mentioned can be directly and causally related to the process of European security. To some extent this has been true also of the intellectual dissent which has received so much publicity since the Helsinki conference in 1975. Dissent, both in the Soviet Union and Eastern Europe, predates the Helsinki accords and in one form or another is as old as the regimes themselves. On the other hand, since it did address itself specifically to this and other related issues of personal freedom, the Helsinki agreement has, at the same time, provided an anchor and focus for dissent and a public framework for its expression. This is discussed in detail in the next chapter.

Although monitoring groups have attracted the attention of the media in the West, their numbers are relatively small and their criticism is directed toward a reform of the existing system. Moreover, their particular goals are nationally oriented; so far, the groups appear to be fragmented and have not established links with each other; rather, they operate by way of contacts in the West. As a consequence, their activities may well prove embarrassing to their regimes but not necessarily threatening. The possible exception to this pattern may be East Germany, where reportedly thousands applied for exit visas to West Germany on the basis of the provisions of the Helsinki accords. So far no major upheavals have occurred to threaten the political stability of the Honecker regime. Here again, the still unresolved national question is bound to increase the sensitivity of the issue, despite the relatively cool and low-key approach maintained by the regime—as witnessed by reactions to the "manifesto" allegedly written by a group within the Socialist Unity Party (SED) and published in the West in January 1978.[44]

It is interesting to note in this context that since the early 1970s there have been rumors that the Soviet Union has been giving serious consideration to reducing the numbers of Soviet troops in Eastern Europe—partly, probably, to test East European reaction before a possible MBFR agreement, but also, it has been suggested, because some regimes have been too ready to rely on the Soviet presence to avoid confronting domestic political and social issues.[45] It is certainly becoming increasingly difficult (though not impossible) for the Soviet Union to ignore the detrimental impact on its image abroad of the apparent continued need to maintain large numbers of divisions on the territory of its allies.

It may be interesting, too, to see what impact the easing of travel and currency restrictions between East European countries over the past few years will have on the pattern of internal dissent. Quite clearly, were the level of dissent to reach threatening proportions, in terms of scope, direction, or coordination, the impact on the present security process in Europe would be considerable—and not just by virtue of the existence of the Helsinki accords.

Conclusions

The answers to the questions posed at the beginning are by no means obvious. In direct terms, the impact of the CSCE and related discussions on Eastern Europe would seem to have been marginal. Changes which have taken place have seemed to be the result of ongoing processes of change which predate the present "era of negotiation." On the other hand, it seems also to be generally accepted that the changed international environment of the 1960s and 1970s has had a more general impact on both alliances, NATO and the Warsaw Pact. Détente has loosened their hierarchical structure and created room for the smaller allies of both superpowers to pursue more nationally minded objectives.

Yet aside from plotting these general trends in international politics, it is hard to pinpoint specific causal relationships in a complex environment. The recent normalization of relations between East and West, and in particular the formal regulation of the German problem have, however, at least stripped away some of the camouflage and may thus enable all the East European states, but especially East Germany and Poland, to establish their relationship with the Soviet Union on a more rational and pragmatic basis. Although the asymmetry of power within the Warsaw alliance remains a fact of military, political, and economic life, short of the outbreak of open hostilities in Europe or the total collapse of one or more of the East European economies, there are evidently practical limits to Soviet capabilities for transforming potential power into practical authority and control.

From their approach to the subject of European security over the past decade it is clear also that each of these regimes has had some quite specific interests in and expectations of the process. In the case of Romania this has taken the symbolic form of a codification of principles to operate in relations between states (and parties) which preserved national autonomy, irrespective of bloc affiliation. For Poland the treaties leading up to the CSCE provided West German recognition of the inviolability of its borders which was given multilateral confirmation at the CSCE. Similarly for East Germany, the much sought for recognition of GDR statehood was settled by a bilateral treaty with West Germany, and international recognition of East German sovereignty was thereafter confirmed by its participation in the Helsinki conference and its membership in the United Nations on a basis of full equality.

To the extent that the East European regimes have achieved these specific objectives, the possible impact of the current formal process of European security on the East European alliance could be considered to be "largely consummated."[46] To some extent, this could work to the detriment of East European national aspirations. Paradoxically, whereas previously Soviet insistence on bloc cohesion was ascribed—in part, at least—to the enmity in relations between the two superpowers, a rapprochement between the Soviet Union and the United States on the basis of a "spheres of influence" approach—in practice, at least, the foundation of the current European security process—could again tend to limit the maneuverability of the respective East European regimes.

Much depends on the ability of these regimes to maintain the process of differentiation in their relations with each other and with the Soviet Union—a relationship which maintains a distinction between national aspirations and systemic obligations, although it is entirely conceivable that the two may happily coincide. In other words, although there is common ideological bond linking the Soviet Union and the East European regimes, the regimes themselves also have common interests, both in preserving national autonomy in their dealings with the Soviet Union (although the particular issues may differ from one regime to another) and in self-preservation.

This second aspect, that of regime security, poses equally difficult problems of analysis. It is conceivable that future developments within Eastern Europe could pose a threat to the security of the Continent, but also to the pattern of relations within the alliance, since the manner in which the East European regimes handle the challenge posed from within their own societies will undoubtedly influence their relations with the Soviet Union, too. For example, the invasion of Czechoslovakia was a reaction to domestic developments within Czechoslovakia and the Czechoslovak party. Although the current domestic unrest in various East European states seems to be qualitatively different and is being treated accordingly, there is no guarantee that a similar situation arising in the future will provoke any different response, particularly if, as apparently happened in 1968, unrest in Eastern Europe spreads to the Soviet Union. (And it is more likely that the experience of the 1968 invasion will prove more effective in preventing a repeat experience than will the Helsinki accords.)

Furthermore, such dangers would increase significantly were the current unrest in Eastern Europe to become intertwined with the various nationalist and minority problems. However, at this point the common interests of the ruling elites would again become an important element. Judging from past experience, minority problems often serve more as a barometer of interparty relations, rather than as contentious issues in their own right.

On the other hand, the current threat to the economic stability of some countries posed by their increasing indebtedness to the West—and their increasing vulnerability to Western-imported inflation and recession—brings with it the dangers implied in increasing financial dependency on the Soviet Union for meeting debt repayments. Indebtedness, as has been demonstrated already in Poland, may also provoke internal unrest in response to relatively harsh economic measures designed to curtail domestic consumption and channel goods into export markets.[47]

The new catchword in both East and West is "economic security." Whether by historical process or coincidence, economic and financial issues have acquired serious implications not only at the domestic level, but also at the systemic (alliance) and international levels.

Leaving aside any considerations of the possible effects on Western economies and banking concerns in the event of an inability or unwillingness on the part of East Europeans and the Soviet Union to meet their financial commitments, serious economic disruption and accompanying social unrest in Eastern Europe could seriously impair the progress of détente in Europe. A point may conceivably be reached in the near future where nominally financial decisions concerning future lending limits and refinancing of existing loans could acquire serious political overtones in the balance of relations between East and West.

Any conclusions regarding the relevance of the current conduct of détente and European security to the political development of the Warsaw alliance as a whole must be equally equivocal. What has been achieved so far in concrete terms with respect to European security is the codification of certain norms of behavior—a framework for the conduct of interstate and interalliance relations, based on the political and territorial status quo. To that extent, future prospects for security in Europe may be said to have been enhanced—they have not been guaranteed—since there is no way of enforcing these norms of behavior. Security is more dependent than ever before on the maintenance of good relations between the two blocs, since the penalties for abrogating an institutionalized, if ambiguous, code are generally greater than if the code had never existed. In the case of Europe this is particularly evident in view of the extreme sensitivity of the region in world politics and the myriad of economic, cultural, and even political ties which have developed in the last five years. The consequences of a breakdown of the process would be serious indeed.

Thus the future of Europe remains uncertain. Having established a procedure for conducting business, Europe is still faced with those "political and power" issues which it was earlier assumed would be settled once the artificially imposed constraints of the ideological overlay were removed. However, it is very likely that in the wake of the Helsinki and Belgrade conferences Europe will experience instead renewed emphasis on precisely this ideological component of the East-West relationship. Provided there is no major breakdown in East-West relations, it may be expected that although the individual East European regimes will continue in the pursuit of nationally determined economic and political objectives—which may or may not coincide with Soviet precepts—their common ideological interests will prevail in dealings with the West. This is a point often lost by confusing the issue of human rights with the notion of polycentrism.

To a certain extent there is already evidence of this common front. While all East European regimes, like the Soviet Union, have shown an active interest in benefiting from the opportunities of East-West trade and access to Western markets, even the most independently minded regimes, the Romanians included, have acted and spoken in concert in warning against alleged Western attempts to use Basket 3 of the Helsinki accords to subvert the leading role of the Communist party in their respective states. And all have denounced the dissident groups within their societies as wittingly or unwittingly being agents of Western imperialism.

There are, then, clear indications that, provided the pattern of relations with the Soviet Union remains relatively stable, and provided they can meet the challenge posed from within their own societies (though from an historical perspective neither is a foregone conclusion), the East European regimes are in a position to confront the ideological challenge from the West, while preserving and promoting the more differentiated relationship with the Soviet Union—and each other—which has evolved, haltingly, over the last twenty-five years.

Given no major catastrophes, the main danger to the East European regimes now seems to come not so much from the rhetoric on human rights as the possibility that détente will revert to being a sport of the superpowers. The danger is clear, if indeed the Helsinki accords and their successors achieve only a summation of lowest common denominators in Europe. Much depends on the attitude of the superpowers. Unfortunately, perhaps, for Europe, at the present time the relationship between the United States and the Soviet Union is more liable to be conditioned by their interactions in other parts of the globe, notably the Middle East and Africa, than by purely European considerations.

To avoid such a situation would require the setting of concrete and realistically achievable goals. This in turn presupposes a degree of common ground. Goals must not only be achievable, they must also be felt to be worthwhile. As things now stand, it would seem possible that what was achievable has been achieved. It is not clear, however, that this has brought either side any closer to what each might consider a worthwhile goal. The polemics since Helsinki suggest that the ideological component of East-West interactions in Europe renders "security" as ephemeral and insoluble as ever. The inability to agree on what constitutes security remains the main source of insecurity and tension in Europe. Although the prospects for military conflict seem remote, Eastern Europe remains a potentially destabilizing factor in East-West relations.

Notes

1. This process is analyzed in J.F. Brown, "Détente and Soviet Policy in Eastern Europe," *Survey* 20 (Spring/Summer 1974):46-58.

2. This attitude has been fostered in the West in part by the institutionalization of West European unity in the EEC; the Warsaw Pact states have consistently proposed new orders for Europe—but rather than reflecting any alternative futures, these have usually been designed as propaganda instruments to manipulate the existing balance.

3. This ideological factor is seen by some authors as the major element distinguishing the present system of alliances in Europe from those of an earlier age. See H. Dinerstein, "The Transformation of Alliance Systems" in Aspaturian, *Process and Power in Soviet Foreign Policy* (Boston: Little, Brown, 1971), pp. 879-900.

4. This hierarchical structure applies in some degree to both alliances. See L. Acimovic, "Cohesion and Conflict in Relations among the East European Countries," *International Affairs* (Belgrade) 1972, pp. 33-47. The

author sees the previous policies of the two superpowers as "trying to stop a natural process of change in the international community and to throttle the resultant aspirations to transform the present system of international relations" (p. 33).

5. As typified by East European and Soviet hostility to "peaceful engagement" (Kennedy), "bridge-building" (Johnson), and, more recently, aspects of West Germany's *Ostpolitik.*

6. Z.K. Brzezinski, *Alternative to Partition* (New York: McGraw-Hill, 1965), p. 75.

7. P. Lendvai, "The Possibilities of Social Tensions and Upheavals in Eastern Europe and Their Possible Effects on European Security" in "Europe and America in the 1970s II: Society and Power," *Adelphi Papers* No. 71, Nov. 1970, pp. 23-29.

8. Aspaturian refers to this pattern as "interpenetrative politics," although he sees pluralization in Eastern Europe taking place within definite bounds. Polycentrism he describes as a "logical absurdity." See his "East European Relations with the USSR" in Toma, *The Changing Face of Communism in Eastern Europe* (Tuscon: University of Arizona Press, 1970), p. 293.

9. One attempt to correlate conformity/nonconformity to Soviet policy with a number of different variables, including East-West trade and cultural interactions, led the authors to assume the existence of a "critical minimum level" necessary before the West could have any significant impact on Soviet-East European relations. See W.R. Kintner and W. Klaiber, *Eastern Europe and European Security* (New York: Dunellen, 1971), chapter 13. Implicit in the authors' conclusions was the assumption that such a level might in practice be reached and even surpassed. However, on the basis of current results it was concluded that "Western practices in these areas have had little causal effect on East European propensities to deviate from Soviet policy [but that] the minimum level at which these interactions have occurred may go far in explaining the absence of relationship" (p. 261). The predictive value of the authors' findings is impaired by their exclusive reliance on quantifiable, and in the case of the indices of conformity, somewhat arbitrary data in Soviet-East European relations.

10. For a more detailed account of the contrasting views of the future of the alliance, represented by Molotov and Khrushchev respectively, see Robin Remington, *The Warsaw Pact: Case Studies in Communist Conflict Resolution* (Cambridge, Mass.: M.I.T. Press, 1971), pp. 25-27.

11. Kiesing's Archives 1966; 21651A.

12. Romanian opposition was given practical effect by the establishment of diplomatic relations with West Germany, Romania's refusal to attend the 1967 Karlovy Vary conference of European communist parties, its refusal to adopt the totally pro-Arab line endorsed by the rest of the alliance after the June 1967 Arab-Israeli war, and its initial refusal to endorse the nonproliferation treaty.

13. For example, the comments by General Prchlik, Chief of the Political Commission of the Czechoslovak Army, as summarized in M. Mackintosh, "The Evolution of the Warsaw Pact," *Adelphi Papers* No. 58, June 1969, p. 10.

14. For a more detailed account of these changes see Ross Johnson, *Soviet-East European Military Relations: An Overview*, prepared for the United States Air Force Project RAND WN-8957-PR, January 1975, pp. 14-17.

15. The Ministers of Defense had met on previous occasions on an *ad hoc* basis for consultations—as had the joint staff. See Johnson, ibid., p. 16. For an account of Western misperceptions of these reforms see R.W. Herrick, "Warsaw Pact Restructuring Strengthens Principle of National Control," *Radio Liberty Dispatch*, 6 March 1970.

16. According to one masterfully understated report, there were no differing opinions "on what was later officially discussed at the session." Bratislava *Pravda* in Slovak, 19 March 1969. Brezhnev had reportedly been pressing for more overt support against China—possibly even in the form of symbolic Warsaw Pact contingents, though this was refused by Romania, Czechoslovakia, and Hungary at least. See *New York Times*, 22 March 1969, and also hints in Bratislava *Pravda*, 19 March 1969.

17. According to the Hungarian Foreign Minister in an interview in *Nepszabadsag*, 10 May 1969, the sovereignty of no member state was violated by the new measures, although he also insisted that "it is natural that there are also comradely debates."

18. For a more detailed discussion of the significance of the reforms for the military structure of the alliance see L. Caldwell, "The Warsaw Pact: Directions of Change," *Problems of Communism* XXIV (September-October 1975):1-19.

19. TASS 1645 GMT in English.

20. Immediately prior to the PCC meeting Brezhnev had paid an official visit of friendship to Bucharest to confer with the Romanian leaders—his first such formal visit since taking over the leadership of the CPSU in 1964. However, on 28 November 1976 the Romanian party paper *Scinteia* emphasized the "consultative character" of the new alliance bodies.

21. This point can be illustrated equally by East German resistance to Soviet policy toward West Germany in the period from 1969 to 1972 as by Romania's more general and public pursuit of an independent foreign policy.

22. Figures for East European division equivalents taken from *The Military Balance 1977-78* (London: I.I.S.S., 1977) p. 102. See also Ross Johnson, *Has East Central Europe Become a Liability to the USSR? The Military Aspect*, RAND Paper Series, P-5383, November 1975, p. 15.

23. The Soviet Union has twenty-seven divisions stationed in these countries, twenty of which are in East Germany. According to *The Military*

Balance 1977-78, p. 106, Poland, East Germany, and Czechoslovakia also have a combined total of twenty divisions available in category one readiness, four in category two readiness, and seven in category three readiness. Alternative figures suggest a slightly different breakdown. According to W.W. Kaufmann, M.I.T., 17 March 1978, there are twenty-three divisions in category one readiness, three in category two readiness, and five in category three readiness.

24. See tables (a), (b), and (c). Figures computed from *The Military Balance 1977-78,* pp. 102-107.

25. Presumably this was a major motive behind Romania's decision to engage in the joint design and manufacture of a prototype fighter aircraft with Yugoslavia for use by their two air forces. This was the first such independent project involving a Warsaw Pact country. See Zdenko Antic, "Productive Results of Yugoslav-Romanian Cooperation," *Radio Free Europe Report*, 25 April 1975.

26. *The Military Balance 1977-78*, p. 109. However, an unconfirmed report in the *Christian Science Monitor*, 1 September 1976, suggested that in January 1976 East German forces began to receive the latest Soviet weapons, including nuclear missiles. Allegedly no other Warsaw Pact member has either been equipped with such sophisticated Soviet planes and missiles or had contingents trained in the use of nuclear weapons. The source for the report was said to be a high-ranking military defector from East Germany. Certainly on several occasions during 1976 references were made in East German statements to the idea of a defensive war against NATO being a just war in which nuclear weapons would be used.

27. M. Mackintosh, "The Warsaw Pact Today," *Survival* XVI (May/June 1974):122-123.

28. The most recent examples were the appointments of General Gribkov as Chief of the General Staff of the Warsaw Pact in October 1976, and General Kulikov as Commander-in-Chief of the Warsaw Pact forces in January 1977.

29. These issues are outlined in Johnson, *Has East Europe Become a Liability to the USSR? The Military Aspect*, pp. 23-28.

30. Some initial evidence of a change of emphasis at least on the part of the Polish regime is presented by Jeanne Kirk Laux, "Intra-Alliance Politics and European Détente: The Case of Poland and Romania," *Studies in Comparative Communism* VIII (Spring/Summer 1975):98-122, who found that in the wake of the Warsaw and Moscow treaties, the Polish regime in its public statements moved away from the extreme protestations of impotence which had characterized the pre-1970 period, toward "a balanced characterization of capabilities" (p. 118). Obviously it remains to be seen how theory relates to practice in this case.

31. For a detailed analysis of the East German-Soviet relationship during this period see N. Edwina Moreton, *East Germany and the Warsaw Alliance: The Politics of Détente* (Boulder, Colo.: Westview Press, 1979).

32. See report in the London *Times,* 31 October 1976.

33. For example, the greater self-assertiveness of the East German defense establishment and its possible nuclear role, as mentioned above. East Germany, along with the Soviet Union and Cuba, is also involved in supplying military and economic support to African liberation movements and some black African governments. See *New York Times,* 4 April 1977.

34. Conference of European Communist and Workers Parties: "For Peace and Social Progress," *Information Bulletin* issued by World Marxist Review Publishers, Vol. 14, No. 12 (316), 1976, p. 15, the implication being also that an uncritical attitude toward the Soviet Union will not necessarily be the only yardstick in the future for determining acceptability and true loyalty.

35. Although the membership of the COMECON is not codeterminous with that of the Warsaw Pact, all members of the Warsaw Pact are members of and provide the driving force behind the COMECON. Since economic factors have demonstrated themselves as being of fundamental significance in the political relations among the Warsaw Pact states, some issues arising within the COMECON framework are directly relevant to the present analysis.

36. As quoted in Z.M. Fallenbuchl, "Comecon Integration," *Problems of Communism,* March-April 1973, p. 37.

37. For example, Romania's initial refusal to join the COMECON Investment Bank, and its only partial participation in the Orenburg gas project in the Soviet Union, as outlined in H. Trend, "The Orenburg Gas Project," RFER. RAD Background Report/165 (Eastern Europe), 2 December 1975.

38. The impact of these issues and others on Romania's position in Eastern Europe is illustrated in greater detail in Stephen Larrabee, "Balkan Security," *Adelphi Papers* No. 135, Summer 1977, pp. 25-29.

39. For a detailed analysis of the hypothetical and actual terms of trade which yield the above conclusions, see M.J. Kohn, "Developments in Soviet-Eastern European Terms of Trade, 1971-75," in *Soviet Economy in a New Perspective. A Compendium of Papers,* submitted to the Joint Economic Committee, Congress of the United States, 14 October 1976 (Washington, D.C.: U.S. Government Printing Office, 1976), pp. 67-80.

40. To a certain extent, though, this imbalance is offset by other means; for example, joint CMEA investment in such Soviet projects as the Orenburg gas pipeline. For a recent analysis see Martin J. Kohn and Nicholas R. Lang, "The Intra-CMEA Foreign Trade System: Major Price Changes,

Little Reform," in *East European Economies Post-Helsinki,* Joint Economic Committee, U.S. Congress, Washington, D.C., 25 August 1977, pp. 135-51.

41. For a concise exposition of the energy issue in East European-Soviet relations since the Second World War see Henry W. Schaeffer, "Energy and the Warsaw Pact. The Political Economy of Interdependence," paper presented at the October 1977 meeting of the American Association for the Advancement of Slavic Studies, Washington, D.C.

42. See report in *New York Times,* 21 November 1977.

43. I. Volgyes, *Limits of Political Liberalization: The Case of Hungary,* monograph. University of Nebraska. One recent development of interest is the joint offshore oil exploration project in the Baltic Sea among East Germany, Poland, and the Soviet Union. Petrobaltic (the name of the tripartite company) has its headquarters in the Polish port of Gdansk. The managing director is a Pole, the financial director an East German, and the technical director a Russian. More details in *New York Times,* 24 January 1978.

44. The manifesto was published in *Der Spiegel,* 2 and 9 January 1978. In addition to its criticisms of the SED leadership and its domestic policies, the document raises the issue of a future reunited Germany. The SED leadership denied the authenticity of the document. The West German cabinet was apparently seriously split over how to react to the document and the issues raised in it.

45. R. Davy, "The ESC and the politics of Eastern Europe," *World Today* 28 (July 1972).

46. R. Lowenthal, "China's Impact on the Evolution of the Alliances in Europe" in "Western and Eastern Europe: The Changing Relationship," *Adelphi Papers* No. 33, March 1967, p. 24. In fact the author argues the point that the emergence of China as a competitive world power has led to a much more rapid disintegration of the Western alliance, because of the one-sided shift in political priorities of the United States toward the Pacific region, whereas the Soviet Union's main priority was still Europe.

47. According to an estimate in the *New York Times,* 4 April 1977, Poland's debt then amounted to $8 billion, and the debt service rate, that is, the proportion of new credit that must be spent just to pay off previous debts, had reached 25 percent—a level comparable to those of Mexico and Brazil. Although total estimates vary, the collective COMECON debt to the West in 1976 amounted to between $32-35 billion, with the Soviet Union accounting for roughly one-third of the total. Furthermore, it should be remembered that such large-scale borrowing only really began in 1972.

9 The CSCE and the Development of Détente

Stephen J. Flanagan

Three years have passed since the thirty-five European heads of state assembled in Helsinki to place their imprimatur on the Final Act of the Conference on Security and Cooperation in Europe (CSCE). During this period, neither the nightmares of cynics in the West nor the dreams of its staunchest advocates on either side of the ideological divide have unfolded. Rather, CSCE has coexisted with several other fora of East-West interaction during a period of diplomatic stagnation. Symptomatic of this state of affairs was the inconclusive communiqué which emanated on March 8, 1978, from the Sava Conference Center in Belgrade at the conclusion of an exhaustive five-month review of the Final Act. Despite its failure to generate new initiatives or adopt a substantive concluding document, Belgrade sustained the CSCE process and set the stage for similar review sessions, the first of which is to convene in Madrid during late 1980. Thus, CSCE has become an enduring feature of the landscape of East-West diplomacy.

In its broader sense, European security involves the entire spectrum of relations among the European states and the way these contacts affect each country's internal stability. CSCE deals with this problem in addressing one of the central disagreements between East and West in the development of détente. For while the Kremlin and its close allies stress the importance of relaxation of tensions and an amelioration of interstate relations on the Continent, the West contends that durable and meaningful security in Europe can only be realized when the barriers to the flow of people and information are sharply curtailed.

Though the Helsinki accord addresses the political, economic, and human dimensions of détente more than specific military issues, the document manifests the security concerns of the signatory nations and is therefore relevant to any discussion of the evolution of Europe. One state's violation or uneven pursuit of any of the Helsinki principles could be inimical to the security of other participants. While CSCE is a facet of the détente process which largely reflects the quality of the entire gem of East-West relations, observance of its provisions does affect progress in other areas. The segments of the Final Act which require affirmative action are test cases of the practicability of détente. Thus, CSCE is both a component and a litmus test of the relaxation of tensions in Europe.

CSCE complements and supplements the other negotiations involving the development of European security: SALT and MBFR. However, a unique aspect of CSCE is its comprehensive representation. It is the only forum where all European states can meet to discuss crucial regional issues and where the neutral and nonaligned (NNA) states on the Continent can voice their security concerns. The Conference's guiding rule of consensus, though hardly an absolute equalizer, does grant each state the power to veto both substantive and procedural actions.

It is these NNA states who have been most forceful in advocating the consideration of certain military issues under the CSCE rubric. While the Conference is not, nor could it usefully serve as, an arms control negotiation, signatories of the Helsinki document do recognize the importance of achieving measures to reduce military confrontation and pledge greater openness in the conduct of selected military affairs.

The Final Act addresses a panoply of issues including guidelines for the conduct of relations between the states of Europe and the reduction of military tension (Basket 1)[1] and for expanded commerce and increased cooperation in industry, science technology, and the environment (Basket 2). However, the focal point of attention with CSCE has become the principle affirming the importance of human rights and provisions calling for humanitarian cooperation and an expanded flow of information (Basket 3). This dramatic turn of events was not foreseen by either bloc at the Helsinki summit. However, when the Final Act was publicized in the East some activists took their governments' pledges seriously and demanded an accounting where there were shortcomings. This development captivated many in the West who viewed CSCE as a newfound tool for realizing rapid and substantial societal change in the Communist world. These individuals have since become disillusioned with CSCE because of the Eastern bloc's erratic observance of the Final Act. Nonetheless, CSCE has evolved in a direction where it forces consideration of fundamental Western security concerns, concerns which the East would rather ignore.

The View from Moscow: A Pandora's Box

The concept of a European security conference had been a recurrent theme in Soviet foreign policy since 1954, but it was advanced with greatest determination in the late 1960s. There were considerable shifts in Moscow's aspirations for the conference over the years in response to the exigencies of international developments and the advance of bilateral diplomacy. The Kremlin's early pronouncements envisioned such a parley yielding a surrogate peace treaty which would affirm the postwar frontiers, legitimize the status of East Germany, and recognize its hegemony in Eastern Europe. Moscow also hoped the fallout from such a pact would arrest the development of West European military integration and the acquisition of nuclear weapons by West Germany. In the late 1960s the Soviets sensed that emerging strains in NATO foreshadowed a major crisis in the West. Moscow believed a major offensive for relaxation of tensions, with the security conference as its leading edge, would expand Soviet influence throughout Europe. To understand the developement of CSCE it is essential to review Moscow's basic security preoccupations before the multilateral talks convened. The Kremlin's proposals for the all-European conference reflect these evolving concerns.[2]

In his March 1966 address to the twenty-third Congress of the CPSU, Brezhnev revived the conference idea and urged the convocation of an all-European meeting on political détente and economic cooperation. This trial balloon was enlarged upon by the Warsaw Pact Political Consultative Committee (PCC) at its July 1966 Bucharest meeting. The Bucharest Declaration suggested that such an all-European gathering could ratify the territorial status quo, undertake the dissolution of at least the military organizations of NATO and the Warsaw Treaty Organization (WTO), replace the European Community with all-European trade associations, and foster continental cooperation in science, technology, and culture.[3] While U.S. participation was not excluded, this parley was clearly designed to be a European enterprise.

The April 1967 conference of twenty-four European Communist parties at Karlovy Vary reformulated some of the Bucharest proposals and affirmed the centrality of resolution of the German question. The Conference's concluding statement berated both Bonn and Washington for pursuing aggressive policies.[4] Brezhnev called on his colleagues to mobilize broad political support in Western Europe for dismantling NATO and establishing of a pan-European collective security system. It was explained that this system would evolve from an expanding web of bilateral East-West treaties. Because of their propogandistic criticisms of the United States and West Germany and their explicit assault on NATO, these proposals were never seriously entertained in the West. Moreover, the Kremlin was somewhat wary of undertaking an opening to the West at that time, fearing an erosion of its control over developments in Eastern Europe.

The invasion of Czechoslovakia smothered any chances of convening a security conference, and exacerbated Western suspicion about the meaning of détente. Thus, a major demonstration of Soviet goodwill became even more urgent. The suppression of Prague's experimentation and the general consolidation imposed on Eastern Europe enabled Moscow to feel more secure in pursuing a *Westpolitik*.[5] Moreover, since relations with the PRC were deteriorating at this time, a relaxation of tensions in the West assumed even more importance.

The PCC advanced a more conciliatory version of the security conference proposal at its March 1969 meeting in Budapest. This new formulation did not suggest abolition of military blocs, allowed for U.S. participation, and removed recognition of the territorial situation as a precondition for initiating talks.[6]

The NATO foreign ministers remained highly skeptical of the purpose of a multilateral conference, although they agreed to review possible topics for discussion. NATO members preferred the resolution of several outstanding issues through bilateral diplomacy. At its December 1969 meeting, the North Atlantic Council linked commencement of the security conference to progress on other East-West issues including: the Berlin situation, other problems related to the division of Germany, and talks for mutual force reduction.[7] NATO's determination in this regard forced the Soviet Union to refocus its détente campaign during the next three years on improvement of relations with individual West European states. This task was somewhat facilitated by the FRG's broadening of its *Ostpolitik* after Willy Brandt's assumption of the chancellorship in October 1969.

During this period, the purview of the multilateral conference was debated in a series of communiqués following NATO and WTO meetings. While NATO wanted to probe the Pact's willingness to expand the conference agenda, the Pact leadership endeavored to keep it to a minimum. First the East bloc declared that the conference would have to address questions of security in Europe, including affirmation of the territorial status quo, trade, and economic, scientific, and technical cooperation.[8] Then in May 1970, two months after the Quadripartite talks on Berlin had commenced, the NATO foreign ministers went so far as to discuss plans for preparatory talks on the security conference, but also noted that the subjects of "freer movement of people, ideas and information" should be on any such parley's agenda.[9] A final item was added when the Warsaw Pact ministers proposed that the conference might establish a permanent organ to expedite East-West cooperation and implement conference decisions.[10] Moscow believed this last point to be a perfect compromise between its desire for a hasty European summit to ratify general principles of relations and the West's demand for substantive negotiations.

By the end of 1971, the time for the security conference seemed at hand and the general issues to be addressed were understood. With the conclusion of the Moscow and Warsaw treaties, the Quadripartite agreement on Berlin, and the impending normalization of relations between the two Germanies, several of NATO's preconditions for the commencement of the multilateral talks had been met. The Soviets launched one final drive for the all-European parley; however, they persisted in ignoring the importance of discussion of humanitarian cooperation and of the force-reduction talks.

The relationship of MBFR to the security conference was the last hurdle the Soviets had to confront. NATO demanded at least concurrent conduct of MBFR and CSCE. Initially obverse to even a loose linkage of these two negotiations, the Kremlin finally succumbed to Henry Kissinger's persuasiveness and threats of further delay of CSCE by accepting the concept of parallelism. Dates and places were established for the initiation of CSCE and MBFR. While progress in one forum was in no way tied to developments in the other, NATO expressed the view that the two parleys were mutually reinforcing.

Yet, by this time, many of Moscow's initial goals for the security conference had been realized through bilateral diplomacy. West Germany's treaties with Moscow and Warsaw had resolved the most contentious border issue in Europe, the Oder-Neisse line. East Germany was on the road to recognition by the world community and an era of East-West cooperation in the commercial sphere was blooming. Nonetheless, the Kremlin attached considerable importance to multilateral endorsement of the territorial status quo, as a further legitimization of its hegemony in Eastern Europe. The basic Soviet goal in CSCE remained the same: broader relaxation of tensions to allow for an enlargement of Soviet influence throughout Europe.

Preparatory negotiations for the CSCE began on November 22, 1972, and dragged on for more than eight months. During the tedious wrangling over the agenda, which often involved semantic or procedural questions, the Soviets made numerous tactical concessions to expedite the proceedings. While Moscow sought a one-stage conference in Helsinki focused on the code of interstate relations and expansion of economic and technical cooperation, it accepted multi-staged deliberations in both Helsinki and Geneva with a greatly enlarged agenda.[11] To further complicate matters for Moscow, Romania joined Yugoslavia in a surprisingly independent stance from the outset of these talks, and Poland and Hungary quietly evinced similar proclivities. As these undesirable developments accelerated during the substantive "second stage" of the negotiations in Geneva, Soviet diplomats acknowledged privately that many of their original aspirations for the conference, particularly the permanent political body, had evaporated.[12] However, abandoning the parley at that point would have been impossible because of the Kremlin's tremendous investment, including the personal prestige of General Secretary Brezhnev, in its successful conclusion.

As the Geneva deliberations droned on for two years Moscow recognized that CSCE was not the ideal instrument for furthering its diplomacy. Nonetheless, it hoped that perseverance would allow realization of the following goals:

Multilateral recognition of the inviolability of the post-World War II borders in Europe;

Codification of the principles of relations between states with *different social systems.*

Expansion of institutionalized cooperation in industry, science, technology.

This scheme would preserve Moscow's hegemonial position in Eastern Europe, suggest durable stability in Europe—hence undermining the impetus of West European integration and "Atlanticism"—and allow for realization of the benefits of exchanges with the West while insulating the Eastern bloc from pressures for liberalization. As Robert Legvold so aptly noted, the Kremlin sought to employ CSCE as a "medium for healing Europe's economic division while sealing its political division."[13]

The Kremlin's Assessment of CSCE

Comparing this outline with the impact of the Helsinki Final Act it appears that Moscow's more modest objectives have been realized. However, even its minor victories in CSCE have been mitigated by undesirable complications. Neither CSCE nor the other components of its détente policy have wrought the Soviets' larger goals: erosion of U.S. influence in Europe and increased control in the East bloc.

At first glance, the Final Act's "Declaration of Principles Guiding Relations between Participating States" seems an incarnation of the Soviets' calls for a code of conduct for interstate relations.[14] The Kremlin found the ten principles (or the decalogue, as it became known) so congenial that they incorporated a slightly reformulated version into the Soviet Union's 1977 constitution.[15] Nonetheless, the declaration is not quite Moscow's optimal formulation.

The first five principles: sovereign equality, refraining from the threat or use of force, inviolability of frontiers, territorial integrity of states, and peaceful settlement of disputes, were greeted by Moscow as the focal point of the Helsinki document. This segment is lauded as a substitute peace treaty affirming the "territorial and political realities" that arose after World War II. Soviet analysts draw heavily on the history of the interwar period, and conclude that unresolved territorial claims are smoldering threats to the peace. Thus the decalogue's affirmation of the inviolability of frontiers is viewed as the "key condition upon which peace can be preserved."[16] Yet even aspects of these cherished principles, as they were ultimately drafted at Geneva, are disturbing to Moscow.

Most importantly, in the preambulary segments of the declaration, the signators declare that the principles are applicable to relations with all

states. This formulation undermines the Brezhnev Doctrine. Despite Soviet
espousal of Socialist fraternalism and persistent claims that the Final Act
only governs relations between states with different social systems, any intervention in Eastern Europe similar to the Czechoslovakian invasion would
violate most of the decalogue's principles. One can hardly expect the Final
Act to restrain Moscow from taking actions to suffocate threatening
developments in its sphere of influence. However, such a move would completely discredit the declaration and jeopardize other aspects of détente. The
Soviet-East German Treaty of Friendship, concluded soon after the
Helsinki summit, reflects Moscow's concern with the impact of the Final
Act on its freedom of action. The treaty incorporates language analogous to
that in Moscow's 1969 treaty with Czechoslovakia, wherein the parties cite
the principles of "socialist internationalism" and pledge to take " . . . the
necessary measures to safeguard and defend the historic gains of
socialism. . . . "[17] This pact is symptomatic of the Kremlin's search
through bilateral treaties for the legal underpinnings of future disciplinary
actions. The pact also includes a clause affirming the importance of "further improvement of political and ideological cooperation and the development and deepening of socialist integration." As will be elaborated later,
this theme is representative of the intensified drive for bloc solidarity which
accompanied the announcement of the Helsinki document in the East.

The record of Soviet restraint in dealing with Eastern Europe during
major foreign policy overtures to the West is mixed. While it is evident that
Moscow refrained from intervening in Poland during the 1970 crisis out of
concern for damaging the emerging détente, the Czechoslovakian operation, though it took place before the web of détente was constructed, stifled
progress on several major East-West negotiations. Still, considering the importance of the European settlement to the Soviet Union, the Kremlin is
likely to exercise caution in order to preserve it. Moreover, another use of
force to repress "deviationist" tendencies in Eastern Europe would undermine Moscow's long-range goal of expanded influence in the West European capitals. The calculus which the Soviets must now consider in dealing
with its allies pits the enduring benefits of the European settlement against
the need to maintain control. The Soviet-East German Treaty's content suggests that Moscow would like to retain both options. The West, however, is
unwilling to accept the validity of proletarian internationalism. Moscow
might find that with the European status quo affirmed and its security
visibly enhanced it would be wiser to allow greater diversity in Eastern
Europe. This strategy would permit resolution of unique domestic problems
in Eastern Europe and might bring even greater stability to the region.
However, the likelihood of this final course of action seems to have
diminished during the present uncertain period in East-West relations.

The Soviet delegation at the Geneva negotiations was unwavering in its effort to realize a separate principle which could be cited at home and in Eastern Europe as validation of the existing borders. The Final Act's principle III, on inviolability of frontiers, represents a departure in international declarations. Previously, the inviolability point had been treated as a corollary of the principle of abstention from the threat or use of force. Adoption of this principle was muted by other tenets of the decalogue and language which suggested that only the use of violence to alter international borders was illegitimate. Nonetheless, the Western media, by branding this principle as simple acquiescence to Communist territorial gains in the aftermath of World War II, in a very real sense enabled Moscow's propaganda triumph.

The tenacious stand of West Germany against any language in the Helsinki document which would suggest finality to the partition of Germany, supported by other members who objected to wording that might compromise Western Europe's ultimate political unification, was successful in minimizing the scope of the inviolability principle. The West Europeans were able to incorporate an additional corollary under the principle of sovereign equality which attested to the right of states to change their frontiers by peaceful means. To ensure a balance between the inviolability principle and the section on peaceful change, and to counteract Soviet claims that the inviolability clause was the overarching facet of the Final Act, the West also pressed for language in the declaration's preamble which noted the equal significance of all principles.

The vortex of controversy over the Declaration has been principles VI, nonintervention in internal affairs, and VII, respect for human rights. The Soviets would have preferred a CSCE document which did not mention civil or cultural rights but recognized that acceptance of such principles was a necessary compromise. From the outset of the multilateral talks Moscow took the high road, noting that the rights and freedoms of peoples in the Socialist states were far beyond those sanctioned in the declaration. Nonetheless, Soviet officials repeatedly cautioned that observance of human rights must be undertaken with deference to the principles of sovereign equality and nonintervention in internal affairs. The Soviets also contend that questions of human rights are solely within a state's domestic jurisdiction, except when their systematic violation presents a threat to the peace.[18] Despite this interpretation, the pledge of the CSCE states to act in conformity with the Charter of the United Nations and the Universal Declaration of Human Rights, as well as other international human rights conventions, makes many of their internal policies matters of international concern.[19]

The Helsinki summit was well publicized in the Soviet Union along with commentaries stressing the Final Act's contribution to securing the irreversibility of détente and the avoidance of war. Very little attention was given to the humanitarian aspects of the accord. Initially, public reaction to the Final Act was largely indifferent; most viewed it as an aspect of Soviet foreign policy remote from their daily lives. However, internal and foreign demands for full implementation of the Helsinki principles in the Soviet Union would soon force the Kremlin to become somewhat disillusioned with CSCE.

Human Rights and Basket 3: Locus of Tension

During the preparatory talks in Helsinki, the Soviets resisted Western claims that a truly meaningful period of détente would have to include an opening of European borders to the flow of people and information. However, after a month of trying negotiations, Brezhnev announced Moscow's willingness to discuss topics such as the enlargement of cultural and information exchanges so long as any agreements would be consonant with the "sovereignty, laws and customs of each country" and served "the mutual spiritual enrichment of peoples, the growth of confidence between them and the affirmation of ideas of peace, freedom and good-neighborliness."[20] The Soviets pursued this line throughout the Geneva sessions and they endeavored to add related qualifications to the preamble and the declaration of the Final Act. However, confronted with a firm stance by the Western and NNA states for expanded contacts, the Kremlin was forced into substantial compromises throughout the declaration and Basket 3.

Yet before the Helsinki summit had even adjourned, Soviet leaders began to assert restrictive interpretations of Basket 3 provisions that were explicitly excluded from the Final Act. During his speech to the summit conference, Brezhnev reiterated warnings that enlarged cultural and personal exchanges would have to serve the goals of "peace and trust"—code words for the ends of the state. In an obvious reference to monitoring compliance with the Final Act, the general secretary emphasized that " . . . no one should attempt . . . to dictate to other peoples how they should run their internal affairs."[21] Other official pronouncements from the Kremlin alleged that cooperation in the humanitarian sphere would have to be governed by the "laws and traditions of each country,"[22] a restrictive phrase which the West and NNA fought to exclude from the Helsinki document. Moscow made it clear that it was not prepared to adopt the West's interpretation of principle VII and Basket 3.

Only weeks after the Helsinki summit, the Soviets' initial enthusiasm about the Final Act faded. The most obvious manifestation of this change was the paucity of media attention to CSCE which had previously been a central item of discussion. There were two developments which precipitated this shift. First, Western leaders served notice that they would assess

Moscow's commitment to détente based on its observance of the Final Act. More menacing to the Kremlin was the fact that Soviet citizens began to cite the Helsinki document in their demands for internal reforms. This course of events triggered a Soviet campaign to counteract Western criticism of its implementation of the Final Act. Dr. Georgi Arbatov, director of the USA Institute, elaborated the offensive's major themes, which have reappeared in Moscow's pronouncements on CSCE over the past several years.[23]

> The West is attempting to distort the meaning of the Final Act and exploit it as "an instrument for interference" in the internal affairs of the socialist countries—contrary to principle VI.
>
> Western leaders are deluded in asserting that the Soviet Union owes something in return for CSCE's sanctioning of the existing European frontiers. All states benefit from the absence of territorial claims.
>
> Détente does not apply to the worldwide ideological struggle nor does it imply Soviet acceptance of the social status quo.
>
> The Soviet Union has far surpassed the West in terms of "objective" fulfillment of the Helsinki accords.
>
> Although the USSR is prepared to implement Basket 3 provisions it refuses to open its borders to "anti-Soviet, subversive propaganda or to materials advocating violence or stirring up national or racial strife. . . . "
>
> The United States has little right, considering its multitude of domestic political scandals and deep-seated social ills to be a champion of human rights.

After dismissing Western criticism with such arguments, Soviet commentators have often proceeded to highlight the "objective data" which allegedly prove the Socialist countries' superior record with respect to Basket 3. Scores of articles have noted that the Soviet Union translates more Western books, imports more Western films and television programs, and that more of its citizens study Western languages than vice versa. These commentaries always manage to overlook the scarce demand in the West for Soviet cultural offerings and attribute the imbalance in these exchanges to restrictive Western regulations governing information for Socialist states. Circumventing criticism of its scarce import of Western newspapers and journals, the Soviets prefer to dote on the size of the Moscow press corps and to excoriate the expanded budgets and transmitting capacities of Radio Liberty, Radio Free Europe, and other Western stations.

With respect to humanitarian provisions of the Final Act, the objective data is less favorable. Thus, the Soviets alleged that the 50 percent decline in Jewish emigration to Israel between 1974 and 1975 was a reflection of a world-wide disillusionment with the practice of Zionism. In a similar vein, the Kremlin has attempted to justify its rejection of a multitude of requests for exit visas under the CSCE provisions on family reunification, with the argument that such emigration usually has an adverse impact on the individual's family in the Soviet Union.[24]

Its overall record of fulfillment of its pledges of greater cooperation in humanitarian endeavors and freer flow of information illustrates the fact that the Soviet Union is unwilling to implement those Basket 3 provisions which would result in significant penetration of Western influence. While cultural and educational exchanges have expanded, these have been of the highly structured nature—which inhibits free interaction between peoples—that the Kremlin prefers. Moderately improved working conditions for Western journalists in the Soviet Union have been offset by arbitrary harassment and the inaccessibility of sources. Though the emigration of Soviet Jews and ethnic Germans has increased above 1975 levels, applying for an exit visa remains a precarious action for most citizens—effectively discouraging any embarrassing wave of departures.[25] It is evident that Moscow consented to Basket 3 and principle VII only to assure realization of portions of the Final Act that it viewed as crucial. However, the Soviet record with respect to these provisions of the Helsinki document has proven an embarrassment to Moscow internationally and stimulated a small, yet menacing, threat at home.

The Threat Within

Unlike its quick defensive reaction to the West's criticisms of its infidelity to the Final Act, Moscow's handling of the new boldness on the part of many domestic dissidents and reformers, which was inspired by CSCE, evolved quite cautiously. The Final Act provided dissidents with an internationally recognized charter which legitimized many of their grievances. This situation made the Kremlin's response more complicated. Soviet leaders recognized that overly repressive measures would provoke an intolerably embarrassing reaction at the Belgrade review conference and might jeopardize progress on other East-West issues. The result was a somewhat indecisive policy with sporadic fits of brutal injustices.

In May 1976, Uri Orlov and nine associates announced the formation of the Moscow Public Group to Promote Observance of the Helsinki Agreements in the Soviet Union—Helsinki Watch—to monitor Soviet compliance with the Final Act. This dramatic action inspired the formation of similar groups in Armenia, Georgia, Lithuania, and the Ukraine. These groups, by virtue of their high visibility in the West and their heterogeneous composition, have proven a particularly thorny problem for Soviet authorities. Orlov was able to forge an alliance of Jewish refuseniks, Christians seeking freedom of worship, artists, academics, reformers, and representatives of several national minorities, some of whom were veterans of earlier human rights struggles. While their total membership is only about forty-five people, these groups represent, according to Andrei Amalrik, but the tip of an iceberg of broad popular discontent. The Public Groups agreed to work in a nonviolent way, utilizing the existing political and legal structures to improve fulfillment of their government's pledges under the Final Act.[26]

The Kremlin's initial response to this development was an intensified propaganda campaign against such activities as well as surveillance of and physical threats to members, all designed to silence these groups through intimidation. Yet for eighteen months after the Helsinki summit, none of the prominent dissidents was arrested or sentenced to a psychiatric hospital. During this hiatus from incarceration, the Helsinki watchers produced over 200 detailed, trenchant reports on such topics as problems of emigration, conditions of political prisoners, and religious persecution as well as general discussions of the impact of the Final Act on Soviet society.[27] These documents found their way to the West and were beamed back to the Soviet people by Radio Liberty and other such organs, making them far more threatening to the Kremlin than any previous enunciations of disaffection. Soon, similar groups began to flourish in Eastern Europe and this, mixed with rising popular dissatisfaction with the economy and the emergence of President Carter's forceful campaign for human rights, seemed to trigger the Kremlin's decision to get tough with the Helsinki watchers. In February 1977 authorities began to arrest and deport central figures in the human rights movement, such that by early 1978, nearly half of the original group was either imprisoned or exiled. Lesser figures were quickly tried in closed courtrooms on trumped-up charges of anti-Soviet agitation, but the trials of more prominent members like Uri Orlov were delayed until after the Belgrade review conference. Despite this repression, the groups have persevered and recruited new adherents. It remains to be seen whether the harsh sentencing of their leadership will end their effectiveness.

The very existence of the Helsinki watch groups is a major achievement stimulated by the CSCE process. Orlov and his associates, bolstered by Western support, forced the Soviet regime to exercise periodic restraint in maintaining internal control. In the future, if CSCE can avoid provoking a siege mentality in the Kremlin, it can effectuate a moderation of certain objectionable Soviet domestic policies. The promotion of such a climate will allow for the painfully slow, evolutionary changes which can lead to lasting liberalization of the Soviet system and greater understanding among the peoples of Europe.

The Soviet Union and Other Provisions

It would be a mistake to view the other major segments of the Final Act, Basket 2 and the military confidence-building measures of Basket 1, as being quite distinct from the human rights and humanitarian provisions. Indeed, Soviet reluctance to fulfill its pledges under these headings can be traced to two central security concerns: a fear of Western penetration of Soviet society and the need to control the flow of information in both the military and economic spheres. Basket 2, by establishing guidelines for cooperation in several fields, serves primarily a hortative function. However, the Confidence—Building Measures (CBMs) are an aspect of the Final Act requiring affirmative action or notification of maneuvers and invitation of military observers and hence are practical tests of good faith.

The goals lauded by Basket 2—increased commercial, scientific, industrial, and technological cooperation—present the Soviet Union with both integrative opportunities and disintegrative threats on the domestic front. As much as the Kremlin would like to reap the benefits of Western capital and technology, it fears the concomitant exposure of Soviet society to capitalist thinking and life-styles. Moscow has endeavored to structure these exchanges so that intercultural interaction is minimized. It is hoped that such dealings will not only strengthen the domestic economy, but also make Soviet goods and services more attractive to their East European allies, thereby abetting COMECON integration. Circumstances external to CSCE have impeded the expansion of trade. There are fundamental structural barriers, such as the severe indebtedness of the Soviet Union resulting from its substantial negative trade balance, which have jeopardized extension of further Western credits.

The first three subsections of Basket 2 affirm the signatories' willingness to promote mutual trade and ease commercial undertakings as a means to reinforce security in Europe. However, Moscow perceives fulfillment of such pledges as dissemination of detailed economic data and expansion of business contacts as potential threats to its security. The segment of Basket 2 urging facilitation of contacts between firms and "sellers and users of products and services" assaults the very heart of state monopoly on economic activity. While there has been a slight growth in end-user participation in trade and industrial cooperation, the Kremlin can only tolerate a very limited degree of such interaction without a disruption of central planning and a growth of capitalist influences among its managerial class.[28] Moreover, there are other provisions such as harmonization of standards and technical regulations which are beyond the capacity of the Soviet economy to fulfill, even if there were the will to do so.

Information on the state of the Soviet economy remains notoriously inadequate, and what does become available is generally presented in a format that makes comparison with analogous Western data nearly impossible. This secrecy is designed to inhibit forecasting of economic trends and to facilitate central control. As one analyst noted:

> Wider foreign dissemination of key economic data may weaken the party control of the economy, foster debate among resource claimants and provide information to those who may use it for purposes otherwise adverse to Eastern state interests.[29]

There are, in addition to this fear, other structural differences such as the tradition of secrecy in state planning, bureaucratic delay, and the absence of an internal demand for such things as marketing information—all of which inhibit timely assembly of data which Western businesses value for their decision-making. Ironically, there is reason to believe that collection of more reliable data could improve Soviet central planning and management, and, if supplied to Western corporations, it might allow lower prices and more favorable credit terms in trade arrangements.[30] However, the Kremlin appears unwilling to experiment at this stage.

In the scientific field there has been a modest increase in the number of Soviet exchange agreements and joint projects with the West since Helsinki. Here again Soviet data necessary for such endeavors are often uneven in quality and quantity. Secrecy in these areas is also related to the need for central control but it is compounded by acute sensitivity about technological inferiority. The Soviets' refusal to allow for free and open exchanges among scientists participating in these projects has dampened hopes that significant advances in research and international understanding might be realized. Nonetheless, the official American assessment of these ventures remains quite favorable.[31]

Irrespective of its poor record in implementation of Basket 2 principles, Moscow has signed a document which affirms the contribution of cooperative undertakings in this sphere of activity to European security. Here again, aspects of Soviet life previously considered as entirely within the realm of its internal affairs are now open to international consideration. Moscow is now accountable for its failure to provide useful economic data, or its reluctance to expand trade or tourism or to enter into antipollution arrangements.

Despite these obstacles to some forms of cooperation, there are areas where East-West interdependence is evident and where societal penetration can be limited to degrees presently tolerable to Soviet authorities. Moscow has advocated convening of all-European conferences on energy, transport, and environmental protection over the past two years, primarily as a ploy to divert attention at the Belgrade conference from review of its implementation of the Final Act. Despite this motivation, exploration of practicable and mutually advantageous cooperative efforts in these areas seems vital, and the UN Economic Commission for Europe (ECE) is the appropriate forum for multilateral talks on these issues. The role of the ECE in advancing European cooperation was recognized by the Final Act, and this has invigorated its work. In addition to the planned conference of experts on transnational environmental pollution, the Soviets may endorse the discussion of other initiatives such as the proposed north-south highway, several Danube basin projects, and multilateral energy exploration and transportation ventures within the ECE framework.

Moscow has manifested increasing interest in pursuing topics addressed in Basket 2 by means of negotiations between COMECON and the EC. After many years of unwillingness to deal with the EC, COMECON advanced a proposal, couched in terms of implementation of Basket 2, for mutual recognition between the two blocs.[32] It is evident that the Kremlin recognized the value of such bloc-to-bloc dealings for enhancing solidarity among its fellow CMEA members. The Community's cautious responses to these overtures have expressed a willingness to negotiate in certain areas of mutual competence, such as compilation of economic and commercial statistics. However, the Brussels Commission has made it explicit that it prefers to deal bilaterally with COMECON members on trade matters. Soviet success along this line is unlikely both because of Western resistance to abetting COMECON integration and because EC-COMECON cooperation will yield few benefits to the West without major Eastern concessions affecting the terms and composition of trade.[33]

CBMs: Small Role in Furthering Military Détente

The Kremlin views the political developments outlined above as the more threatening aspects of CSCE, but it has also shown little interest in the military confidence-building measures mandated by the Helsinki accord. Nonetheless, it has implemented the letter, though not the spirit, of this title of the Final Act. Since the Helsinki summit, Moscow has accelerated its often propagandastic campaign for military détente to complement the political detente fostered by CSCE. While the focus of this drive has been measures for arms control and disarmament—to be taken by the West—the Soviets do include certain ''measures in the military-political sphere that

would help to enhance confidence among states, avert the threat of conflicts . . . and reduce military spending.''[34] Recognizing this perspective,
Soviet observance of the CBMs can be better understood. Since military
détente is a central element of its post-Helsinki European policy, the
Kremlin feels obliged to fulfill nominally the CBM provisions.

Nonetheless, the Soviet military remains deeply suspicious of the openness urged by the Final Act. Moscow has generally refused to send observers
to NATO maneuvers, has been very selective in extending invitations to
Warsaw Pact exercises, and NATO military observers have been subject to
a constricted purview when in the Soviet Union. It was not until late 1977
that the United States was invited to send observers to a Soviet exercise, and
while the U.S. team enjoyed exemplary treatment, it remains to be seen if
this was simply a ploy to ease the Belgrade review process.[35] Indeed, it is in-
auspicious that the Kremlin did not even announce the first major Red Army maneuvers undertaken after the Belgrade conference, which were held
in East Germany during July 1978.

One disturbing Soviet practice involving implementation of CBM provisions suggest a potential liability. Moscow has generally only invited
observers to maneuvers from states bordering on the location of a given
maneuver. Nonetheless, it seems more than a geographical coincidence that
Greece and Turkey, two states Moscow is anxious to pry away from NATO,
were the only Western nations invited to observe the ''Kavkaz'' maneuver
in Georgia and Armenia during January 1976. Whether Moscow intended
to demonstrate its military prowess to Athens and Ankara by this move is
debatable. Nonetheless, the incident suggest a possible misuse of the CBMs
which runs directly counter to their objective—exhibition of goodwill and
reduction of tension.

Thus, characteristic of Soviet compliance with other uncherished provisions of the Final Act, Moscow has been most scrupulous in observing the
CBM stipulations when such action is useful for other political ends.

The Kremlin's Balance Sheet on CSCE

CSCE has been only marginally supportive of Soviet objectives in Western
Europe. The process begun at Helsinki has not reduced U.S. involvement
with affairs on the Continent. The unified NATO-EC negotiating positions
at Helsinki and Belgrade suggest that ''Atlanticism'' and West European integration were actually reinforced by preparations for CSCE. Moreover,
the eruption of tensions between the Kremlin and the Eurocommunist parties has diminished the impact of such ''fraternal'' associations on affairs in
the West. While economic cooperation between the two halves of Europe
has expanded in recent years, this trend anteceded CSCE.

Ironically, this major foreign policy initiative has inadvertently yielded Moscow disturbing, though thus far quite manageable, developments at home. Nonetheless, the Kremlin still asserts, but in a more subdued fashion, the centrality of the Helsinki documents to the maintenance of peace and security in Europe. Moscow relished the Helsinki summit but it fears what the ongoing CSCE process will bring. This concern is most evident with respect to events in Eastern Europe.

The Hopes of East European Regimes: Greater Independence, Enduring Control

The ruling elites of Eastern Europe have often-disparate goals in CSCE which reflect unique national circumstances such as their degree of dependence upon the Soviet Union, their relationship with their citizenry, and general economic conditions. Nonetheless, these regimes share, to greater and lesser degrees, many of Moscow's fundamental concerns with the CSCE process. All these officials fear a common threat arising from the Helsinki documents: an erosion of their ability to control political developments among their citizenry. This problem is more acute in Eastern Europe than it is in the Soviet Union because of the region's cultural and geographical proximity to the West as well as its dependence on foreign commerce. Thus, all these regimes approach their Helsinki commitments to freer flows of people, information, and ideas and to expanded civil and cultural rights with considerable trepidation.

Conversely, what sets several of these regimes apart from their patron is a common aspiration that CSCE will enhance Moscow's sense of security and thereby allow them greater freedom of maneuver in the formulation of their domestic and foreign policies. Many Eastern European officials believe that such a development would grant them greater legitimacy among their citizenry. Other leaders are eager to seize such an opportunity to break away from the Kremlin's Socialist solidarity campaigns, particularly in the conduct of their relations with the West. It is instructive to highlight some of the diverse interests in CSCE among the East European states.

Most East European governments, particularly Poland and East Germany, placed great stock in Helsinki's multilateral ratification of the postwar frontiers. While most of these countries welcomed the prospects of greater East-West trade inspired by the Helsinki spirit, the East Germans feared a consequent erosion of their leadership position in intrabloc commerce. Romania has been in the vanguard of Eastern nations asserting the universality of the Final Act's Declaration of Principles. Moscow has persistently alleged that the Helsinki document governs only relations between states with different social systems, yet this qualification is noticeably absent in many East European commentaries on the subject.[36]

Romania's views on European security are unique among members of the Warsaw Pact, closer to those of nonaligned Yugoslavia than to those espoused by the Kremlin. Bucharest's assertion of its independence from the very opening round of negotiations at Helsinki is a striking illustration of what might be labeled the maximalist East European aspiration for CSCE. The Romanians have championed multilateral endorsement of various principles of interstate relations to inhibit Soviet encroachment on its singular foreign policy.[37] Bucharest has also stressed the importance of actualizing these pledges through the adoption of far-reaching arms control measures.[38] In pursuing this policy, the Romanians have advanced such two-edged proposals as the liquidation of blocs and withdrawal of all foreign troops under the mantle of the Soviet-endorsed pan-European security system. Though this deviationist course was quickly denounced by other Warsaw Pact members anxious to curry favor with the Kremlin, Bucharest's continued success along this line has made such a stance attractive to Poland and Hungary.

There has also been considerable variation in East European implementation of all facets of the Final Act. Despite this diversity, all these regimes recognize that there is a point at which interests in the rights of individuals, economic development, and a liberalized flow of people and ideas must be subjected to their need to exercise firm control. It is also understood that determination of this firebreak is not necessarily a decision which each state can make independently, because a threat to the "advance of socialism" in one country often concerns all fraternal states. Thus, the more orthodox regimes—East Germany, Bulgaria, and Czechoslovakia—share most of Moscow's views and practices with respect to CSCE. Two of the progressive states, Hungary and Poland, have consequently demonstrated great caution, fearful that if the Helsinki process becomes intolerably threatening to the hard-liners it could trigger a reaction which would stifle their limited autonomy. In this regard, several of these regimes may cooperate with Moscow's post-Czechoslovakia drive for bloc cohesion—which has been intensified since CSCE began—in order to avoid much sterner disciplinary action.[39]

The Impact of the Final Act

Assessing the effect of the Final Act on the political situation in Eastern Europe is complicated because of CSCE's synergistic relationship with several other developments. Nonetheless, there are several trends which can be specifically traced to the Helsinki summit. The Final Act was signed at a time of economic decline and swelling social malaise in Eastern Europe such that it found many advocates among a citizenry anxious for change.

In early 1975, the Soviet Union gravely impaired the East European economies by imposing steep price increases on raw-material exports to its Socialist allies. At the same time, the "stagflation" which had inflicted the West a few years earlier was beginning to be felt in the Socialist countries as a result of increasing East-West trade.[40] These developments, coupled with the enduring structural problems of these command economies, caused a reversal of gains in the consumer sector. This period also witnessed the emergence of the Eurocommunist phenomenon in the West which precipitated internecine strife in the international Communist movement and presented East Europeans with an alternative model abhorred by the Kremlin. Hovering in the background of all this turbulence are the impending succession struggles in the Soviet Union, Yugoslavia, Hungary, and Bulgaria. The infusion of the Final Act's civil, humanitarian, and cultural provisions into this volatile environment helped ignite unanticipated social unrest.

The numerous official pronouncements emanating from East European capitals during the first few months after Helsinki echoed the Kremlin's praise. The media in these countries provided substantial coverage of the Conference proceedings as well as exegeses on the Final Act. The general themes of the Soviets' post-Helsinki propaganda campaign were sounded, but with noticeable differences in emphasis.[41] Accompanying the familiar phrases emphasizing the primacy of the declaration, berating the West for distorting the meaning of the Final Act, and noting the importance of moving toward military détente, two points were given particular prominence:

Détente does not extend to the ideological realm despite capitalist attempts to demand such capitulation. During a period of relaxed tensions the Socialist community must pursue an even more vigilant ideological struggle and greater *coordination of its foreign policy and ideology.*

The West overemphasizes Basket 3 and principle VII and exploits them as a guise to interfere in the internal affairs of the Socialist states.

This promotion of increased Warsaw Pact integration at all levels of social and economic life, designed to halt the onslaught of pernicious bourgeois influences, was speedily intensified after Helsinki.

The first manifestation of this drive was a plethora of intra-Pact ventures in cultural and scientific cooperation. In the months after Helsinki there were dozens of ministerial-level conferences on such topics as cultural cooperation, journalism, social science research, and many more. Secretaries for ideology from the Warsaw Pact countries CP central committees convened in January 1976 to discuss the strengthening of bloc collaboration. In his address to the twenty-fifth Congress of the CPSU Brezhnev confirmed this renewed "drawing together of the Socialist countries.''[42] The drive for solidarity reached new heights when the WTO's Political Consultative Committee, traditionally the forum for foreign policy coordination, announced the formation of a committee of foreign ministers.[43] The establishment of this foreign ministers committee can be partially linked to Moscow's rebuff by a vocal minority of Eurocummunist parties at the East Berlin CP Conference the preceding June. Indeed, the Kremlin seems to have resolved that if the disease of separate routes to communism could not be arrested in Western Europe, then at least the East could be immunized with a heavy dose of conformist pressure. But this move also reflects the general post-Helsinki tightening-up which was designed—in the short term—to bolster the Pact's solidarity going into the Belgrade conference. The PCC's communiqué set out practical steps to counter the West's challenge to socialism, and advanced several disarmament proposals for consideration at the CSCE review session.

Internal Dissent

The confluence of these political and economic developments set the stage for a flurry of protest in the East bloc. The Helsinki spirit provided new impetus to the civil rights movement in Poland and the emigration phenomenon in East Germany, both of which are primarily outcroppings of social dysfunction in these states. In contrast, the Final Act and the consequent blossoming of international interest in human rights have actually enabled the long-isolated voices of dissent in Czechoslovakia to be heard. A glimpse at these most prominent human rights movements illuminates the way in which CSCE influenced the evolution of dissent in the East.[44]

The initial outburst of post-Helsinki protest surfaced in Poland during late 1975. Hundreds of intellectuals and the Catholic Church hierarchy denounced, and ultimately succeeded in altering, several constitutional amendments advanced by the party which would have tightened Warsaw's alliance with Moscow and further subjected the rights of the individual Pole to state interests. However, it was the extraordinary food price increases proposed by the Warsaw regime in June 1976 which triggered a workers' strike that had ripple effects throughout Polish society. The government rescinded the pricing decree but its harsh actions against the strikers, including a series of trials, spurred other protests. Intellectuals formed a defense committee—known by its Polish acronym, KOR—to aid workers who were harassed or imprisoned in the aftermath of the strikes. KOR joined with the Church in a successful campaign for amnesty for the strikers, but their demands for a full inquiry into charges of police brutality toward dissenters went unheeded. In an event more directly related to Helsinki, a nationalist group, the Movement for the Defense of Human

Rights (Ropco), was formed in early 1977 with the objective of bringing Polish law into conformity with international human rights conventions.[45]

In early January 1977, a document entitled Charter 77, signed ultimately by more than 900 Czechoslovakian citizens—including several prominent figures in the 1968 reform movement—emerged from Prague. The "chartists" eschewed characterization as an opposition political movement, and declared their desire to enter into a "dialogue with political and state authorities" on observance of the Final Act and the human rights conventions which have been incorporated into Czechoslovakia's legal system.[46]

There are very few overt dissidents in East Germany, most of whom became visible in the West during protests of the repressive actions taken against the most prominent critics of the regime, folksinger Wolf Biermann and physicist Robert Haveman. However, the East Berlin government was confronted with a much more explosive problem: over 100,000 East Germans applied for exit visas during 1976, most of whom invoked their rights under the Helsinki accords.

To the surprise of the East bloc governments and the protesters themselves, these phenomena have had extraordinary repercussions because of their emergence as international *causes célèbres*. While foreign support has bolstered the viability of these movements, the internal conditions in each country have determined the character of the governmental response.

The Final Act provides these movements with further objective criteria by which to assess their government's performance in observing human rights. Most of these East European dissidents, like their counterpart Helsinki watchers in the Soviet Union, have undercut the regime's traditional justification for cracking down by characterizing themselves as nonpolitical citizens concerned about observance of international legal obligations. Moreover, many of these dissidents have received the blessings of the European Communist parties, and this support is not only a legitimizing factor but a moderating influence on the response of Eastern regimes anxious to avoid further fissures in international Communist unity.[47] Thus the official response to dissent in the post-Helsinki environment is much more complicated than before. The governments cannot easily brand such individuals as subversive or antisocialist—not with much credibility. An overly repressive action against the dissidents will sully the country's image in the West and thereby jeopardize crucial trade concessions and other benefits of détente. Confronted with this dilemma of exercising firm control or maintaining good relations with the West, most East European governments have demonstrated a willingness to engage in a cost/benefit analysis, although a strong bias toward control persists.

Consider the variety of responses to Helsinki-inspired activism in the East. Most regimes have preferred a low-keyed strategy of harassment to intimidate dissidents and have been willing to make concessions on humanitarian issues when there is some political or economic reward. Hungary and Poland have undertaken firm but hardly oppressive action in coping with dissent. In Romania, President Ceausescu has felt obliged to yield ground on several humanitarian questions in order to maintain Bucharest's good image in the West. East Germany, uncertain of its popular support and confronted with increasing exposure to Western influences in this era of détente, has displayed this insecurity in fairly stern actions against its small group of dissident intellectuals. The most distressing violator of human rights has been Czechoslovakia. After an initial debate between Husak and hard-liners within the regime over the severity of the response, the latter faction prevailed and so the cautious probings of the Charter 77 reformers were greeted with what one expert on Eastern Europe called "an hysterical overreaction" of reprisals.[48]

Thus, the impact of CSCE as a force for internal liberalization in Eastern Europe varies considerably in each country. While international monitoring of the human rights situation sustains Charter 77, the momentum of internal forces is likely to determine the development of civil liberties in Poland. In East Germany, the emigration movements are protected by the general relaxation of tensions of which CSCE is a part. However, no regime has been reluctant to squelch the dissident voices that have emerged in these countries. The restraint exhibited by Budapest in coping with limited protests can be attributed to the much less threatening nature of these groups and to Hungary's determination to avoid any provocation of the West which might jeopardize trade expansion. The importance of economic relations with the West and the interrelationship between Basket 2 and Basket 3 issues are examined below.

Eastern Europe and Basket 2

The East Europeans have even more to gain from expanded economic, scientific, and technological cooperation with the West than do their Soviet allies. These countries must confront not only the aforementioned structural problems which inhibit East-West trade, but also a striking dilemma. For, while joint commercial and industrial ventures and access to Western science and technology are crucial to the modernization efforts—and hence the stability of most COMECON states—the impact of their attendant human contacts is a potential hazard to this same stability. The distinct opportunity that full implementation of many Basket 2 principles presents to Eastern Europe is a lessened dependence on COMECON and hence the stifling aspects of the Soviet economic model. These societies have been placed in an economic straitjacket by Moscow, and expanded trade and joint commercial and industrial projects are viewed by many East European planners as a means to infuse new stimuli into their modernization process.

Here again there is by no means an East European consensus on these issues. The East German leadership may see a negative balance for their country in extensive cooperation with the West. East Germany could lose its privileged status in trading with the EC as well as its position as the leading producer of high technology items for its COMECON partners. Moreover, East Germany is perhaps most vulnerable to the pernicious influences that an influx of capitalist businessmen and technicians would bring. Czechoslovakia's ambivalence toward economic contacts contrasts sharply with the disposition of its allies Romania, Hungary, and Poland, who are manifestly eager to increase their export earnings through trade and to explore the feasibility of a variety of ventures with the West. COMECON's favored means of circumventing the attendant undesirable influences of economic cooperation with the West is the outright purchase of technology. Nonetheless, even such "neutral" absorption of technology often necessitates political and institutional changes in planning and management.

The Soviets have recognized the benefits of East-West trade to stability and regime legitimacy in Eastern Europe. However, the Kremlin has endeavored to avoid the unwanted political consequences by fostering greater COMECON integration and by pressing for bloc-to-bloc trade negotiations between the EC and its COMECON partners. But there are rather formidable hurdles in Moscow's way. All the East bloc countries, with Romania being the most vociferous, have argued the importance of national planning within the context of COMECON plan coordination. On the question of trade, the EC Commission has held firmly to its preference—for both economic and political reasons—to negotiate agreements with individual East bloc states.

Another liability of expanded economic contacts with the capitalist world confronting Eastern Europe is the concomitant exposure to Western economic trends. The stagflation which has flowed east with commerce exacerbated the general economic decline in the COMECON states. This problem, coupled with their mounting indebtedness to the West, may force the East Europeans to reassess the value of such trade and will certainly render them more dependent on the Soviet Union for fulfillment of their financial obligations. The East bloc also has its complaints about Western compliance with Basket 2 provisions. Restrictive trade policies such as U.S. linkage of most-favored-nation (MFN) status to emigration policies and EC import quotas have been repeatedly decried by East European officials as violations of the Final Act. MFN is primarily of symbolic importance to the Soviet Union, whose principal exports to the West are raw materials not subject to tariffs. However, MFN status is of considerable value to the East Europeans, who have certain finished goods that can be competitive on Western markets when duties are removed, as Romania and Poland have demonstrated. While this is not the place to explore the impediments to trade expansion such as Eastern dumping and Western demands for reciprocity, one consideration is noteworthy in the current context. Increased East European export earnings could help reduce the regions' indebtedness to the West and its financial dependency on the Soviet Union.

CBMs Downplayed

Despite calls for the development of military détente, the East European Warsaw Pact members, with the exception of Romania, have shown little inclination to observe the military CBMs in the "spirit of reciprocity" extolled by the Final Act. Although these countries have provided notification of all maneuvers above the mandatory 25,000 troop threshold, they have been less forthcoming about smaller exercises and major redeployments. Similarly, until just before the Belgrade conference, the Warsaw Pact members had declined all invitations to observe NATO maneuvers and have often limited the purview of NATO observers attending exercises within their borders. Most Warsaw Pact members joined in Soviet efforts to disparage CBMs while endorsing Moscow's grandiose disarmament schemes as more effective for realizing military détente. Only Romania has placed much emphasis on CBMs, and Bucharest has advanced various proposals for expanding these measures, although some of their ideas actually fall under the rubric of arms control.

Conclusions

In the view of the region's ruling elites, CSCE has done little to enhance security in Eastern Europe. It has proven to be a catalyst for a number of disturbing, and potentially destabilizing, developments in an already uncertain climate. East European leaders have been confronted with new problems of adaptation, and often the changes have been away from liberalization. Moreover, the renewed campaign for Socialist integration in the wake of the Helsinki summit has actually restrained the evolution of more independent foreign and domestic policies. The marginal improvements in the humanitarian sector have generally been stimulated by more tangible interests than fulfillment of Final Act pledges. While Helsinki-inspired dissent may be manageable for the Eastern regimes, rising economic dissatisfaction, ethnic struggles, and the attraction of Eurocommunism are quite likely sources of instability in the region. The way these governments assess the benefits of détente will be reflected in, and influenced by, the CSCE process.

It would be unfair to disparage the new hope CSCE has provided for

Eastern reformist movements. Eastern Europe has returned to the front rank of Western foreign policy concerns and popular consciousness, rather than being forgotten, as some feared, behind the frontiers recognized at Helsinki. So long as this situation persists without an overly zealous liberationist tone, CSCE can contribute to the vicissitudinous struggle of improving human rights and fundamental freedoms in the region. While this process does involve inherent East-West conflicts, it is the only way a more enduring peace can be forged on the Continent. The ultimate causes of insecurity in Eastern Europe are not generated by Western interference, but by Moscow's hegemony and the absence of broad popular support for the region's regimes.

The Neutral and Nonaligned States: Common Stake in CSCE

One of the surprises of the CSCE process has been the vigorous, constructive role played by the neutral and nonaligned states since the outset of the multilateral negotiations. Much to the Kremlin's dismay, the NNA have been neither docile nor particularly supportive of Soviet efforts to skirt human rights issues. Indeed, while they have acted as intermediaries between the two blocs, frequently advancing compromise proposals, more often than not the NNAs have been supportive of the West's designs for CSCE.

This diverse agglomeration, ranging from neutral Switzerland, Austria, and Sweden to nonaligned Spain to Communist, nonaligned Yugoslavia, can hardly be said to constitute a third bloc. However, the NNA have become a driving force behind CSCE, united in their interest of sustaining the process. The NNA have used their considerable collective influence both in forging reconciliation between East and West and in spurring both these parties to strive for more comprehensive accords, particularly in the area of military confidence-building. Because of their diversity, it is impossible to assess herein their individual goals in and reactions to CSCE. However, it is instructive to examine the impact of their common devotion to the success of the process.

For the NNA, CSCE represents the one forum addressing their security concerns where the consensual basis of decision-making grants them much more impact on these questions than might otherwise be possible. This common, though quite broad, focus of CSCE participants gives the process a unique character. The several NNA states that are geographically situated between the two major blocs—Austria, Finland, Sweden, and Yugoslavia—have a critical stake in the progress of détente. These four states, as well as Romania, have been the foremost advocates of innovative

CBMs and other military security measures. For Finland, Yugoslavia, and Warsaw Pact member Romania, CSCE is important in buttressing their independence from Moscow's dictates. The Final Act provides further affirmation of Yugoslav and Romanian sovereignty while the Finns believe that it provides an additional guarantee of their present degree of autonomy.

These states have been generally pleased with the fruits of CSCE but have expressed concern with what they regard as Western overemphasis of compliance with Final Act provisions. Most of the NNA fear that preoccupation with such accounting inhibits progress toward new measures and jeopardizes those established at Helsinki. Finland, Yugoslavia, and Sweden have also cautioned the West that focusing attention on principle VII and Basket 3 could have similar repercussions. Nonetheless, all these states endorsed efforts for a balanced review of implementation at the Belgrade follow-up session.

Other major members of the NNA group—Austria, Ireland, Spain, and Switzerland—have taken positions quite similar to those of the European Community, and several have undertaken new initiatives within the CSCE framework. For example, the Swiss successfully lobbied at Helsinki for a meeting of experts to discuss their draft "Convention on a European System of Peaceful Settlement of Disputes." This conference convened at Montreaux in October 1978 to discuss Berne's concepts for both binding settlement procedures in justiciable disputes and also new formulas for arbitration of political conflicts. Austria has taken a particularly vigorous stand in defense of the humanitarian and informational segments of the Final Act, going so far as to offer political asylum to signers of Charter 77. CSCE also nudged the Dublin government, which is actually a member of the EC caucus, toward normalization of relations with East European capitals.

The disposition of the NNA states toward CSCE are related more to dominant trends in the dealings between the two blocs than to any consideration of group solidarity. When debate polarizes them, these states tend to shift toward the bloc with which they are closest ideologically. Nonetheless, the keen interest of these countries in avoiding such bifurcation in order to sustain the CSCE process as a meeting of individual states was felt at Belgrade and has important implications for future review sessions.

For the West, Pleasant Surprises

While the members of the European Community approached CSCE with hopes of realizing a moderately valuable code of détente, the U.S. delegation arrived at Helsinki with very low expectations and a negotiating strategy best described as damage limitation. While quite active in the agenda-setting, preparatory talks, Washington's low-keyed participation in the Geneva deliberations until the final stages was testimony to the fact that the United States was involved in the CSCE primarily as a concession for progress in other areas, such as MBFR, which were viewed as more vital. However, after an initial national trauma about the alleged signing-away of Eastern Europe's freedom at Helsinki faded and the full potential of the Final Act was appreciated, the United States began to reassert its influence on CSCE matters. Indeed, by mid-1976 these two roles had become somewhat reversed. Washington became the most intense champion of CSCE's human rights and freer exchange provisions, while the West Europeans counseled restraint to ensure that the fragile process could be sustained. Despite these differences, two surprising dimensions of the CSCE undertaking have been the solidarity of the Western participants and the degree to which the Final Act has actually advanced Western interests in Europe.

Western Europe's ardent interest in CSCE flowed from the hope that the conference would set the framework and provide the impetus for a multilateralization of the European détente initiated by West Germany's *Ostpolitik*. Also, in this period of Soviet-American predominance in East-West diplomacy, the West Europeans value CSCE as a forum where their interests are directly represented.

Western Goals

The first objective of the Western states at Helsinki was to expand the conference agenda from a simple endorsement of platitudes on interstate relations and the territorial status quo to a much broader scheme for regularizing transnational relations and expanding human contacts. This concern for Basket 3 items is influenced to varying degrees by domestic political considerations in the allied states, but there is Western consensus that durable security is impossible so long as half of Europe remains sealed off from the other half. The philosophical underpinning of this position is the conviction that ignorance of each other's societies and governmental interests is largely responsible for the present degree of apprehension in Europe. Thus, the West contended at Helsinki that if CSCE were to make a genuine contribution to European security it would have to provide for a more liberal flow of people and information across the continent's international frontiers.

The EC Nine, particularly Italy and the Benelux countries, pressed successfully during both the preparatory sessions and the two years at Geneva for inclusion of Basket 3 on the agenda and for the substantiation of both this segment and principle VII of the declaration.[49] Washington feared that the lengthy negotiations at Geneva which were necessary to obtain Eastern concessions in these areas, but which also forestalled the European summit that Moscow craved, was impeding progress on SALT and MBFR.

The West also wanted to insure that CSCE would not only ameliorate interbloc diplomacy but also relations between the various East European states and the Soviet Union. The West battled for principles in the Declaration on sovereignty and nonintervention to help erode the basis of Soviet hegemony in Eastern Europe and to provide a sound rebuke to the concept of united sovereignty implicit in the Brezhnev doctrine.

Another major concern in Western planning for CSCE was the development of expanded contacts and information flows in the military domain. Western negotiators contended that certain military confidence-building measures and exchanges would reduce tensions and promote trust in Europe. The British and West Germans presented the EC's position that the CBMs, like the provisions on human contacts and freer information flows, were useful tests of the practicability of détente. Despite the successful inclusion of all the above items on the agenda, the Western governments still exhibited certain apprehension about the impact of CSCE.

Western Misgivings

The most prominent fear in NATO capitals was that involvement with CSCE would exacerbate the problems of maintaining adequate military force levels, much less increase outlays for defense. There was considerable anxiety that an overdose of the era of negotiations would dull public support for military preparedness. While CSCE may have contributed to the initial euphoria about the promise of detente, the continued Soviet military build-up has counteracted this effect.

Another source of trepidation in the West concerned the impact that endorsement of the territorial status quo on the Continent would have on relations with Eastern Europe. Some policy planners asserted that CSCE would further isolate Eastern Europe from the West by affirming Soviet hegemony and facilitating Moscow's integrationist policies in the region. In fact, the aftermath of Helsinki witnessed a revival of interest in East European affairs not only in Western capitals but among the general population. While some of this attention is the result of expanding bilateral political and economic relations, it is concern for human rights and Basket 3 provisions which really turned the spotlight on Eastern Europe.

A related concern, which preoccupied West German planning for CSCE, was avoidance of any actions at Helsinki or Geneva which might undermine the arrangements established by its carefully drafted "Eastern treaties." Bonn also confronted domestic concern with the impact of CSCE with an intensity unique in the West. The CDU/CSU opposition, long critical of *Ostpolitik*, was anxious to launch a major attack on the SPD/FPD government if it acceded to any CSCE provisions which could be depicted as undermining German interests. Most sensitive was the Declaration of Principles, which addressed the territorial and political situation in Europe. West Germany fought successfully to exclude any language in the declaration which would suggest finality to the borders on the Continent. Bonn preferred a text which would approximate the terms of its "Eastern treaties," all of which allow for ultimate reunification of Germany. Thus, when East and West agreed on the inviolability principle (III) it was West Germany negotiators who were instrumental in realizing the mitigatory provisions for peaceful change of frontiers in principle I and the preambulary formula on the interrelationship among principles. With Moscow eager to assert the overarching importance of the inviolability principle these qualifying phrases were critical. In a similar vein, while West Germany favors an expansion of human contacts in Europe it has likewise remained attentive to the East's sensitivity about these interactions. Bonn's cautiousness in this regard is designed to avoid any tensions which might jeopardize its agreements on reunification and repatriation with several Eastern countries.

A universal source of anxiety among members of the European Community was that CSCE would undermine West European integration. This threat was two-pronged: disruptive factional struggles might erupt among the Nine and would certainly be cultivated by the Soviets, and/or alternative pan-European institutions might be established which would, at best, distract members from involvement with Community affairs. It was well understood in Brussels that the Soviet campaign for a European security conference had increasingly emphasized inclusion of trade and economic cooperation issues on the parley's agenda. Moreover, Moscow's pronouncements on détente stressed its importance in helping to "liquidate any discrimination, nonequality and artificial barriers" in trade and inveighed against enlargement of the Community.[50] As it became evident that the CSCE would address issues within the EEC's purview, member states began to plot how the Community's interests could be best represented.

In ironic contrast to these fears, the effort of charting a Community strategy for CSCE proved to be the singular major success in policy coordination. The Nine's Political (Davignon) Committee and its various subgroups have forged common EEC positions on both political and economic aspects of the CSCE. At the various CSCE deliberations the Community's interests have been represented by the delegation of the member currently occupying the chairmanship of the Council of Ministers. This harmony was evident at the preparatory talks and lingered right through the Belgrade review. The EEC also collaborated with the NATO Political Committee in such a way that Western initiatives at both Geneva and Belgrade were usually advanced under the joint sponsorship of the Community and NATO. However, it should be noted that the Nine did object to any efforts by the superpowers to manipulate the course of negotiations on the Final Act by means of extraneous bilateral discussions.[51] Nonetheless, Western policy coordination was instrumental in expanding the scope of the Final Act in the areas of military confidence-building and Basket 3.

The Impact of the Final Act

Implementation of the Final Act is not really an issue in the West because the document's principles generally reflect common governmental practices. Nonetheless, the allied governments have undertaken a concerted effort to develop exemplary records by fulfilling not only the letter but the spirit of the Helsinki document. Thus, Western governments have announced military maneuvers below the 25,000 troop level, liberalized travel restrictions and visa requirements, expedited family reunification cases, and expanded cultural, scientific, and educational exchanges. Though this record is hardly flawless, it has set a standard for comparison with the East, and several practices that were not consonant with the Final Act were altered.[52] All these measures were crucial to the principal task of the West in the wake of Helsinki: monitoring the East's fulfillment of its pledges.

The Ford administration and several other Western governments confronted bitter criticism from a broad range of the political spectrum in the wake of the Helsinki summit. It is evident that this reception of the Final Act gave impetus to the West's decision to assess compliance in the East. The U.S. Congress felt the public hostility most acutely. Moreover, members of Congress and other Western officials were encouraged by East bloc dissidents to be outspoken in reviewing the Communist governments' observance of Final Act provisions. These factors provided the stimulus for legislation establishing the Commission on Security and Cooperation in Europe. This commission, composed of members of legislative and executive branches, has a mandate to review compliance with the Final Act, and to aid it in this task the president provides semiannual reports on the records of the thirty-four signatory states. The commission has conducted study missions in Europe, held extensive hearings on implementation of Baskets 2 and 3, assembled the documents of Eastern human rights groups, and had its professional staff serve on the U.S. delegation at the Belgrade conference. Moscow protested the commission's formation, asserting that it is an illegal instrument for interference in the internal affairs of the Socialist states, and study groups sponsored by the panel have been denied entry into the East bloc countries.[53] However, this resistance has not prevented indirect contacts with dissidents in the region. The commission's activities have abetted Helsinki watchers in the East and spawned formation of analogous groups in the West. The renewed public and governmental interest in human rights has also reinvigorated groups long active in the field. While the West has focused its monitoring activities on the human rights and Basket 3, it has not overlooked other facets of the Final Act.

Looking to Basket 2, the East's provision of economic and commercial data and efforts at facilitation of trade and industrial cooperation arrangements have generally fallen short of Western standards. However, in response to criticism, the Eastern governments have gone on the offensive with complaints about the West's withholding of MFN trade status, EC tariff barriers, and antidumping regulations.

Strict fulfillment of the guidelines established in Basket 2 does present the West with some problems. These governments fear the economic dislocation often caused by the long-term trade agreements preferred by the COMECON states. Similarly, there is the problem of determining market value of certain Eastern exports for which, in many instances, there is no domestic demand. In the case of scientific and technological cooperation, Western participants have agreed that the exchanges are useful for advancing international understanding and monitoring developments in East bloc research. However, in most instances the flow of new technical information has been to the East.[54] Furthermore, civil rights practices have often interfered with the conduct of these exchanges. All these issues are part of the entire framework of a détente diplomacy, and realization of the Final Act's guidelines for cooperation will require extensive bilateral and multilateral negotiations.

A similar offensive was undertaken by some of the East bloc countries in response to criticism of their human rights policies. As noted previously, the Eastern media emphasized the failings of the West in implementation of Basket 3 provisions calling for increased dissemination of information. Similarly, economic and judicial injustices in the West, particularly in the United States, have been assailed as violations of the Final Act. The West welcomed these exchanges as a legitimization of its contention that the Helsinki accords had elevated such matters to the agenda of interstate diplomacy. However, as the Eastern countries appreciated the cogency of this argument, their charges of civil rights violations in the West became less visible.

Conclusion

The general assessment of CSCE in the West has been positive. Most Western capitals agree that their "Eastern" policies have been well served by CSCE. There is some concern in Western Europe that the tenor of the U.S. human rights campaign and the emphasis on criticizing the East bloc's implementation of its Helsinki pledges may have contributed to the recent stagnation in East-West diplomacy. Yet, most Western leaders recognized the inherent conflicts of interests which would arise once the superficial aspects of the détente relationship had run their course. The Final Act does call for undertakings that are inimical to unfettered regime control in closed societies, but which are crucial to enduring peace in Europe. If the Final Act is to become an effective instrument for realizing this goal, disregard for its provisions must be noted. But the West must shun expectations that CSCE can achieve a transmutation of Europe in a few years. Despite uneven implementation of the Final Act, CSCE has evolved into an effective agent for shaping European détente in the Western mold. Thus, by the time preparations for the Belgrade conference were undertaken, it was evident that Moscow would be a less than enthusiastic participant in the review proceedings.

Battle Lines Are Drawn

The polarization of Eastern and Western goals at the Belgrade review conference was evident early in the preparatory stages. The West favored a thorough, though not overly accusatory, accounting of signatory states' compliance with the Final Act. The Soviet Union and its allies, with the exception of Romania, argued that the Helsinki document envisioned the Belgrade session as an opportunity to explore new and expanded measures of cooperation in Europe. While Moscow successfully inhibited adoption of a substantive concluding document, the West realized its objectives of a frank assessment of implementation of Final Act provisions and the construction of a framework for a continuing series of similar conferences. While none of the dozens of new proposals advanced during the parley was adopted, it seems unlikely that, given the extant state of East-West relations, alternative strategies by either side would have yielded different results.

In contrast to the deliberations leading to the Helsinki summit, the United States took a leading role in Western planning for and negotiating at Belgrade. This transition was attributable to developments on the Continent and to the Carter administration's renewed attention to European affairs and the state of human rights throughout the world. The Western governments had fairly uniform goals, but there were differences over the manner in which they should be pursued. Although the European allies were willing to express support for the U.S. quest of a thorough human rights review in private conversations, several governments believed it was more constructive, or were pressured by domestic political considerations, to be somewhat restrained in criticizing the East's record in this regard.[55] The Kremlin attempted unsuccessfully to exacerbate these disagreements by playing to European fears that an "aggressive" review session would indeed hinder progress in other areas of détente diplomacy.[56] However, consultations between the EC and NATO caucuses maintained allied unity.

This unity was not evident among Warsaw Pact members. The West provided several East European nations with incentives to break ranks with the Kremlin. The selective criticism of observance of human rights and humanitarian provisions left Hungary and Poland (because of their more enlightened internal policies) relatively unscathed, and also inhibited formation of a unified resistance to the West on these issues. Moreover, Hungary, Poland, and Romania all feared that such a tough Pact response might jeopardize their arrangements with the West in trade and other areas. Thus, Hungary and Poland reportedly pressed for moderation during Pact consultations. If this experience at exercising national interests in WTO caucuses is repeated in other such deliberations, then a central Western goal in CSCE, the evolution of greater independence for East European regimes, will have been promoted.

The Soviets undertook a propaganda offensive nearly a year before Belgrade in order to avoid the appearance of being a defendant at the review session. Moscow's principal goal was to limit the scope and duration of the conference, thereby down-playing the parley's significance and avoiding an embarrassing inquiry into its human rights policies. After the November 1976 meeting of the Warsaw Pact's Political Consultative Committee, the East began to reveal these objectives and to advance a barrage of new and recycled proposals for consideration at Belgrade. These schemes, most of which were patently designed to undermine Western security, were advanced in an effort to divert attention from a review of implementation.[57] However, with the support of the NNA states, the West was successful in eliciting Eastern agreement to an organizational framework, outlined in the so-called "Yellow Book," which assured a thorough review at Belgrade and established precedents for future reviews of the Final Act.

The NNA states and Romania were particularly vigorous participants at Belgrade, advancing more than one-fourth of the new proposals brought before the gathering. Most NNA proposals were practicable supplements to the Final Act, particularly in the field of CBMs, although some members of this group did pursue particularist objectives. Most of these countries echoed the concern of several NATO members that an acrimonious confrontation at Belgrade would be inimical to the progress of the détente so vital to their security. Indeed, it was the NNA delegates who were most disappointed with the denouement of the conference.

The Fruits of Belgrade

Looking solely to the concluding statement of the Belgrade conference the results of these lengthy negotiations seem meager. In the document, participating states reaffirmed their commitment to détente, acknowledged that exchanges on implementation had taken place and that there had been disagreement over the degree of success in this regard, noted new proposals examined, but not adopted, and agreed to meet again on Thursday, November 11, 1980, in Madrid. Such a perspective is inappropriate for assessing a conference which was not intended to have immediate, substantive consequences. Belgrade was part of an ongoing process. The precedent-setting nature of this review of the Final Act is a significant achievement. Despite the fact that no participant state was censured officially, the most egregious East European violators of human rights felt the heat of the conference's spotlight, and are confronted with the prospect of similar embarrassment in the future.

The real measure of Belgrade's success will be developments in Europe over the next several years. The review process will be effective if the East bloc remains sensitive and occasionally responsive to Western pressure for fuller implementation of their Helsinki pledges. The effect of the Belgrade deliberations on the overall condition of East-West relations is another indicator of CSCE's value.

Despite the disturbing nature of the Belgrade sessions for the Soviets and their closest allies, these governments have taken a fairly positive view of the conference. Commentators noted that the proceedings reaffirmed the centrality of the Final Act in the process of détente, while minimizing the significance of the parley's other activities.[58] Moreover, the Eastern states have not suggested that Belgrade had an adverse impact on other aspects of the détente process. Indeed, according to a U.S. National Security Council study of the Carter administration's human rights campaign, PRM-28, the Kremlin has not allowed this activism to inhibit negotiations on other issues. Clearly underestimating the depth of the U.S. commitment to human rights, Moscow regards the Carter policy as a propaganda ploy which should be countered with analogous agitation. Hence, Moscow's extensive media blitz decrying the enhanced radiation (neutron) warheads appears designed to meet this need.[59] While the East does not assert the existence of a linkage between CSCE and progress in other areas of mutual interest, this is not so in the West.

Belgrade did seem to provoke a new round of ideological tightening-up among Warsaw Pact members. A flurry of intra-alliance conferences and high-level visits was evident during the first few months after the review conference. Brezhnev's visit to Czechoslovakia, an apparent gesture of support for the hard-line faction of the Prague regime, also signaled endorsement of forceful repression of dissidence. WTO foreign ministers meeting several weeks after Belgrade sounded what may be the keynote of an intensified "struggle against the imperialist policy of interference in the internal affairs of the [Socialist] states."[60] Moscow may not impose a linkage between CSCE and other issues on the East-West agenda, but it is not willing to take any chances on maintaining stability in its client states.

As for the impact of Belgrade in the sensitive area of human rights, the results are ambiguous. It was hardly expected that Belgrade would in some way shame the more repressive Eastern governments to alter their domestic policies. The West was hopeful of drawing these regimes into a dialogue on relevant provisions of the Final Act. The East bloc delegations began the conference with a determination to avoid any such exchange and they therefore avoided comments of the state of human rights in the West. However, when Western criticism shifted to specific instances of repression, the Soviet delegation opted to respond with countercharges about shortcomings in the extension of economic and civil rights in the United States. This move was a tacit acknowledgment of the legitimacy of addressing human rights practices in the conference framework, as was the fact that the East bloc delegations continued to participate in these exchanges.

The NATO delegations, plus Ireland, advanced a proposal to enhance implementation of the human rights provisions by reaffirming a clause in principle IX which recognizes the "role which institutions, organizations and persons as well as governments" play in this endeavor. This measure was designed to protect and sanction both the activities of Helsinki monitoring groups throughout Europe and the right of the individual to invoke the Final Act in dealing with his government. The Soviets did not respond to this proposal directly; rather, they attempted to squelch its consideration by advancing three human rights proposals which were patently unacceptable to the West. Despite this setback, Charter 77 signators issued a statement on Belgrade which asserted that the conference proceedings had "enhanced the possibility that [human rights] movements will grow."[61] Even if the reformist movements in Eastern Europe were strengthened by Belgrade, the harsh sentencing of Helsinki Watchers Orlov, Shcharansky, and Ginzburg only weeks after the conference adjourned suggests that the Soviets are not deterred from taking whatever measures are perceived as necessary to liquidate dissent, although they are sensitive enough to international criticism to have delayed these actions until after the review session. Moreover, it is doubtful that the Kremlin can ever totally repress these manifestations of discontent which have been buoyed by the process set in motion at Helsinki.

For the West, the circumstances of Belgrade were quite different from the Helsinki and Geneva rounds of CSCE. No longer could concessions be exacted from Moscow in exchange for the summit it craved. Rather, the

West was now the demander and it had few bargaining chips. Soviet intransigence prevented adoption of a substantive concluding document, and as a result the West opted for a skeletal statement which outlined what had transpired while setting the framework for continuing reviews.

Nonetheless, the events at Belgrade rekindled public and governmental interest in the CSCE process and stimulated consideration of the scope of détente. Future sessions should accomplish this and possibly much more. The new proposals advanced at Belgrade remain open to consideration and provide a guide for preliminary discussions.

Belgrade did not inject new vigor into détente, but it may have provided a more useful service. The conference helped remind the CSCE states of the complexity and vulnerability of the new relationship they are attempting to forge. Belgrade was a striking example of the dual strains of cooperation and confrontation—with somewhat greater evidence of the latter—that are intertwined in this détente relationship. There remain several issues which CSCE might address. However, the direction of political developments in Europe will decide not only whether these problems can be broached, but also the evolution of the entire CSCE process.

The Future of CSCE

Assessing the future of CSCE is a complicated task because of its interrelationship with a multitude of political, economic, and diplomatic phenomena. The progress of other major East-West negotiations will greatly influence CSCE's evolution, as will the domestic political situations in the participating states. The next several years portend to bring considerable change to Europe, particularly in the Communist states. CSCE will both reflect and affect these developments.

The Warsaw Pact governments are unlikely to abandon CSCE; indeed, their restrained reaction to Belgrade is testimony to their tremendous investment in the process. These states would, however, like to steer CSCE away from its present focus on human rights and Basket 3. The Eastern regimes will probe the limits of Western tolerance in their dealings with domestic dissent, and the ideological and political stiffening evident in the wake of Helsinki and Belgrade will persist throughout any period of relaxed tensions. The Soviets would also like to isolate the military aspects of CSCE. Recent proposals for special conferences on security are designed to enable Moscow to advance propagandistic schemes for disarmament without the encumbrance of dealing with other segments of the Final Act. Nonetheless, the Eastern regimes recognize that the West links their implementation of the Final Act to progress on other issues, and this situation is certain to figure in their policy calculations.

The impact of a succession crisis on Soviet attitudes toward CSCE presents many possibilities. During such periods, the Kremlin has traditionally been so preoccupied with consolidation of its power base that it has neglected regulation of the pulse of political developments in Eastern Europe. The Kremlin's indecisiveness during these periods has allowed social experimentation and drives for greater autonomy to develop among its allies, only to be arrested by Soviet invasion and/or intensified Pact integration campaigns, as demonstrated in the wake of the crises of 1956 and 1968.

The Soviet Union is not the only Eastern state with an impending succession problem. Sometime in the not-too-distant future, Yugoslavia, Bulgaria, and Hungary will have to find new leaders, and each is confronted with a unique set of variables. Tito's passing will raise the specter of disintegration of the Yugoslav state, encroachment on its nonaligned status, and a number of related geopolitical problems. Kadar's demise will bring into question the durability of his new economic mechanism and openings to the West. Zhikov's death might allow some shift in the policies of Moscow's closest ally. These destabilizing developments are likely to take place in an environment where the Eurocommunist model remains attractive to many East Europeans, where consumer shortages continue to plague the COMECON economies, and where increasingly bold human and civil rights movements are growing under the more repressive regimes. In the midst of such changes, CSCE would function as only one influence on the evolution of East European security.

It is apparent from the pronouncements of Western governments, particularly the United States, that their approach to CSCE over the next several years is likely to remain focused on monitoring the East's compliance with its Helsinki pledges. The U.S. Commission on Security and Cooperation in Europe evinces a determination of maintaining its Helsinki watch, and its work is likely to be complemented by other official and private efforts.

One element of the Carter administration's foreign policy which will influence the evolution of CSCE is its strategy of differentiated relationships with the various East European states. This policy, championed by National Security Advisor Brzezinski, emphasizes the amelioration of the relations with Eastern Europe apart from the context of Soviet-American détente. The policy guidelines call for making overtures to regimes which have undertaken internal reforms and/or have strayed from the Kremlin's foreign policy line, and for expansion of contacts with the leaders of reformist movements in these states. This strategy met with considerable success at the Belgrade conference when Hungary and Poland, spared of criticism of their human rights policies because of their more enlightened rule, refused to join with their Warsaw Pact allies in a unified response.

While expanded contacts with the West disturb the Kremlin, it also recognizes its inability to meet the economic needs of its allies. Moscow may continue to strive for expanded economic relations between its allies and the West on a bloc-to-bloc basis. However, this scheme runs contrary to the differentiation concept and will likely meet continued resistance from the West.

Events in the Mediterranean and the Balkans, which have been addressed in the CSCE context, will greatly influence the development of European security over the next several years. The Balkans present a host of uncertainties for the development of European security. This volatile region has few of the bilateral underpinnings of stability that exist in northern Europe. The Balkan states' quest for regional cooperation, which was rekindled at the CSCE-inspired Athens Conference, has been historically thwarted by external intervention.[62] The next few years seem likely to repeat this experience. While CSCE-related undertakings could enhance stability in the Balkans, its involvement with Mediterranean problems would be diversionary and should therefore remain minimal.

Belgrade's major liability was that its deliberations stretched over a nine-month period. A repetition of this timetable would certainly dull the interest of all parties in continuation of the review process, and it could probably be avoided by extensive bilateral and multilateral consultation before future conferences. It would also be wise for the NATO and EC caucuses to focus their efforts on a few specific initiatives. Several proposals for expanded CBMs were advanced at Belgrade, and these, as well as other schemes, will remain worthy of consideration as palpable links between political and military détente.[63]

CSCE can remain a vital element in the amelioration of European security if it is pursued with a wider appreciation of its potential. Western opinion must be familiarized with the limitations of détente so as to avoid the unrealistic expectations which led to the bitter disappointment with Belgrade's results. Similar disillusionment after Madrid could result in abandonment of CSCE and consequently the loss of a major source of influence in the East bloc. The Western public should be educated to realize that CSCE will be a long, frustrating endeavor and that efforts to realize overnight liberalization of the Communist states would actually be self-defeating.

The crucial task ahead will be to engage the Eastern participants in a dialogue on the state of implementation and the justifications for certain failings. Mutual indictments will only fan Eastern fears of Western goals. A sustained dialogue would provoke both sides to examine their relationship and isolate those areas which do actually threaten their security. Those which have been exposed as secondary can then be the subjects of accommodation, and a new awareness of the security needs of both sides will arise. Such a slow chipping-away at selected problems will not solve others, but the political climate on the Continent will be enhanced.

Notes

Note: Some of the material cited herein was substantiated in confidential interviews with U.S. officials during February and March 1978. Acronyms used: CDSP, Current Digest of the Soviet Press; FBIS, Foreign Broadcast Information Service.

1. The chapters of the Final Act were dubbed "baskets" during the Geneva negotiations. The Final Act is a solemn political document. It is morally, not legally, binding upon signatory states. Nonetheless, the human rights conventions reaffirmed under principle VII are documents in international law and it is expected that the Final Act will become a source of customary international law.

2. For a thorough examination of Soviet views on European security see: Robert Legvold, "The Problem of European Security," *Problems of Communism*, January/February 1974, pp. 13-33. Soviet goals in Western Europe are explored in Blacker chapter in this volume.

3. Marshall P. Shulman, "Soviet Proposals for a European Security Conference, 1966-1969," *Studies for a New Central Europe*, No. 3-4 (1968-69), pp. 70-71; "Declaration on Strengthening Peace and Security in Europe," in United Kingdom, Secretary of State for Foreign and Commonwealth Affairs, *Selected Documents Relating to Problems of Security and Cooperation in Europe, 1954-1977*, Command Paper 6932 (London: H.M. Stationery Office, 1977), pp. 38-43.

4. "Statement on Peace and Security in Europe Issued by a Meeting of European Communist Parties in Karlovy Vary, Czechoslovakia, 26 April 1967," in *Documents Relating to Security and Cooperation in Europe*, pp. 44-47.

5. Pierre Hassner, "Europe in the Age of Negotiation," *Washington Papers*, No. 8 (Beverly Hills: Sage Publications, 1973), p. 67.

6. Mojmir Povolny, "The Soviet Union and the European Security Conference," *Orbis*, Spring 1974, pp. 210-211.

7. "Declaration of the North Atlantic Council, Brussels, December 4-5, 1969," *Documents Relating to Security and Cooperation in Europe*, pp. 64-67.

8. "Statement of Warsaw Pact Foreign Ministers, Prague, October 30-31, 1969," *Documents Relating to Security and Cooperation in Europe*, pp. 61-62.

9. "Communiqué of the North Atlantic Council, Rome, May 26-27, 1970," *Documents Relating to Security and Cooperation in Europe*, pp. 73-75, par. 16.

10. "Memorandum of the Warsaw Pact Foreign Ministers Meeting, Budapest, June 21-22, 1970," *Documents Relating to Security and Cooperation in Europe*, pp. 77-78.

11. For a fuller discussion of these sessions by a member of the FRG delegation, see Gotz von Groll, "The Helsinki Consultations," *Aussen-*

politik, 2/1973, pp. 123-129, and "The Foreign Ministers in Helsinki," *Aussenpolitik*, 3/1973, pp. 255-274.

12. This is noted in an article by one of the U.S. delegates. See Harold S. Russell, "The Helsinki Declaration: Brobdingnag or Lilliput," *American Journal of International Law* LXX (April 1976):246.

13. Legvold, "The Problem of European Security," p. 26.

14. The Final Act of the CSCE is reprinted in the *U.S. Department of State Bulletin*, September 1, 1975, pp. 323-350.

15. *Draft Constitution of the USSR*, Article 29, Supplement to *International Affairs* (Moscow), 11/1977.

16. For a Soviet interpretation of the Final Act's ten principles see Y. Rakhmaninov, "Europe: Principles of Security and Cooperation," *International Affairs*, 2/1976, pp. 41-50.

17. "Soviet/GDR Treaty of Friendship, Cooperation and Mutual Assistance, Moscow, October 7, 1975" in *Documents Relating to Security and Cooperation in Europe*, pp. 285-289, Article 4.

18. Rakhmaninov, "Europe: Principles of Security and Cooperation," p. 27.

19. The several basic UN documents on human rights: the "Universal Declaration of Human Rights," the "International Covenant on Economic, Social and Cultural Rights," and the "International Covenant on Civil and Political Rights," are collected in the *Bulletin of Peace Proposals*, 3/1977, pp. 276-288. The United States has recently signed, but not ratified, the two covenants.

20. "Brezhnev Address to Meeting of the CPSU Central Committee," *Pravda*, December 22, 1972, pp. 2-5 (*CDSP*, XXIV/51, January 17, 1973), p. 13.

21. "Brezhnev Speech at Helsinki, August 1, 1975," in *Pravda*, August 1, 1975, p. 1 (*CDSP*, XXVII/31, August 27, 1975), pp. 12-14. Excerpts from the statements of all thirty-five heads of state at the Helsinki summit are compiled in *Bulletin of Peace Proposals*, 4/1975, pp. 309-335.

22. Communiqué of the Politburo of the CPSU, "On the Results of the Conference on Security and Cooperation in Europe," *Pravda*, August 7, 1975, p. 1 (*CDSP*, XXVII/31, August 27, 1975), pp. 14-15.

23. Georgi Arabatov, "Maneuvers of the Opponents of Détente," *Izvestia*, September 4, 1975, pp. 3-4 (*CDSP*, XXVII/36, October 1, 1975), pp. 1-6.

24. Characteristic of this line of argument is an article by L. Maximov, "Fulfillment of the Helsinki Understandings," *International Affairs* (Moscow), 10/1976, pp. 22-31.

25. For a detailed examination of Soviet (and East European) compliance with Basket 3 and the human rights principles endorsed in the Final Act see U.S. Congress, Commission on Security and Cooperation in

Europe, 95th Cong. 1st Sess., Hearings, *Basket Three: Implementation of the Helsinki Accords*, Parts I-IV, February-June 1977. A summary of the commission's monitoring of implementation of all facets of the Final Act is its *Implementation of the Final Act of the CSCE: Findings and Recommendations Two Years after Helsinki*, Committee Print, House Committee on International Relations, September 23, 1977.

26. See U.S. Commission on Security and Cooperation in Europe, *Implementation of the Final Act. . . ,* p. 21. A roster of public group membership and their positions as of early 1978 is included in Radio Liberty Research Report 44/78, "Fact Sheet on Public Groups for Furthering the Implementation of the Helsinki Agreements in the USSR," February 25, 1978.

27. The U.S. Commission on Security and Cooperation in Europe has compiled some of these documents. See *Reports of Helsinki Accord Monitors in the Soviet Union*, Vol. I, February 24, 1977; Vol. II, June 3, 1977; and *The Right to Know, the Right to Act: Documents of Helsinki Dissent from the Soviet Union and Eastern Europe*, May 1978, pp. 70-119.

28. Paul Frere, "The Lost Basket of Helsinki," *Atlantic Community Quarterly* XV (Spring 1977):46.

29. Testimony of Dr. John Hardt, Congressional Research Service in Commission on Security and Cooperation in Europe, Hearings, *Basket II—Helsinki Final Act East-West Economic Cooperation*, January 13 and 14, 1977, p. 17.

30. Ibid.

31. U.S. Commission on Security and Cooperation in Europe, *Implementation of the Final Act. . . ,* pp. 60-63.

32. U.S. House of Representatives, Committee on International Relations, 94th Cong. 2d Sess. and 95th Cong. 1st Sess., Print, *Semiannual Reports by the President to Commission on Security and Cooperation in Europe*, First-December 1977, p. 36; and Second-June 1977, p. 19.

33. John Pinder, "The Community and Comecon: What Could Negotiations Achieve?" *World Today*, May 1977, pp. 176-185.

34. As cited in F. Stephen Larrabee, "Soviet Implementation of the Helsinki Agreement: The Military Dimension," Radio Liberty Research Report 1/77, January 1, 1977, p. 1.

35. Interview with participant in observer group.

36. See, for example: Janusz Symonides, "Declaration on Principles Guiding Relations between States," in Polish Institute on International Affairs, *Conference on Security and Cooperation in Europe: A Polish View* (Warsaw: Polish Scientific Publishers, 1976), pp. 67-118.

37. For an official summary of Romanian positions on CSCE see Romulus Negagu, *European Security: A Romanian Point of View* (Bucharest: Meridiane, 1977).

38. Robert R. King, "Romania: The Difficulty of Maintaining an Autonomous Foreign Policy," in Robert R. King and Robert W. Dean, eds., *East European Perspectives on European Security and Cooperation* (Washington: Praeger, 1974), pp. 179-182.

39. For an elaboration of this point see J.F. Brown, "Soviet Policy in Eastern Europe," *Survey* XX (Spring/Summer 1974):50-51, 57.

40. See testimony of James F. Brown in U.S., Commission on Security and Cooperation in Europe, *Basket III: Implementation of the Helsinki Accords*, p. 276.

41. Radio Free Europe Research, Background Report 46, "The East European Response to Helsinki," February 18, 1976, p. 14.

42. "Brezhnev's Report to the CPSU Central Committee," *Pravda*, February 25, 1976, pp. 2-9 (*CDSP*, XXVIII/8, March 24, 1976), p. 6.

43. PCC's Bucharest "Declaration on Security and Cooperation in Europe," November 26, 1976, in *Documents Relating to Security and Cooperation in Europe*, pp. 319-326.

44. For a more detailed survey of these developments in Poland, Czechoslovakia, and the GDR see Thomas Henneghan, "Human Rights Protests in Eastern Europe," *World Today*, March 1977, pp. 90-100; and in all Eastern Europe U.S. Commission on Security and Cooperation in Europe, Hearings. *Basket III . . . ,* Vol. II, pp. 273-439.

45. Nicholas Carroll, "The Dissident Movement in Poland," *Sunday Times* (London), April 9, 1978. Excerpts reprinted in U.S. Commission on Security and Cooperation in Europe, *Documents of Helsinki Dissent . . . ,* pp. 30-32.

46. Text of Charter 77 manifesto appeared in the *New York Times*, January 27, 1977.

47. See Jiri Valenta, "Eurocommunism and Eastern Europe," *Problems of Communism*, March-April 1978, pp. 41-54; Heinz Timmerman, "Eurocommunism: Moscow's Reaction and the Implications for Eastern Europe," *World Today*, October 77, pp. 376-385.

48. Testimony of James F. Brown, U.S. Commission on Security and Cooperation in Europe, *Basket III . . . ,* pp. 278-279.

49. Karl E. Birnbaum, "East-West Diplomacy in the Era of Multilateral Negotiations," in Nils Andren and Karl Birnbaum, eds., *Beyond Détente: Prospects for East-West Cooperation and Security in Europe* (Leyden: Sijthoff, 1976), pp. 145-146.

50. Michael Palmer, "The European Community and a Security Conference," *World Today*, July 1972, p. 302.

51. Richard C. Longworth, "East and West Talk," *European Community*, December 1973, pp. 14-16; and U.S., President, *First Semiannual Report to the Commission of Security and Cooperation in Europe*, pp. vii-viii.

52. See U.S., President, *Semiannual Reports to the Commission . . . ,* passim; and speech by Ambassador Arthur J. Goldberg at the opening Belgrade session, in U.S., Department of State, *The Belgrade CSCE Meeting: U.S. Delegation Statements, October 6 to December 22, 1977,* pp. 1-9.

53. Yuri Zhukov, "Self-Appointed Inspectors," *Pravda,* October 28, 1976, p. 6 (*CDSP,* XXVIII/42, November 24, 1976, p. 6).

54. See testimony of Professor Loren R. Graham, in U.S. Commission on Security and Cooperation, Hearings, *Basket III . . . ,* Vol. III, pp. 81-4.

55. For illustration of West German thinking on this issue see Johann G. Reissmuller, "Cautious Line Best for Bonn at Human Rights Talks," *Frankfurter Allgemeine Zeitung,* June 15, 1977, p. 1; for a thorough discussion of British views of Belgrade, see United Kingdom, Secretary of State for Foreign and Commonwealth Affairs, *The Meeting Held at Belgrade 4 October 1977 to 9 March 1978 to Follow Up the Conference on Security and Cooperation in Europe,* March 1978, Command Paper 7126, p. 2.

56. S. Vishnevsky, V. Zhuravky, "Belgrade: Businesslike Approach Prevails," *Pravda,* October 23, 1977, p. 5 (*CDSP,* XXIX/42, November 16, 1977, pp. 3-4.

57. "Declaration on Security and Cooperation in Europe by the PCC of the Warsaw Treaty Organization," Bucharest, November 25, 26, 1976, in *Documents Relating to Security and Cooperation in Europe . . . ,* pp. 319-326; *Pravda,* May 27, 1977, p. 4 (*CDSP,* XXIX/21, June 27, 1977, p. 18).

58. See Press Conference of Soviet delegation chairman Yuri Vorontsov in *FBIS—Soviet Union,* March 17, 1978, p. BB1 and "Belgrade Said to Benefit Cause of Peace, Détente," *Pravda,* March 25, 1978 (*FBIS—Soviet Union,* March 29, 1978, pp. BB1-3).

59. See *Washington Post,* March 21, 1978. Reprinted in U.S. Commission on Security and Cooperation in Europe, *The Belgrade Followup Meeting to the CSCE: A Report and Appraisal* (House International Relations Comm. Print), May 17, 1978, where this assessment was confirmed by Ambassador Goldberg, pp. 86-87.

60. "Communiqué of the Meeting of the Committee of Foreign Ministers of the Warsaw Treaty Member States," *Tass,* April 26, 1978 (*FBIS—Soviet Union,* April 27, 1978, p. D2).

61. U.S. Commission on Security and Cooperation in Europe, *The Right to Know . . . ,* pp. 12-13.

62. F. Stephen Larrabee, "European Security and the Problem of Balkan Security," in King and Dean, eds., *East European Perspectives . . . ,* pp. 218-22. For an assessment of the 1976 Athens Conference on Balkan cooperation see: Robert King and others, "The Athens Conference and Regional Cooperation in the Balkans," in King and Brown, eds., *Eastern Europe's Uncertain Future,* pp. 31-34.

63. For a comprehensive examination of CBMs see: Johan J. Holst and Karen A. Melander, "European Security and Confidence Building Measures," *Survival*, July/August 1977, pp. 146-154.

Part IV
Alternative Perspectives

10 Eurocommunism: Between East and West

Kevin Devlin

So-called "Eurocommunism"—like its lively younger brother, "Eurosocialism"—is a vague, inaccurate, and misleading term which veils rather than describes complex realities. It is vague and misleading because it does not refer, as one might suppose, to a clear grouping of West European Communist parties with common positions, an agreed body of doctrine, or organizational links, but rather to a process of change, to recognizable transitional tendencies affecting certain Communist parties. It is inaccurate because these tendencies are also found in some other Communist parties outside Europe. But we need it: it is a word whose time has come; and the steadily increasing flow of articles, books, conferences, lectures, and study courses on the subject in the past few years, on both sides of the Atlantic—though, of course, only on one side of the Iron Curtain—suggests that it is here to stay.

But what do we mean by it? The Eurocommunist phenomenon should be examined against the background of a wider historical process: the process of sociopolitical adaptation to environmental realities that has been developing—gradually, unevenly, and in greatly varying degrees—among Communist parties operating in advanced capitalist democracies over the past two decades (although its origins can be traced even further back, in the case of the Italian CP). And the first and most fundamental characteristic of that gradual, uneven process was the abandonment by these Western Communist parties, at first in practice and then increasingly also in theory, of revolutionary Leninism. With the onset of the cold war and the consequent division of Europe into adversary camps, Leninism—the doctrine of the vanguard revolutionary party of the working class—had become for Western Communist leaderships a geopolitical irrelevance, even if for ideological reasons they could not admit this. The only exception to this practical abandonment of the revolutionary option was the Greek Communist party (KKE), which did attempt to seize power first through a *coup d'état* in late 1944 and then through a bitter civil war from 1946 to 1949. And one could perhaps describe as neo-Leninist the tactics of the Portuguese CP, in alliance with the ultra-leftist military, from 1974 to 1975—behavior, we may note, which brought it sharp criticism from the Italian and Spanish CPs and fraternal support from the French CP.

The outbreak of the Sino-Soviet conflict—revealed to the scandalized leaders of the minor parties at the eighty-one-party Moscow Conference of November 1960—gave decisive impetus to the post-Stalinist transformation of the international Communist movement in general, and to autonomous tendencies among the Western parties in particular. The challenge to Soviet authority posed by the only Communist regime with comparable revolutionary prestige, and the ill-advised efforts of the CPSU to meet that challenge by rallying loyalist parties for a collective condemnation of the Chinese at a world conference, offered other parties, ruling and nonruling, an increased freedom of maneuver which some of them began to exploit. The ouster of Khrushchev in October 1964, and the uncertain touch which his successors brought to interparty and international affairs for a few years, considerably strengthened tendencies in many Western Communist parties toward more independence, especially in domestic policies, and adaptation to national circumstances.

With the Italian CP in the vanguard, these parties were becoming more aware of their own political interests and opportunities in economically advanced societies of pluralistic, constitutional democracy, and also more conscious of the need to seek political allies and to extend their electoral base by presenting a more acceptable public image. Both considerations led them to stress that their goal was a national path to an indigenous type of socialism. This in turn led them, on occasion, to dissociate themselves from unpopular developments in Eastern Europe.[1] And this was not only a matter of political opportunism (although that was certainly often a factor): the extent to which genuine rethinking was involved was suggested by the often stormy internal ideological debates which went on in various West European Communist parties in the mid-1960s (and sometimes, as in Sweden and Finland, led to a prolonged factional struggle between "progressives" and "dogmatists").

At the same time a new sense of *regional* and not just national identity was affecting even conservative or pro-Soviet Communist parties in Western Europe (and we note in passing that they have always constituted the majority, even if they have not included the most important). This sense of regional identity found expression in the conferences of West European CPs held in Brussels in June 1965 and in Vienna a year later. More important was the more carefully prepared regional conference held in Brussels in January 1974, because it has been followed by a prolonged series of thematic West European Communist conferences on such subjects as agricultural policy, the motor industry, or the condition of women, to which interested parties send delegations.

The Czechoslovakian Invasion

Between the two earlier West European conferences and the later one, however, the regional consciousness of the Western parties and relations

between them and the Eastern regimes had been profoundly changed by
another watershed event in the history of communism—the invasion of
Czechoslovakia by troops of the Soviet Union and four other Warsaw Pact
allies in August 1968. The unexpected and largely spontaneous flowering of
"Socialist democratization" in Czechoslovakia in April-August 1968, and
the coercive reaction of the probably divided Kremlin leadership (prodded
by Ulbricht and Gomulka) to this infectious example revealed a deep and
enduring divergence of political interests between bureaucratic-
authoritarian regimes, which could brook no challenge to the power of the
apparat, and nonruling parties, which had to compete for votes in open,
pluralistic democracies.

With some exceptions—the Portuguese, Luxembourg, West Ger-
man/West Berlin, and Cypriot CPs, plus the Greek "Exterior" CP—the
West European parties reacted to the invasion with a chorus of criticism and
condemnation. Ten years later, only the small Austrian CP has reversed its
stand on the invasion (at the cost of losing its best and brightest), although
some others have tacitly accepted the "normalization" of Czechoslovakia.

In July 1968 three West European Communist parties warned the
Soviets in advance that they would publicly oppose any armed intervention
in Czechoslovakia. Is it a coincidence that these three—the Italian, French,
and Spanish CPs—are now the major exemplars of Eurocommunism?

Yet there are significant differences between these three parties with
regard to their record on postinvasion Czechoslovakia, and it is worth
glancing briefly at these differences, because they fit into a wider pattern. A
student of the Eurocommunist phenomenon finds that on other important
issues besides Czechoslovakia there is a significant gap in substance and
style between the positions of the Italian and Spanish CPs on the one hand
and those of the French CP on the other. For the first two, condemnation
of the invasion was a matter of principle, and they demonstrated this by
consistent criticism of the repressive "normalization" that followed. In the
Italian case the sincerity of the PCI's sympathy for the "Socialist opposition" in Czechoslovakia and the firm editorials with which *Unità* met invasion anniversaries received negative confirmation from the other side,
through the Husak regime's expulsion of the Prague correspondent, of the
party daily, *Unità* (1972), and of Italian Communist employees of the
Czechoslovak Radio (1976). But perhaps the most striking example of the
PCI's attitude was the publication in 1977 of the book *Prague: An Open
Question* by the leading (and persecuted) Czechoslovak dissident Zdenek
Mlynar, with a preface by Lucio Lombardo Radice of the PCI Central
Committee. With this book the Italian CP was in effect serving notice that it
would continue to regard postinvasion Czechoslovakia as an "open ques-
tion"—an unresolved problem—for the whole international Communist
movement.[2]

For the Spanish party (PCE), the invasion was a major
turning-point—"the last drop that made the vase overflow," as Secretary-

General Santiago Carrillo put it later in his book *Eurocommunism and the State*. Since 1956 the Spanish CP had maintained "revisionist" (or what would later be called Eurocommunist) positions in domestic affairs—urging other anti-Franco forces, including even "the civilized right," to join it in a "pact for liberty" on the basis of "national reconciliation." But the PCE had combined all this with traditional pro-Soviet attitudes. After August 1968 the PCE emphasized an independence which frequently involved vigorous criticism of the East European regimes for their lack of democracy, their repression of human rights, or their dealings with the Franco government. This stress on independence was strengthened by Moscow's covert and ultimately ineffective support of Enrique Lister's pro-Soviet splinter party in the early 1970s; it also found significant expression in the visit which a Spanish Communist delegation under Carrillo made to Peking in September 1971 in an unsuccessful effort to reestablish normal relations with the Chinese CP. The lasting strength of the PCE's stand on Czechoslovakia is indicated by the fact that when it held its historic ninth Congress, it did not invite what Carrillo slightingly calls "the official Czechoslovak party," although he had shortly before received exiled representatives of the "Socialist opposition," Mlynar and Pelikan.

Contrast the record of the French party (PCF). It is true that it never withdrew its "disapproval" of the Warsaw Pact intervention in Czechoslovakia. Again, it joined many other Western Communist parties in criticizing the political trials held in Czechoslovakia in the summer of 1972. But this and similar *ad hoc* stands, intended to dissociate the PCF from manifestly unpopular developments in Eastern Europe, could plausibly be regarded as "cosmetic" opportunism—at least until the historic change of course in late 1975, to which we must return later. Closer inspection reveals that the PCF actually played an ignoble role in the process of pro-Soviet normalization in Czechoslovakia during one crucial stage. In late November 1969 a PCF delegation led by Etienne Fajon visited Prague for talks with a solidly conservative CPCS delegation, and (it was learned later) took the occasion to hand over the protocol of Waldeck Rochet's discussion with Dubcek on 18-19 July 1968. This material, the pro-Soviet spokesmen Alois Indrea, Vasil Bilak, and Pavel Auersperg made clear in statements in January 1970, was then used against Dubcek by the Husak regime.[3] It may be that an incident such as this should be borne in mind when it comes to considering the credibility of certain positions adopted in later years by the French Communist party.

The Western Communist reaction to the invasion of Czechoslovakia marked one important stage in a wider, uneven process—the post-Stalinist erosion of Soviet authority in the international Communist movement. This erosion was due partly to Soviet efforts to reassert that authority in profoundly altered circumstances—notably, as mentioned earlier, by trying to rally other Communist parties for a collective denunciation of the Chinese. It was an important sign of the changed times that the green light for the first post-Khrushchev world conference came from the Italian CP, in a series of articles (October-November 1967) in which Secretary-General Luigi Longo in effect laid down the PCI's conditions for participating in such a conference.[4]

Even then, the conference was delayed, and the procedural conditions were further changed; when the conference finally did take place in June 1969 after repeated editorial sessions and hundreds of amendments, it brought not a restoration of Soviet influence but a further weakening of Soviet authority: the giant was now being increasingly restrained by a network of precedents of high tensile strength. The pro-Chinese and neutralist parties boycotted the conference, of course, but out of the seventy-five parties present, fourteen expressed opposition to, or reservations about, a collective document that already contained important Soviet concessions—for example, the failure to assign any special status to the CPSU, the new interparty principle of noninterference in the affairs of others, and the statement that there was no longer any "leading center of the international Communist movement." Five did not sign the text at all; four (including the PCI) signed only the section on antiimperialist unity of action; and five (including the PCE) signed only after having expressed reservations of various kinds. Since the document was, in any case, not binding upon the signatory parties, it could well be said that this 1969 conference marked the institutionalization of diversity, and even of dissent, in the international Communist movement.

A salutary lesson for the Soviets, one would have thought; yet four years later they were off on the conference trail again. This time the vicarious calls that came from pro-Soviet leaders beginning in late 1973 were for a pan-European conference of Communist parties, to be followed by a world conference, the calls coming within the context of attacks on Maoism. The Soviets eventually got the first conference, the European one—although I doubt very much that they would have wanted it if they had known in advance the price they were going to pay for it. They never did get the second, even though more than two-thirds of the world's Communist parties had backed the project by June 1975.

The Emergence of Eurocommunism

With regard to the second pan-European conference,[5] the Soviets wanted to cast their net as widely as possible. In particular, they wanted—with an eye to the approaching post-Tito era—to obtain the return of independent, nonaligned Yugoslavia to what one may call "conciliar communism." The main price they paid for Yugoslav participation was the adoption, at an initial, consultative meeting in Warsaw in October 1974, of a new procedural rule of "decision-making by consensus." From the Russian viewpoint, that turned out to be a disastrous mistake.

There followed a prolonged struggle between an independent minority and the conservative majority of the twenty-eight parties represented, a struggle fought out behind closed doors in at least fifteen "editorial" sessions over twenty months—so that the conference finally took place a full year behind the original schedule. Against the pro-Soviet majority was ranged an alliance of convenience grouping two independent Eastern regimes, Yugoslavia and Romania, and the Western nonruling Communist parties of Italy (plus San Marino), Spain, Great Britain, and Sweden—later to be joined, at least on some issues, by the French.

Taking their stand upon the new principle of consensus, this independent alliance resisted successive attempts (made by the East Germans, who as hosts were charged with producing the successive drafts for a collective document) to impose upon the European parties something like a "general line," expressed in ideological terms.[6] Against this pressure to close the ranks, the independent parties stood by their demands: if there was to be a collective document at all, it must be based upon genuine consensus; it must emphasize the principles of autonomy, equality, and noninterference in interparty relations (the corollary being that no special status should be granted to the Soviet party); it must contain no criticism of any party, present or absent (for example, the Chinese); it must deal with political action, not with ideology; and in any case it was not to be binding upon any party.

In this long struggle over the character and content of the collective document, which ended in East Berlin at the end of June 1976, the old Field Marshal Tito out-generaled the new Field Marshal Brezhnev, so to say: the independent alliance had its way on almost every point of importance, even to the extent of getting the sacrosanct formula "proletarian internationalism" replaced by an anodyne reference to "voluntary cooperation" between equal and autonomous parties. But during the process there had been several developments of importance to our theme. One was that the independent Western parties had acquired a greater sense of their community of interests, of what they had in common ideologically and politically, of the goals which they could set before members and electors within the framework of national and regional realities, and, not least, of their ability to resist Soviet pressures. At the East Berlin conference Enrico Berlinguer of the PCI insouciantly used the new term "Eurocommunism"[7] in noting that other West European CPs now shared the PCI's perspective of a Socialist society based upon "the principles of the secular, nonideological nature of the state and its democratic organization; the plurality of political parties and the possibility of alternation of government majorities; the autonomy of trade unions; religious freedom, freedom of expression, of culture, and of the arts and sciences."

The other important development was the French CP's quite abrupt shift in the closing months of 1975 from its traditional solidarity with Moscow to an ostentatious independence that found expression in unprecedented criticism of the Soviet regime—for example, the PCF Politburo's condemnation of Soviet labor camps in December 1975, the later attacks upon Soviet cultural policies, or the denunciation of individual acts of repression.

Despite the French CP's habitual stress on continuity, there was no doubt that this dramatic change did take place. In May-July 1975 the PCF was on the pro-Soviet side of a balanced "subgroup" of four loyalist and four independent parties which vainly tried to reach a compromise agreement on the pan-European conference text. In September a Central Committee member, J. Chambaz, signaled the change with an article rejecting the Soviet spokesman Zarodov's criticism of what were about to become known as "Eurocommunist" positions. In mid-November Secretary-General Marchais and Secretary-General Berlinguer signed in Rome a "Eurocommunist" communiqué expressing their common commitment to pluralistic democracy and civic liberties. Both signed similar communiqués with Secretary-General Carrillo of the Spanish CP, and the bilateral network subsequently spread to include others, such as the British and the distant Japanese CP.

From the first, the French CP wore its revisionist rue with a difference; and we shall have to consider later the credibility of this Eurocommunist commitment. At this point we may pause to consider the term briefly again, to see what and whom it covers.

Eurocommunism implies a certain consensus among the Communist parties concerned about what the characteristics of a "Socialist" (that is, postcapitalist) society in an advanced Western country ought to be—and, equally important, ought not to be. On the positive side, the extract from Berlinguer's East Berlin speech cited above listed most of the bourgeois liberties that were to be maintained and extended in a pluralistic regime with full opposition rights, no official ideology or philosophy, and so on. On the negative side, this pluralistic-libertarian perspective also involved the explicit rejection of existing "models" of a Communist society—a rejection to be made credible (especially in the case of formerly loyalist parties like the PCF) by "principled," and preferably also systematic, criticism of the undesirable aspects of these regimes.

It is when one applies this second criterion—independence of Moscow, rejection of the East European model, and readiness to criticize the Soviet regime—that the number of Eurocommunist parties is reduced to some half-dozen in Western Europe: the Italian, French, Spanish, British, Swedish, Icelandic, and San Marino CPs. There are, in addition, a few more with the same characteristics in other parts of the world: the Japanese and Australian CPs, the dissident-Communist MAS (Movement to Socialism) in Venezuela, and perhaps the Mexican CP.

As far as Europe is concerned, the ones that matter—the ones that present a serious challenge both to the capitalist West and to the bureaucratic-authoritarian East—are the "Big Three" of Italy, France, and Spain. Their preeminence was symbolized by the "Eurocommunist summit" of Berlinguer, Marchais, and Carrillo, held in Madrid in early March 1977 (when the Spanish host-party was still formally illegal!). That meeting, however, also drew attention to limitations in the Eurocommunist evolution and differences among the three parties. Thus, the challenge to the "real socialism" of the regimes was muted—significantly so, in view of the fact that the Central Committee secretaries of the East European ruling parties were holding what had to be viewed as a rival conference on the same days, March 2-3, in Sofia. The Berlinguer-Marchais-Carrillo communiqué did, indeed, stress commitment to an impressive list of bourgeois liberties within the framework of the "will to build socialism within democracy and freedom"—but it said nothing at all about the lack of these liberties in Eastern Europe. To journalists covering the Madrid summit it was an open secret that this reticence was reluctantly accepted by Santiago Carrillo under pressure from his French and Italian guests; and, indeed, the three made this plain enough at their press conference.

During the past two years the differences in the national situation of the three major Eurocommunist parties have been accentuated, as have been their differences with regard to ideology, politics, foreign affairs, interparty relations, internal life, and what one might call collective temperament. During the year the Italian CP took on greater responsibility for tackling Italy's profound crisis in collaboration with other political forces, without entering government or achieving the full "historic compromise" with Christian Democracy. The French Communist party, which had seemed certain to return to governmental power in March, spent much of the year feuding with its Socialist ally/rival, with the result that the expected leftist victory was transformed into defeat, with far-reaching consequences for France and Europe. The Spanish CP, legalized in April 1977, did disappointingly in the June elections, but rallied to become an important force in the process of post-Franco democratization, gaining ground particularly in the trade union area, and ended the year with an historic congress at which, amid an unprecedented display of internal democracy, it outraged the Kremlin once more by formally abandoning Leninism. A brief survey of some of these developments may provide guidelines for discussing tendencies and limitations of the Eurocommunist evolution, as well as the nature and extent of the challenge that these parties pose to the capitalist West and the Communist East.

Spain: Defying the Kremlin

In an article published in January 1976 on the new triangular relationship between the Italian, French, and Spanish CPs, the Austrian dissident-Communist Franz Marek said: "The Spanish say what the Italians think; and the Italians say more than the French think." The quip has lost much of its point, largely because some French Communists have been thinking and saying rather startling things since then. It is nevertheless true that of the three the Spanish Communists are the most outspoken—particularly when it comes to saying what they think of the Soviets.

The most famous example of this is Santiago Carrillo's book *Eurocommunism and the State*, which he wrote during 1976 while in hiding in Madrid. Published in April 1977, just as the PCE was legalized shortly before Spain's first elections since the civil war, this was the first attempt by a Western European Communist leader to examine at length the ideological, political and international implications of Eurocommunism. It is also, and not at all incidentally, a principled critique of the Soviet "model," which Carrillo rejects because of its "deformations and degenerations" (*inter alia*). Despite some progress since Stalin's time (offset by persisting "forms of oppression and repression"), the Soviet Union still cannot be considered a "workers' democracy"—at best, Carrillo suggests provocatively, it may "represent an intermediate phase between the capitalist state and the authentic Socialist state." After describing Stalinism, he declares: "This system has not been transformed, it has not been democratized, and it still retains many coercive aspects in its relations with other Eastern socialist states, as was brutally demonstrated by the military occupation of Czechoslovakia."

An important point is that in Carrillo's perspective the double challenge of Eurocommunism—to Western capitalism and to the authoritarian Eastern regimes—must be kept in harmony with a continuation of that East-West balance of power in Europe which alone (he indicates justly) has made the emergence of Eurocommunism possible. Not only must Eurocommunism try to demonstrate that "democracy is not the same thing as capitalism, but that its defense and development demand the passing of that system"; it must also demonstrate that

> the victory of socialist forces in Western Europe will not in the least augment Soviet state power, or mean the extension of the Soviet model of the one-party state: it will be an independent experience, with a more advanced socialism which will have a positive influence on the democratic evolution

of the existing socialist regimes. . . . In this connection, what is essential is the independence of the Communist parties with respect to the Soviet state, and the development in theory and practice of an unequivocally democratic way.[8]

From the Soviet viewpoint, the Carrillo affair did have the useful effect of revealing some fissures in the Eurocommunist front. The Italian Communists criticized the "tone" of the Soviet rejoinder, as the French did with considerably less emphasis, but neither of them defended the substance of Carrillo's argument: he had gone a good deal further, it seemed, than either Berlinguer or Marchais was prepared to go. It should also be noted, however, that the PCI issued an Italian translation of Carrillo's book through its own publishing house—which is more than the French CP did.

Over the past two decades the Italian CP has built up, sporadically and piecemeal, a more impressive body of dissociative criticism of the Soviet regime than the other two major Eurocommunist parties; but no single authoritative and systematic critique that can be compared with Carrillo's book comes to mind. This could perhaps be linked with the PCI's habitual tendency to follow a *politica di presenza* (policy of presence) not only in Italian and West European institutions but also in the international Communist movement. If it refuses to contemplate the "excommunication" of the Chinese Communists or anyone else, it equally refuses to consider anything like a "break" with the Soviet party.

As for the French CP, it seems to me that since its dramatic shift in late 1975 (which surely involved a decision henceforth to give its own political interests consistent priority over those of the Kremlin), its criticism of the Soviet regime has largely been expressed either by *avant-garde* individuals, like Jean Elleinstein, or in small-circulation publications like *La Nouvelle Critique*, or in ostentatious gestures, as when Georges Marchais refused to attend the twenty-fifth CPSU Congress because of differences between the two parties on Socialist democracy and French foreign policy, adding that the conditions for a meeting between himself and Brezhnev "do not exist today." Similarly, Marchais has frequently stressed that for the French CP socialism and liberty are indivisible; he has sometimes deplored the lack of liberty in the Soviet Union; but he cannot go on from major and minor premise to the syllogistic conclusion that the Soviet Union is not a true Socialist society.

Even the most radical French Communist critic of the Soviet regime, the anti-Stalinist historian Jean Elleinstein, deputy director of the party's Center of Marxist Study and Research, has the same difficulty. In a long interview which he recently gave to George R. Urban of Radio Free Europe/Radio Liberty, Elleinstein said flatly: "There is in the Soviet Union no democratic opposition, no free press, no freedom of association, no freedom of assembly, no freedom of opinion." But then a little later, discussing "the question of whether or not the Soviet Union and its client states in Eastern Europe are Socialist countries in our definition of the term," he said: "I would say they represent a certain type of socialism—I would hesitate to say that they are *not* Socialist."[9]

That hesitation in a man of Elleinstein's intellectual courage—shown most recently in his articles in *Le Monde* after the French Left's election defeat, criticizing his party's policies—may perhaps be seen as reflecting a wider problem of identity among Eurocommunists. They may be taking a reformist, constitutional road paralleling that of the Social-Democrats, but it then becomes psychologically all the more important for them to preserve their *communist* identity as part of a world revolutionary movement that has its historical origins in the Leninist October.

France: The Lessons of a Defeat

Political developments during late 1977 in Italy, France, and Spain brought out important differences among the three major Eurocommunist parties, with particular reference to their relations with noncommunist forces, of the Left and of the Center. Briefly put: the Italian and Spanish parties were moving, if unevenly and hesitantly, in roughly the same direction, while the French CP was on a clearly divergent course. Or again: the first two, in different ways and for different reasons, had rejected (at least for the time being) "the leftist alternative"; the French, having for more than a decade based their political strategy on the idea of a leftist alternative, were about to be responsible (as most observers now agree) for blocking its advent.

Consider the events of fall 1977. The PCI, having kept a minority Christian Democratic government in office for more than a year, and supporting an austerity program, until its own supporters began rebelling, was calling for a further step toward sharing power *and* responsibility with the traditional adversary through the "historic compromise"—while being prepared to settle for entry into a "programmatic majority." In Spain—only half a year after the Communist party was legalized—Secretary-General Carrillo was insisting on the need for an all-party "government of democratic concentration" to tackle the country's problems; failing that, he enthusiastically accepted as next-best the all-party programmatic agreement known as the "Moncloa Pact," which he had also urged, and which he aptly described as a Spanish version of the *compromesso storico*. The PCE has shown itself considerably more ready to cooperate with the centrist UCD of Premier Suárez than the Socialist PSOE, and has actually complained of the latter's efforts to work for a "leftist alternative."

While the Italian and Spanish CPs were thus trying to build up their image as reasonable and responsible partners in a broad and substantially cooperative array of forces covering most of the political spectrum, the French CP was behaving in a very different manner. It was displaying toward its own Socialist and Left-Radical allies an aggressive militance which in late September caused the collapse of the negotiations over the updating of the Common Program signed in 1972—and this only six months before the crucial elections of March 1978 that until then had seemed certain (according to opinion polls) to bring the Union of the Left to power with a clear majority.

The PCF promptly launched a massive publicity campaign aimed at demonstrating that it was in the right and had always been in the right: that, as *the* party of the working class (by Communist definition), it was the only guarantee and the indispensable instrument of genuine social change in France—change which the Socialist party (PS), having "swung to the right," was blocking through its refusal to update and implement the Common Program. Now the differences between the PCF and the PS—notably over the number of firms to be nationalized and the degree of control over management—should have been open to settlement by negotiation, if the will to reach a settlement had been there. But the bitterness of the polemic (especially on the Communist side) and the efforts of each side to outmaneuver the other were such that many observers saw the central issue not as a dispute over the program on which the Left hoped to win the election, but rather as a struggle for predominance of power within the alliance. To put it more plainly: by mid-1977 it had become fairly obvious that the Communist leadership was concerned over the prospect that the PCF would be the *junior* partner in a *leftist* government—and that, entrenched behind the dogmas of its "proletarian vanguard" tradition, it was prepared to put a leftist victory in question in order to avert that outcome.

This was, indeed, what happened. Contrary to the opinion polls, the Union of the Left failed to gain its expected victory, and the Socialist party failed to gain a commanding lead over the Communist party. The first round on March 12 showed the French electorate to be divided into two roughly equal camps—each of which in turn consisted of two major components of roughly equal strength: Socialists and Communists on the left facing Gaullists and "Giscardian" centrists, with only a few percentage points separating all four. The most disappointed were the Socialists, with only 22.6 percent instead of the 28 percent or more that recent polls had indicated. Having for years been regarded as the strongest party not only on the Left but also in France, the Socialist party was now shown to be only slightly ahead of the PCF (20.6 percent) in electoral strength, while the latter remained much stronger in terms of organization, finances, and trade-union influence. The second round, with its direct confrontations between Left and Center-right, showed more clearly how the leftist alliance had suffered electorally both from its open disunity and from the widespread distrust of the Communist party when it became a question of its entry into national government. The "majority" vindicated its title if narrowly by taking 50.49 percent to the Left's 49.29 percent, with a more decisive margin of 290 to 201 seats in the Chamber of Deputies.

From the Communist leadership's viewpoint, the trouble was that the ally it ended up with was not the one it had started out with. Foreign observers who commented on "the advance of the Left" in France in recent years should really have been speaking of the advance of the Socialist party founded in 1971 under Francois Mitterrand. When the Socialists and Communists signed their Common Program in June 1972, the Socialist party was by a considerable margin the weaker of the two—but within a few years the power relationship was reversed. While Communist electoral strength stagnated at around 20 to 21 percent,[10] the Socialist party drew in other leftist elements and steadily increased its electoral appeal. As a result, Communist attitudes regarding the Socialists shifted back and forth in accordance with the party's perceived political needs—bitter polemics from the fall of 1974 to the fall of 1975, fairly good relations until both parties had profited from partnership in the local elections of March 1976, then a gradual shift back to the feuding which ended the Left's chances in the 1978 elections. Now the Common Program lies on the scrap-heap of history; and, as for the disunited Union of the Left, the recriminations flying back and forth between the Communist and Socialist leaders indicate that it may be impossible to put Humpty Dumpty together again.

We may be less surprised at this if we recall that the centrifugal strain was there from the beginning: from the first each ally also saw the other as a rival. This competitive element in the partnership was demonstrated by the events of three successive days in June 1972. On June 27 Mitterrand and Marchais signed the Common Program. On June 28 Mitterrand said bluntly in an address at a meeting of the Socialist International in Vienna that "our fundamental objective is to demonstrate that, of the 5 million PCF voters 3 million might vote for the Socialist party." On June 29 Georges Marchais delivered at a PCF Central Committee meeting a "secret" report—published by the Communists three years later, in a context of anti-Socialist polemics—in which he expressed strong and distrustful criticism of his new ally.

Marchais warned against "the least illusion" that the Socialists could be trusted to stand by the Common Program and not "break the Union of the Left after the elections to go over to an alliance with right-wing parties"; the "only guarantee" against that was the action of the PCF among the masses. Rejecting any idea of *"ideological rapprochement"* between the two parties, he said that basically the PS remained "absolutely reformist . . . totally alien to scientific socialism"; its permanent characteristics included fear of working-class action, hesitation to join in the fight against big capital, "the tendency to compromise with the latter and to engage in class collaboration."

Attitudes of this kind, whether openly expressed or not, account for a widespread mistrust of the PCF which, in the last analysis, dragged down the Socialist vote. The mistrust emerged clearly from a poll conducted for

Le Nouvel Observateur in January 1976—as the PCF's propaganda machine was incessantly proclaiming its liberal-independent commitment in preparation for its 22nd Congress. The key question asked for reactions to the proposition that, if the Union of the Left came to power, the PCF "would seek to govern alone by eliminating the other parties"; and 46 percent agreed with this brutally Leninist hypothesis as against 31 percent who disagreed, while 23 percent were undecided. Similarly, only 33 percent thought that the PCF was "a party like the others," while 48 percent judged it "very different from the others," with 19 percent undecided. In these figures we find the most obvious explanation of the defeat of the Left two years later.

For the PCF leadership, of course, the party line was correct all along; but this habitual triumphalism is beginning to prove counterproductive in more ways than one. Immediately after the elections the Politburo announced that the Communist party had no responsibility whatever for the defeat of the Left—all the blame was to be assigned to the Socialists. But this produced an unprecedented ferment of protest and indignation in the ranks of the party, among both intellectuals and workers. Marchais admitted that "a debate of unprecedented scope" was going on, but explained lamely that, according to the statutes, contributions to such a debate could only appear in the party press before a congress. So they appeared in the nonparty press—a flood of challenging letters and articles that criticized the party's policies with regard to the Socialists and other matters, and complained of the lack of internal democracy. In the past, such rebellion, by outstanding figures like Jean Elleinstein and the philosopher Louis Althusser, would have been met by expulsion; but now Marchais had to promise that "no heads would roll." Creaking at every aclerotic joint, digging in calloused heels, the PCF *was* moving jerkily along the Eurocommunist road, if a considerable distance behind the other two parties.

Meanwhile, these other two were justifiably concerned over events in France, and the behavior of the PCF vis-à-vis the Socialists. Manuel Azcàrate of the Spanish CP was more outspoken than the diplomatic Italians: "The French Communists have not applied the basic principle of Eurocommunism, which consists in seeking a very wide agreement between the most underprivileged classes and the middle classes." For the defeat of the French Left cast shadows also over Italy, where the Communist party is much stronger than the Socialist party, and over Spain, where it is considerably weaker. The question remains unanswered: Can a Communist party collaborate loyally and on mutually profitable terms with a social-democratic party of comparable strength?

Italy: The Regional Option

The prolonged drama of the kidnapping of Aldo Moro by the Red Brigades is a reminder that Italy's profound and complex crisis manifests itself on many levels—societal, economic, political, moral, and administrative (to list the more obvious categories). This systemic crisis has been aggravated in recent years by more widespread problems affecting the capitalist countries in general, particularly since the Arab oil boycott of late 1973 (high inflation and unemployment rates, trade imbalances, and so on), but in Italy its national roots are deep and intertwined: the cultural-economic gap between North and South, the parasitic bureaucracy, the anachronistic institutions, the dense network of corrupting customs that lies behind such phrases as *clientelismo* or *sottogoverno,* the chaotic frustration of higher education, the ludicrously inadequate tax system, the growth not only of lawlessness but of random violence—these are some of the more obvious surface manifestations.

The Italian Communist party's slow and cautious approach to positions of political power on the national level (as distinct from the local and regional levels) is now based primarily on the claim that its contribution is needed if the country's formidable socioeconomic problems are to be tackled with any prospect of success. One should perhaps note here, however, that to a considerable extent this is already happening, and has been happening for years. Even before the local elections of June 1975 brought the Communist vote to within a few percentage points of the Christian Democratic party and gave Communist-dominated coalitions new power bases in most large cities and in many regions and provinces, the PCI was in effect already helping to govern Italy, since its parliamentary collaboration (particularly in the closed legislative "commissions" of both chambers) had become necessary for the passing of important laws. The present "programmatic majority" is simply another step in a process that has been going on for years.

The PCI has a supplementary argument of international relevance, and that is that it is in the interests of Italy's Western allies that the country's social and economic decline be halted and reversed—which again (it is said) means Communist entry into government. Whatever validity there may be in this argument—and one can accept the need for the PCI's contribution to the government of an Italy in enduring crisis while still regarding it as a *potential* threat to pluralistic democracy—it is clear that the problems which the political advance of the PCI pose for the Western community of nations lie mainly on the level of foreign policy, and this with particular reference to the EEC and NATO.

But these are two very different issues. The PCI's positions with regard to the EEC (and to West European integration in general) are much clearer and, more important, have been established for a much longer period, than with regard to the Atlantic Alliance, and by this time there is little reason to question the credibility of its "regional option." It is more than a decade and a half since its positions on this began to diverge substantially from those of the Kremlin and of the other West European Communist parties (notably the French). As early as 1962 its program for the tenth party congress accepted West European integration through the EEC as an "irreversible reality," and acknowledged that it had been "a fundamental factor in Italy's economic leap forward," as Luigi Longo put it. True, this increasingly positive attitude to the EEC (responding the perceptions of the Italian electorate) contained a marked anti-American element, and specific EEC policies (notably regarding relations with the COMECON) were frequently criticized. Essentially, however, the new line adopted in the early 1960s—and developed steadily in the face of direct and indirect Soviet and French Communist criticism—represented an effort to transfer to the regional level the domestic strategy of a "long march through the institutions," through gradual involvement in decision-making processes.

In this process of adaptation to regional realities, Communist trade-union leaders went ahead of the party itself. In 1963, the Italian Communist-Socialist CGIL labor federation set up an office in Brussels to seek liaison not only with the EEC bureaucracy but also with the local headquarters of the "free" (non-Communist) and Christian international labor organizations; a few years later it sought and got representation on the economic and social bodies of the the EEC Commission. For several years the PCI itself knocked at the door of the European Parliament, so to speak, but its application was vetoed by the Italian government. In 1969 the Christian Democrats finally gave way to persistent Communist pressure, and the PCI sent an active delegation under Giorgio Amendola to Strasbourg, where it was joined in 1973 by a distinctly less enthusiastic delegation of the French CP. It appears that the Italian Communist contribution to the European Parliament (as also, since 1976, to the Western European Union) has on the whole been a distinguished and useful one, and it is significant that it was one of the first delegations to give strong support to the proposal for direct elections to the Parliament—unlike the French CP, which vigorously opposed direct elections until 1977.

The belief that the PCI's efforts to involve itself in West European integration—for its own political purposes of course—is strengthened by the contributions made to a private seminar on foreign policy held at the party's Palmiro Togliatti Institute of Communist Studies in December 1972, and particularly two interventions by Giorgio Amendola. The party's policy, he said, was "to participate in the Community to make it an open Community, organized democratically . . . not dominated by the bureaucrats and the 'Eurocrats' . . . nor dominated by the national executives of the governments . . . with a Parliament elected by universal suffrage." Later Amendola said that "the final objective is . : . a Socialist Europe, truly united from the Atlantic to the Urals." But he immediately stressed that this could only be an "historic"—that is, a long-term—objective; and it was, moreover, a goal that could be reached eventually only through "a profound process of transformation—a transformation of the capitalist countries, and also a transformation of the institutions of the Socialist countries . . . more socialism in the West and more democracy in the East." Against this long-term, "ideological" background he presented a more immediate regional goal: "Western Europe . . . faces the objective of arriving at political unification and also economic and monetary unification."

(It might be added that on this as on other issues there is a gap between the positions of the PCI and PCE on one hand and those of the PCF on the other. Carrillo declares that for Spain there is no alternative to West European integration; the PCI supports the candidacies of Spain, Portugal, and Greece; the PCF warns zealously against any encroachment by the EEC on French sovereignty, and opposes the entry of all three countries into the Community.)

Compared with its stand on the Common Market, the PCI's present (outwardly) accommodating attitude to the Atlantic Alliance is a relatively recent development—and to that extent invites skepticism. As this decade opened the PCI's slogan was still: "NATO out of Italy, Italy out of NATO." At the thirteenth party congress in 1972, Berlinguer was still speaking of "the struggle against the Atlantic Pact," and stressing the need to free Italy from "the bond of subordination which links it to NATO," as part of a broader struggle to "liberate Europe from American hegemony." But in 1974 there were signs of rethinking, and at the fourteenth party congress in March 1975 Berlinguer announced that the PCI was "not raising the question of Italy's departure from the Atlantic Pact," and was in fact opposed to "any other unilateral departure from one bloc or the other"—a stipulation that he explicitly applied to nonaligned Yugoslavia, expressing his party's "profound interest" in having that neighboring country stay out of the Warsaw Pact.

The opportunistic element in this new position was obvious enough. But it should also be noted that Berlinguer affirmed this position subsequently at international Communist gatherings, notably in his speeches at the twenty-fifth CPSU Congress in February 1976 and at the pan-European Communist conference in June 1976. On the latter occasion he stressed that the Italian road to a Socialist society lay "within the framework of the international alliances to which our country belongs." This reassuring message was emphasized during the campaign for the crucial elections of June 1976, and was symbolized by the presence among the independent candidates on the party's lists of Air Force General Nino Pasti, who for several years had been responsible for nuclear affairs at SHAPE headquarters. During this campaign Berlinguer touched upon another thorny argument—that only the existence of NATO made it possible for Western Communists to speak plausibly of struggling to achieve a democratic socialism. In an interview he said that he had no fear of meeting the "unjust" fate of Dubcek, because "even if the [Soviet] will were there, there does not exist the least possibility that our road to socialism can be hindered or conditioned by the USSR. . . . I feel that since Italy does not belong to the Warsaw Pact, there is absolute certainty that we can proceed along the Italian road to socialism without any conditioning"—and he even accepted the description of NATO as a "useful shield" for this purpose.

While this argument rests on political logic, it is equally true that the NATO allies still have cause to be concerned about the PCI's eventual role as a governing party. One solid reason for this is the fraternal link that still exists between the Italian CP and the Soviet regime. Does the "critical solidarity" of which Italian Communists like to speak mean that eventually solidarity will prevail? In particular, is it true that the PCI has always sup- ported Soviet *foreign* policy (as is often said of the Eurocommunist parties in general)?

During a discussion with Sergio Segre at PCI headquarters in Rome in the autumn of 1976, I received from him two booklets containing the un- published texts (compiled for internal distribution) of contributions to two party seminars held in December 1972. One of them contains an il- luminating passage in which Segre (the Central Committee official responsi- ble for foreign affairs) had suggested the need to work for a convergence with other Italian parties on foreign policy. He said:

> It seems to me, then, that we must examine how, even in this area of Atlan- tic policy, within a perspective which clearly calls for the dissolution of the blocs, we can indicate intermediate phases, so that this problem may no longer be a cause of vertical division between the [Italian] political forces. . . . If we want to go ahead along this line, we must at a certain point develop a dialogue with the forces of the West, with the democratic forces of the Left, with the West as a whole.

Within a few years his call at that seminar for the development of "what might be called our Westpolitik" began to be answered by international and national events which together promoted a process of convergence among Italian parties on foreign policy. Thus, the drastic effect of the Arab oil boycott of later 1973 on Italy led the Christian Democrats quietly and gradually to revise their positions on the Middle East—until they became substantially compatible with those of the Communists. On the other hand, the grave deterioration of Italy's economic situation made it clear to all but the political extremists on either flank that the country's international situation was, and would continue to be, one of "asymmetrical interdependence"—the weak partner in a network of economic and political relationships.

Thus, as the Communists modified their stand on some issues (the EEC, the Atlantic Alliance), the Christian Democrats modified their position on others (the Middle East and the Third World) until the convergence became unmistakable. In a lecture given in August 1976 Segre was able to rephrase his remarks of December 1972, but this time as a public affirmation, not a tentative and private proposal: "In recent years the PCI has made an effort, even through revising its own previous attitudes on some major questions of international policy, to contribute to the construction of an Italian foreign policy which would be a factor of national unity and no longer, as in the lacerating years of the cold war, a factor of vertical division between the political forces of this country." Nor was this only a Communist opinion. It was a Christian Democratic foreign minister, Arnaldo Forlani, who told the UN General Assembly on October 1, 1976, that "on the basic options [of Italian foreign policy] there exists a full measure of agreement in our national parliament, between our political forces and throughout the country." This consensus was given institutional expression recently, when the Christian Democrats, the PCI, and the four smaller parties of the "constitutional arc" adopted a common statement on foreign policy.

We have already noted how the PCI diverged substantially from Soviet foreign policy positions on the Common Market. Other divergences have dealt with the international Communist movement—Yugoslavia and China, for example. More recently the list has been growing. The PCI took up a neutralist attitude toward the Ethiopian—Somali conflict, in which the Soviet Union was involved on the Ethiopian side, and apparently made a vain attempt at mediation. Similarly, the Italian Communists have remained on good terms with tthe Eritrean rebels, and declined to join the Soviets (and the PCF) in attacking President Sadat's peace initiative.

In the spring of 1978, the PCI's Central Committee emphasized the growing importance which the party now places—or at least wishes to be regarded as placing—on "consensual" foreign policy by setting up a new "Center for the Study of International Policy." On this level, as on that of domestic affairs, it seems to be a safe bet that the Italian CP will give primacy and priority to its own political interests, even when they conflict with those of Moscow.

Eurocommunists between East and West

The defeat of the *Union de la Gauche* in the French elections of March 1978 drew attention, as we have seen, to significant differences in the political and ideological positions of the three major Eurocommunist parties—or, rather, between the Italian and Spanish CPs on the one hand and the French on the other. It also gave relieved Western policymakers occasion to ponder the nature and extent of the threat which the PCF, whether alone or as part of a leftist alliance, posed (or might one day pose) to the existing order in France, and hence to the wider community of economically advanced Western democracies.

The central question here is not whether the French Communist party is now "independent" of Moscow (a term which in this context would need careful definition). It is whether the advance of the PCF toward at least a share of national power would in practice promote Soviet strategic interests by weakening or destabilizing the NATO alliance in particular and the West in general. The potential threat which the PCF poses to the existing order in France and in the Western community can, of course, be considered on various levels—for example, the strategic level, the international, the economic, or the societal. The most obvious of these, though not necessarily the most important, is the strategic level; and here we must deal with the possible effect of the party's rise to power, or partial power, on France's defensive strength, on its relations with the Atlantic Alliance, and on the East-West balance of power in Europe.

On this as on other levels we find marked differences both in substance and in style between the positions of the PCF on the one hand and those of the Italian and Spanish CPs on the other. The changes in the PCI's attitude to NATO may legitimately be regarded with caution or even skepticism by Western governments; but one cannot deny the party's present efforts to persuade all concerned that the alliance has nothing to fear from its participation in government. Similarly, Santiago Carrillo would allow U.S. bases to remain in Spain as long as Soviet troops are in Czechoslovakia (whereas the Socialist leader Felipe Gonzalez demands their removal); and, while he is against Spain's entry into NATO, he says that he would accept even this if a majority of the population votes for it in a referendum.

As against the Eurocommunist evolution of the Italian and Spanish Communist parties with respect to the Atlantic Alliance, the hostility of the PCF to the alliance has hardly diminished. With regard to NATO (and, indeed, foreign policy in general), it might be more fitting to speak of the PCF's "Gaullo-communism." This PCF concept reflects a Gaullist emphasis on French national sovereignty combined with "antiimperialism" directed particularly against the United States and the Federal Republic of Germany.

This traditional, not to say visceral, hostility to the "imperialist" West was quite clearly expressed in Marchais's "secret" Central Committee speech of June 29, 1972, on the signing of the Common Program. The concession obtained from the Socialists that France must be ready to face *any*

Eurocommunism: Between East and West   255

aggressor meant, he said, that "the military policy and the very orientation of France's foreign policy would escape, in an essential area, from the global strategy of imperialism," adding later that the PCF would profit from the fact that in international affairs "the Socialist system is henceforth the real determining factor."[11]

Recent shifts in the party's positions—notably the sudden acceptance of the *force de frappe* and of direct elections to the European Parliament—had to be viewed against the background of Communist-Socialist maneuvering for political advantage, and in any case hardly amounted to substantial change in a bloc orientation that for so long was an essential element of the PCF's identity. Similarly, the PCF's habitual hostility to the United States and West Germany is hardly veiled by its blatant appeals to Gaullist sentiment—accusing President Giscard d'Estaing of betraying the General's heritage by "creeping Atlanticism," and making French sovereignty its watchword with regard to defense as well as West European integration. The PCF has, indeed, said for many years that it is for France staying in the Atlantic Alliance but against its return to the military organization. Yet on all questions where Communist defense policies differ from those of the Socialist party (PS), the Communist positions would in practice seriously weaken Western defense capabilities if implemented.

Thus, the PCF now says that it favors the maintenance of France's nuclear force, but calls for a defense strategy *tous azimuts*, with missiles targeted against *all* potential aggressors—including, party spokesmen have specifically said, the Federal Republic of Germany. It also wants the use of the nuclear weapon to be subject to a "collegial" decision by the government (which might be one way of ensuring that the deterrent did not deter). Again, the PCF rules out the possibility of a West European defense community, while the Socialist party keeps this option open—and Santiago Carrillo for his part, has expressed interest in it.

If this is a potential threat to the security of the West, however, it is one which should be viewed in its true proportions. We are dealing here with a strategically and economically important country whose development in recent decades has been decisively affected, through a network of interdependent relationships and despite the distorting pressures of Gaullism, by its memberships in the Atlantic Alliance and the European Community. Even if the Left had won an inevitably narrow victory in the March 1978 elections, is it reasonable to suppose that a party representing only one-fifth of the electorate could have imposed, against the opposition of a stronger coalition partner, such serious changes in defense and foreign policy?

If the Union of the Left had won, France and the Western community of nations would, indeed, have faced a serious threat, but it would surely have come to the socioeconomic level (through the flight of capital, inflation, and social conflict) rather than on the military-strategic level. On both levels, moreover, the Communist leadership suffered from an inability to shed dogmatic attitudes and respond adequately to new realities (and here, perhaps, we come to the most significant difference between the PCF and the other two major Eurocommunist parties). The PCF's visceral anti-Americanism on one level was matched on the other level by a visceral anticapitalism which prevented it from adopting a rational and realistic approach to France's economic situation: while Italian Communists were urging on the working class the need for austerity, their French comrades were lapsing into the crude simplicity of "Let the rich pay!"[12]

The process of adaptation to the sociopolitical realities of the advanced, pluralistic democracies of Western Europe, which we take to be the core of Eurocommunism, imposes upon the Eurocommunist parties a convergence with social-democratic positions in many areas (the commitment to the preservation of bourgeois liberties and to respect for constitutional democracy). Yet this very convergence emphasizes the need for the Eurocommunist parties to maintain their *communist* identity and the demarcation between themselves and the social-democrats. While pursuing in practice policies of gradual reformism, and doing so (if they are to have any hope of success) in collaboration with social-democratic and/or centrist forces, they must insist that their ultimate goal remains the social revolution, giving political power to the working class, even in a multiparty democracy, and ending capitalist exploitation.

In accordance with this latter imperative, it is also of basic importance for them to continue presenting themselves as part of an international movement of revolutionary "Marxist-Leninist" parties, some of which have already come to power and, by Communist definition, introduced "socialism." But here lies the other arm of the dilemma. The Eurocommunist commitment to pluralistic democracy and human rights involves explicit rejection of the Soviet/East European model of socialism—a rejection that must be made credible to electors by "principled" and continuing criticism of the repressive aspects of these regimes and of their lack of democracy. At the same time, however, there are other reasons for West European Communist parties to be cautious about undertaking such systematic criticism. One is that criticism draws public attention to the pro-Soviet and Stalinist past of the Western Communist party concerned, and also to its continued fraternal links with the regimes being criticized, so that the political profit to be gained is questionable. Secondly, the criticism, if it is sufficiently vigorous and sustained, may cause divisions within the party by offending conservative or pro-Soviet elements—a situation which the Soviets may attempt to exploit by encouraging these elements, examples being the Kremlin's all but overt backing of the Spanish secessionists headed by Enrique Lister in 1969-74, or of the Swedish "Workers' Communist Party" founded in 1977.

There are, of course, corresponding restraints on the Soviet side. The victory of the strategic alliance between the Eurocommunist parties and the two independent East European regimes in the prolonged struggle over the pan-European conference document (1974-76) demonstrated the continuing erosion of Soviet authority. The fact was that the international Communist movement was no longer an international Communist organization: there was no center of authority, no guardian of orthodoxy empowered to deal with heretics by expelling them from the Marxist-Leninist "church," and no means of obliging other Communist parties to subordinate their own interests to those of the CPSU.

In these circumstances, the uneven process of adaptation to Western sociopolitical realities which we call Eurocommunism seems likely to continue, and to affect in particular those West European Communist parties that have already become important factors in national political life—which, we recall again, means a very small minority of them. Their chances of making political progress within the framework of constitutional democracy might be strengthened by a continuation or intensification of the general Western economic crisis, but probably only to a limited extent: in the event of anything like a catastrophic collapse of the Western economic system, they too would surely be among the victims, as the Italian Communists are quite ready to admit—and the Eastern regimes would not be spared, either. Meanwhile, as the 1978 French elections demonstrated, the Eurocommunists carry the burden of their past, and must repeatedly seek to establish their credibility.

Maintaining credibility means subjecting the Soviet Union and other Eastern regimes to at least sporadic criticism. The level of generally indirect ideological polemics between Eurocommunists and regime dogmatists will rise and fall: a direct confrontation (let alone anything like a formal split) would not be in the interests of either side. But, even if the polemics were to cease altogether, the challenge which Eurocommunist ideas represent for "real socialism" would remain. In the past few years the "subversive" effect of these ideas upon East European societies has combined with the unexpected impact of the Helsinki Conference ("Basket 3") to produce a new wave of dissent and unrest in most East European countries.

The fact is that both parts of a divided Europe are constantly being subjected, in very different ways and in varying degrees, to destabilizing influences. Perhaps the question to ask is which system is better equipped to withstand pressures that cannot be entirely eliminated—which is better fitted to cope with the inevitable challenges of change? One thought seems relevant: that rigidity has a hidden weakness, and flexibility a hidden strength. In a time of trial, the Western democracies can surely draw comfort from the memory of a contrast—between the way NATO reacted in 1975 to the presence of the strongly pro-Soviet Portuguese Communist party in the government of a member-state, and the way the Warsaw Pact reacted in 1968 to Communist Czechoslovakia's ill-starred experiment in "socialism with a human face."

Notes

1. One notable example of this was the chorus of criticism with which West European CPs met the Soviet trial of Siniavsky and Daniel in early 1966.

2. The further significance of the book lay in the fact that it in fact consisted of the text of a long memorandum which Mlynar, a former secretary of the Czechoslovak CP's Central Committee, addressed to the leaderships of the European Communist parties in early 1975, within the framework of the preparations for the pan-European conference, arguing that it would be in the interests of the very regimes that had taken part in the invasion to reverse the course of repressive "normalization" in Czechoslovakia.

3. Waldeck Rochet, having just visited Moscow (with Italian CP envoys) to warn the Soviets against intervening in Czechoslovakia, went on to Prague to lecture Dubcek on the folly of overdoing liberalization! See Kevin Devlin, "Rewriting Secret History: the PCF and Czechoslovakia," Radio Free Europe research/Free World No. 0583, Munich, 13 May 1970. For further testimony on the PCF's acceptance of normalization in Czechoslovakia see Roger Garaudy, *Toute la verité* (Paris, 1970) and Pierre Daix, *Prague au coeur* (Paris, 1974). Garaudy was expelled from the PCF in May 1970 and Daix left the party in 1974—both mainly on account of their anti-Soviet stand on Czechoslovakia.

4. The PCI's main conditions were that the conference must be consultative, with no binding programmatic content; the principle of the autonomy of each party must be strictly respected; nonattendance must not affect a party's status as part of the international Communist movement (that is, no "excommunications"); any party must have the right "not to accept, or to accept only partially or with reservations any eventual (collective) decision"; and a basic purpose of the meeting should be to establish "new forms of unity and collaboration," which should extend to noncommunist forces. All of these conditions, with the exception of the latter part of the last one, were in fact implemented at the Moscow Conference of June 1969. In retrospect, it seems hardly an exaggeration to say that Soviet acceptance of them marked the initiation of a new era in the history of the international Communist movement.

5. The first pan-European conference of Communist parties was held in Karlovy Vary, Czechoslovakia, in April 1967. It was boycotted by the

Albanian, Yugoslav, and Romanian parties from the East, and by the Dutch, Icelandic, and Norwegian parties from the West, while the independent Swedes sent only an observer.

6. In an interview given to the Rome weekly *Espresso*, August 31, 1975, Sergio Segre of the Italian CP's delegation to the preparatory meetings said that the second East German draft (as unacceptable as the first) said of the Communist parties that "they play a vanguard role, pursue identical objectives, and are guided by a single ideology."

7. There has been some controversy over the origin of the term "Eurocommunism." It seems to have been coined in June 1975 by the exiled Yugoslav journalist Frane Barbieri, former editor-in-chief of the Belgrade weekly *Nin,* and then writing for the Milan newspaper *Il Giornale Nuovo.*

8. While visiting Rome in February 1976 (instead of attending the twenty-fifth Congress of the CPSU) Carrillo gave an interview in which he spoke of the "primitive stage" of socialism in the USSR. Asked if he did not fear that such ideas would be condemned by Moscow, he replied: "By what right can they condemn us? They can criticize us, as we criticize them. Condemnation is excommunication from a church, and the Communist movement was a church but now no longer is one."

9. Compare this with Elleinstein's earlier statement in his book, *Le P.C.* (Paris, 1976): "We want neither Gulag nor the banning of artistic exhibitions, nor the censorship of literary works, nor psychiatric hospitals for political crimes, nor the persecution of Christians or Jews, and we condemn that with as much firmness as anyone, even if we do not reduce the whole reality of the Socialist countries to these facts" (p. 154).

10. The myth of Communist political progress in France fades in the light of one striking fact: the PCF's *best* electoral performance under the present Fifth Republic (22.5 percent in March 1967) has been worse than its *worst* performance under the Fourth Republic (25.6 percent in January 1956), and this despite a general shift of the electorate to the Left, and despite the PCF's energetic efforts over the past decade to build up its image as an independent, progressive, trustworthy party committed to democratic liberties, and so on.

11. *Le Monde*, 9 July 1975.

12. In an early Italian Communist commentary on the result of the French elections Claudio Petruccioli said in *L'Unità* of March 21, 1978, that the French Left had failed to "make its candidature for government entirely convincing to the electorate," and that it would have to abandon the illusion that the country's grave economic crisis "can be resolved through the simple substitution of the ruling class."

11 Is European Security Negotiable?

Jane M.O. Sharp

A favorite epithet of the Nixon administration at the beginning of its ill-fated second term was that the world was entering an "era of negotiation" as distinct from the ugly confrontations of recent years. All this was thought to be highly auspicious for continued stability and security in Europe, the more so since three sets of negotiations had been established to codify various aspects of the new spirit of détente; the strategic arms limitation talks (SALT) between the United States and the Soviet Union; the Conference for Security and Cooperation in Europe (CSCE), a Warsaw Pact initiative involving Canada and the United States and all European states except Albania; and the Mutual and Balanced-Force Reduction talks (MBFR) between selected members of NATO and the Warsaw Pact.

Writing in 1973, just as the MBFR talks were getting underway in Vienna, the French scholar Pierre Hassner suggested one criterion by which these negotiations might be judged:

> The positive value of MBFR and of the whole negotiating process lies not in dismantling a relatively safe military balance for which there is no substitute in sight, but in changing the character of political relations. It will have been worth all the trouble and the risk if, by becoming a permanent feature of the process of East-West communications it contributes directly or indirectly to modifying the behavior of its participants in the direction of restraint. For, more than mutually balanced force reductions, what European security needs is a process of mutually balanced interpretation and non-intervention, and a mutually balanced reduction in the role of force.[1]

Pursuit of formal arms control agreements in the past, however, has rarely lowered force levels or restrained behavior. On the contrary, negotiations seem as likely to generate armament and exacerbate international tensions.[2]

Much has changed in recent decades; not only Europe's position in the hierarchy of world power and influence, but also the hierarchy of states within Europe itself. Since World War II, nuclear weapons have made possible sudden annihilation against which there is no defense; a fact which substantially alters perceptions of adequate security requirements. Yet much in international politics remains the same, and earlier arms control efforts suggest the following general propositions about the relative costs and benefits of seeking formal rather than flexible security arrangements:

The Resistance of the Status Quo. Formal agreements can serve to codify, but cannot easily change, the political, territorial, or military status quo. The most valuable agreements appear to be those which codify a mutually acceptable situation, complementing a relaxation of tensions brought about by independent unilateral means. By contrast, where attempts are made either to codify a status quo which many states find unacceptable, or to negotiate changes in the status quo, results have often been counterproductive.

The Tendency to Discriminate. To the extent formal agreements create different classes of states, they generate resentment in those states who feel discriminated against. This resentment leads to a desire for redress which can take many different forms, with more or less destabilizing impact.

The Tendency to Generate More Armament. Negotiations between former enemies or potential adversaries, which focus narrowly on military capabilities, tend to exacerbate international tensions and generate the acquisition of more armaments; as a hedge against failure to reach an agreement, to correct newly perceived asymmetries, and to support particular negotiating positions.

This chapter seeks to assess the impact of contemporary arms control diplomacy on European security in light of these propositions.

The Resistance of the Status Quo

Agreements to limit military forces presuppose the solution, acceptance, or rationalization of other major territorial and political differences between the parties involved. Treaties which essentially do no more than codify an already acceptable situation are the easiest to achieve and the most stable over time, but history is replete with frustrated efforts to negotiate change. Witness the attempts in Europe through the 1950s to negotiate changes in the post-1945 territorial boundaries, disengage foreign troops, and unite the two halves of Germany—efforts which not only failed but in the process heightened tension both between East and West and among the states of the Western alliance.

Once West Germany had joined NATO and the Soviet sphere of influence in Eastern Europe was embodied in the Warsaw Pact in 1955, a certain stability was established. This stability was threatened on several occasions over the vulnerable and ambiguous status of Berlin, and Soviet hegemony was challenged more than once in the East; but no Western support was offered in East Germany (1953), Hungary (1956), or Czechoslovakia (1968).

The essential feature of Willy Brandt's *Ostpolitik* in the late 1960s and early 1970s was the recognition of political and territorial realities in Europe, however painful these were in terms of perpetuating the division of Germany. A series of mutually reinforcing concessions by West Germany on the one hand, and East Germany, Poland, and the Soviet Union on the other, made possible the rapid (at least in diplomatic terms) conclusion of a set of treaties which are widely held to have made a positive contribution to peace and stability in Europe. The concessions, for the most part, took the form of explicit acceptance of formerly contentious issues.

For the Federal Republic it meant burying the Hallstein doctrine and abandoning the insistence on progress toward reunification as a precondition of further progress in détente, which had been implicit understandings in Bonn through the mid-1960s. Acceptance of the Oder-Niesse line as the border of East Germany explicitly recognized postwar territorial gains by Poland, which paved the way for the West German treaties with Poland and the Soviet Union in 1970. The tacit acknowledgement of Soviet domination in Eastern Europe as a whole and over East Germany in particular, as well as Brandt's ingenious concept of two states within one nation, made possible the Basic Treaty between the two halves of Germany in 1972, followed by UN membership for both in 1973.

These concessions were balanced by a more secure Western position on Berlin following Soviet accession to the 1972 Four Power Agreement, and by Eastern bloc recognition of a sovereign West Germany as a legitimate member of the NATO alliance.

The conference for Security and Cooperation in Europe is dealt with in depth elsewhere in this volume and will only be touched upon here, insofar as it illustrates the proposition that formal international agreements are more likely to reflect than affect political relations.[3]

In 1966, when the Warsaw Pact invited the West to participate in a European security conference, the primary objectives of the Soviets appeared to be consolidation of their political hegemony over the East and confirmation of post-1945 borders in Europe; it was to be, in effect, the World War II Peace Conference. Another Soviet objective in the early 1960s seemed to be dissolution of the two military blocs to reduce American influence on the Continent, and the establishment of an alternative pan-European security system. After the "Czech Spring" of 1968 the Soviets seemed less inclined to press for a rapid reduction of U.S. military forces and more ready to embrace the status quo, viewing the United States as something of a partner in the management of European security.

By 1972, when the CSCE was just getting underway in Helsinki, the *Ostpolitik* treaties had already accomplished most of what the Soviets had hoped to achieve at a security conference and CSCE became a more general multilateral confirmation of the status quo in Europe.

For example, the Helsinki Final Act, concluded in July 1975, set the seal on East European and Soviet acceptance of the political and economic reality of the European Economic Community. But the GDR had been a de facto partner in the Community for years by virtue of special inter-German trade relations, and pragmatic agreements, for example between Euratom and the Soviet Union on nuclear fuel supplies, had already been arranged with little fanfare. Furthermore, since January 1975, Eastern countries doing business with EEC members were supposed to deal with the commission in Brussels rather than by way of bilateral deals with individual countries.

Assessments of the value of the CSCE process depend to some extent on prior expectations. The West German government was well satisfied with the result, not having expected any radical change, but viewing the exercise as a means to consolidate what had already been achieved in the Eastern treaties, to facilitate further East-West interaction, and perhaps create a basis for increased personal contacts. Continued steady progress in political and economic relations between Bonn and Moscow was reflected in the twenty-five year trade agreement signed by Breshnev and Schmidt in Bonn in May 1978.

The French, on the other hand, who, to many observers, both at Helsinki and Geneva, seemed to use CSCE as a means of enhancing their own prestige in both halves of Europe, were less enthusiastic. French tactics during the 1972-75 phase of the conference, and particularly in Geneva in the spring and summer of 1975, were a source of irritation to her West European colleagues as well as to the East. Other members of the EEC and NATO were upset by moves to represent France as the spokesman for the West; and both East and West were distressed by the manner in which the French seemed to hark back to the 1940s to emphasize their status as one of the "Victorious Powers" of World War II—this particularly with reference to the status of Berlin.

Other members of the EEC were, in general, well pleased with the opportunity afforded by the CSCE process to demonstrate their capability to conduct a common foreign policy; indeed one of the more gratifying aspects of CSCE for those who wished to deemphasize military bloc confrontation in Europe was the fact that the EEC rather than NATO was the caucus which thrashed out Western positions.

For the neutral and nonaligned, this was an important pan-European gathering which many hoped would develop into a permanent multilateral process.

For the Soviets, who had initially conceived the conference and pushed hard for it throughout the previous decade, results were mixed. To the extent that postwar frontiers were declared inviolable and commitments made to improve East-West cooperation in scientific, technological, and economic affairs, the Kremlin was presumably well satisfied. But the Soviets were also clearly worried by the tendency of some Western delegates to use the CSCE as an instrument for changing the political status quo by increasing social and human contact to encroach on Soviet domestic policy. To the extent that the West wanted to push the human rights issue beyond where the Soviets felt they could safely go, there was considerable resistance; reflected in the conscious Abrenzung policy of the GDR, and increasingly harsh treatment of dissidents in the Soviet Union.

The United States government in general and Henry Kissinger in particular were openly skeptical of the CSCE process from 1972-75, and especially of the human rights issue. But between the Helsinki Final Act and the Belgrade Conference in 1978-79, the new Carter administration had made a vigorous stand on human rights the cornerstone of its foreign policy. Too vigorous for most West European governments. The West Germans were particularly uneasy with President Carter's tactics on this issue, believing they could rebound and undo the steady progress of recent years. In 1977 Chancellor Schmidt reminded the United States that the Bonn government had succeeded in repatriating approximately 50,000 Germans from Eastern Europe through "quiet diplomacy."

In sum, the most useful aspects of the CSCE were those which recorded progress on issues of cooperation and security and established a firm base for further achievements, rather than the effort to push hard for dramatic new breakthroughs. The series of trials which followed the Belgrade Conference, including those of Ginzburg and Shcharansky, were hardly more humane than the ordeals of earlier dissidents in the Soviet Union. Indeed one has to ask whether some of the CSCE rhetoric did not have a negative impact.

MBFR and the Status Quo

MBFR was originally proposed by NATO with two limited objectives in mind; to discourage unilateral reductions of U.S. and West European troops and to counter a recurrent but somewhat vague Warsaw Pact proposal for a European Security Conference, with a more pragmatic means of securing reductions in Soviet forces in Eastern Europe.

In 1968 when NATO formally invited the Warsaw Pact to "join in a process leading to mutual and balanced force reduction," four principles were suggested which implied that a genuine disarmament measure was contemplated. Reductions were to:[4]

be reciprocal and balanced in scope and timing;

maintain the present degree of security at reduced costs without destabilizing the situation in Europe;

create confidence in Europe generally;

be consistent with the vital security interests of all parties.

Terms like "mutual" and "balanced" seemed to imply that forces in
Europe were essentially matched and that the purpose of NATO at MBFR
was merely to reduce the levels on either side. The prospect of arms control
negotiations, however, always stimulates a reassessment and a recounting
of the opposing forces, and by the time MBFR exploratory talks began in
Vienna in January 1973, NATO delegates spoke not of maintaining but
"improving" the balance. The term "balance" took on special meaning;
for the West it came to imply proportional reductions to achieve balance.
NATO claimed three main disparities in need of correction: Warsaw Pact
advantages in manpower, tanks, and geography, the latter in the sense that
troops could more easily be reintroduced into central Europe from the
Soviet Union than from the United States.

The Soviet view of the balance is somewhat different. Since accepting
the invitation to participate in MBFR in 1971, the Soviets have consistently
maintained that the force relationship established in Europe since World
War II is essentially balanced, and as such contributes to peace and stability
on the Continent. The primary Soviet motivation in MBFR is thus to
preserve the status quo, and doing so does not necessarily defy the four
principles NATO laid down in 1968. Given the asymmetries in alliance force
postures, precise measurement of military capability is in any case impossible, but the Pact has not used MBFR to seek additional advantages as
much as to preserve and legitimize its position relative to NATO.

Reductions could still be reciprocal and balanced in scope and timing;
nor does maintaining the present degree of security at reduced costs present
any problems. Furthermore, if Europe is deemed to be stable, the
maintenance of the status quo can hardly be said to undermine confidence
or be inconsistent with the vital security of any state. Indeed, it has been
argued that if the Warsaw Pact were to give up any of its current advantages
in, say, numbers of tanks, its security would be diminished according to the
NATO principles.

The proposals each side has made in Vienna reflect their fundamentally
different approaches, with NATO seeking negotiated change and the
Soviets aiming to codify the status quo.

NATO seeks to correct a manpower imbalance through asymmetric cuts
to achieve common alliance ceilings, and to offset the Soviet preponderance
in tanks with excess NATO nuclear systems. The initial NATO proposal
called for a first stage reduction of 29,000 U.S. and 68,000 Soviet troops. A
second stage would reduce other national forces down to common alliance
ceilings of 700,000 ground troops each for NATO and the Pact. According
to NATO estimates, this would entail reductions of 199,000 for the Pact and

92,000 for NATO. In December 1975 this proposal was amended with an offer to withdraw 1,000 tactical nuclear warheads, fifty-four F-4 nuclear-capable aircraft, and thirty-six Pershing medium-range ballistic missiles, in exchange for a Soviet tank army to include 1,700 tanks, and new manpower ceilings of 900,000 to include ground and air forces.

By contrast, the Pact asserts that the East-West balance must be maintained by equal cuts in all force categories. The initial Pact proposal was a first-stage reduction of 20,000 troops each for the United States and the Soviet Union, to be followed by equal percentages of ground and air forces and nuclear delivery systems. In February 1976, responding to NATO's December 1975 proposal, the Pact amended its position to include equal reductions of one army corps headquarters and 300 tanks on each side; fifty-four U.S. F-4 and fifty-four similar Soviet nuclear-capable aircraft; thirty-six U.S. Pershing and thirty-six Soviet Scud B missiles; and an unspecified (but presumably equal) number of air defense systems on each side.[5]

Another point at issue was whether to establish common alliance ceilings for manpower, or national subceilings. NATO has consistently sought freedom to adjust national forces within common overall alliance limits, whereas the Pact has insisted on National subceilings to preclude any movement toward a West European Defense Community.

While West Germany, for reasons discussed below, is likely to resist all efforts to establish subceilings, a status quo manpower agreement might be feasible. For example, recognition that Western Europe feels most threatened by the preponderance of Soviet troops in the Pact, and Eastern Europe by the Bundeswehr in NATO, suggests a need to establish de facto limits for Soviet and West German forces within overall alliance ceilings. This could be achieved by freezing current manpower levels and setting at 50 percent the maximum any nation could contribute to manpower ceilings in the MBFR guidelines area. Such an agreement would simply codify the current Bundeswehr contribution to NATO and current Soviet deployments in the three northern tier countries of the Pact, and should be relatively easy to accomplish.

This would be—as most arms limitation agreements have been—in the nature of a cosmetic treaty, arbitrarily selecting a component of the force posture which is measurable and codifiable, in order to forge a political agreement. Though it may seem a minimal accomplishment after almost a decade of effort, previous experience indicates this may be the maximum level of agreement possible, at least in terms of setting quantitative limits.

The Tendency to Discriminate

While states are manifestly not all equal, either in their military capabilities or their power to influence world affairs, measures which emphasize these inequities will tend to destabilize political relationships. One reason why it has been so difficult to negotiate arms limitation in Europe is that states like France and Germany which have been subject to humiliating treaty provisions in their recent past, are hypersensitive to the discriminatory potential of international agreements.

From its inception, NATO was plagued with problems of status. Less than equal partnership was implied for West Germany by the 1954 Paris and London treaty limitations on rearmament, and the complete integration of West German armed forces under the alliance command structure. The French, in addition to their fears of German revanchism, also bitterly resented the special Anglo-American relationship, particularly as it prevailed in nuclear matters. Before withdrawing French forces from NATO's military structure in 1966, De Gaulle on several occasions tried to institute a triumvirate directorate of the alliance with the United States and Britain, efforts which not only failed but did nothing to ease Germany's self-image.

Other tensions derived from the fact that, as former "Great Powers," some European states had difficulty adjusting to a more subdued role in the balance of power generally, and to being dependent on the American nuclear deterrent for their ultimate security. Both Britain and France sought to elevate themselves in the alliance hierarchy by developing independent nuclear forces, thereby emphasizing Germany's nonnuclear status.

As the Federal Republic contributed more and more to NATO in terms of manpower and defense support costs, its second-class membership became increasingly irksome and led *inter alia* to demands for nuclear sharing in the alliance and bitter debates over the ill-conceived multilateral nuclear force (MLF). This concept especially disturbed the Soviets, and negotiations aimed toward a nonproliferation treaty were begun in 1965 largely to solve the impasse in East-West relations following the MLF debacle.

Both France and West Germany soon came to regard the NPT talks as discriminatory; an attempt by the established nuclear powers to impose a nonproliferation regime on the others. Resentment surfaced during the negotiations as West German leaders strove to avoid being set apart from their alliance partners. In 1967, recalling earlier humiliations, Finance Minister Strauss referred to the draft text of the treaty as a "Versailles of Cosmic Dimensions," and former Chancellor Adenauer called it a "Morgenthau Plan squared." Assessing the impact of the NPT negotiations in 1974, one German political analyst wrote:[6]

... American nonproliferation policy turned the Soviet Union into what many Americans considered a co-responsible partner in the control of United States allies in Western Europe. It also helped to induce the French retreat from NATO and subsequently damaged Atlantic relationships in ways which led even heads of West European governments to perceive Soviet-American cooperation on nonproliferation as "nuclear complicity."

An apparent U.S. willingness to accede to Soviet demands that the language of the NPT should preclude nuclear sharing in NATO was particularly disturbing to Bonn. While not necessarily advocating the Multi-Lateral Force *per se,* it was felt that such options should not be freely given up but traded in exchange for appropriate Soviet concessions—a familiar argument which would be repeated in the 1970s with respect to neutron bomb and cruise missile options.

In addition to purely military concerns, leaders of the nuclear industry in West Germany feared that the NPT system of inspection and control, to which only nonnuclear weapons states were subject, might encourage industrial espionage. Not only did the FRG seem doomed to second-class status with respect to nuclear weapons but also to risk losing out in the fierce competition to sell nuclear technology worldwide. These anxieties were manifest again in 1977 in response to American criticism of the sale of sensitive technology to Brazil.[7]

Though not as bruising to the alliance as the NPT, the SALT negotiations have also been a source of recurrent anxieties that the superpowers will settle their own problems at the expense of European interests. The centerpiece of the first SALT agreement was a treaty limiting ABM. This was well received in Western Europe because constraints on Soviet ABM seemed to enhance the value of independent French and British deterrents. The other part of the agreement was an interim agreement on offensive missiles, about which the NATO allies were far from enthusiastic. The paradox of SALT was that the closer it came to its objective of codifying strategic parity between the superpowers, the more nervous the Europeans felt about American security guarantees. For example, it was even suggested that the 1973 Soviet-American Agreement on the Prevention of Nuclear War was an abrogation of the U.S. commitment to NATO to respond appropriately to Soviet aggression in Europe. Far from diminishing over time, and with improved intra-alliance consultation, these concerns appear to have been exacerbated by the continuing SALT process and the concurrent MBFR talks.[8]

Discriminatory Potential of MBFR

When MBFR was first proposed, little serious thought had gone into devising negotiating strategies or reduction schedules for the simple reason that NATO planners saw the negotiations as an end in themselves, in preventing unilateral reductions. Once the Warsaw Pact responded positively and the serious dialogue began, several potentially divisive problems were envisaged—in particular, that different classes of European states might be created depending on the verification procedures instituted to monitor an MBFR treaty. For example, some states might have to reduce their forces, others merely to freeze at current levels, and still others be unrestricted. In the first two cases, there would presumably have to be more intrusive inspection schemes than for the third category—reminiscent of the troublesome provisions in the NPT in which nuclear weapons powers are not subject to as stringent IAEA inspections as the nonnuclear weapons powers.

The exploratory talks which lasted from January to June 1973 witnessed much frenzied jockeying for position, and intra-alliance concern for status and rank. Two tiers of participants were eventually established. Direct participants with forces deployed in the geographical region designated as the "guidelines area" in which initial reductions are being considered; and "special" or observer-status participants who sit in at the Vienna talks on a rotating basis and are sometimes referred to as "rotating flanks."

The direct participants in NATO are the United States, Canada, Britain, West Germany, and the Benelux countries; and East Germany, Poland, Czechoslovakia, and the Soviet Union in the Warsaw Pact. Whether or not to include Italy and Hungary was the most serious dispute of the preliminary talks, settled temporarily by eliminating both.

Setting up an obvious hierarchy of participants might seem like a blueprint for disaster at subsequent negotiations. However, when formal talks began in October 1973, and perhaps because of belated sensitivities to the alliance discord associated with the NPT and SALT, there was an impressive effort to maintain NATO cohesion and present a united front in Vienna. An elaborate system of intra-alliance consultation was established in Brussels where negotiating positions were thrashed out in the Special Political Committee at NATO headquarters, then approved by the North Atlantic Council before formal presentation to the Warsaw Pact. Thus even "rotating flanks" theoretically had a veto over items in alliance statements which appear at plenary sessions in Vienna. But if and when any hard bargaining starts it will presumably take place informally in (the sort of) "back channel" dialogue between the major powers, a feature of arms control negotiations to date; and the apparent NATO cohesion could easily break down if the consensus on initial positions is only skin deep. Motivations, attitudes, and final objectives vary considerably, not only among the direct participants, but between those in the Central region and those on the flanks, as well as between alliance members and the nonaligned in Europe, who have no input to the negotiations but whose security would inevitably be affected by an MBFR agreement.

The northern and southern flank states in each alliance as well as the neutrals (Austria, Finland, Sweden, Switzerland, and Yugoslavia) have all expressed varying degrees of anxiety lest an MBFR agreement simply reduce Soviet forces in Central Europe to be redeployed nearer their own borders. The only kind of MBFR agreement likely to satisfy Norway, for example, would be one which established a ceiling on Soviet forces deployed in the Kola peninsula. Italy, Greece, and Turkey are nervous that their alliance partners, to the north and west, might conclude an agreement which does not sufficiently cater to their interests; and some reports suggest that these states have already vetoed both procedural and substantive positions agreed to by other members of the alliance in Brussels. As with the NPT, however, the country most sensitive to discrimination associated with MBFR is West Germany.

Historical experience and two world wars have conditioned some members of the Eastern bloc, notably Poland and the Soviet Union, to be particularly wary of German militarism. Despite the advances toward normalization of political relations in recent years, the specter of the Wehrmacht still haunts the East and there is a lingering tendency, however unfair, to view the Bundeswehr as the direct descendant of earlier war machines. There is a suspicion in the East—and force levels tend to confirm the impression—that the Federal Republic strives for hegemony in Western Europe. MBFR negotiations are therefore viewed in the East primarily as a means of curbing the growth in German strength.

Thus, Warsaw Pact proposals in Vienna have emphasized national subceilings on alliance forces and restrictions on any new defense arrangements, in order to limit the growth of the Bundeswehr and moderate any reduction of the American influence in NATO. Above all, the Pact has sought to prevent development of a West European Defense Community led by the Federal Republic—a prospect which has long been anathema in the East. The Soviets want to maintain their ambiguous role as something of a superpower security manager containing the Germans in collusion with the United States.

Ever sensitive to infringements on its sovereignty, Bonn has firmly resisted subceilings in favor of collective alliance limits. While NATO, in general, opposes subceilings because they seem to preclude development of an integrated defense entity in which one member could make up for another's deficiencies, West German leaders nevertheless found their alliance partners relatively insensitive to the implications of Soviet interference in the size of the Bundeswehr. Only belatedly did the alliance as a whole come out for collective ceilings in deference to German anxieties.

As the only major power on either side whose territory lies wholly within the guidelines area, and whose total force will therefore likely be subject to whatever limitations comprise a final MBFR agreement, and as the battle-ground on which any future European conflict would almost certainly be fought, the Federal government has much to be anxious about. The point here is that pursuit of the kind of formal agreement underway in Vienna seems to emphasize rather than alleviate these anxieties.

The Tendency to Generate More Armament

Several mutually reinforcing pressures of the negotiating process combine to generate incentives to acquire more armament, in most cases defeating the original arms control objective.

The Urge for Symmetry. States become hypersensitive to newly perceived imbalances and inadequacies and tend to correct them by leveling up to parity in a variety of force categories not previously considered important. Agreements may then only be possible when limits are set high enough to permit all participants to attain comparable force levels. These newly established ceilings soon come to be regarded as "floors" to be attained, thereby providing the rationale for increased force acquisitions regardless of objective security requirements.

Attempts to match forces are complicated by asymmetric defense needs which are determined by a complex mix of geopolitics, historical experience, and level of industrial development. Accounts of early disarmament debates are full of frustrated attempts to distinguish between "offensive" and "defensive" systems and to establish mutually acceptable ratios of force or "war potential," problems which continue to plague contemporary arms control forums.

The Acquisition of Forces to Support Negotiating Positions. These so-called "bargaining chips" come in several varieties. One example is the kind of weapons program about which opinion is divided in the defense bureaucracy, and the bargaining rationale tips the balance in favor of development or deployment; decisions affecting the Safeguard ABM, Trident submarine, neutron bomb, and cruise missile programs were profoundly affected by the negotiating process.

Sometimes forces are deployed which a government might want to retain but which in the absence of negotiations might have to be relinquished in the face of public or legislative pressure; U.S. manpower and theater nuclear force levels in Europe would almost certainly have been reduced but for MBFR.

Scheduled programs are often accelerated or funded more generously if there is a negotiation in progress, and obsolete or superflous systems are often retained for bargaining purposes which in the absence of negotiations would be reduced, withdrawn, or dismantled. Finally, there are some systems which seem to be procured for the primary purpose of being bargained away.

The Displacement Effect. When arms agreements threaten to foreclose a weapons program, there is a tendency both to rapidly acquire that particular system before the treaty is concluded, and to divert resources into other areas to compensate for lost capability. In this sense, arms control often stimulates military innovation.

There are many historical examples of this, sometimes within the letter, if not the spirit, of the law and occasionally in direct contravention of international agreements. For example, Versailles Treaty prohibitions on naval warships displacing more than 10,000 tons led to the development of smaller, but equally well armed "pocket battleships"; restrictions on heavy bombers in the same treaty stimulated the Germans to design smaller aircraft like the Stuka. The United States managed to circumvent a 1922 Naval Treaty requirement to scrap two battleships by converting them to aircraft carriers instead. More blatant evasions of the Versailles Treaty included illegal German military formations on the Eastern border, relations between the Reichswehr and the Russian Army for training purposes, and production of weapons specifically forbidden, such as heavy artillery and tanks.

Compensation for lost capability is often the domestic price demanded for international agreements. Such an effect manifests itself during the ratification process when deals are struck between the executive and special military and industrial interests to gain acceptance of the treaty. These can take the form of commitments for increased strength in other areas, more vigorous military research and development programs, or some pet project of those most in need of persuasion.

SALT, MBFR, and the European Military Balance

In trying to assess the impact of contemporary arms control efforts on Europe, it is sometimes difficult to separate the effects of SALT from those of MBFR. A ripple of concern generated in one forum over a specific imbalance has a tendency to spill over into other areas and even into a general anxiety about the East-West global balance. Thus while MBFR was proposed as a forum to deal with general-purpose forces in a narrowly defined area of Central Europe, and SALT was intended to limit intercontinental strategic nuclear systems; in practice both forums have generated concern across a broad range of weapons, missions, and geography. In particular, the urge for symmetry has created new anxieties about those "gray area" systems which do not yet fit unto formal negotiating structures.[9]

Impact on NATO Conventional Force Planning

Before the search for a formal MBFR agreement became official NATO policy in June 1968, member states adjusted their forces unilaterally, more in accordance with national priorities than alliance commitments, and were able to do so without causing undue alarm, because, to quote Madariaga, "there was a free future in which to revise." After the 1961 Berlin crisis, NATO governments acted in response to perceptions of a steadily diminishing threat from the East, growing economic pressures, and in several cases, extra-alliance demands on military forces. The trend, except for West Germany, was toward reduced defense budgets and lower force levels in Europe.

The 1968 MBFR proposal then stimulated a wave of reassesments of the East-West military balance in Europe. Defense analysts, particularly in the United States, Britain, and West Germany, began to assert that NATO forces postured to sustain a protracted conflict were dangerously inappropriate to counter Warsaw Pact forces for a blitzkrieg type of attack. Expressions of considerable equanimity about the balance in the late 1960s gave way to a growing concern with Pact advantages followed by increasingly alarmist exhortations to correct deficiencies.

NATO improvements through the 1970s, parallel with MBFR, focused on increasing combat-to-support ratios, precision-guided antitank munitions, and close-in air support. Meanwhile, Warsaw Pact improvements appeared to emphasize enhanced support facilities, longer range interdiction capabilities, tanks, and a new family of sophisticated tactical aircraft.

Impact on U.S. Force Planning

As the formal stage of the negotiations approached, there was no shortage of official declarations that the objective was to achieve a mutual lowering of forces. But congressional hearings on U.S. forces in Europe, in the summer of 1973, reflected growing skepticism.

Senator Mansfield, who had urged withdrawal of U.S. troops from overseas bases since the mid-1960s, denounced the negotiations as nothing more than a delaying tactic. In September 1973 Mansfield again pressed for unilateral reductions, only weeks before formal talks were scheduled to begin in Vienna. This effort came very close to success; a proposal calling for a 40 percent reduction of all U.S. overseas forces, to be phased out over three years, passed the Senate, 49-36. Only after intensive White House lobbying, claiming that such action would undermine the Vienna talks, was this reversed by a qualifying amendment. Later a compromise measure calling for a 23 percent cut also passed, but that too was nullified by a joint Senate-House committee.

From the mid-1960s until the early 1970s, congressional action on the issue of U.S. forces in Europe was largely a matter of reacting to the initiatives of the unilateralists. This situation began to change, however, after Senator Mansfield's retirement and with the election of Senator Sam Nunn from Georgia, who increasingly adopted the NATO cause as his special concern, arguing that increases in alliance strength would help the other side to take MBFR more seriously.

MBFR illustrates how arms control negotiations can distort both the gathering and consumption of intelligence. Comparisons between civilians who serve the defense establishment of one side with the uniformed military who perform a similar function for another would be difficult under any circumstances, but such comparisons between political adversaries contemplating an agreement to readjust their military force levels are almost certain to be misinterpreted. The tendency is to underestimate one's own and allied strength and to exaggerate that of the adversary. "Support" and "combat" categories become redefined so that cooks and bottle-washers on the other side, not to mention cadets in their military academies, come to be included in estimates for their crack fighting troops, while one's own support categories and reserves tend to be played down.[10]

Thus while some Western intelligence estimates indicate a massive build-up of men and equipment in the Pact countries since the mid 1960s, more sober assessments revealed substantial increases of military strength by both alliances. In manpower, for example, much was made in the Western press in the mid-1970s of a reported 140,000-man increase in Soviet troops in Eastern Europe over the past decade. But 70,000 of these represent the five divisions moved into Czechoslovakia in August 1968, which clearly remain to serve more of a police function than to spearhead an attack westward. The other 70,000 moved into East Germany to bolster the Group of Soviet Forces in Germany (GSFG) were perhaps of more genuine concern to NATO planners, though they could reflect a Soviet effort to increase their bargaining position for MBFR, and in any event have been more than matched by the combined increases of American and West German troops in the Federal Republic.

In 1974, Senator Nunn sponsored legislation calling *inter alia* for a restructuring of U.S. forces in NATO to increase the combat-to-support, or teeth-to-tail, ratio. Hearings on the implementation of this legislation the following year suggested the coercive impact of this force restructuring on the MBFR process.[11] As one Pentagon spokesman testified:[12]

> The Nunn amendment . . . . has been helpful to us in the MBFR negotiations. We have demonstrated to the Soviets that we can and are increasing our combat power, and that they cannot just wait around for unilateral cuts in the American combat forces.

However, while in favor of increasing combat strength, the military were not happy about the proposed cuts in support personnel. A former commander-in-chief of the U.S. 7th Army in Europe claimed that impending changes in the teeth-to-tail ratio would reduce self-sufficiency and flexibility while adding very little to on-the-ground combat power. Reports in 1975 suggested that military pressure against restructuring forced cancellation of a scheduled withdrawal of 8,000 support troops from West Germany.[13] The net result of the restructuring program was then simply to insert more "teeth." During 1977, for example, 18,000 more U.S. combat troops were sent to Europe—and 8,000 more are promised before the end of FY 1979—without any support personnel being withdrawn.[14]

Impact on European Force Planning

During the late 1960s allied governments were conscious that support for Senator Mansfield's efforts for unilateral American reductions reflected considerable resentment of a perceived shortfall in the European contribution to the alliance, and recognized that both the appearance and the reality of greater European effort would complement the political value of MBFR. Several NATO defense ministers, under the leadership of Britain's Dennis Healey, met informally in November 1968 to discuss how their individual contributions might be more effectively coordinated. In addition Healey strongly believed there was a need to develop common West European positions to balance the United States in NATO councils,—"to talk back to teacher," as he put it.[15] Signs of Soviet-American duopoly in the recently completed NPT negotiations had led to serious concern that European interests may not be properly taken into account at the forthcoming SALT and MBFR talks.

This Eurogroup, as it came to be known, served several different functions but focused initially on development of a coordinated program of force improvements designed to boost NATO defenses before MBFR talks began formally. A five-year European Defense Improvement Program (the EDIP) was launched in December 1971 and had three main elements; financial contributions to develop a common NATO infrastructure, additional improvements to national forces and increased intra-European military aid, notably from West Germany to Turkey. West Germany added three combat brigades to increase her army combat strength from thirty-three to thirty-six brigades, and raised her financial contributions to the alliance substantially more than any other Eurogroup member, but from 1971 Belgium, the Netherlands, Norway, and Denmark all maintained steady increases in defense spending, in real terms.

An important Eurogroup function was to act as a ginger group to prevent alliance members from reneging on their defense commitments. Canada was the first to receive a Eurogroup broadside, for the unilateral withdrawal of troops from West Germany in 1969—the first alliance member, and only direct MBFR participant, to do so since the proposal was first mooted in 1968. Since that time Canada has been subjected to recurrent pressure from Brussels and Washington to increase her military presence in Europe, even to the point of being threatened, in late 1975, by the withholding of special EEC trade concessions.

In September 1975, former U.S. Defense Secretary James Schlesinger asked Canada to upgrade her forces in Europe to their pre-1969 level, and NATO Secretary-General Joseph Luns caused considerable irritation in Ottawa by roundly criticizing the Canadian forces as underequipped. While no manpower increases were immediately announced, Canada did renew an earlier pledge not to withdraw more troops unilaterally from Europe, and a 1976 defense review recommended a 12 percent increase in the defense budget. There have also been major Canadian purchases of military aircraft from Lockheed, plans to purchase new tanks, and, since October 1975, participation in NATO exercises in Europe.

Britain and The Netherlands were both under domestic pressure to reduce defense spending in the 1970s, which provoked strong Eurogroup counteraction to avoid cuts in the politically sensitive MBFR guidelines area. The Dutch announced a 15 percent reduction in military personnel in 1974, but later announced that implementation of the cuts would be contingent on a successful MBFR agreement—effectively putting the cuts on ice for an indefinite period. Under pressure from Brussels, the cuts were in any case to be in the Dutch Navy rather than in ground forces which national priorities would have indicated. To compensate for the modest active-duty strength of the Dutch Army, a new mobilization scheme was introduced in which conscripts on release from their normal period of national service active duty are assigned to a parallel reserve unit for the next fourteen months.

Britain reduced both its capability to patrol the Eastern Atlantic and its presence in the Mediterranean, while maintaining minimal naval facilities in Cyprus, Malta, and Gibraltar, but actually improved the combat strength of the British Army on the Rhine (BAOR). A 13 percent increase in the combat-to-support ratio was planned by converting three divisions of two brigades each into four armored divisions, one artillery division, and one infantry formation. This occurred against the better judgement of some defense analysts who argued that Britain should concentrate on what she does best, namely, maritime defense, and preferably of the exposed northern flank, rather than improving ground forces on the Continent. But pressure from the allies not to disrupt MBFR, and the political importance of balancing the French presence in West Germany, combined to preclude any significant reductions in BAOR force levels. Indeed, despite an overall reduction in military personnel of more than 40 percent over the past two decades, there have been no cuts in BAOR, except for temporary redeployment of some units to Northern Ireland. Furthermore, for all her economic difficulties and withdrawal from overseas military commitments, Britain still devotes a greater proportion of her gross national product to military spending than any other West European ally. There was thus considerable resentment in late 1977 when Secretary-General Luns sent an unusually caustic note to British Defense Minister Fred Mulley, complaining about the inadequacy of Britain's contribution to NATO and suggesting that, with North Sea oil revenues about to flow, the United Kingdom could well afford to do more.

Given Western Europe's economic problems, MBFR was probably the only rallying point around which reductions could be blocked and new

defense programs generated. NATO members not participating directly in
the Vienna talks, for example, do not seem to have been subject to the same
degree of peer pressure. Italy was able to reduce her armed forces by 50,000
in 1975 without any obvious recrimination from Brussels, and France—ever
independent—announced the withdrawal of 10,000 troops from West Germany in 1977. Perhaps in a conscious effort to compensate for this latter
reduction from the crucial guidelines area, Portugal was granted a $34.5
million grant from the United States in May 1977 to help equip a brigade
committed to NATO.[16]

The Long-Term Defense Program

NATO cohesion reached new heights with the Carter administrations's enthusiastic bolstering of U.S. commitments to the alliance; a policy directed
largely by Robert W. Komer, special assistant to Defense Secretary Harold
Brown for NATO affairs and a defense analyst closely involved with the
early contingency planning for MBFR. Komer designed a NATO-heavy
U.S. defense budget for FY 1979 with about $60 billion earmarked for
NATO-related programs and equipment. This included 5,000 new tanks,
24,000 new antitank precision guided missiles, and more than 2,000 advanced tactical aircraft. In order to man this new equipment, President
Carter promised an additional 8,000 troops.[17]

Encouraged by these signs of renewed American interest in the alliance,
NATO ministers meeting in Washington, D.C., in May 1978 reiterated and
confirmed what had been a somewhat tentative pledge the previous year;
namely, a commitment to increase their defense budgets by 3 percent annually. At the same time, a new and ambitious set of force goals, the Long
Term Defense Program (LTDP), was announced. The genesis of this LTDP
initiative, which focuses on ten areas of NATO's force posture deemed in
special need of upgrading, can be traced directly back to the RAND studies
of the NATO-Pact balance which Komer undertook for the Nixon administration as the United States was gearing up for the Vienna talks in the
early 1970s.[18]

Whatever its merits, the LTDP was launched at what seemed a singular-
ly inappropriate time, with many of the European allies understandably em-
barrassed to have the proposed force build-up loudly trumpeted in
Washington, but roundly condemned by delegates to the UN Special Session on Disarmament meeting concurrently in New York. The Turkish
prime minister, Bulent Ecevit, in particular, questioned the need for increased defense spending in an era of détente.

There were other negative spin-off effects from the LTDP. The Soviets,
for example, lost no time in exploiting the much-publicized plans for a
NATO build-up to rationalize further increases of their own, and specific-

ally to demand greater defense contributions from their East European allies. This came to light after the November 1978 meeting of the Warsaw Pact political consultative committee in Moscow, when the Romanian president, Nicolae Ceausescu, made public his refusal to comply with the Kremlin's request. Ceausescu objected to three specific proposals: to match NATO's 3 percent budget increase, to fully integrate the East European national armies under a unified Pact (presumably Soviet) command, and to sign a declaration condemning the regime in Peking.[19] In remarks reminiscent of the Turkish premier in Washington some months earlier, Ceausescu claimed that increases in defense spending were unjustified in terms of the international situation and would be damaging to Romania's economic development.

Predictably, the Romanians were taken to task for their intransigence by *Pravda,* and also at a Moscow state dinner honoring a visiting delegation from Afghanistan, where President Brezhnev warned of the dangers awaiting Socialist states which embarked on steps of unilateral disarmament.[20] These admonitions, in turn, were not unlike those of Secretary-General Luns to recalcitrant NATO members.

Thus it appeared that in both alliances—parallel with MBFR—flexibility in force planning gave way to a ratchet effect in which the only acceptable adjustment was upward. Certainly within NATO, unilateral reductions in manpower or equipment by those states directly participating in the Vienna talks were virtually eliminated and domestic attempts to curtail any aspect of defense activity generated severe criticism from Brussels. Pact politics are not so transparent, but there were hints that MBFR was used in much the same way to pressure the Soviet satellites to increase their defense efforts.

The Impact of SALT and MBFR on Theater Nuclear Forces in Europe

Because of the ambiguity and inconsistency which surround theater nuclear weapons in NATO, there has been no shortage of proposals within the alliance, both from national defense establishments and more traditional arms control and disarmament circles, to reduce, even in some cases to eliminate, the stockpile. Ironically, these efforts have been frustrated rather than helped by arms control diplomacy. Not only has the withdrawal of obsolete and superfluous systems been precluded, but controversial new programs, like the neutron bomb, may have been kept alive primarily because of their perceived utility as bargaining chips.

Studies conducted in the mid-1960s by the Systems Analysis division of the Pentagon indicated the feasibility of a conventional NATO defense of Western Europe. But, despite the withdrawal in 1967 of some of the smaller and more vulnerable battlefield weapons like the Davy Crockett cannons, Defense Secretary McNamara had little success in reducing the build-up of theater nuclear forces, though he did manage to level off the stockpile in the mid-1960s at approximately 7,000 land-based warheads. Once this figure was made public in late 1966, it became a symbol of the U.S. security commitment to the alliance and especially to West Germany, a symbol which took on even greater significance with the 1968 proposal to negotiate an MBFR agreement.

U.S. anxiety about nuclear weapons stationed abroad increased during the early 1970s for a variety of reasons, not least the reassessments of the NATO-Warsaw Pact balance stimulated by MBFR which underscored anomalies in NATO's nuclear posture. Theater nuclear weapons appeared to present impossible complications for battlefield commanders since no one had been able to devise a nuclear war-fighting doctrine which would not result in total chaos on the battlefield, unacceptable collateral damage to civilians, and enormously high combat fatalities to combat troops. Analysts noted a surfeit of warheads of excessive yield, stored in sites vulnerable both to sabotage and preemptive attack and subject to dubious command and control procedures. Attention was also drawn to the fact that substantial numbers of troops and dual capable aircraft were tied up in a nuclear role which might better be released for conventional contingencies. In the U.S. Congress, Senator Stuart Symington, an outspoken critic of what he considered excessive and indiscriminate deployment of nuclear weapons overseas, and of the secrecy which surrounds most discussions of nuclear policy, was instrumental in airing the issue in a number of hearings and studies.

These congressional investigations confirmed what many had suspected; namely, that ever since the initial deployments to Europe in the 1950s, determinants of nuclear force levels had been more political than military/strategic. Several Defense Department officials indicated that nuclear force levels there do not reflect assessment of defense needs as much as the availability of fissile material for weapons use.[21]

Proposals to reform theater nuclear force planning have included pulling back weapons from provocative positions along the East German border, tightening security at storage sites, replacing obsolete systems and—on the assumption that the deterrent function is paramount—drastic to moderate reductions. Testifying as a private citizen in 1974, Paul Warnke asserted that only a few hundred warheads were necessary for a credible deterrent posture. Alain Enthoven, a former Defense Department analyst from the McNamara era, recommended a stockpile of 1,000 warheads, that is, a reduction of 6,000. Jeffrey Record, while an independent analyst at the Brookings Institution, recommended cutting back to 2,000. When the simmering dispute between Greece and Turkey erupted again over Cyprus in the summer of 1974, and the domestic crisis worsened in Italy, Defense Secretary Schlesinger recommended removal of U.S. nuclear weapons from all three countries.

All these proposals, and any others which implied tampering with the quantitative level of the nuclear stockpile, were opposed by the State Department on the grounds that reductions conducted unilaterally would not only undermine the alliance position at MBFR, but could also complicate SALT by giving away potential Forward Based System (FBS) leverage.[22]

Congressional concern about European nuclear forces was embodied in legislation which required freezing the U.S. NATO nuclear stockpile pending a Defense Department review of:[23]

the overall concept for the use of TNWs in Europe;

the relationship of TNW use to deterrence and a strong conventional defense;

reductions in number and type of nuclear warheads not essential for the defense structure of Western Europe;

steps to develop a rational and coordinated posture by NATO, consistent with a proper emphasis on conventional defense.

Responding to this directive in 1975, a Pentagon report emphasized the need to reduce vulnerability, increase accuracy, and improve command and control procedures with respect to theater nuclear weapons. More invulnerable Poseidon missiles were to be deployed in the Mediterranean and assigned to the Supreme Allied Commander in Europe (SACEUR), but no corresponding reductions were anticipated in vulnerable land-based systems. Indeed, with respect to proposed reductions the report reflected State Department caution against "acting unilaterally and precipitously," in the interest of preserving alliance solidarity.[24]

A January 1977 Congressional Budget Office report on theater nuclear forces recommended the "reduction or elmination of marginally useful or highly destabilizing theater nuclear systems such as Honest John, Atomic Demolition Mines, nuclear Nike-Hercules, Quick Reaction Alert forces", and pursuit of "more survivable peace-time basing modes such as sea-basing. . . ." The report further suggested that a better delineation of NATO's deterrent objectives could produce a smaller and differently configured theater nuclear force.[25]

Implementation of these recommendations was hampered by the fact that Stanley Resor, chief of the U.S. delegation at MBFR, resisted all changes to force levels in the MBFR guidelines area, presumably on the basis that any systems potentially useful as bargaining chips should be retained on a contingency basis. (The reverse logic does not seem to apply; namely, that no new forces should be introduced during negotiations.) Such a policy makes for rigid force planning and seriously complicated a U.S. Air Force plan to replace F-4 nuclear-capable aircraft on Quick Reaction Alert with the less destabilizing conventionally armed F-15. The F-15s were deployed to Europe as planned (a wing in 1976 and a squadron in 1978), but pressure from the MBFR delegation reportedly blocked removal of the F-4s on schedule, despite the fact that the aircraft were needed back in the United States for reserve training purposes. The F-4 issue was particularly sensitive because fifty-four of these aircraft were part of a package of nuclear systems and troops, offered at the Vienna talks in December 1975 in exchange for a Soviet tank army.

It could be argued that such a proposal might be compromised by unilateral reductions, but priorities appear misplaced if arms control initiatives which stand on their military and strategic merits are precluded by bargaining tactics in negotiations which, some would claim, are already stagnant. This seems to be a recurrent problem of arms control diplomacy; namely, that the agreement pursued becomes an end in itself, often at the expense of the more fundamental objective of sensible force planning.

Nevertheless, some reforms were implemented in theater nuclear forces which did achieve minimal arms control objectives. As more obviously second-strike systems, the extra Poseidon missiles assigned to SACEUR were presumably both less destabilizing and less provocative than more land-based systems would have been. Storage sites for nuclear weapons were consolidated and moved away from the border with East Germany and made more secure against sabotage, theft, and preemptive attack. Honest John and Sergeant missiles were replaced by the longer-range Lance, which could be deployed farther back in less vulnerable and less provocative positions.

Other attempts to modify the force posture, however, seemed more likely to have a negative impact. In particular, the rush to develop more discriminate nuclear weapons—attributable in part to the displacement effects and bargaining tactics of SALT and MBFR—threatened to lower the firebreak between nuclear and nonnuclear weapons. Development of the controversial neutron bomb is a case in point.

The Neutron Bomb Controversy

Development of nuclear weapons for discriminate use on the battlefield has long been debated in NATO. Two reduced blast/enhanced radiation prototypes of the 1950s rejoiced in the code-names "dove" and "starling" and were designed to explode above ground, killing everyone within a certain range but with minimal damage to buildings or to personnel a short distance away. Though energetically promoted by the U.S. weapons laboratories at Livermore and Los Alamos, these early neutron bombs were firmly resisted by national defense establishments through the 1960s.

A neutron warhead was used in the U.S. Army Sentinel antiballistic missile system—in the short-range Sprint missile, which was designed to intercept incoming enemy missiles as they entered the atmosphere, with minimal damage to cities. But Defense Secretary McNamara insisted on preserving a clear firebreak between nuclear and nonnuclear use, and refused to develop low-yield nuclear weapons for the battlefield.This caution was mirrored in West Germany, notably in the writings of Helmut Schmidt, who argued that a nuclear exchange could never be confined to the battlefield and that nuclear weapons would not defend, but only destroy, Europe.

McNamara's successors, however, were more inclined to regard nuclear artillery as a useable component of the general-purpose forces, and both Melvin Laird and James Schlesinger invoked SALT and MBFR to rationalize a renewed effort to improve the limited nuclear warfighting capabilities of nuclear weapons. Secretary Laird asserted in the spring of 1972, for example, that with strategic systems likely to be limited at SALT and conventional forces at MBFR, it was necessary to improve NATO's theater nuclear capability, and increase support for research and development programs to reduce the yield, improve the accuracy, and lower the collateral damage of battlefield nuclear weapons.

After SALT I, which placed limits on ABM deployment, some elements in the U.S. Army, fearful of losing their hard-won nuclear responsibilities, were looking for a new mission for the now redundant neutron warhead of the Sprint missile. Additional pressure for another look at the feasibility of enhanced radiation warheads for battlefield weapons was a logical consequence, and the preponderance of Soviet tanks in Central Europe, highlighted in the reassessments of the NATO-Pact balance prompted by MBFR, provided a convenient antitank rationale.

Writing in 1973, General James Polk, a former commander of U.S. forces in Europe, invoked three sets of negotiations—SALT, MBFR, and CSCE—to rationalize extensive modernization of NATO's nuclear stockpile:[26]

> We need to get over the "fire-break" mentality and initiate a vigorous program to modernize our European based stockpile.
>
> Just as the SALT talks demand that we push ahead with MIRV and Trident, so the MBFR talks require that we modernize our hardware, our thinking, and the tactical options available and required at the lower end of the nuclear spectrum. To do otherwise is to continue drifting, aided and abetted by the euphoria of détente and false hopes that may be generated by East-West negotiations on European security and cooperation.

While some of the military accepted the weapons technologists' claim that enhanced radiation effects were ideal for incapacitating enemy tank crews, NATO field commanders were anything but unanimous about the utility of any battlefield nuclear weapons. Many expressed the view that nuclear munitions only served to complicate military planning for the defense of densely populated Europe, and that once the nuclear threshold had been crossed there was high risk of all-out nuclear conflict, a judgment borne out by nuclear war games conducted since 1954.

The U.S. Congress several times denied the Nixon administration funds to produce ERW warheads for European theater nuclear forces: $15 million was cut out of the FY 1974 budget and $904 million denied in FY 1975. Research proceeded apace, however, and, while it still had not been found feasible to miniaturize a neutron core to fit the 155mm shell, in 1976 President Ford signed an authorization to manufacture and stockpile ERW warheads for the Lance missile and the eight-inch artillery piece. No arms control impact statement was issued and funds for the new warheads were buried in a $10 million item in the Energy and Research Development Agency (ERDA) section of the public works bill for FY 1978, an item which was apparently overlooked in the initial Carter administration review of the budget on taking office in 1977.

The Carter administration seemed confused over the merits of the case and began by bullying congressional liberals into approving funds so as to keep ERW options open, then caused great confusion among the allies by requiring European governments to make the final deployment decision. This was particularly embarrassing for West German Chancellor Helmut Schmidt, who had long argued for a more cautious nuclear policy in Europe. The subsequent outcry against the neutron bomb in West Germany included not only the majority of the SPD, but also several CDU/CSU spokesmen and military leaders. The risk that any nuclear weapons might be released from alliance control and fired on the initiative of field officers was thoroughly alarming to most West Germans.

Indeed, it is widely held throughout Europe that American reluctance to initiate a nuclear exchange with the Soviets has a restraining influence on the first use of nuclear weapons by NATO commanders. To the extent that the neutron bomb, or any other discriminate nuclear weapon, might tempt a NATO officer to initiate a nuclear exchange on the battlefield which might be deemed *not* to require an American response, it is regarded as dangerously destabilizing. Here the security interests of the two halves of Europe converge, as neither wants to contemplate a conflict which leaves the two superpowers as nuclear-free sanctuaries while Central Europe is reduced to ashes.

Thus, in the absence of the bargaining rationale and intra-alliance pressure, there would have been little, if any, justification to change long-term SPD policy against the deployment of systems which could lower the nuclear threshold. Yet the Carter administration acted as though it were unaware of the sensitivity of these nuclear questions in West German domestic politics and pressed Chancellor Schmidt hard for his formal approval of neutron deployment. Eventually the chancellor gave his consent on two conditions, that the alliance as a whole must approve deployment, with at least one other continental member of NATO willing to deploy the system. He could not have been less enthusiastic, yet even this reluctant endorsement had been at enormous cost in domestic political terms.

The lessons of the neutron bomb controversy confirm previous arms control experience. Not only did negotiations encourage the modernization of battlefield nuclear weapons which led to the current generation of ERWs, but the arms talks also distorted the decision-making process with respect to production and deployment. The case against deployment in Europe appeared overwhelming but for the slight possiblity that a threat to deploy might conceivably encourage concessions by the Soviets. But, as amply demonstrated in the past, coercive bargaining tactics are more effective to keep recalcitrant allies in line than to produce restraints in an adversary.

Impact of SALT and MBFR on Gray-area Systems

Anticipation of a SALT II agreement which would codify Soviet-American parity in some key strategic indices, together with increased sensitivity to the conventional force balance through MBFR, have focused attention on asymmetries in European-based weapons which do not fit into either negotiating forum; namely, NATO systems which threaten Soviet territory, and Soviet systems which threaten Western Europe.

On the Western side these include American forward-based nuclear-capable aircraft, principally F-4s based in Central Europe, A-6s, A-7s, and F-4s deployed with the Sixth Fleet in the Mediterranean, and F-111s in the United Kingdom. The Pershing missile, while usually categorized as a theater nuclear weapon, could also be considered a gray-area system by virtue of its range, which U.S. Army spokesmen variously estimate at between 400 to 700 miles. Cruise and intermediate-range ballistic missiles currently being developed in the United States, if deployed in Europe, also represent potentially threatening gray-area systems for the Soviets, as do independent British and French nuclear weapons.

From a Western perspective the principal Soviet systems which threaten the Eurostrategic balance are the mobile intermediate range ballistic missile, the SS-20, deployed in the Western military districts, and the swing-wing supersonic Backfire bomber. Less threatening are the older SS-4 and SS-5 medium- and intermediate-range ballistic missiles and medium-range bombers Blinder and Badger.

Forward-Based Systems. Just as NATO's conventional force planning was more flexible before MBFR, so American forward-based systems (FBS) were frequently adjusted before the initiation of SALT. For example, Thor missiles were removed from Britain, Jupiter missiles from Italy and Turkey, and B-47 and B-57 bombers from various bases. Early-model cruise missiles like Mace and Matador were also withdrawn, and under the "Crested Cap" program in 1967 Secretary McNamara redeployed ninety-six nuclear-capable fighter airplanes from West Germany to the United States.[27]

These systems took on new political and diplomatic significance, however, at the first SALT negotiating session in November 1969, when the Soviets claimed that all U.S. systems capable of delivering nuclear weapons onto Soviet territory should be considered strategic. The American position was that only weapons of intercontinental range would be dealt with at SALT, and while this view prevailed through SALT I and II, the possibility that the Soviets will insist on including FBS at some future stage effectively precluded any downward adjustment of these forces. Indeed, NATO's nuclear strike aircraft were substantially augmented in the 1970s.

Cruise Missiles. From the Soviet perspective, one of the most troublesome aspects of U.S. force planning parallel to SALT has been development of the family of small pilotless low-flying subsonic winged aircraft known as cruise missiles. Initially developed by Germany in the 1940s, these weapons were first deployed as the V-1 buzz bombs which wreaked such havoc on London and Antwerp at the end of World War II. After the war, both the United States and the Soviet Union experimented with cruise technology and deployed a number of nuclear-armed systems during the 1950s and 1960s. By the early 1970s, the Soviets were still deploying short- to medium-range cruise missiles, but in the United States the role of delivering nuclear warheads had fallen almost exclusively to bomber aircraft or land- and sea-based ballistic missiles, because of their greater speed and penetration capabilities, and the cruise missile program was gradually being phased out.

Resuscitation and refinement of the U.S. cruise missile program began during the ratification process of SALT I. Immediately after the accords were signed in May 1972, Defense Secretary Laird submitted a supplementary defense budget, which was essentially his "price" for approval of the agreement. To compensate for limits on submarine-launched ballistic missiles, Laird requested funds to develop a long-range submarine-launched cruise missile—in effect to maintain a strategic role for the Polaris submarines which would otherwise have been lost under the terms of the Interim Agreement. As a displacement effect of arms control diplomacy, this is reminiscent of the 1922 Washington Naval Treaty in which a number of

U.S. capital ships scheduled for demolition under the terms of the agreement were converted to aircraft carriers instead.

Additional pressure to develop cruise missiles came from Secretary of State Kissinger, in search of bargaining chips for SALT II. Kissinger went to Moscow in September 1972, hoping to upgrade the Interim Agreement into a long-term treaty in time for the Nixon-Brezhnev summit scheduled for 1973. But the Soviet response was generally negative. Brezhnev would agree neither to a numerical reduction of missile launchers nor to a ban on MIRV deployments.

Kissinger returned home in search of new negotiating tactics and settled on cruise missiles as the most appropriate bargaining chips with which to move the Soviets into a more conciliatory position. As one navy spokesman revealed:[28] "We have been asked to provide a demonstration of capabilities of all the elements of strategic cruise missiles in time relationship to the SALT negotiations."

Initially, those in the Defense Department and the White House who were pushing cruise missiles for their bargaining potential were more enthusiastic than the services. After a period of intense lobbying by the cruise missile project manager, however, by 1974 the armed services were arguing for acceleration of the program into the production stage. This view, disdainful of bargaining chips until they pass from research and development into production, went beyond Kissinger's original concept of a useful negotiating tool; to the point where he eventually came to regret his initial enthusiasm for cruise. "How was I to know the military would come to love it?" he complained to the press in February 1976, by which time the damage was done.[29]

From an arms control perspective it was unfortunate that cruise missiles should be revived for negotiating purposes just as technological advances in propulsion and guidance had reached the point where such systems could be produced relatively inexpensively. Whereas early cruise missiles were thought of as inaccurate and useful only as short-range tactical weapons, in the 1970s they emerged as essentially new means of accurately delivering conventional or nuclear warheads over short tactical or long strategic ranges. Thus, while emphasized primarily because they looked like attractive bargaining tools to a budget-conscious defense establishment, they soon came to be regarded as a particularly cost-effective addition to the permanent-force posture.

Just as the development of MIRV proved a counterproductive bargaining chip at SALT I, serving only to encourage Soviet MIRV development, so cruise seems destined to run out of control to complicate not only SALTs II, III, and MBFR, but any future efforts to control gray-area systems in Europe.

The Vladivostok Understanding: Spotlight on Cruise and Backfire

In late 1974, President Ford and Mr. Brezhnev met in Vladivostok to establish the framework for a second SALT treaty. An aide-memoire outlined ceilings of 2,400 offensive strategic missile launchers for each side, of which not more than 1,320 could be MIRVed. This was an attempt to comply with assurances, made to the U.S. Congress during the SALT I ratification process, not to conclude unequal agreements. It did not, however, restrict the freedom of either the United States or the Soviet Union to proceed with their scheduled strategic programs. Europeans were relieved that American FBS were explicitly excluded from the new ceilings, but apprehensive about how two other gray-area systems were to be limited—American cruise missiles and the new Soviet swing-wing supersonic Backfire bomber.

United States negotiators initially argued that cruise missiles were exempt from the Vladivostok ceilings but that Backfire should be included. The Soviets predictably argued the opposite. The Soviets have always insisted that Backfire is a medium-range nonstrategic bomber which should be excluded from consideration at SALT (paralleling the U.S. argument on FBS). In statements following the Vladivostok summit, U.S. officials accepted this understanding. But when SALT negotiators met again in Geneva in early 1975, the American position had been reversed, reflecting both hard-line domestic criticism of the Vladivostok accord and new intelligence estimates suggesting a strategic potential for Backfire; that is, against targets in the continental United States.

The Soviets continued to insist that the plane was only of intermediate range, a judgment with which many defense analysts in the West concurred, since for United States targets the Soviets would either have to refuel Backfire en route, fly one-way missions, or fly at subsonic speeds, none of which made much sense given the design of the aircraft. Even former Defense Secretary James Schlesinger admitted that including Backfire in SALT II was "fundamentally and ultimately a question of the image of equality and a political issue."[30]

Previous arms control experience indicates that the lowest common denominator of agreement on the Backfire-cruise issue will be at the highest common denominator of forces. Either both systems will be completely exempt or both will be included, but within limits high enough to permit scheduled deployments.

In an attempt to reconcile these differences—and perhaps hoping to cash in some of his cruise "chips"—Henry Kissinger went to Moscow in January 1976 to offer a compromise. In exchange for Soviet constraints on production rates, the United States would exclude Backfire from Soviet strategic launchers in SALT II. In addition, the United States limit its air-launched cruise missiles (ALCMs) to a range of not more than 2,500 km, with aircraft deploying them to be counted in the 1,320 MIRV allowance. Although this proposal was unacceptable to the Soviets at that time, it was profoundly disturbing to several NATO defense ministries, because it suggested that SALT II could deny them a cruise missile option in the future.

Anxieties reached new heights when it was learned that the Soviets not only wanted to limit U.S. cruise missiles, but also to ban the transfer of cruise technology to the allies. For West Germany this was uncomfortably reminiscent of the NPT negotiations and provoked similar intense lobbying from Bonn to modify the language of the agreement.[31] But the assumption that cruise missiles were necessary, or even useful, for the defense of Western Europe did not seem to be based on serious analysis. British defense experts, in particular, were skeptical of the relevance of cruise for the European theater, despite isolated suggestions of replacing their aging Polaris with nuclear-armed cruise missiles. While in the United States, a 1977 Los Alamos Weapons Laboratory study noted that, in terms of both cost effectiveness and penetration of Soviet air defenses, cruise missiles did not compare well with existing ballistic missile systems. A plausible case was made for deploying air-launched cruise missiles as relatively nonprovocative second-strike weapons, but many analysts raised serious doubts about the value of short-range sea- or ground-launched systems.[32]

Despite these shortcomings, the NATO desire to maintain a cruise missile persisted, suggesting perhaps that the desire was based less on rational defense planning than on fears of deprivation and discrimination.

Meanwhile, back in Washington, the hard-liners in Congress and the Joint Chiefs showed an unfortunate tendency to manipulate and exploit these European anxieties as they assembled their package deal for approval of SALT II. For, just as in 1963 and 1972 the U.S. defense establishment had insisted on certain military programs as their price for supporting the Limited Test Ban and the SALT I accords, so new demands were being made in anticipation of a ratification fight over SALT II.

To compensate for the lack of restraints on Backfire, for example, General David Jones, Chairman of the Joint Chiefs, exacted a promise of White House support for a new American bomber of comparable capabilities—probably a larger version of the FB-111—as well as additional squadrons of F-15 jet interceptors.[33]

Similarly, to compensate for restraints imposed on cruise and to counter the still unrestrained Soviet SS-20, and again playing on European anxieties, the U.S. Air Force called for a new intermediate-range mobile ballistic missile for use in Europe. Development funds for such a system authorized in the FY 79 budget, in addition to an army program to extend the range of the Pershing missile.[34]

While NATO officials concerned themselves with maintaining cruise missile options, and applauded the efforts to deploy more Eurostrategic systems, many Europeans doubted whether all this extra hardware would actually enhance their security. Despite claims by proponents of their defensive and nonprovocative nature, the special properties of cruise blur the traditional nuclear/conventional and strategic/tactical categories of weapons and missions, and so complicate the task of European arms control efforts. Furthermore, the promise of new capabilities tends to generate tension and anxiety among those states who feel others may be gaining a military advantage, creating new imbalances, and stimulating new spirals in the arms competition. Perhaps the most serious implication for European security was the pressure to deploy systems in West Germany which seemed to decouple Western Europe from the American strategic umbrella, and so undermine basic assumptions of current deterrence doctrine.

Often obscured by the predominantly Soviet-American and intra-NATO debates was the East European concern about cruise missiles, which parallels their anxieties about the neutron bomb. It must be small comfort to the northern-tier countries of the Warsaw Pact to learn that SALT II limits potential cruise missiles in NATO to a range of 600 km. A conventionally armed cruise missile of such a range, for example, could give the Bundeswehr a capability for strategic strikes into Eastern Europe outside the NATO constraints which operate in the case of nuclear weapons.

Conclusion

To return to Pierre Hassner's criterion for the negotiating process, it can hardly be claimed that SALT and MBFR have modified the behavior of the participants in the direction of restraint. On the contrary, the increases in force levels throughout Europe in the 1970s suggest that arms control diplomacy has not begun to keep pace with the momentum of technological innovation in weaponry, nor relieved the concomitant pressures to deploy the most modern and most lethal equipment.

Perhaps the most obvious lesson of the past decade is the extremely limited utility of formal agreements. While it has been relatively easy to conclude treaties which codified a comfortable status quo, attempts to negotiate changes, or to cement conditions which are not generally acceptable, have usually been too costly, both in terms of eroded trust and increased armaments.

Not only the negotiating process, but also the treaties themselves can have a negative impact. An accord which may have merit in itself nevertheless often discriminates against third parties, as the SALT accords are perceived by many Europeans to be against their best interests. In addition, multilateral treaties generate resentment if some states appear to impose limitations on others, or create different classes of states with respect to their obligations and privileges under international law. The NPT is a notable example, but MBFR could also prove discriminatory if it goes beyond a simple status quo agreement.

To suggest that codifying the status quo is the most that can be achieved by formal agreements is not to say that present political conditions and military balances should be frozen for all time, but rather that changes might be better implemented by other means. At the very least, that traditional arms control diplomacy ought to be supplemented by more independent initiatives.

Fluctuations in both nuclear and nonnuclear force levels in NATO, prior to the initiation of SALT and MBFR, indicate that, in the absence of negotiations, manpower and military hardware can be adjusted without causing undue alarm to alliance partners; but they also indicate that such flexibility tends to vanish in the effort to maintain a cohensive bargaining position.

Without the pressures inherent in the negotiating process, any urge for symmetry in a defensive alliance like NATO operates more with respect to sharing the economic burden of defense than keeping score in the trappings of military power with the adversary. This moderates rather than escalates force levels, as each state tries to shift the burden to others. Hence the recurrent offset disputes among the United States, West Germany, and Britain, and the general trend toward lower force levels during the 1960s, when perceptions of the Soviet threat were at their lowest since 1947.

As Madariaga observed at the League of Nations, in the absence of agreements implying reciprocal obligations, a state is more willing to rely on the "internal compromise between the ambitions of its fighting departments and the sobering influences of its exchequer." In effect, pursuit of an interalliance arms agreement contrives a conflict and imposes a ratchet effect on force planning in which the only acceptable adjustments are upward. Thus, in stark contrast to the *Ostpolitik* and the CSCE, which were based on the whole gamut of social, political, and economic relations, MBFR has reemphasized the bloc-to-bloc structure in Europe, encouraging states to measure their security in military terms at the expense of improving relations in more productive spheres.

In conventional forces, for example, what to many Western observers were no more than routine Warsaw Pact reequipment schedules were interpreted by others, sensitized to the asymmetries in the East-West balance by the Vienna talks, as a deliberate push for military dominance of the Continent. This in turn led to perceptions of inadequacy among some NATO countries, as well as fears by conservative elements that the West would not drive a hard enough bargain at MBFR. All of this generated pressure for special efforts to match the Pact in a variety of force categories, at a pace which would have been unthinkable in the 1960s, and which many found unwarranted in the 1970s. Some of the increases—more tanks on the central front for NATO and more logistic support in the Pact, for example—would perhaps have been requested by the military in each alliance in any event. But the frequency with which extra forces were rationalized to maintain a cohesive bargaining position in Vienna suggests that MBFR accelerated, if it did not always initiate, many of the increases.

More troublesome than increases in conventional hardware has been the impact of the negotiating process on nuclear and dual-capable weapons. SALT and MBFR not only precluded several initiatives which could have substantially reduced NATO's nuclear stockpile, but also spurred the search for more usable battlefield nuclear weapons, and spawned new anxieties about the "Eurostrategic Balance" and inadequacies in a "gray-area" systems like cruise missiles and shorter-range ballistic missiles.

An important point, often lost in the minutiae of counting hardware on both sides, is that Western Europe has been relatively sanguine under an awesome Soviet threat of nuclear-capable, medium-range bombers and missiles for two decades. It is primarily the consciousness-raising effect of SALT and MBFR, with their relentless probing of interlocking force balances, which has created perceptions of a new problem in need of solution.

With President Carter calling for a separate negotiating structure for European nuclear systems and President Giscard calling for a new forum to cover European arms control "from the Atlantic to the Urals," there is a real danger that a new generation of defense analysts and diplomats will want to build careers in correcting the Eurostrategic balance. Nothing could be more detrimental to the long-term prospects for security in Europe, since a forum dealing exclusively with gray-area systems would inevitably stimulate appetites for more and better hardware in those categories. It behooves governments everywhere to analyze carefully what the impact of arms control diplomacy has been before contemplating any new forums. Previous experience, and especially that of the recent past, suggests that efforts should be directed toward more tacit and flexible arrangements for controlling force levels.

Long-term security policy for Europe would ideally seek the benefits of codified stability without incurring the costs of the negotiating process. One test of when the time is ripe for formal diplomacy might be to ask whether all the participants in a proposed arms control forum are prepared to begin the exercise with a force freeze. If they are not, then the minimal degree of mutual confidence and trust is probably lacking and the process of negotiation is likely to generate more, rather than less, of the forces under consideration, thereby exacerbating tensions and further reducing prospects for security.

Finally, in addition to being wary of embarking on new negotiations, NATO and Warsaw Pact governments should reassess the wisdom of continuing SALT and MBFR in their current forms. The prognosis for SALT III is for increasing European unhappiness with superpower management of the strategic balance. The new hysteria about gray-area systems was reflected in the West European reaction, in late 1977, to information that the text of SALT II would incorporate guidelines for SALT III. NATO officials, reportedly, began immediately to formulate some SALT III guidelines of their own, which the *German Tribune* summarized in January 1978 as follows:

> Modernization of NATO's nuclear armament must be neither abandoned nor crucially curtailed unilaterally unless the Soviet Union makes appropriate counter-concessions. (Since there would always be disagreements on the "appropriateness" of a Soviet response this is tantamount to saying, "No unilateral adjustments of U.S. nuclear stockpiles."
>
> Eurostrategic systems should only be included in the SALT III agenda with European consent and participation in the negotiations.
>
> There must be no Soviet advantage in the Eurostrategic balance.
>
> SALT III must not restrain intra-alliance transfers of technology.

Any negotiation hobbled with such prerequisites seems doomed to fail. A more prudent arms control policy for both strategic and gray-area systems would be to quietly and informally assess existing forces to see if current levels could be stabilized in a treaty, relying thereafter on unilateral restraints in force planning to control future deployments.

As for MBFR, widespread dissatisfaction with the lack of progress has produced a fairly broad consensus in the West for shifting the focus of the negotiations away from seeking quantitative limits. If anticipated limits were to go much beyond some form of status quo agreement, Eastern governments would probably concur; there has already been informal grumbling, to Western visitors in Moscow, that the Vienna talks are ill-conceived. One way to salvage the MBFR exercise might be to pay more attention to the "associated measures" which are included on the official agenda, but which were not discussed in any detail during the first five years of the talks.

Such measures are functionally related to the CSCE confidence-building measures (CBMs) which, in general, seek to curtail the use of force rather than effect reductions; for example, measures to reduce the risk of surprise attack by establishing a pattern of prior notice and exchange of observers at all military maneuvers and troop movements over a certain size. Better exchange of data on military budgets and procurement has also been suggested as a means of reducing the arms competition generated by uncertainty about the adversaries' capabilities.[35]

The principal virtue of this approach is that a system of European CBMs need not be formally negotiated and embodied in binding treaty commitments, but could be developed gradually as a code of conduct for acceptable military conduct in both halves of Europe. By contrast, as long as MBFR is limited to the pursuit of an agreement on force levels, there will be continued exhortations from Brussels and Washington for the NATO allies to improve their combat capability, which in turn can only encourage the Pact to continue its build-up in Eastern Europe.

Notes

1. Pierre Hassner, *Europe in the Age of Negotiation* (Beverly Hills: Sage Publications, 1973), pp. 47-48.

2. Salvador de Madariaga, *Disarmament* (New York: Coward, McCann and Geoghegan, Inc., 1929), p. 31, writing of disarmament efforts at the League of Nations describes problems of the negotiating process which parallel those of contemporary forums:

> In the absence of a definite agreement implying reciprocal obligations, each state feels itself free to maintain a force which is a compromise between the ambitions of its fighting departments and the sobering influence of its exchequer. This internal compromise is relatively easy because there is a free future in which to revise it. If and when a definite agreement, of an international and solemn and binding character, is envisaged, such a freedom tends to vanish and three sets of forces come into play, all tending to increase the figure to be offered: the tendency to reserve a margin against possible contingencies in international negotiation; prestige; and the necessity to provide a margin for discussion with the national exchequer. Such is the explanation of the warning often heard in League disarmament discussions to the effect that a conference for the reduction of armaments may well result in all-round increases.

3. See chapter 9.

4. Annex to NATO communiqué, June 1968, Paragraph 7. Reprinted in *Survival* (London IISS), September 1969.

5. W.B. Prendergast. *MBFR: Issues and Prospects* (Washington, D.C.: A.E.I., 1978), p. 29.

6. Uwe Nerlich, in Larus and Lawrence, eds., *Nuclear Proliferation Phase II* (Kansas City: Univ. of Kansas Press, 1974), p. 89. Reprinted with permission.

7. See Theo Sommer (Editor of the Hamburg weekly *Die Zeit*) in *Newsweek*, October 11, 1976.

> Haven't the Americans themselves through their atoms-for-peace program, been the most profligate proliferators . . . and aren't they on top of that the most unrestrained peddlers of conventional arms? Don't they even today sell enriched uranium to India? Is it logical for Washington to decry the export of European nuclear facilities and at the same time to sell to South

Africa the computers without which Vorster's secret enrichment plant could not operate? . . . Finally, isn't it reasonable to suspect that the Americans employ lofty nuclear theology simply to cover up rather down-to-earth interests—if not to say base commercial ones?

8. See Helmut Schmidt's October 1977 speech to the International Institute for Strategic Studies, reprinted in *Survival*, January/February 1978, pp. 2-10.

9. See, for example, "Equaliser, please," *Economist*, August 26, 1978, pp. 10-11.

10. This kind of arithmetic occasionally comes to light in legislative hearings on military spending. Witness the following exchange between Sullivan of the Senate Armed Services Committee and Wood of the Department of Defense:

> Sullivan: You mention we are devoting a lot more attention than we had in the past to try and find out what they have. That growth does not represent increase in our knowledge as opposed to real growth in their capability, does it?
>
> Wood: That is an excellent point. I think we would have to say that in part the intelligence capability has improved and we may have simply found more things that have been there all along. To some extent these figures probably reflect that sort of thing.

United States Congress, Senate Armed Services Committee, *Hearings on FY 1976 Military Appropriations*, March 1975, pp. 2241-2242.

11. Public Law 93-365.

12. United States Congress, Senate Armed Services Committee, *Hearings on FY 1976 Military Appropriations*, March 1975, p. 2269.

13. *New York Times*, September 14, 1975.

14. Col. Phil Stevens, "NATO and the Warsaw Pact—An Assessment." *Military Review* (The Professional Journal of the U.S. Army) LVIII (September 1978):40.

15. Harlan Cleveland, *The Transatlantic Bargain* (New York: Harper and Row, 1970), p. 23.

16. IISS, *Strategic Survey*, 1977, p. 125.

17. Edward Walsh, "Carter Pledges NATO Funds: Vows More Troops," *International Herald Tribune*, January 7/8, 1978 (also, FY 1979 Posture Statement, page 39).

18. Robert W. Komer, "NATO's Long Term Defense Programme. The Origins and Objectives," *NATO Review* III (June 1978):9-12.

19. Hella Pick, "Romania Suggests Buffer Zone," *Manchester Guardian Weekly*, December 10, 1978.

20. *Pravda* article, December 16, 1978. Brezhnev quoted in *Aviation Week and Space Technology*, December 11, 1978, p. 13.

21. *Nuclear Weapons and Foreign Policy*, Hearings before the Senate Foreign Relations Committee, 1974, p. 163.

22. *New York Times*, July 24, 1975.

23. PL 93-365.

24. James Schlesinger, *The Theater Nuclear Force Posture in Europe. A Report to the Congress in Compliance with PL 93-365*, Department of Defense, 1975.

25. Congressional Budget Office, *Planning U.S. General Purpose Forces: The Theater Nuclear Forces*, Washington, D.C., January 1977, pp. 39-40.

26. James Polk, "The Realities of Tactical Nuclear Warfare," *Orbis*, Summer 1973. Reprinted with permission.

27. See Uwe Nerlich, *The Alliance and Europe: Part V. Nuclear Weapons and East West Negotiations*, Adelphi Paper #120, IISS, Winter 1975/1976, especially pp. 20-28.

28. Waterman testimony, United States Congress, Senate Armed Services Committee, Hearings on FY 1974 Military Appropriations, 1973, p. 3274.

29. Leslie Gelb, *New York Times,* February 17, 1976.

30. Quoted by Bernard Weinraub, "Russia's Backfire Bomber: Red Threat or Red Herring?" *New York Times*, May 7, 1978.

31. Richard Burt, "U.S. Agreed with Soviet to Limit Cooperation with Allies," *New York Times*, May 2, 1978.

32. Robert S. Metzger, "Cruise Missiles: Different Missions, Different Arms Control Impact," *Arms Control Today* VIII (January 1978).

33. Richard Burt, "Carter Deal Said to Win Military over to Arms Treaty," *New York Times*, July 14, 1978.

34. Walter Pincus, "Conferees Back Long-Range Mobile Ballistic Missile System," *Washington Post*, August 3, 1978.

35. The best survey of confidence building measures is J.J. Holst and K.A. Melander, "European Security and Confidence Building Measures", *Survival* (IISS, London), Volume XIX, No. 4, July/August 1977, pp. 146-154.

Index

About the Contributors

Stephen J. Barrett is Counsellor, British Embassy, Ankara. He has been head of the Science and Technology Department at the Foreign Office. Earlier, he was principal private secretary to the foreign secretary, head of the South West European Department, and political advisor in Berlin. Mr. Barrett was a fellow at the Center for International Affairs, Harvard University from 1977 to 1978.

Coit Dennis Blacker is a research associate in the Arms Control and Disarmament Program, Stanford University. He was affiliated with the Center for Science and International Affairs, Harvard University, from 1975 to 1977.

Robert W. Dean is on the senior staff of the Rand Corporation. He has been an analyst in the Office of Political Research, Central Intelligence Agency, and from 1970 to 1974 he was a senior analyst with Radio Free Europe in Munich. Dr. Dean has taught at the University of Southern California European Graduate Program, and during 1976-1977 he was in the mid-career program of The Kennedy School of Government, Harvard University. He is the author of *West German Trade with the East: the Political Dimension,* as well as other books and articles on European security.

Kevin Devlin has been a political analyst for Radio Free Europe in Munich since 1961. He has published widely on European communist parties, and his articles have appeared recently in *International Security* and *Problems of Communism.*

Stephen J. Flanagan is a staff member of the U.S. Senate Select Committee on Intelligence. Dr. Flanagan was a fellow at the Center for Science and International Affairs, Harvard University, from 1976 to 1978.

Linda B. Miller is adjunct research fellow, Center for Science and International Affairs, and professor of political science, Wellesley College. She has published articles on American-European relations in *World Politics, The World Today, Journal of Common Market Studies,* and *International Security.* She was a Rockefeller Foundation Fellow in International Conflict, conducting research on the politics of energy, during 1976-1977.

N. Edwina Moreton teaches in the Department of Political Science, University College of Wales, Aberystwyth. She has been a Harkness Fellow of the Commonwealth Fund of New York, and during 1977-1978 she was a postdoctoral fellow at the Center for International Studies, Massachusetts Institute of Technology.

Jane M. O. Sharp is a research fellow at the Center for Science and International Affairs and is affiliated with the Institut Universitaire de Haute Etudes Internationales, Geneva. She is a director of the Council for a Livable World, Washington, D.C. Her articles have appeared in *Alternatives, Arms Control Today,* and *Bulletin of the Atomic Scientists.*

Henry Stanhope has been defense correspondent of *The Times,* London, since 1970, and has written extensively on the superpower military balance and international security problems. He has been a visiting fellow at the Center for Science and International Affairs. Mr. Stanhope is also author of *The Soldiers: An Anatomy of the British Army.*

About the Editor

Derek Leebaert has been a research fellow, Center for Science and International Affairs, since 1975, and he is also affiliated with the Department of Political Science, Massachusetts Institute of Technology. He serves as managing editor of *International Security,* having previously worked in the United Nations Institute for Training and Research, New York. He directed CSIA's European Security Work Group, 1976-1978.